Social Change and Development

Social Change and Development

Emerging Issues in the North-East India

Editor

D.V. KUMAR

RAWAT PUBLICATIONS

Jaipur • New Delhi • Bangalore • Hyderabad • Guwahati

ISBN 978-81-316-0486-1

Published by
Prem Rawat for **Rawat Publications**
Satyam Apts, Sector 3, Jawahar Nagar, Jaipur 302 004 (India)
Phone: 0141 265 1748 / 7006 Fax: 0141 265 1748
E-mail: info@rawatbooks.com
Website: www.rawatbooks.com

New Delhi Office
4858/24, Ansari Road, Daryaganj, New Delhi 110 002
Phone: 011 2326 3290

Also at *Bangalore, Hyderabad* and *Guwahati*

Typeset by Rawat Computers, Jaipur
Printed at Nice Printing Press, New Delhi

Contents

List of Tables

Contributors

T.K. Oommen is presently Professor Emeritus at the Jawaharlal Nehru University, New Delhi. During his distinguished career he held important positions such as the President of the International Sociological Association and also of the Indian Sociological Society. He has been a Visiting Professor at the University of California, Australian National University, Institute of Advanced Studies (Budapest), etc. He has published extensively. Some of the books which received wide acclaim include *Citizenship, Nationality and Ethnicity: Reconciling Competing Identities (1997), Pluralism, Equality and Identity: Comparative Studies (2002).* He has won prestigious awards in the field of Sociology such as V.K.R.V. Rao Prize in Sociology (1981), G.S. Ghurye Prize in Sociology and Anthropology (1985) and the Swami Pranavananda Award in Sociology (1997). He was also a member of the Prime Minister's High Level Committee (2004–2006) for the study of Social, Economic and Educational Status of the Muslim Community in India. He was conferred upon the Padma Bhusan, in 2008.

Prasenjit Biswas is currently Associate Professor at the Department of Philosophy, North-Eastern Hill University, Shillong, Meghalaya. He has authored The *Postmodern Controversy* (2005) and *Ethnic-Life Words in North-East India* (2008). He has also published in leading national and international journals across disciplines of humanities and social sciences.

A.C. Sinha is former Dean, School of Social Sciences, North-Eastern Hill University, Shillong. Trained in anthropology and sociology, he has researched into the areas of politics, ethnicity, environment, youth, religion and issues of development of North-East India in general and Sikkim and Bhutan in particular. He has published extensively. His latest publications are on *Sikkim: Feudal and Democratic (2008)* and *Indian Nepalis: Issues and Perspectives* (edited with T.B. Subba) (2008).

N. Vijaylakshmi Brara is Reader, Centre for Manipur Studies, Manipur University. Her major academic interests are gender, culture and grassroots political institutions. Her recent publication is *Politics, Society and Cosmology in India's North-East* (2007). She has published a number of articles in academic journals.

Manorama Sharma is presently Professor and Head, Department of History, North-Eastern Hill University, Shillong, Meghalaya. Her research interests include modern Indian history with special focus on historical developments in North-East India. Her recent publications include *Social and Economic Change in Assam; Middle Class Hegemony (1990),* History *and History Writing in North East India* (1998) and *Society and Social Forces in North East India (1999).* She has published articles in scholarly journals and edited books on the North-East.

C.L. Imchen is Professor at the Department of Sociology, North-Eastern Hill University, Shillong. His areas of interest span polity formation and nation-state and native systems. He has co-edited a book on *Nagaland* (with K.S. Singh and N.K. Das). He was a Visiting Fellow at the Department of Anthropology, Harvard University during 1993–1994 and also a Teacher Fellow at the Department of Public Administration, Carlton University, Ottawa.

D.V. Kumar is Associate Professor, Department of Sociology, North-Eastern Hill University, Shillong. He has been investigating issues of modernization and development, social change and ethnicity. He has published research articles on these issues in such journals as the *Sociological Bulletin.* His *Modernisation and Ethnicity* (2006) is widely used as a text in universities.

N.K. Das, former Deputy Director and currently Visiting Fellow, Anthropological Survey of India, Kolkata, has published over a hundred research papers in national/international journals on themes of ethnicity, social movements, social stratification, kinship, legal anthropology, and cultural syncretism. Of late his areas of research are Identity, cultural pluralism and State, tribal ecological and livelihood issues, indigenous knowledge systems and belief systems. His major books are *Ethnic Identity, Ethnicity, and Social Stratification* (1989), *Kinship Politics and Law in Naga Society* (1993); *Anthropology of Weaker Sections* (with Surajit Sinha, 1993), *Identity, Cultural Pluralism and State: South Asia in Perspective* (with V.R. Rao, 2009), *Tribes, Cultural Adaptations and Belief Systems (2009), and Cultural Diversity, Indigenous Knowledge and Biodiversity Conservation (2009).* He is currently the Chief Editor, *Journal of Social Anthropology.*

Tejimala Gurung is Associate Professor at the Department of History, North-Eastern Hill University. Her research interests include social formation and human development. She has edited (with Sajal Nag and Abhijit Choudhury) the *Making of the Indian Union: Merger of Princely States and Excluded Areas* (2007).

I. Lanu Aier is Associate Professor at the Department of Sociology, North-Eastern Hill University, Shillong. He has researched into the areas of politics and religion and ethnic relations. He has recently published the *Contemporary Naga Social Formations and Ethnic Identity* (2006). He has also edited books and published a number of articles.

P.M. Chacko, formerly with the Department of Sociology, North-Eastern Hill University, Shillong, has been interested in the issues of tribal development and social change. His publications include *Tribal Communities and Social Change* (ed.) (2005) and *Studies of Tribes in Kerala: A Trend Report* (2007).

P. Nayak is Professor at the Department of Economics, North-Eastern Hill University, Shillong. His research interests include development economics in general and the issues of development in North-East India in particular. Currently he is engaged in working in the area of human development and women empowerment. His latest publications include *Human Development and Deprivation in Meghalaya* (2007) (with E.D. Thomas) and *Growth and Human Development in North East India* (2009).

S.K. Misra is presently Professor of Economics, North-Eastern Hill University, Shillong. His areas of interest span quantitative economics and microeconomics. He is currently engaged in the study of biologically inspired global optimization methods. He has over a hundred research articles to his credit. His publications include *Computer Applications in Social Science Research* (1991).

B.N. Borthakur, formerly with the Department of Sociology, Dibrugarh University, has been working on the issues related to industrialization and development. His latest book is *Sociological Aspects of Economic Development* (2004).

D.K. Nayak is Professor, Department of Geography, North-Eastern Hill University, Shillong. His research interests include demography with special reference to ageing. He has widely published a number of articles in national and international journals.

K. Debbarma is Associate Professor, Department of Political Science, North-Eastern Hill University. His areas of interest include human rights and development and migration politics. Besides a number of articles in research journals on these issues, he has recently published a book on *The Chakma Refugees in Tripura.*

B. Panda is Reader at the Department of Sociology, North-Eastern Hill University. His areas of research interests include voluntary sector, development and sociological theory. He is widely published.

Rekha M. Shangpliang is Assistant Professor, Department of Sociology, North-Eastern Hill University, Shillong. Her research interests and publications are in the areas of sociology of environment and gender studies.

Acknowledgements

I sincerely wish to thank the Indian Council of Social Science Research (Delhi), the North-Eastern Council (Shillong) and the Indian Council of Social Science for support grants for organising a National Seminar on Social Change in North-East India: Processes and Responses in Shillong. The articles in this edited volume are revised versions of papers presented in the seminar.

I am very thankful to the contributors who despite their academic engagements have revised papers in the light of discussions in the seminar.

I am extremely grateful to my colleagues C.L. Imchen and I. Lanu Aier of the Department of Sociology, NEHU, for encouraging me to undertake this present volume. Without their unstinted support, I would have found it extremely difficult to do. They were always there whenever I needed their help.

I would also like to thank my colleagues at the Department Rekha M. Shangpliang, B. Panda, A.K. Nongkynrih and Nikhlesh Kumar for all help.

My thanks go to Rawat Publications and Pranit Rawat, in particular, for taking enormous care in brining out the volume.

Needless to add, without the support from my wife Radhika and my children, Lahari and Pranay, this work would not have seen the light of day. I am deeply thankful to them.

Introduction

Social change has been a central concern with sociological theory. Changes which have been taking place in societies engaged the attention of some of the outstanding minds in Sociology since the times of Marx, Durkheim and Weber. For instance, great social transformations in the social, economic and political fields in the wake of the French Revolution, the Industrial Revolution and the Intellectual Revolution (which had inalienable links with the Project of Enlightenment) became the subject-matter of profound sociological writings. In fact, the very genesis of Sociology was located in the context of these transformations. Sociology became the main field of enquiry engaging itself in a study of social changes that were sweeping across Europe. Social change became one of the important preoccupations for sociologists who were trying to understand its ramifications and consequences for human society. Marx and Engels (1968) were deeply engrossed in examining the dialectical nature of transformation of societies from one stage to the other as a result of changes taking place in the forces and relations of production, and visualized the possibility of a just and humanitarian social order emerging. Weber in his magnum opus *Protestant Ethic and the Spirit of Capitalism* (1967) gave us an elaborate account of the growth of capitalism given the right motivational framework embedded in the Protestant ethic. Durkheim (1964) was engaged in looking at the transformation of societies characterized by mechanical solidarity into societies of organic solidarity through the instrument of division of labour, understood in social terms rather than economic terms (Aron, 1965). They were also intellectually alive to the emergence of 'pathological' tendencies that would accompany these transformations. Marx would talk about alienation, Weber referred to disenchantment and Durkheim pointed to the question of *anomie*.

Questions related to increasing structural differentiation and functional specialization (Parsons, 1966), deepening of the process of democratization, growth of industrialization (Black, 1966; Levy, 1966; Smelser, 1959) and urbanization, growth of rationality (Habermas, 1971), growing instrumentalization of social relations (Horkheimer and Adorno, 1972; Marcuse, 1972) became intrinsically connected to the study of social change following the writings of Marx, Durkheim and Weber.

Social change is a ubiquitous phenomenon and its pace has increased considerably in the modern times. The past looks rather placid by comparison with the present, characterized as *modern* in some of the sociological writings, in terms of the pace at which social change is occurring. Modernity has lent great poignancy to the study of social change. Questions related to how one makes 'sense' of what modernity is have been dealt with elsewhere (Kumar, 2008).

Dwelling upon the nature and characteristics of social change, Moore (1994) would argue that social changes occur frequently or constantly and that they are neither temporally nor spatially isolated. Further, changes in contemporary times are much higher than in former times and it is inconceivable that any part of society would be exempt from social change. S. Vago in his highly lucid summary of different definitions of social change looks at social change as changes taking place in terms of group activity (Gerth and Mills, 1953), structure of society (Ginsberg, 1958), structure and functioning of society (Davis, 1959), social relationships (MacIver and Page, 1949), social structure and social relationships (Nisbet, 1969). Thus, as one can see there are different ways of making 'sense' of what social change is.

The phenomenon of social change has been theorized variously. Different theoretical traditions have emerged at different points of time and sought to engage themselves with an interrogation of the nature and processes of social changes taking place in the societies. In this context, one can refer to evolutionary theories (Comte, 1915;

Morgan, 1964), conflict theories (Coser, 1956; Dahrendorf, 1959; Marx and Engels, 1968), structural and functional theories (Parsons, 1966; Ogburn, 1964), socio-psychological theories (Weber, 1967; Hagen, 1962; McClelland, 1961). They identified different sources of social change and traced the different trajectories that social changes would follow. For instance, for evolutionary theories of social change, the endogenous factors account for social changes which would assume a gradual and progressive form. Conflict theories would locate class struggle as the main factor responsible for social transformations and look at social changes taking place in a violent and sudden fashion. For socio-psychological theories of social change, socio-psychological factors (McClelland's n Achievement, for example) would be the main source of social changes.

Coming to the situation in India, social change has been the main preoccupation of some of the leading sociologists. They sought to make a systematic sociological study of what are called the basic social institutions in the country such as the caste system, village community and family structure and the changes taking place in them. The study of caste has attracted, quite understandably so, enormous attention of sociologists working on India (Bailey, 1957; Beteille, 1965; Dumount, 1972; Leach, ed., 1960; Mayer, 1960; Srinivas, 1962, to mention a few). Village community and family structure too were studied in earnest. Sociologists have devoted considerable amount of effort to make a systematic study of these structural features of the Indian society. Changes taking place in the village community have been studied both intensively and extensively (Dube, 1955 and 1958; Ishwaran, 1966; Lewis, 1958; Majumdar, 1958; Marriot, 1955; Srinivas, 1955). The nature of joint family and significant changes which have occurred and continue to occur therein have been the subject matter of scholarly sociological writings (Desai, 1965; Kapadia, 1958; Ross, 1961). Along with the above changes taking place at the level of macro-structure such as political institutions, bureaucracy, the processes of industrialization and urbanization have also been studied (Berna, 1961; Bottomore, 1965; Lambert, 1963; Park and Tinker, 1959; Pocock, 1967; Weiner, 1961).

However, one of the important problems of these studies, as pointed by Y. Singh (1973), is that scholars have focused exclusively on changes taking place at the level of structure to the neglect of changes taking place at the level of cultural traditions or vice-versa.

His book *Modernisation of Indian Tradition* (1973) which has made an important contribution to the study of social change in India seeks to rectify this anomaly and interrogate changes taking place both at the level of structure and culture (as a result of both what he calls orthogenetic and heterogenetic sources).

The context of North-East India remains curious in the sense it has been studied more for its spectacular instances of militancy, insurgency, terrorism and social unrest rather than the gradual but important social changes which have been taking place (Baruah, 2005; Chaube, 1973; Misra, 2000; Singh, 1987). Any understanding of social changes taking place in the North-East is an equally challenging task given the enormous diversity that prevails in the region. In fact, some would go so far as to question the very use of the term 'North-East' as a homogenous category considering the immense socio-cultural diversities that obtain here. A systematic understanding of these diversities and changes taking place in them would be of great sociological interest.

Changes taking place both at the level of social institutions, organizations, social groups and at the level of culture demand equal attention. From the point of view of assessing changes in structural and cultural aspects, one of the most critical moments in the context of North-East was the inroad of British administration followed by missionaries. It led to significant changes in the social, cultural, economic and political framework of the North-Eastern societies. Introduction of a different religious world view (Christianity), changes in the land holding patterns, increasing commodification of the land, imposition of the modern system of administration and new political culture, introduction of modern educational system, are some of the aspects of change which happened as a result of the contact with the British. In post-independent India, the emphasis has been on a developmental paradigm which essentially focused on the industrialization of the region, greater exploitation of the natural and mineral resources and the need for transition from shifting cultivation to settled agriculture. It resulted in the growth of a middle class, accentuation of socio-economic inequalities, deepening of regional disparities and changes in the value system, the ramifications of which have not been sociologically explored in an adequate manner. The vanishing significance of the principle of egalitarianism and the gradual entrenchment of the principle of hierarchy could be cited as one of such ramifications. Further, the introduction of a federal political structure and the deepening of the process of democratization have led to a new dialectic in the political reality of the North-East in terms of traditional political structures coming in conflict with the modern political structures.

A comprehensive treatment of the above would no doubt entail discussion on the trajectory of social changes and the related issue of values. The question of values is integrally connected to the explication of direction of social changes. Social scientists have long remained indifferent and disengaged from the question of values. It is now being increasingly felt that social scientists, given the knowledge base they have, need to express their point of view and spell out the direction in which societies could meaningfully move forward. In the context of the North-East, for example, while some desirable changes have taken place such as growth of literacy, greater health facilities and greater political awareness, other changes have certainly not been progressive in nature. The growth of socio-economic inequalities and greater exploitation in the hands of the dominant sections could be cited as examples.

It is also vital that we need to have a proper understanding of the responses of the communities to both the agencies and processes of social change. While some changes have been accepted quite willingly (the introduction of modern educational system, for instance), others have been resisted quite strongly. The systematic exploitation of natural and mineral resources of the region for the benefit of powerful sections including business people and government contractors, imposition of a developmental model without taking the sensitivities and sensibilities of the people of the region into account, gradual marginalization of their traditional political structures, the continued immigration of outsiders which disturbs their demographic profile, structural/institutional and cultural aspects are some of the issues which have led to frequent articulation of their discontent and alienation. These articulations more often than not assume violent and aggressive style as manifested in the growth of secessionist and separatist movements in the North-East. The granting of political autonomy in the form of states has, to some extent, contributed to diminishing of the sense of deprivation and neglect and greater willingness on the part of communities in the North-East to have a dialogue with the so-called 'mainstream' India. Still simmering fears persist regarding the long-term health of their institutional and cultural features such as family structure and values etc. in the context of influx of 'outsiders' into the region. For example, one of such anxieties expressed frequently by the people concerns the higher rate of inter-community marriages and their critical sociological impact on their very existence as a community. The value of egalitarianism, too, is coming under increasing pressure due to the ascendancy of different structures of hierarchy. The inexorable entry of forces of modernization is also being viewed suspiciously by them as they would constitute a threat to their cultural patterns. The issue of identity which is central to their existence as a community assumes greater poignancy in the context of their belief that it is being increasingly delegitimized by the logic of modernity. This drives them to uncritically romanticize their traditions without looking at the possibility of having an engagement with modernity (Kumar, 2008). Thus, as one can see, any study of social change in the North-East needs to locate itself in the context of the above-mentioned wide-ranging sociological issues in order to be meaningful and relevant.

Considering the inadequacy of the research done on the above issues and the limited knowledge available on the problem of social change with reference to the North-East, there is a long-felt need to bring studies together which would reflect on these issues. It is hoped that this volume would make a meaningful and useful intervention in such reflections concerning social change in the North-East India.

T.K. Oommen, in his usually incisive style, before looking at the situation in the North-East, examines the conceptual confusion that results from conflation of nation and state. This also leads to conflation between nationality and citizenship undermining the empirical reality in South Asia in general and India in particular where one does not fail to notice a disjuncture between the two, a product of a long historical process brought about by conquest, colonialism and immigration. Even in the context of Europe, where this conflation first began to be articulated, it was not conceptually meaningful to conflate the two. The cultural diversities there were too significant to permit such a luxury. The situation becomes more complicated in the context of India where the range of diversities becomes enormously huge making it almost impossible to conflate nation with state. Any such conflation becomes highly problematical in nature. The wide gap between the empirical reality of India and the concept of nation-state needs to be recognized. The systematic denigration of the idea of multi-national state needs to be resisted. The idea of nation-state sits uncomfortably with the reality of cultural diversities. The federal political structure that has been institutionalized is a device to articulate and protect the federal quality of our society.

Coming to the North-East, he argues that the state-society dichotomy is substantial. There are only eight states but a greater number of societies in the North-East, and then proceeds to examine the nature of social change in the North-East. Before doing so, he problematizes some of the popular misconceptions about the North-East. One of such misconceptions is that the North-East is predominantly inhabited by the tribes whereas in reality there are only four states (out of eight) which are dominated numerically by the tribal communities. In this context he makes a distinction between a tribal society and peasant society by saying that tribal societies are autonomous in terms of social structure and culture, whereas peasant societies are part-societies. Further tribal societies are stratified whereas peasant societies are both stratified and hierarchical. Then he argues against viewing the entire population of North-East as having been converted into Christianity. Only three out of eight states in the North-East have a Christian majority while four are Hindu majority states. He proceeds to dispel another couple of such misconceptions about the North-East.

Any study of social change should identify the point of departure or the base line from which social changes begin. In the context of North-East he identifies three such base lines – the advent of Ahoms in Assam, the colonial intrusion and the achievement of independence. Changes brought about by these three forces, singly or conjointly, should be part of any study of social changes in the North-East. Finally, in his keynote address, he identifies certain actual processes of social changes in the North-East. For example, the complete displacement of cultural patterns is usually not noticed in the tribal societies of the North-East. What one finds is accretion. Similarly changes in material conditions, as popularly assumed, are not always faster as compared to cultural changes. The spread of education is greater in tribal North-East as compared peasant societies in the North-East. He also notes the declining influence of secessionist forces in the North-East possibly because of deepening of the process of democratization and its institutionalization in suitable political structures (village councils, for example) and introduction of developmental policies and programmes in the North-East.

Prasenjit Biswas, in his philosophically-informed article, interrogates the very idea of the 'social'. He argues that the nature of social change needs to be understood in conceptual terms. One of the critical aspects concerning social change is an understanding of the interplay between social structure and the social agency. This can be interpreted and theorized following the canons of Marx, Althusser and Weber. It can be argued that these three leading pathfinders of Social Sciences have advanced epistemic and praxiological notions of the 'social', there arises an ontological and ethical view of the 'social' that surpasses any deterministic notion of 'society' as a 'context'. This different and not yet fully received theoretical move within Social Sciences rearticulates an idea of the 'social' as a domain of 'freedom' that is filled in with many possibilities of 'change', both material and immaterial. The paper mobilizes some of the positions that are already contested within Social Sciences in order to arrive at a different ontology of the 'social'. The paper elaborates on this transitional notion of the social in the context of the North-East India to suggest that the 'politics of self-preservation' in the realm of political economy and culture have resulted into a skewed notion of change that needs a correction. In terms of disciplinary bounds of understanding, such transitions require de-disciplining and deterritorializing the idea of the 'social' into 'social change' as an experiential category that discloses more than it declares. Such a shift in our disciplinary orientation could lead us to quite a few home truths that currently unsettle us in the realm of development as well as in our knowledge of the society in the context of the North-East of India.

A.C. Sinha, in his elaboration of factors of social change which he defines as recurrent, repetitive and relatively long-term alterations at different levels, identifies coming of missionaries, introduction of British administration, exposure of the North-East to the world wars, achievement of independence and inauguration of welfare state in India. The missionaries introduced the Roman script so that different dialects spoken in the North-East could be converted into languages. They provided valuable contribution to education and modern health care system. Similarly monetization of land introduced by the British administration had proved to be a highly influential factor of social change in the North-East changing the nature of ownership pattern. Participation of the people of the North-East in the world wars resulted in their being exposed to the modern ideals of equality, justice and faith. After independence democratization of polity and introduction of welfare state resulted in heightened political consciousness and mobilization among the people of the region.

N. Vijaylakshmi Brara interrogates the very notions of 'development' and 'modernization' and tracing the growth of these terms from their western roots argues that these have been uncritically adopted to understand the process of social change taking place in the Third World countries. What these concepts have done is that they have hierarchized the dualism that exists between the western countries and the Third World countries, with the former being put on a higher pedestal. Coming to the North-East, she contends that for a better understanding of the situation in the North-East, comparative framework would be very meaningful. Development needs to be measured not only on the basis of one component but different components. Human development index should be a vital component of any notion of development. She finally calls for a democratic framework of development instead of alienating the hegemonic frameworks which are currently in place.

Manorama Sharma's paper on *Social Change and Women: Has She Acquired a New Identity in North-East India?* is extremely relevant in a volume of this kind as it fills in the gap by interrogating the issue of gender relations, an issue which has not been given adequate importance in the studies on the North-East. One generally looks at the structural aspects (such as matriliny in Meghalaya, for example) without necessarily looking at the processual aspects in terms of how gender relations are played out on the ground. The experiences of women, which are generally oppressive in nature, go unaddressed. She tries to examine if social changes taking place in the North-East have had an effect on the perception of others on women, their perception of themselves and finally the way their identity is constructed.

C.L. Imchen, in his incisive article, *Construction of Tribal Identity from a Socio-Historical Perspective*, interrogates the nature of discourse that has been the mainstay of constructing the other in European scholarship which has led to the current problematic of understanding the issue of identity concerning the marginalized indigenous groups.

He underlines the colonial roots of such a discourse and looks at how it continues to be employed in contemporary times in the context of the Nagas. He does this by first looking at the relationship of the Nagas with the British which was determined by the principle of 'immemorial possession'. The post-colonial Indian State without considering whether the Nagas consider themselves as part of 'Indian Civilization' incorporated them in its jural-politico administrative structure. The right of self-determination articulated by the Nagas continues to be delegitimized in numerous ways contributing to the continued tensions between the Nagas and the Indian State

D.V. Kumar, in his paper, *Ethnicity and Social Change: The Context of Mizos*, locates the ethnic movement as part of a wider process of social change. He argues that one can make a meaningful appreciation of ethnic movements if they are viewed as a process of social change taking place in the North-East. He makes use of the Lacanion notions of *imago* (the self-image in times of tension) and correlative space (the accompanying perception of social reality) in the understanding the growth of ethnic movements. He takes up the Mizo ethnic movement that took place from the 1960s upto 1980s as case study. The essential argument he offers is that the Mizo ethnic movement was the result of changes which took place in *imago* and correlative space which were in turn caused by the politics of deprivation and neglect which the Mizos were subjected to both by the Centre and the Assam government. While he contextualizes his arguments by referring to the Mizo ethnic movement, he hopes to provide important insights which would be usefully employed in understanding ethnic movements elsewhere too.

N.K. Das looks at the emergence of identity/ethnic politics, separatist movements, sub-regional movements as essentially an expression of perception of deprivation, marginalization and social exclusion. The growing incapacity of the state to address the legitimate needs and aspirations of communities of the North-East in terms of greater political decentralization (in substantive not merely in formal terms), equalitarian distribution of economic resources and measures to protect and promote the cultural identity of communities have been the main factor responsible for the eruption of the numerous socio-political movements in the North-East. They constitute the major component of changes taking place in the North-East. These various movements should not be seen as something dysfunctional for the society. Rather they need to be viewed as constituting a plea for undertaking necessary and appropriate socio-economic and political measures for the alleviation of deprivation and a feeling of neglect among the communities located in the North-East.

Tejimala Gurung gives a historical account of migration of the Nepalese into India since colonial times. She would argue that migration which can be taken as a manifestation of the process of social change has emerged as an important economic and political issue in South Asian countries. Factors responsible for migration could vary from case to case. But migration of any group from one area to the other has deep sociological implications both for the group which is migrating and also for the host group/s. Migration of a group should not be viewed purely in physical terms. It also needs to be viewed in sociological terms for the implications it will have in terms of diverse cultural patterns coming into contact and affecting each other and different political and economic tensions emerging as a result of this. She contextualizes her discussion by looking at the situation of the Nepalese in the North-East.

I.L. Aier looks at the interaction between the Naga traditional authority structure and the modern state structure. Some important changes have been noticed in this interaction between the two. In order to do this, he makes use of Golman's framework of the study of evolution of Polynesian society in terms of linear passage from traditional (the past) to open (transitional phase) and to stratified (culmination point), though he does notice that there are obvious differences between the Polynesian society and the Naga society

Pariyaram M. Chacko's article looks at the relevance of entrepreneurs for the question of generating employment in the North-East. Given the inability of the government to provide employment to every youth, it is necessary to focus on the development of entrepreneurship which has an immense potential for ensuring economic prospect and generating employment opportunities. Its absence can be a serious handicap for development and growth. Then he dwells upon some of the cultural explanations of entrepreneurship (Weber, for example). He examines the growth of entrepreneurship in the North-East among the indigenous communities who for a long time failed to develop a sense of entrepreneurship (as manifested in the absence of big enterprises) thus leaving the field open for the 'outsiders' to come in and occupy it.

P. Nayak and S.K. Misra in their joint paper on *Structural Change in Meghalaya: Theory and Evidence* refer to structural changes as an essential component of economic changes. Globalization is a recent pronounced instance of structural changes taking place in the economy. Structural changes are essentially long-term in nature and involve some important changes in policies and investment patterns. They seek to construct their case by taking Meghalaya as an illustration. They contend that an examination of various socio-economic components such as economic participation and dependency ratio, sectoral distribution of income, changes in demographic attributes etc. would point to structural changes taking place in the Meghalaya economy.

B.N. Borthakur in his paper *Industrialization and Socio-Cultural Transformation of Rural Community in Assam* adopts a structural-functional framework to examine the changes taking place in a community in terms of occupational structure, education levels, family structure, food habits, attitudes towards religion and greater exposure to means of mass communication, dress patterns and so on as a result of establishment of Oil India Ltd. This is an empirical study which establishes in a typical structural-functional framework a close relation between economy and society.

Debendra Kumar Nayak's article examines a powerful demographic transition that is sweeping across the globe (India is no exception) and its impact on the size and age structure of population of the world. The number of the elderly is rising substantially all over the world. The North-East India, too, is witnessing such a significant demographic shift. In this context he makes a sociologically interesting comparative study between areas of tribal dominance and areas which have a predominance of non-tribal communities on the basis of data collected from successive census enumeration from 1971–2001. He concludes the paper by identifying some of the important issues and challenges that this kind of demographic transition throws up concerning the aged.

K. Debbarma looks at the highly fluid situation in Tripura caused by migration of 'outsiders' into the state. The growing incidence of militancy in the state, may be attributed to a great extent by the increasing incidence of migration. He argues that unless appropriate steps are taken by the state in this regard, the situation will be bound to worsen and become more volatile.

Biswambhar Panda in his article looks at the NGOs as instruments of social change in terms of promoting education, creating awareness and empowering the disadvantaged sections of the society. He makes an empirical examination of the contribution made by the NGOs and the role played by them in ensuring people's participation in developmental process. The analytical framework he uses for this purpose is that of collective action framework. He also takes up issues such as accountability of the NGOs for a critical discussion.

Rekha M. Shangpliang engages herself with an understanding of organic linkages between society and nature in the context of the Khasis of Meghalaya. The linkages between nature and the Khasis are explored in the tribal folklores and legends. The harmonious and peaceful co-existence between society and nature has come under a lot of pressure in the recent past owing to several forces such as British rule, advent of Christianity, heightened process of modernization etc. The natural resources of the region over which communities in the North-East in general and the Khasis in particular depend are being plundered and exploited for commercial purposes. This has serious implications for man-nature relationship and these are dealt with at length in this paper.

A perusal of the articles in this volume would clearly point to the central theme that runs through all of them. Whether one is interrogating aspects of change in the North-East, or engaged in understanding the process of identity construction or looking at the demographic transition experienced in the North-East, or examining the impact of movement of the non-tribals into the tribal areas, the central dialectic that informs all the articles is that of social change. It is the basic analytical variable that is used to deal with wide-ranging issues concerning the societies of the North-East. It is hoped that this volume would prove a useful and meaningful intervention in the current interrogation of social changes that are occurring in the North-East and about which very few sociological accounts are available.

References

Aron, R. 1965. *Main Currents in Sociological Thought.* Vol. I. Harmondsworth: Penguin.

Bailey, F.G. 1957. *Caste and the Economic Frontier.* Manchester: Manchester University Press.

Baruah, S. 2005. *Durable Disorder: Understanding the Politics of North-East India.* New Delhi: Oxford University Press.

Berna, J. 1961. *Industrial Entrepreneurs and Entrepreneurship in Madras State.* Bombay: Alice Press.

Beteille, A. 1965. *Caste, Class and Power.* Berkeley and Los Angeles: University of California Press.

Black, C.E. 1966. *The Dynamics of Modernization: A Study in Comparative History.* New York: Harper & Row.

Bottomore, T.B. 1965. 'Modern Elite in India', in T.K.N. Unnithan et al. (eds), *Towards a Sociology of Culture.* New Delhi: Prentice Hall of India, 180–188.

Chaube, S. 1973. *Hill Politics in North-East India.* Bombay: Orient Longman.

Comte, A. 1915. *The Positive Philosophy.* Translated and edited by Harriet Martineau. London: George Bell.

Coser, L.A. 1956. *Functions of Social Conflict.* Glencoe, Ill.: Free Press.

Dahrendorf, R. 1959. *Class and Class Conflict in Industrial Society.* Stanford: Stanford University Press.

Davis, K. 1959. 'The Myth of Functional Analysis as a Special Method in Sociology and Anthropology', *American Sociological Review,* 24(6): 757–772.

Desai, A.R. (ed.) 1961. *Rural Sociology in India.* Bombay: Popular Book Depot.

Desai, I.P. 1965. *Aspects of Family in Mahwa.* Bombay: Asia Publishing House.

Dube, S.C. 1955. *Indian Village.* London: Routledge and Kegan Paul.

—. 1958. *India's Changing Villages.* London: Routledge and Kegan Paul.

Dumount, L. 1972. *Homo Hierarchicus.* London: Paladin.

Durkheim, E. 1964. *The Division of Labour in Society.* New York: Free Press.

Gerth, H. and C.W. Mills. 1953. *Character and Social Structure.* New York: Harcourt.

Ginsberg, M. 1958. 'Social Change', *British Journal of Sociology,* 4: 205–229.

Habermas, J. 1971. *Towards a Rational Society.* London: Heinemann.

Hagen, E.E. 1962. *On the Theory of Social Change: How Economic Growth Begins.* Homewood, Ill.: Dorsey Press.

Horkheimer, M. and T. Adorno. 1972. *Dialectic of Enlightenment.* London: Allen Lane.

Ishwaran, K. 1966. *Tradition and Economy in Village India.* London: Routledge and Kegan Paul.

Kapadia, K.M. 1958. *Marriage and Family in India.* New Delhi: Oxford University Press.

Kumar, D.V. 2008. 'Engaging with Modernity: Need for a Critical Negotiation', *Sociological Bulletin*, 57(2): 240–254.

Lambert, R.D. 1963. *Workers, Factories and Social Change in India.* New Jersey: Princeton University Press.

Leach, E.R. (ed.) 1960. *Aspects of Caste in South India, Ceylon and N.W. Pakistan.* Cambridge: University of Cambridge Press.

Levy, M.J. 1966. *Modernization and the Structure of Society.* New Jersey: Princeton University Press.

Lewis, O. 1958. *Life in a North Indian Village.* Alabama: University of Illinois Press.

MacIver, R.M. and C.H. Page. 1949. *Society: An Introductory Analysis.* New York: Holt, Rinehart & Winston.

Majumdar, D.N. 1958. *Caste and Communication in an Indian Village.* New York: Asia Publishing House.

Marcuse, H. 1972. *One-dimensional Man.* London: Abacus.

Marriot, M. 1955. 'Social Structure and Change in a UP Village', in M.N. Srinivas (ed.), *India's Villages.* Bombay: Asia Publishing House, 95–121.

—. 1955. *Village India.* Chicago: University of Chicago Press.

—. 1960. *Caste Ranking and Community Structure in Five Regions of India and Pakistan.* Poona: Deccan College.

Marx, K. and F. Engels. 1968. *Selected Works.* London: Lawrence & Wishart.

Mayer, A.C. 1960. *Caste and Kinship in Central India.* Berkeley and Los Angeles: University of California Press.

McClelland, D.C. 1961. *The Achieving Society.* Princeton, NJ: Van Nostrand.

Merton, R. 1968. *Social Theory and Social Structure.* New York: Free Press.

Misra, U. 2000. *The Periphery Strikes Back: Challenges to the Nation-State in Assam and Nagaland.* Shimla: Indian Institute of Advanced Study.

Moore, W.E. 1994. *Social Change.* 2nd edn. New Delhi: Prentice Hall of India.

Morgan, L.H. 1964 (1877). *Ancient Society.* Cambridge: Harvard University Press.

Nisbet, R.A. 1969. *Social Change and History.* New York: Oxford University Press.

Ogburn, W.F. 1964. *On Culture and Social Change.* Chicago: University of Chicago Press.

Park, L. and I. Tinker. 1959. *Leadership and Political Institutions in India.* New Jersey: Princeton University Press.

Parsons, T. 1951. *The Social System.* London: Routledge.

—. 1966. *Societies: Evolutionary and Comparative Perspectives.* Englewood Cliffs, NJ: Prentice Hall.

Pocock, D.F. 1967. 'Sociologies: Urban and Rural', *Contributions to Indian Sociology*, IV: 52–69.

Ross, A.D. 1961. *The Hindu Family in its Urban Setting.* Toronto: University of Toronto.

Rowe, W.L. 1963. 'Changing Rural Class Structure and the Jajmani System', *Human Organization*, 22(1): 41–44.

Singh, B.P. 1987. *The Problem of Change: A Study of North-East India.* New Delhi: Oxford University Press.

Singh, Y. 1973. *Modernization of Indian Tradition.* Faridabad: Thomson Press (India) Limited.

Smelser, N.J. 1959. *Social Change in the Industrial Revolution.* Chicago: University of Chicago Press.

Srinivas, M.N. 1955. *India's Villages.* Bombay: Asia Publishing House.

—. 1962. *Caste in Modern India and Other Essays.* Bombay: Asia Publishing House.

—. 1972. *Social Change in Modern India.* New Delhi: Orient Longman.

Turner, R. (ed.) 1962. *Urban Future.* Berkeley: University of California Press.

Unnithan, T.K.N. et al. 1965. *Towards a Sociology of Culture in India.* New Delhi: Prentice Hall of India.

Vago, S. 1989. *Social Change.* New Jersey: Prentice Hall.

Weber, M. 1967. *The Protestant Ethic and the Spirit of Capitalism.* London: Unwin.

Weiner, M. 1961. 'Changing Leadership in West Bengal', in A.R. Desai (ed.), *Rural Sociology in India.* Bombay: Popular Book Depot, 72–91.

1

Social Change in the North-East India

Some Methodological Issues

T.K. OOMMEN

It is a truism that for the analysis of social change 'society' should be the unit. And yet, this self-evident truth poses extremely complex issues because of the efforts to link societies and states. States and societies have always existed; if societies are viewed as products of gradual evolution, states are believed to be consciously constituted structures for regulating the behaviour of the relevant population as and when required. Although some western anthropologists referred to 'tribal' communities as 'stateless societies' it is a conceptual nullity in that all societies have had legitimized authority structures. They manifested in a wide variety of forms – tribal chiefs, council of elders, ecclesiastical heads, emperors, monarchs, dynasties, city-states, party-states and democratic states. If states and societies were co-terminus there would not have been any issue in endorsing them as units of analyses. But this is not true.

It is widely acknowledged that the effort to establish isomorphism between state and society began only 360 years ago when the Treaty of West Phalia gave birth to the institution of nation-state. Ever since that as Zygmunt Bauman, the Polish social scientist, had aptly observed, '... with hardly any exception, all the concepts and analytical tools currently employed by social scientists are geared to a view of the human world in which the most voluminous totality is a 'society', a notion equivalent for all practical purposes, to the concept of 'nation-state' (1973: 78).

I suggest that the conflation of society and nation-state sowed the seeds of initial confusion. Gradually, the institution of nation-state came to be endorsed as an ideal and nation-state and state became equivalents. Thus, the conflation of society and nation-state and hyphenation of nation and state are the twin sources of the prevailing conceptual confusions and the problems in identifying an appropriate unit for the study of social change.

Diametrically opposite articulations are made about linking state and nation/society. Let me illustrate it by recalling the views of two British authors. J.S. Mill held: 'It is in general, a necessary condition of free institutions that the boundaries of government should coincide with those of nationality ...' (cited in Smith, 1971: 9). But Lord Acton differed violently: 'Nationality does not aim at either liberty or prosperity, both of which it sacrifices to the imperative necessity of making the nation the mould and measure of the state; its course will be marked with material and moral ruin' (cited in Smith, 1971: 9). I can go on with this exercise of recalling both positive and negative pronouncements regarding linking the state and the nation and its consequences. But these excursions will not be helpful in arriving at a consensus. And as Tilly (1994: 137) reports after analysing states and nationalism for five centuries, 'only a tiny proportion of the world's distinctive religious, linguistic and cultural groupings have formed their own states, while precious few of the world's existing states have approximated the homogeneity and commitment conjured up by the label 'nation state'.

Independent India, after some initial hesitation, decided to re-constitute its politico-administrative units on linguistic basis. This was based on the recommendations of the State Reorganisation Commission (SRC) which submitted its report in 1956. This was indeed a giant leap forward in improving the governability of India. At the time of the reorganization of the states in the 1950s two broad views were articulated. One view was that the unity of India must not be imposed but must be a fundamental unity recognizing its social pluralities and cultural diversity; the strength of Indian Union must be the strength that it derives from its constituent units, an approximation of J.S. Mill's view and an implicit endorsement of the idea of a multi-national state. The other view was that in the past India had not been an integrated political unit and so the effort should be to create a united India; the new concept of unity cannot be based on the re-affirmation or re-enunciation of old values such as religion and language which are divisive rather than cohesive. Therefore, the unity of India should transcend community (read religion) and language and recognize the nation as one integrated unit. This view reflects an acknowledgment of Lord Acton's position and endorses the homogenization project of nation-states.

However, Indian political praxis does not neatly fit either of these positions. Both empirical reality and political expediency called for a cautious approach. There are four important bases of socio-cultural identity in India – religion, caste, tribe and language. Of these the first two are not viable for the formation of politico-administrative units (see Oommen, 2005: 142–52) and language and tribe are accepted as the bases for the formation of provincial states.

The purpose of this short exercise in conceptual history is to suggest that there is an enormous gap between the empirical reality of India and the concept of nation-state. Therefore, it is appropriate to designate India as a multi-national state. But even those who used to invoke the notion in the past have abandoned it because it is not viewed as politically correct any more. Perhaps the disintegration of multi-national socialist states and the emergence of mono-national states in their place has accelerated the process of rejecting the notion of multi-national state. As I see it there exists a conceptual vacuum created by (i) the lack of fit between the concept of nation-state and society, and (ii) the delegitimation of the idea of multi-national state. However, there is no serious effort made in political theory to grapple with this issue (see Oommen, 1997, for an exception).

If India's complex empirical reality cannot be denoted by the concept of nation-state and if the notion of multi-national state is no more in vogue, what is an appropriate designation for India? Charles Tilly's coinage, namely, *national state* seems to be helpful. However, his definition of national states as '... relatively centralized, differentiated and autonomous organizations successfully claiming priority in the use of force within large, contiguous and clearly bounded territories' (1990: 43) fits more the bureaucratic structures of states and completely ignores the emotional appeal implied in the idea of nation. Further, national states are viewed as transitory structures; they are nation-states-in-the-making in Tilly's rendition, which does not fit the Indian reality. Therefore, I have suggested that national states should be viewed as entities which not simply accommodate but consciously celebrate cultural diversities in contrast to nation-states which are perpetually engaged in creating mono-cultural states. This would require the co-existence of federal political structures along with social and cultural diversities (see Oommen, 2008: 21–36). The essence of federalism lies not in the constitutional or institutional structures but in the society itself. Federal government is a device through which the federal qualities of the society are articulated and protected (Livingston, 1966). Therefore, what Smith (1979) designated as 'methodological nationalism' an offshoot of treating nation-states as the ultimate units of analysis is utterly unsuited for comprehending Indian social reality. This also poses methodological issues in treating India's North-East region as a unit of analysis to understand the ongoing process of social change.

II

The theme of this paper is social change in North-East India. Four issues need to be kept in mind while undertaking this task: one, the nature of the unit being analysed; two, the point/s of departure, three, the process of displacement, and four, the direction of change. I have hinted above that the territory encapsulated within the national state of India consists of numerous societies but all of them may not be appropriate units for analyses. However, the provincial states and union territories established on the bases of language and tribe provide the requisite methodological justification to be treated as appropriate units of analysis. In the case of the North-East the state-society disjunction is substantial; while there are only eight provincial states (including Sikkim) there are numerous societies. Therefore, it is more appropriate to conceptualize the North-East as a 'region'. But there are several misconceptions about the North-East not only in popular imaginations but also in scholarly imageries which do not lend themselves for rigorous analyses. It is necessary to dispel these naïve notions.

First, the North-East is invariably visualized as a region inhabited predominantly by tribes. But of the 461 Scheduled Tribes (STs) of India only 196 live in the North-East and most of them are tiny. In fact, only 13 per cent of India's tribal population lives in the North-East. Further, of the eight states of the North-East, only four – Arunachal Pradesh, Meghalaya, Mizoram and Nagaland – are tribal majority states and the remaining four – Assam, Manipur, Sikkim and Tripura – are populated mainly by the peasantry. It is very pertinent to remind ourselves here of the great sociological relevance of the distinction between tribes and peasants.

Peasant societies are part-societies and tribal societies are autonomous in terms of social structure and culture. Therefore, they should be recognized as two distinct types of societies (see Oommen, 1967: 85–99). which is to say the North-East consists of two ideal types of societies based on the characteristics of reciprocity (peasant) and autonomy (tribe) vis-à-vis the world outside. It could however be argued that the tribal societies are no more autonomous in terms of social structure and culture. Be that as it may, it is necessary to unfold the factors and forces which contributed to the transformulation of tribal societies from autonomous to part-societies. If the starting points of tribal and peasant societies were different the patterns and consequences of social change occurring in them are bound to be different. In an adequate analysis of social change in the North-East this point should be kept in mind.

There is another crucial difference between tribal and peasant societies. As all societies, tribal societies too are stratified based on gender, age, class, power distribution, rural-urban differences. This is true of the tribal North-East too. But the peasant societies of the North-East as elsewhere in India are characterized also by hierarchy. That is, tribal North-East is stratified but peasant North-East is both stratified and hierarchical. This is a crucial difference. True, inequality exists in both these types of societies but in India's peasant society inequality is not only sanctioned but also sanctified through theological doctrines, social values and behavioural norms of Hinduism. The tendency on the part of analysts to overlook this vital fact has obliterated our understanding of the differences in the nature of social change among the tribal and peasant societies in the North-East. It may be that tribal North East is influenced by the caste system through its interaction with peasant North-East. Conversely, the rigidity of caste system in peasant North-East might have got reduced because of its proximity to and interaction with tribal North-East. But these need to be investigated and established.

The second misleading conception about the North-East India is that the region is largely populated by tribes converted to Christianity at the instance of foreign missionaries. But only three out of the eight states in the North-East have Christian majority while four are Hindu majority states. In Arunachal Pradesh 37 per cent of population profess Hinduism which is numerically the biggest religious community. Further, the imagined elective affinity between the tribes of the North-East and Christianity is a myth; Arunachal Pradesh with 80 per cent tribal population have only 10 per cent Christians. Does this disjunction between Christianity and tribal identity affect the patterns and processes of social change in Arunachal Pradesh is what needs to be asked and answered. The relative weak presence of Christianity in Arunachal Pradesh is also important because the argument that the spread of Christianity among those people who were animists and nature worshippers and whose religion was castigated by Christian missionaries does not hold in the case of Arunachal Pradesh. An explanation of this exceptionalism is significant because analysists of social change should also unfold the why of non-change.

The widespread belief that Christianity in the North-East is a colonial transplant is also contrary to facts. Christianity was first introduced into the North-East India during the Mughal period. In 1901 there were only 33,783 Christians which increased to 560, 987 by 1951. But the number of Christians increased fivefold in the first four decades in North-East after the British left India. That is, the phenomenal increase of Christians in the North-East is a post-colonial phenomenon. While before 1950 the great majority of Christians were found in Meghalaya, Nagaland, and the hill areas of Manipur and Mizoram, during the second half of the twentieth century significant conversion movements spread to Tripura and Arunachal Pradesh (see, Downs, 2003: 381–400). Thus both in terms of numbers and spread to new areas the expansion of Christianity in the North-East is largely a phenomenon of Independent India and not colonial India.

The third misconception about the North-East is that it is a den of tribal secessionist movements inspired and/or led by Christian missionaries. This imagery about the North-East instantly stigmatizes the entire region as 'anti-national' and pro-Christian. But what are the facts? Of the six secessionist movements of independent India the three bigger ones crystallized outside the North-East and they have/had explicit link with religion. The Tamil secessionist movement was based on Tamil language and Dravidian Hinduism, the demand for Sikhistan/Khalistan was/is based on Sikh religious identity and Punjabi written in Gurumukhi script and the Azad/Autonomous Kashmir movement is based on Islamic identity reinforced by Urdu language. Of the three secessionist movements in the North-East the two – Naga and Mizo – explicitly invoked tribal nationhood, and the third movement under reference is led by the United Liberation Front of Assam (ULFA) which is non-tribal and non-Christian. In fact the density of social movements in the North-East is disproportionately high as compared with other regions in India (see, Oommen, 2005: 181–95) but only the leaders of the Naga movement highlight their Christian identity. This being so, the stigmatization of secessionist movements of the North-East based on their attributed association with Christianity brings in prejudices in the analysis of social change in the region.

A fourth misconception about India's North-East is that the region is populated by a racially distinct type of people. It is true that some of the communities, notably the Manipuris, the Mizos, the Nagas and the Sikkimese have a different pigmentation but the vast majority of the people in the region are very similar in their physical appearance to the rest of Indians. And curiously, while those with darker pigmentation are discriminated against in the rest of the world, it is the fairer group of the North-East which feels discriminated in India. But the internal phenotypical differences are invariably ignored in media reports. Thus, a recent newspaper report had the caption: 'Our Seven Step Sisters? (*Hindustan Times,* January 13, 2008).

On the other hand, the discriminations which exist within the North-East is perhaps equally acute. For example, an earlier newspaper report (*Hindustan Times,* January 26, 2004) had the caption: 'We are strangers at home'. However, having remarked that 'we are all racist, but it is more palpable between North-East and the mainland', this report noted that the non-Khasis are branded as *'dkhars'* in Meghalaya and non-Mizos are labeled *'Vais'* in Mizoram, i.e., outsiders. Similarly, the Assamese propensity to pre-fix 'naga' to anything extreme is well known. Examples are *'naga jolokia'* for the hottest chilli or *'naga tenga'* for the sourest vegetable. These clearly indicate the prevalence of prejudices among the peoples of the North-East. While the Kuki-Naga clashes are well known, what is not so well known is the stigmatization to which Manipuri Nagas are subjected to by the Nagas of Nagaland by referring to the former as Kachcha Nagas. One can go on pointing out other examples but the point to be noted is that there exists tensions not only between the 'North-East periphery' and the 'Indian mainstream' but also within the North-East – between tribes and peasants and between the tribes. An informed analysis of social change cannot ignore these matters which vitally affect everyday life. Do the prevailing stereotypes and articulated prejudices which trigger off conflicts, increase or diminish due the ongoing process of social transformation is a question to be addressed now.

India is the proverbial land of immigrants; immigration into India started in the hoary past. But, over a period of time most of the immigrant groups got domesticated. But, the persisting conflicts between insiders (nationals) and those who are perceived as outsiders (ethnies) result in instability and change, and Assam is a prime theatre of this (see, Oommen, 1982: 41–64). Assam has two major blocks of nationals – Assamese Hindus and the plain tribes (the Bodos) who consider the state as their ancestral homeland. There are several blocks of immigrants – the tribal population brought from Bihar and Orissa during the colonial period, Bengali Muslims and Hindus who came from Bangladesh and West Bengal, and the Nepali Hindus – who look upon Assam as their adopted homeland. But those who consider Assam as their ancestral homeland contest the claims of those who consider Assam as their adopted homeland. Needless to say that the immigrants are invested with varying degrees of legitimacy.

The immigrants from the rest of India do not consider Assam as their homeland – ancestral or adopted – and hence remain ethnies, that is outsiders, in the perception of the locals. To complicate matters the North-East has several linguistic/tribal communities which consider themselves as 'nations'. However, only a few are state-seeking nations (as noted above) and aspire to establish sovereign states. While most are state-renouncing nations and demand only politico-administrative units – provincial states, Regional Councils, District Councils – and have reconciled to remain within the Indian Union. But both secessionist and autonomist aspirations have triggered off socio-political movements which have differing implications for the state and society in the North-East (see, Oommen, 2005: 181–95). It could be stated without the fear of being contradicted that social movements have contributed substantially to the process of social change in the North-East. But a full-fledged analysis of this is awaited.

III

The purpose behind calling into question the widespread misconceptions about India's North-East is to alert the analysts of social change the tortuous task that awaits them. The prevalence of misconceptions often tend to adversely affect 'objective' analysis. Let me now turn to the point of departure or the baseline from which change started in the North-East. The general impression that one gets is that history remained suspended in the North-East till British colonialism. To get out of this impasse one must make a distinction between replicative and retreatist colonialism (Oommen, 1991: 67–84).

Replicative colonialism creates settlement societies as in the New World of Americas and Australia. The colonizers settle down in the new region which was 'discovered' and replicates their social structure and culture through political and economic domination completely marginalizing, through genocide and culturocide (the systematic destruction of the cultures of the local population). A variant of this happens when the immigrant community establishes its hegemony over the geographical space into which it comes without indulging in genocide and culturocide. This is illustrated by the Ahom advent in Assam much before British colonialism and Bengali immigration into Tripura after India became independent. The Ahom advent in Assam has an interesting parallel in Northern India – the Aryan advent. But the domestication and domination of the Aryans and the Ahoms is so complete that analysts refuse to cognize these intrusions as alien to their respective regions. The analytical consequence of not distinguishing between replicative and retreatist colonialism is disastrous because the real baseline from which social change started gets eclipsed. Further, the baselines seem to be different for peasant North-East and tribal North-East – the Ahom advent for the former and British colonialism for the latter with attendant consequences. For example, Ahom kings permitted preaching of Islam in Assam in the seventeenth century which partly explains the strong Muslim presence in the peasant North-East. A long duree analysis of social change in the North-East cannot ignore the differing starting points and the differences in the orientations of the type of colonialisms involved.

British colonialism was retreatist in that after two centuries the colonizers had to withdraw, certainly not willingly but due to the enormous pressure mounted on them through the anti-colonial movement. At any rate, it does not seem to be correct to attribute Christianization of a few major tribal communities to the proselytization policy pursued by the British state. It is pertinent to recall the 1858 proclamation of the British Queen in this context: 'Firmly relying ourselves on the truth of Christianity and acknowledging with gratitude the solace of religion, we disclaim alike the Right and Desire to impose our convictions on any of our subjects' (quoted in Firth, 1976: 189). I am not arguing that the British adhered to the announced policy, nor am I suggesting that some of the colonial officials have not facilitated conversion to Christianity. But I insist that the analyst should recognize the distinction between official policy and practice because it has serious implications for understanding the texture of social change.

If the British policy were one of systematic proselytization the Christian population in India would not have remained as low as it was on the eve of colonial exit. And, the expansion of Christianity increased several fold in the North-East after the British left as I have already noted. This being so the widespread popular perception that Christianization of the North-East is attributable solely or at least largely to British colonialism needs to re-examined because the spread of Christianity is widely endorsed as an important factor of social change in the North-East. The role of Christian missionaries also needs to be objectively examined because at least a section of Indian social scientists hold that they were here not simply as propagators of Christianity but were also agents of imperialism (see, for an example, Sinha, 1972: 410–23).

There is a third baseline the analyst of social change in the North-East should keep in mind, that of Indian Republic's massive effort to integrate the region into the 'national' mainstream, the euphemism invoked being nation building. There is a colossal perceptual gap between mainstream India and the North-East periphery, particularly those who challenge the hegemonic orientation of the Union. What is perceived as national integration from the centre is cognized as internal colonialism by the periphery. These variations in cognitions have profound consequences for the analysis of social change.

There is another aspect to 'integration' of the tribes into the mainstream. In the 1931 census of India, there was an entry under religion referred to as animist, primitive or nature worship. But in 1951, the first census of independent India all those who did not convert into one of the world religions – Buddhism, Christianity, Islam – were absorbed into Hinduism. This route to cultural absorption shattered the religious identity of millions of tribal Indians. In the North-East it is not an acute problem given the fact that most of the tribal population has embraced one of the established religions. But yet the problem persists. For example, in 1991, 36 per cent of the people of Arunachal Pradesh and 17 per cent in Meghalaya did not identity themselves with Hinduism, Islam, Christianity, Buddhism, Sikhism or Jainism. What are the implications of this?

Since the benefits of reservation are available to all tribal communities irrespective of their religious identity, identifying with one of the less established religions may not adversely affect their economic privileges or political prospects. But is it likely to affect their social standing and cultural identity within their communities? Is it not appropriate to investigate the variations in the nature and quality of social change taking place among those groups which retain their primal vision and those who embraced one of the established religions?

The project of cultural homogenization, the mission of nation-state, is singularly unsuited for India which I designate as national state, an entity which celebrates cultural diversity within the framework of the federal polity (Oommen, 2008: 21–36). That is, 'integration' of the North-East, particularly tribal North-East, can only mean political and economic integration. But the federal structure should concede the requisite political and economic autonomy to all its constituent units. In turn the provincial states should vertically transmit political and economic autonomy to the structures below it. On the other hand, the social structural and cultural specificities of the linguistic and cultural communities cannot be tampered with. Such a dual process, reciprocity in political and economic contexts and retaining autonomy of culture and social structure would throw up a process of social change which is specific to the North-East, particularly the tribal North-East. The examination of this specificity should be an important item on the agenda of the study of social change in the North-East.

The three baselines I have identified – the Ahom advent, the colonial intrusion and the birth of independent India – have differing reverberations and varying impacts on the North-East. Some of these are complimentary but others are contradictory and pull in opposite directions. Their impact, singly and conjointly, needs to be recognized and analysed to understand social change in the North-East.

IV

Let me now refer briefly to what I have called the process of displacement and the point of destination. The tendencies observed in the West in the context of social change are mainly two. One is displacement anchored to western epistemological dualism. And, the second is the differential rate of change occurring in different dimensions of society which gave birth to the notion of culture lag. Neither of these tendencies seem to be applicable as they are in the Indian case. Thus, as against displacement it is accretion which results in the co-existence of the old and new elements that usually occurs in India. Similarly, it is not that the change in material dimensions is faster as compared with the realm of values; it could be reverse. And, these tendencies have their specificities in the peasant North-East and the tribal North-East given the variations in their points of departure.

For example, the incorporation of Assam into the world tea market had affected the peasantry more. But, the arrival of Christianity made greater inroads into the tribal world. The structure of joint family of the peasantry is gradually giving way to nuclear family but not disappearing. Similarly, monogamous marriages have not completely displaced polygamous unions among tribes. The folk legal system and the state legal system co-exist among tribes in different contexts and with differing legitimacy. In contrast, the religious legal systems and the state legal system co-exist in the case of peasantry. But, both the peasantry and tribes have a common criminal legal system along with their co-citizens in India.

The spread of education differs across the different politico-administrative units. In general, the spread is better in the tribal North-East with Mizoram achieving full literacy. In contrast the peasants lag behind in education; the case of Muslim peasantry being particularly worrisome. As for gender equity the tribes have been better off traditionally as compared with the peasantry. In turn this indicates that patriarchy has been less oppressive among the tribes. But in some tribes (e.g., the Khasis) the women have had an edge over men traditionally because of matriarchy and the inheritance system of property from mother to daughter. This is gradually disappearing with the modernization of economy and men taking employment in the non-agricultural sector. But, the customary advantage of the Khasi women in the economic context did not facilitate their wielding political power. Indeed there has been a gap in the status of Khasi women between the economic and political sectors and that is persisting; they are not much visible in the political space even today.

From the brief narration that I have attempted it is clear that one cannot speak of a uniform set of changes in social structure and culture. On the other hand, certain broad trends are visible in political and economic contexts. For example, the extremist tendencies in the sphere of political mobilization are gradually disappearing. The Mizos have reconciled to the idea of finding their fortunes within the Indian Republic. The secessionist tendency of the Naga National Movement has blunted and to-day the focus is to consolidate the Naga Nation within the territorial ambit of India. The secessionist streak in ULFA has always been ambiguous and the ultimate objective seems to be to wrest a place of dignity for the Assamese people under the political roof of India.

Even as secessionist tendencies are dwindling the proclivity to pursue political autonomy for the different nations (read linguistic groups and tribes) within the Indian state system is proliferating. This can be contained within the framework of a federal polity which recognizes and respects cultural identities. At the same time, the predatory tendency of the state, particularly the Indian state, comes for intense interrogation because of its perceived proclivity to violate human rights. The civil society becomes an important agent of social change in this context and this manifest in the numerous tribal associations which assert their base anchored to tradition to secure citizenship entitlements.

Social change in the North-East India today, as elsewhere, seems to be primarily technology-driven and market-prompted. Even education is adapting to this emerging ethos. Thus skill-oriented, encashable education which can provide quick huge monetary returns is preferred. The newly enunciated look-east policy is providing intense motivation to become efficient and prompting migration. A small segment of the North-East elite youth is migrating to different parts of India as well as beyond the borders. They are gradually entering the brain pool of the world. However, the economic mobility experienced by the youth of the North-East does not seem to be uprooting them from their traditional attachments. A new hybridity – economic prosperity, political assertion and cultural rootedness – is emerging. Needless to say different permutations and combinations of this hybridity depending upon points of departure and processes through which society passes through would emerge. For the student social change of the North-East the present moment poses a huge challenge and provides an exemplary opportunity.

References

Bauman, Zygmunt. 1973. *Culture as Praxis.* London: Routledge and Kegan Paul.

Downs, F.S. 2003. 'Christian Conversion Movements in North-East India', in R. Robinson and S. Clarke (eds), *Religious Conversion in India: Modes, Motivations and Meanings.* New Delhi: Oxford University Press, 381–400.

Firth, C.B. 1976. *An Introduction to Indian Church History.* Madras: Christian Literature Society.

Livingston, W.S. 1966. *Federalism and Constitutional Change.* Oxford: Clarendon Press.

Oommen, T.K. 1967. 'The Rural Urban Continuum Re-examined in the Indian Context', *Sociologia Ruralis,* 7(1): 85–99, reproduced in T.K. Oommen, *Social Transformation in Rural India: Mobilization and State Intervention.* New Delhi: Vikas Publishing House, 1984.

—. 1982. 'Refugees, Foreigners and Outsiders in the Indian Context', *Sociological Bulletin,* 21(1): 41–64, reproduced in T.K. Oommen, *State and Society in India: Studies in Nation Building.* New Delhi: Sage, 1990.

—. 1991. 'Internationalization of Sociology: A View from Developing Countries', *Current Sociology,* 39(1): 67–84, reproduced in T.K. Oommen, *Knowledge and Society: Situating Sociology and Social Anthropology.* New Delhi: Oxford University Press, 2007.

—. 1997. *Citizenship, Nationality and Ethnicity: Reconciling Competing Identities.* Cambridge: Polity Press.

—. 2005. 'State and Social Movements in Northeast India', in T.K. Oommen (ed.), *Crisis and Contention in Indian Society.* New Delhi: Sage, 181–195.

—. 2008. 'Nation Building and Diversity', in R.L. Watts and R. Chattopadhyay (eds), *Building and Accommodating Diversities.* New Delhi: Viva Press, 21–36.

Sinha, Surajit. 1972. 'Tribal Solidarity Movements in India', in K. Suresh Singh (ed.), *Tribal Situation in India.* Shimla: Indian Institute of Advanced Study, 410–423.

Smith, A.D. 1971. *Theories of Nationalism.* London: Duckworth.

—. 1979. *Nationalism in the Twentieth Century.* Oxford: Oxford University Press.

Tilly, Charles. 1990. *Coercion, Capital and European States, A.D. 990–1990.* Cambridge: Basil Blackwell.

—. 1994. 'States and Nationalism in Europe, 1492–1992', *Theory and Society,* 22(1): 131–146.

2

On the Idea of 'Social Change'

Towards a Conceptual Response to Transitions in North-East India

PRASENJIT BISWAS

The idea of 'social change' has received several interpretations from a variety of schools of thought. The present paper follows a rather simpler pathway: it proceeds from the very idea of the 'social' to the idea of 'change' and examines how 'social change' divides the conceptual terrain into a structure versus agency kind of debate. The idea of 'social' emerges as a paradigm for social theories since late 50s and it is handed down as a manufactured notion within the interpretative movements of Social Sciences. Beyond these received frames of epistemic and praxiological notions of the 'social', there arises an ontological and ethical view of the 'social' that surpass any deterministic notion of 'society' as a 'context'. This different and not yet fully received theoretical move within Social Sciences rearticulates an idea of the 'social' as a domain of 'freedom' that is filled in with many possibilities of 'change', both material and immaterial. The paper mobilizes some of the positions that are already contested within Social Sciences in order to arrive at a different ontology of the 'social'. Further, a conceptualization of 'change' in terms of non-linear and dynamic alterations of what an existential shift signifies gives rise to a concept of change that assumes a great sense of 'freedom' and 'creativity'. Understanding 'social change' in such a decoded manner is a mode of understanding how change touches itself and how it phenomenally fritters away its potentialities for 'freedom' in drawing boundaries and limits. This understanding shall develop a responsive account of 'social change' as a 'category of experience' in North-East India that demands a greater concern by being different for the conceptual straight-jackets of the 'mainstream' disciplinary Social Sciences.

De-disciplining and De-territorializing the 'Social'

If society is looked upon as 'non-totalitizable' that has in-diffusible diversity of 'segments', it cannot be given a singular 'meaning'. Rather the meaning of the term 'society' would be plagued by a plurality that is neither a representation of many faces of the so-called social reality nor a collection of shades of its constituents. The plurality inherent in society cannot just be explained in terms of various constituents and their historical pathways to a kind of maturity, it needs to be explained only in terms of including that which has been excluded. The craft of being social thereby becomes inclusionary without an agenda of inclusion and exclusion; as such an agenda would do the opposite of what it means. The reason being an over determined/underdetermined agenda of change ending up in constructing dualities and binaries that only privileges the one side over the other. It is rather the case that the inner potential for change that lies at the heart of a society does not make itself readily available for an agenda or programme of change. A programmatic vision of change cannot take itself beyond a few steps of institutional reforms, it cannot bring forth a change of signification that can be attached to an experience of change. Therefore liminality of an agenda of change in the 'social' can pave the way for a big change in the very concept of change, which in turn evolves into a different notion of 'social change' by reorienting the very concept of the 'social'.

Let us consider, to start with, the ranging debate between Marx and Weber on the very idea of the 'social'. Marx of *Grundrisse* and Weber of *Protestant Ethic* are in a potentially volatile contrast. For Marx, production of value and the time needed for such a production are nomologically related. For him, 'circulation time is not time during which capital creates value, but rather during which it realizes the value created in the production process. It does not increase its quantity, but rather transposes it into another form, from the form of product into that of commodity, from commodity to that of money etc. (...). Thus circulation time appears as time which does not determine the price; and the number of turnovers, in so far as it is determined by circulation time, appears not in such a way that capital brings in a new value-determining element, an element proper to it, *sui generis*, as distinct from labour; but rather as a limiting, negative principle. The necessary tendency of capital is therefore *circulation without circulation time,* (...) the highest result it achieves in this line is, on one side, *fictitious capital;* on the other side, credit only appears as a new element of *concentration*, of the destruction of capitals by individual, centralizing capitals' (Marx, 1973: 46).

Weber's *Protestant Ethic* allows capital a circulation time in order to add values to it and provides a positive principle of changing the systems of exchange that are based on outmoded values. Weber's notion of 'value' does not depend on circulation or circulation time, it is primarily an 'instrument' of rationalization of any productive activity and its consequences. Contrastingly, for Marx, the social character of capital gets its motion as well as its rest from the time of its circulation, which gets arbitrarily terminated. Capital, for Marx can become 'fictitious' as it circulates in time to appropriate its own use-value, while for Weber, any amount of time spent in circulation only adds to the value, without any distinction between 'use-value' and 'exchange value'. Weber's *Protestant Ethic* developed an idea of 'labour' that 'orders world content according to some plan' (Gerth and Mills, 1946: 293–94) and emphasized on 'gain spirit', which as the very coinage suggests, is an outcome of rationalized human work. In contrast to Marx's granting the capital almost an autotelic capacity, Weber subjects it to a larger project of rationalization of the economy and society. From a Weberian point of view, circulation time of capital is the time taken to 'rationalize' its achievements, which relies on a complex connection between labour and strategies of managing production. A kind of Weberian Marxism arose in USSR affirming 'Taylorism' and pursuance of principles of efficient management, which is a reverent admission of productive capacity of capitalism. In other words, circulation time of capital is the source of its productive capacity that would shape the process of rationalization of the political economy of surplus and profit. This mixing of political economy and the process of rationalization is the *unresolved* paradigmatic perspective on the very notion of the 'social' that is both economic and ideological.

This leads us to an understanding of the 'social' in terms of ideology critique. Ideology as a category of articulation and representation encompasses a structure of 'social' that is not just constituted by its components, but it is a complex transformation of actors and their perspective on themselves. 'Ideology' as a category of understanding establishes a culture of reproduction of the past practices in the form of a 'structure', where the relationship between agents and their action is determined by the possibility of reproduction of 'past practices'. In other words, practices meant for changing a structure of ideas and actions do not change on its own because of collective will of the agent, but it continues reproducing itself in various ways. This is how an ideological reproduction of a set of practices goes along the capitalist machine of production that ensures cultivation of a certain moral and cultural kind of human labour that capitalist production requires. 'Reproduction' in Marx meant reproduction of not only the social relations of capitalist mode of production that largely depends on a willing acceptance of ideological dominance of capital, but it also meant 'ideas' that can make it run. Such 'ideas' are collaborative to institutions and organizations that can produce a 'social' or 'collective' affirmation of the mode in which capital reproduces itself and circulates. As the whole, idea of the 'social' becomes only an element in the whole mechanism of capitalist reproduction, any possibility of change is inscribed within the material existence of an ideological apparatus (Althusser, 1970: 158). Ideas are 'material' as they are inscribed in practices of reproduction, which in turn, is an outcome of institutional and organization processes that follow the same logic of reproduction. Such a logic of reproduction creates ideas in terms of its system of meaning and representation that gives significance to 'practices' that reproduce the logic of capital, hence, it is not possible to think of 'change' outside this system of representation of ideas that collaborate with capital. This bring us to what Weber stated as 'rationalization', which in Marxist framework would be those functioning and collaborating ideas that guide the logic of capital and vice-versa. The only difference between Weber and Marx lies in the fact that Marx 'dialectically' subjects ideas to the logic of capital, while Weber privileges the abstract force of reason by actors in providing justification for practices.

All these could be considered as pre-Lacanian, pre-Foucauldian and pre-Derridean notions of the relationship between ideas and 'representation of the social world' as determination of ideas by the structure. Such prevailing mode of rationalization presupposes the logic of the capital. Lacan, Foucault and Derrida break through this thesis of structural determination of ideas by taking into account the *freeplay* between idea and structure as it happens within a complex relationship of mutual and reciprocal relationship between ideas, events and structure. One can list out the major moves within this trajectory of breaking and disentanglement from Structuralism of both Marxian and Weberian kind.

A break from Weberian kind of structuralism required 'disenchantment' with forms of rationalization. The intertwinement of social action and economic rationality that give rise to large economic order develops an idea of totality or structure that is an outcome of various material and other interests. Contrarily, a Marxist understanding of 'totality' as an ensemble of the social and exchange relations gives rise to a dominant discourse shaping every particular articulation. What needs to be read off from this Weberian and Marxian understanding of totality is the rationality and its determinants in order to do justice to a possible alternative to their inherent dichotomies such as universal vs. particular, economy vs. social and other such irreconcilable theoretical output. As an alternative, one may propose a Foucauldian-Lacanian-Derridean essentially incomplete and emergent pictures of social discourses that locate various effects of subject positions in the web of power relations within which they are formulated. The very idea of the 'social' gets liberated from determined set of totalities and settles into a complex web of human relations that alter centres of power and subjectivity as it evolves as phenomenon. Of course, a strong sense of revealed history maps this emergence without succumbing into a warped path of historical prejudgments and rational evaluations. A 'sufficiently interpretable historical rationality' guides a more complex framework of rationality as a response mechanism to 'subject effects' of power. As Althusser frames it 'the identification of specific effects has revealed the existence of specific discourses as their condition' (Althusser, 2003: 75).

The specific discourses as the ideological-material condition for change has the effect of being 'internal' to the mechanism that produces it, which is the specificity of power relations. Such an internal effect of power relations constitutes the historical rationality in terms which the subjects articulate and express a notion of change. Much of the social-scientific notion of 'change' separates the material and the ideological from each other and reduces human sciences to a practice of legitimation (ibid.: 204). Weberian disenchantment with social theory and Marxist understanding of processes of reproduction of the dominant are responses to such practice of legitimation. What Weber considered as a process of rationalization, which is disenchantment with reason itself reappears in Marx's formulation of 'reproduction' with an ascent of reason that 'develops' itself in the processes of appropriation and expropriation.

One must read-off a complicated movement of thought within the Western canon of social theory at this point. Despite the distinguishing differences and contradistinctions between Weber, Marx, Althusser and the post-structuralists in their arguments about material, ideological and legitimational social processes, one notices a transformation of ideas into reality and vice-versa. This can be understood in terms of various moves and counter-moves within the acts of reason. The moves within reason such as thoughts on legitimation that separates the material and the ideological reaches the positionality of 'power' within reason and this is where reason serves the function of state. Countermoves within such functionality of reason undermines the state in order to recover an 'autonomy of thought', which is nothing but recreating 'a space for reason' within the existing modes of material production. This strategy assumes first of all a place of power for thought within reason, which in turn, seeks a place of power in the material sites and forms of production of power itself. Weber's disenchantment with reason begins from this self-acquired position of power by reason. Marx had seen how 'real appropriation' happens within such 'sites', which quite contradictorily and self-destructively appears in a process of expropriation of reason as value-producing activity that makes its own products devalued (Marx, 1973: 538). Countermoves within reason to give it an autonomy relegates itself into an expropriating act that devalues the potential of reason itself. This converts reason from an instrument of legitimation to a mere symbolic form that augments and sustains itself by cutting itself off from real processes of appropriation. This brings us to a self-glorifying moment of Western modernity that debunks the instrumentality of reason in favour of its symbolic, communicative and other such expropriationary roles that conform to the objectives of the state. Such conformism is established in thinking apriori a homology between space of reason and the space of power, both creating a subject by disengaging the self and the world from each other. This diminution and decline of Western modernity is right now characterized in the apparent disjunction between social agency and the subjectivity that results into a mechanical acceptance of certain foundational norms. The subject loses its apriori sense of the social world in which s/he lives, it is rather the case that with respect to an already determined and normatively found world, s/he exists and this alone gives her the reasons for existence. Moves and countermoves within reason has been a device of adjustment within the rule that announces its sovereign and free subjects as 'out of bounds'. Such moves within social theory recapture its legitimizing role that does not foreground a theory of change. There is grudging recognition to the 'vulnerability' of crucial theoretical notions such as 'autonomy' and 'right' within the authority of reason that guaranteeing rights does not ensure autonomy directly but rather supports autonomy *via* the support for self-respect (Brink, 2000). This vulnerability arose from a search for a strong centre of gravity within the very conceptualization of the social.

Such a vulnerability manifests in the boundary crossing between structuralism and post-structuralism in social theory. The structuralist notion of a field of struggle, which is conceived as a 'process without a subject' (Lukacs, 1971: 83–84) brought back an idea of transcendence that situates the subject as an unconscious tool of history. Post-structuralist correction to this by recognizing the immanence of the field in terms of relations that constitute the play of subject positions heightens the annulment of a fixed subject. This has resulted into an identity between the subject and the event making the subject vulnerable to its own experience of struggle. The discipline now moves between the standstill situated subject within the field of struggle and a variety of effects that it produces at the time of its arrival and annulment. This kind of a subject acts as the 'constituent of power' (Badiou, 2003: 34) that affects the network of relations in modernity. For both Marx and Weber, such a subject as power herself is an agent and hence both of them commit themselves to a transformational role by the agent as such. Such a notion of agency is caught up between the centralizing tendencies of reason to find itself as *sui generi* within the very faculty of reason such that it can play a legitimizing role. The agent is always in excess of herself that produces a process of change in the 'social' by way of ideas and opinions. Production of such a process of change by the subject by way of arrival and annulment in a state of continuous emergence and evolution leads it into a de-disciplined subjectivity that moves beyond territories and locales. Such is the paradoxical formation of power that does not retain the place of the subject as fixed and hence keeps it in an incipient stage of becoming. The journey of the subject is such that its place within reason as a place of power is essentially destabilizing and hence emergent to the extent that it defies 'disciplining' and instead affects a freewheeling subjectivity that appears in the stage of the 'social'. Such a journey entails a conversion of subjectivity from its singular sentinent determination and differentiation *to* an embodied reflexive self that connects itself with the other that constitutes an outside for itself. Reflexive subjectivity as a praxis for overcoming subjection acts as an antidote of 'subject-effect' that reduces the subjectivity of the subject to a product of a regime of power, while neither such a subjectivity nor its origin in power can be an agent, author or master of the processes of emergence of new forms of subjectivity. This moment of an abnegation of authority and agency of the subject grounded in the 'subject-effect' frees the disciplinary description of society in terms of 'process' and 'product' and instead brings in a discursive suspension of the operative reason that sets the boundaries of discipline.

This moment has been theorized by a good number of social theorists. For example, Anthony Giddens and Pierre Bourdieu theorized on the notion of reflexivity in terms of the subject's agentative capability to reflect on normative and power relations in a conjuncture. Giddens's leaves out the 'subjectivity' into what he called 'life politics', a politics of self-actualization. This politics, for Giddens, is determined by 'normative and power relations' that exists at a certain conjuncture. These relations, as per Giddens often interrogate conditions of their own production by getting entrapped into irresolvable paradoxes and thereby opening up undefined possibilities of their transformation. Such relations gave rise to a duality between external social conditions and internal creativity of the subject (Giddens, 1995: 56–109). This produces a sense of 'ontological insecurity' that goes into forming a destabilizing interior of subjectivity that runs the risk of just becoming a cog in the wheel, or it either de-traditionalizes or re-traditionalizes itself (Giddens, 1991). One may say that the politics of self-actualization involving an essentially unstable subjectivity leads to both a possibility of being constrained as well as being transformed. Pierre Bourdieu further problematizes this 'politics of self-actualization' in terms of 'weight of the world' that breaks up the enduring values and dispositions (Bourdieu, 1999: 435–37). The phenomenology of experiencing the weight of the world throws the subjects in the world without the capacity to reconstitute them as 'social selves'. One can call this deterritorialization of the subject following Emmanuel Levinas in the sense that the subjectivity of the subject is constituted as an Other that responds to the call of the Other. This is an ethico-political phenomenology of the subject, who is no longer the master of its own subjectivity.

Neo-liberal Transitions in North-East India

Contemporary state of North-East India can be best described as a state of 'rogue democracy' that stifles democratic action by those actors who draw up a narrow agenda of power. The continuation of Armed Forces Special Powers Act and the extermination by state and non-state actors constitute a different politics of self-preservation which is blind, self-directed and intransitive (Habermas, 1984: 388). Such a politics of self-preservation is a by-product of not just the weight of the world but it is also an instrumental end that serves a symbolic and ideological reproduction of the agenda of power. Power, in this context, is a mobile army of strategies, policies and interests that can relieve actors from reproducing themselves in their lived experiences. There is a recovery of the agency not in the realm of actual acts of the subject, but in the realm of subjectivity that constitutes self-preservation subsumed by power. Reflexivity in the acts of conscious imagining of one's own self and situation de-substantializes itself by dissociating reason and action in such a way that the cognitive-instrumental ends of power are satisfied. Such satisfaction produces a conflation of means and ends, as self-preservation can be both when reason and action are dissociated from each other. Such a dissociation results into asking politics to change our lives, which has a great invasive consequence.

Such a 'politics of self-actualization' is presented in the economy of North-East India. Politics of self-actualization has its deeper ontological grounding on multiple economic and political strategies. The so-called 'Look East' policy trumpeting a dream investment of 1,20,000 million INR in the next five years is one such deployment of ontology. Such a huge dose of public investment is a neoliberal strategy of inducing artificial demand in the market. When there is going to be soaring price rise due to recession in the national and the world economy, how such artificial inducement of demand can generate income and employment in the region? The plausibility of desirable consequences is now substituted by an artificial simulation of market demands that keeps politics of self-preservation going.

The total absence of a macro-economic understanding of dwindling agricultural productivity in terms of major crops such as rice in the North-East further compounds this unresolved policy failure of the Indian State. Suffice to say that the tomtomming of foreign investment, virtual auctioning of tea, trans-Asian highways and opening of new seaports merely produce the fiction of an economic boom. What ails the key and basic sectors of economy such as agriculture and maintenance of existing infrastructure does not find any place in any policy formulation of DONER or World Bank. Proportionate to the impending recession, there is also a slump in the quality of understanding in the think tank.

The triviality of the talk of strengthening the security mechanism without any semblance of human security in terms of strengthening the agency and the voice of the public has been mooted over last few years. A disjunction in the security discourse between human security and insurgency, human capability and terrorism is part of the strategy of mainstreaming the North-East India. Nobody probably thought the cost of such blinding discourse can be heavy in times of recession. Already, the cent per cent grant dependent states of the North-East are looked down upon by the Centre and how they are treated in the case of a national slowdown is a matter of commonsense. One of the news items says that establishing of AIIMS like institute has been ruled out by the Centre. The Centre also denies the possibility of irrigating the downstream areas of Assam from the reservoir of the lower Subansiri Hydroelectric Project. The downstream impact study of the proposed Tipaimukh dam is not to be carried out. The natural resource rich India's North-East is looked as 'power house' or as an important link in the supply and communication chain with East, South and South-East Asia.

The Lower Subansiri Hydroelectric Project, according to the Central expert will regulate the reservoir storage between 720 m cum and 1,365 m cum with a dam height of 116 metres to handle flow of 35,500 cusecs of water. This very difference between full storage and minimal requirement of storage will depend on full flow of the river in the downstream, which is estimated at beyond 50,000 cusecs of water during the rainy season. Out of this flow, the dam will contain only the minimum at the risk of other seismic and tectonic factors. As the dam is planned to block the free flow of lower Subansiri, the flood plains are bound to be dispersed alongwith an increased silting and quasi-tectonic perturbations of the river strata. The experience of flooding of the plains of Lakhimpur in Assam due to release from NEEPCO dam is stoutly denied by the concerned central ministries and the case is the same in the Subansiri hydroproject. The stout denial of any such adverse impact and then virtual auctioning of the one of precious product such as tea is like controlling the outflow of resources from the North-East by pump priming as well as setting up an auction driven economy. This is outsourcing both the supply and demand sides of the economy to the calculated control by the Centre and the international market. Central policy towards North-East's natural, cultural and human resources are that of a benevolent king, who gives monetary bounties and prepares to take away its exploits.

This state of denial and manipulative methods of running the economy and polity comes with a price tag on the people concerned. The move by Oil India Limited to explore and survey Dibru-Saikhowa national park at the cost of losing many wild species has recently come to light. Despite NGOs pointing out the prima facie absence of environmental clearance, the OIL is conducting geo-magnetic survey for exploration endangering one of the most significant biodiversity hotspot of the world. The sanctity of the Dibru-Saikhowa National Park, which is supposed to be outside the pale of any such exploration, is openly violated by a government agency by citing some petty legal brownie points. Once again in a state of denial, both the Assam government and the Centre do not see what is going on in the national park.

How does one come out of this state of denial? Is it a *fait accompali* for the people who are never an equal partner in making development decisions, rather they are looked upon as beneficiaries by a giant state. The market further reduces them to the guinea pigs of neo-liberal financial manipulation.

Did we develop sensible ears to listen to voices from below in last sixty one years of independence? Or, as the time flows in a manner that below the daze and rattle of mega dams, superhighways, swanky malls and staged beauties shall the rants of the flooded, maimed, butchered and the displaced due to fratricides die an ignominious death? Is it a renewed Darwinism that pits every form of identity as an instrument of domination? Does freedom to choose and articulate mean here a self-enclosed, self-serving and arrogated sense of the self that undercuts any attempt to understand the other?

The intransigent sense of achievement in mustering a mandate for an orchestrated policy on any essential aspect of development-power, health or connectivity assumes a Hobbesian power in neutralizing the voices of responsible dissention. Be it implementation of dams in Arunachal Pradesh by NHPC with resultant floods in Assam, be it peddling of the controversial power and uranium deals in Meghalaya with the blessings of NGOs, and be it Assam health minister's pro-active admonition to young doctors for not serving the public institutions are not entirely different episodes as they look like. They are the seedy outcome of being a part of a development framework that comes as one of the many gifts of modern statecraft.

Development frameworks also act as security and stability mechanisms for a shaky establishment. The work of the bogeyman in terms of a propaganda of 'silent invasion', politics of demography in threatening terms and organization of ethnic divide keeps ranting the sky in the region. It repeats, ironically, the same paralanguage of adding fuel to the already fractured social spaces of Assam by once again dividing them between ethnic majorities, tribes and minorities. Larger students' body such as AASU's cobbling of an alliance between ethnic majority and tribes against minorities will always remain internally fragile as it merely balms off deep the seated divisions between the plains and the tribes of Assam. Across these jaws of ethnic fracture, Khasi Students' Union's demand for 30 per cent reservation of medical seats in the NEIGRIHMS in 2008 and its boycott of entrance examination seeks a greater equity and justice for local tribes that prima facie marks claims of representation. KSU's protests show that mere institution building without a desirable level of representation only gives rise to homogenized mills of 'opportunities' to be exploited by a smart clientele. The insensitivity of bureaucratic machinery constitutes a form of structural violence that often meets here with a possibility of resistance in terms of 'local interests' that again subverts larger question of impartiality and neutrality. The supposedly neutral space of employment, education and access to human development gets fractured in a failure to address issues related to claims of autonomy and justice.

All over the country, the so called clientele of the meritorious from the social background of upper castes and creamy layers is questioned for its readiness to corner all the privileges. Replicating such a model of high brow elitist development in the North-East only seeks to strengthen the class of opportunity seekers cutting across really existing social hierarchies. If the constitutional machinery cannot ensure equity and a desirable level of representation, then play up the social hierarchy in the right or the wrong way. Be it tribal vs. non-tribal, hills vs. plains and national vs. regional, a reverse playing of the hierarchy becomes the key to social engineering for a growth-seeking national economy. Further internal divisions within larger communities also speak for itself in fratricidal terms in many occasions. In-fighting among Bodos, Nagas and secret killings in Assam portray a politics of mutual extermination.

There is also a deep nexus of political opportunism and neo-liberal economic gains, be it within the nation-state or beyond it. Witness the praise for such model of development in the speech made by NPF Member of Parliament as well as by the B.L.T supported independent during the trust vote.[1] While NPF member was vocal about Naga right to unification, the Bodo member was gaga about the promises of a central university and central funds for Bodoland area. Cash-for-vote and funds-for-development mingle in the vote-for-trust that made the two MPs proclaim how dependent Nagas and Bodos are on central assistance. One implication of such dependency is the readiness to agree to centrally designed policies and schemes and join in the so called 'consensus' that sidesteps people's own choices.

What is happening here is a phenomenon of silencing of people's voices through a politics of self-actualization that does not lead to expansion of democratic choices. It rather banks on an ontological shift from reproducing material and social lives from situated practices to economic dominance that simultaneously transposes self-actualization into self-preservation. This leads to a set of divided, traumatized and objectified subjects who are simultaneously defiant and yet a part of the process of being dominated.

The promised impact of 'Look East' policy on the North-East merely reduces the cultural and economic North-Eastern spaces to a corridor through which mainland India's cherished dream of connecting itself with South-East Asia is realized. Within the borders of the nation, clamour for rights of scheduled tribes, their access to higher education, industry and employment are all put up as items of a giant leap that enlightens the episcope of development. The freedom of each of the collective group-identities must have the freedom to choose their paths of self-development. If neo-liberal policies of the state subject such fundamental freedom to the vagaries of market, it builds up a 'structural violence' of institutions. Governments, institutions and agencies appropriate and monopolize the space of development as if they are authorized to replace peoples' expressions of choices. If such institutions engage themselves in this fractured terrains of the social space by prioritizing one group's proclaimed interest over others, it ends up by shrinking liberties to the pre-decided set of economic and political options.

Custodial killings by the keepers of law, fake encounters, peace manoeuvres and lack of any semblance of human dignity go unabated with the indifferent character of economic boom. Scripting the story of growth in ethnocentric terms condones itself from victimizing the Other. The talk of opening up the borders with South-East Asia and fencing of Bangladesh borders stand as logical contraries. The rage against the immigrant Bangladeshis, the fight against the so-called Jihadis and counter-insurgency operations against ethnic militants are all mixed up in the unholy link between peace and development. Irony of the irony is that it marks an absence of adequate self-representation and unreserved acceptance of the Other. The future conjures up a ghastly image of extermination and desensitized consumerism in the progress of globalization that would swing between war, terror and despotic accumulation. Can the vision of economic progress face the human cost of survival without falling into the trap of neo-Darwinianism?

Changed Images of the North-East India

Quite contrary to this repeatable and prolonged sense of agony, there is an image make over of the region as an icon of diversity that now replaces the old image of 'ethnic cauldron'. There is a significant change of phrases, from a strange admixture of terrorism and tranquillity to a transborder gateway to the East and South-East Asia. Such a change is reflected in ascriptions like 'a tourists' paradise', 'post-frontier blues', 'home of tribes', 'endangered authenticites' etc. and descriptions such as 'land of the rising sun', 'abode of clouds', 'abode of thirty-three crores gods' and many such metaphors. Such images contest each other in terms of finesses and accuracy. It is also a play of poetic imagination on the sensible and the mythological that cuts deep roots in native minds. The best part of such a free flowing and mobile army of metaphors is that it replaces the old and the outworn metaphors of 'native' and 'outsider'; it rather includes the larger neighbourhood and sends across the message that the North-East is no longer an isolated island. This gives it an internal resilience to tolerate the 'other', the new cult of the other that allows a better representation of the 'self'. The whole of the North-East can now represent itself better to the outsider and to the nation as it opens itself to tourists, national and foreign. There is also a substantial 'museumization' of ethnic cultures, artifacts and traditional tribal looms and products that not only represent but provide lasting touch to invaluable diversity of the region.

There is a new language of imagination that engages a technique of boundary crossing. The historical past is pressed against the diving lines of political boundary. If the play of history over politics produces novel cultural imaginations, it is the play of cultural metaphors in an ethnically contested political terrain that widens imagined spaces. Widening of identity spaces in relation to a globally expanding value of plurality and hybridity finds a renewed vigour in claims of justice and autonomy. There is a process of expanding imagined spaces of lived territories in one's language such that one overcomes the spatial limits of a territory. In case of the North-East, legends and parables of migration by communities and tribes is relived in the everyday crossing of spatial limits fixed on ethnically and politically defined territories. Learning from each other's histories has always been a part of narrative construction of selves in the case of the North-East. If violence and counter-violence shapes the relation between the self and the other, then cross-cultural appreciation is also equally a plausible means to shift the ethnic boundaries in everyday lives. For example, Khasis talking about the impact of Presbyterian Church among the Mizos and comparing similar such impact on the Khasis as an aftermath of Mizo success establishes an imagined ordering of lives that recounts the traces of commonality with not so near brethrens. Nagas talking about the Mizo struggle and trying to assess the impact of 'permanent peace' is also a quest for a wholesome self beyond a monochromatic vision of war against the Indian State. The incidence of *Mautam* in the areas inhabited by Mizos and Hmars brings back the memory of MNF struggles in a retrospectively altered understanding of the national struggle. All these are not just a flow of indigenous knowledge in a comparative context, but it marks a crossing of boundaries. This crossing of boundaries is reflected in not just standing together as distinct entities but in giving rise to a joint presentation of cultures in the national and international forums.

In contrast to this new regime of imagination, the statecraft of the region still has many deep mazes that divert and derail every initiative: peace and development. Peace processes in the region has been so fragile that it threatens to be a game of deferring conflicts. Development programmes are like playing a second fiddle to the larger politicization of governmental power and economy. In this, the State and the market exist as collaborators. One effect of this collaboration is a new language of representation and description, while it commodifies the traditional economy only to give a field for a mercantile corporate economy. This produces a contrast between the social and cultural ethos and the economic practices. On the one hand the contrast affects the very perception of material needs and on the other, it forces a distortion of values. For example, marginality of the *Jhumias* ironically becomes the bare minimal sustenance for them in the hills. The contest between ethnic elites gets resolved in rage against immigrant peasantry.

Marginality becomes the key parameter in pursuing policy of pump-priming that leaves practices of social discrimination unaffected. Shift from pump-priming to utilization and acquisition of land, forest, mineral and water resources are part of a strategy of getting the North-East incorporated in the global funding networks that seeks the consent of the community. Privatization of shared and community resources acts as the beckon for private investments in public sectors such as energy, power and communication. The new metaphors give a soothing balm to the 'damaged life' of the community as stakeholder and manage to give a new picture of progress, peace and prosperity. The idea of the North-East as a space of encounter between the native and the nation with its fragments of similarities across South Asia marks a series of culturally hybrid locales that poses challenges to the singularity of the nation-state.

When would our flawed and unimaginative statecraft start seriously decoding the new meanings from the enormous fund of concept-metaphors that the North-East throws up in an otherwise emancipated space of nation-state? Before we catch up with this long revolution, can there be a rethinking about cultural crossings that would give its rich pay-off towards political imagination(s) of the North-East?

A Conceptual Response

What is probably needed at this point of time is a steady conceptualization of various shifts that have happened within the North-East due to external interventions. The problematique of state versus insurgency and its gradual dissolution in a development paradigm that alters the very social space needs to be conceptualized. Given the above description of the very idea of the 'social' that effectively leads us to a deterritorialization of the idea of the 'social' poses fresh theoretical challenges in understanding the transition from local to the global in the North-East.

The transition can be characterized as the North-East being thrown overboard 'outside itself (it was trying to claim independence and/or trying to become one with nation) as if it belongs to the Other, the South-east ... it is no longer itself, a strategy of exteriorization, you see what happens to your core by withdrawing as an 'onlooker'. As an 'onlooker', you are nothing but an already appropriated subject who has merged her self with the 'global'. A new faith of sovereignty is generated through the catered ideas by negating roles of rationality, freedom and choice. Seemingly, political freedom is no longer essential for informed economic choices, as choices are already given as 'options'. One needs to opt for and not choose with a definite sense of determination and satisfaction. This recalls Marx's description of advancement of capital through concentration that purges out the region into the global and redeems it as a 'fiction'.

India's 'Look East' policy reduces the actual process of choosing as a 'look beyond'. The look 'connects' India's North-Eastern borderlands with South-East Asian markets. It presents a complicated mechanism of 'maintenance of national boundary' and its 'suspension' necessitating a 'theoretical' linkage between 'deterritorialization' and 'logistics of global capital'. Look East policy's endorsement of trans-Asian highways, sub-regional integration between India's North-East and South-East Asia, a common currency within ASEAN, etc., are supposed to also play the role of binding diverse cultural identities within a South-East Asian landscape. Remembrance of historical migration of the most of North-East Indian tribes from South-East Asia and the second world war memory of building 'roads' through Myanmar is *converted* into a 'cultural consumption' of a free market of South-East Asian economy. Does it capture the imagination of being 'truly Asian', a de-territorializing effect of substituting what is 'truly Indian' or 'other Asian'?

The effect of the de-territorializing act of 'suspension of sovereignty' (pace Agamben) in the *embedded* relations between North-East Indian identity(ies) and their memory that 'contextualizes' the post-national 'politics of the governed'. One needs to investigate into the logic of suspension of sovereignty that stands in a contrary relationship to the 'constitution' of 'consumer-citizen' within a political economy frame of globalization. As the political boundary suspends the sovereign choice of movement of the people outside of a designated 'territory', the state of exception further 'suspends' juridically the operation of the 'boundary' in order to evolve protocols of trans-border trade and inter-state relationship. Such a suspension assumes a double meaning of allowing a freedom to cross the border as well as contain such a freedom only in the direction of the 'economic destinations'.

The project of the states and multilateral global bodies in connecting the borderlands mobilize selective memories of 'labouring, war and exodus' that invokes the 'disrupted and interrupted' cultural memory of respective tribes and communities. Ironically enough, such colonial memories give strength to building roads, connecting frontiers and developing market niches between the North-East India and South-East Asia. Is there then a possibility of an alternative memory of uninhibited sharing of lived experiences that may defy the colonial and post-colonial forms of repression? The project seeks to retrieve the possibility of an un-colonized sharing of between, say, Kachins and Kukis, Apatanis and Semas working together in building roads in Ledo-Myanmar-China sector during 1942–44 that now promises a revival. This will involve grafting the past memories into the present through a complex network of oral histories of migration of various tribes of the North-East through Pungsau pass and Shan state serving as an umbilical chord to the memories of colonial forced labour, exodus and migration. As stated by many memoirs, the exodus of people from Myanmar during Japan's aggression originated in a Myanmar village called Myitkina and ended in a village called Shamlung right below the Pungsau pass. What needs to be interrogated here is, (a) whether a project of retrieval of 'colonial memory' jibes with 'oral histories' of migration in terms of routes and stories of hardship; (b) to what extent pre-colonial cultural connections between tribes across the current political borders between the North-East India and Myanmar find its latent salience in the contemporary project of building a strong state and market based co-operation; (c) whether transmission of cultural and economic goods in today's context fits into an already existing history of trading between border communities, and (d) does a suspension of sovereignty in economic exchanges mean privileging 'sovereignty free actors' as stateless but firmly entrenched into a trajectory of historical and cultural memorabilia?

Contemporary narratives of globalization establishes a ready fit between cultural memories of the past with the present re-connection between estranged kins through transport, electronic communication and the overall possibility of trading and value addition. The availability and construction of such a 'narrative fit' in India's 'look east' policy needs to be re-contextualized. It needs to be inquired how fitting of memory at the transnational conjuncture erases distinction between 'agency' and 'power'? The erasure between 'agency' and 'power' in the case of belonging within a shared space takes the form of 'forgetting' that allows us to draw a 'contrast' between 'lived experience' of/beyond the 'border' and 'cultural memory' that one speaks of without disruption. Can memory re-construct a political subjectivity that makes transnational economic and cultural exchange possible between the North-East India and South-East Asia as envisaged in India's 'Look East' policy? The supposed link between memory and economy is pregnant with a new understanding of the possibility of social changes that are foretold in policies of development.

Such policies and politics of development encounter a dichotomy between cultural self-description and its representation in various discursive and epistemic paradigms. For example, most of the tribes and communities in the North-East is assigned a name by exogenous sources. Exo-ethno-names such as Naga, Khasi, Mizo etc. tell a story of 'subsumption' within an influential dominant paradigm of knowledge. Especially the colonial construction of a tribal identity along with its social and cultural boundaries as observed by ethnographers not only wielded fixed notions of who the tribe was, but it produced knowledge claims in terms of concrete anthropological and cultural sciences. In contrast to such representational moves, indigenous communities attempted to represent their own cultural resources as a living tradition, but most often without much of a departure from the so-called colonial ethnography. This has resulted into such divergent outcomes as (i) an attempt to return to roots by way of reclaiming one's past through indigenous ethno-narratives, and (ii) repudiation of the past for the purpose of justifying the present existential strategies of re-description of the self over and against an Other. In effect, the uneven and diversified histories of self-development appear ethnocentric with a claim to an exclusive distinctness that dovetails 'internal differences' and resists the possibility of an inter-cultural inter-community transaction between oneself and another. Ironically, this gives a closure to an authentic self-identity in narrow terms of belonging and non-belonging and passes it with a counter-hegemonic label against any opening to the outside world. Another facet of this closure is a selective self-representation in a chosen discourse that reflexively highlights identity concerns.

The co-existence of close-kin groups across cultural boundaries present a challenge for discovering common and shareable sources of history. For example, the two tribes such as the Bodos and the Garos belong to Sino-Tibetan linguistic origins, but at present they inhabit different areas. This results in dissociation of cultural memory from shared historical past. Most of the time, various tribes express an yearning for their long lost cousins in the course of migration while they still share same linguistic and cultural roots. Much of this hidden history of shared roots of tribal cultures and communities need to be retrieved through an interpretation of their memory. Such interpretations happen in a state of being territorialized and localized and hence it cannot overcome the material limits of immediate socio-cultural presence. The effect of the loss of one's history is felt in the ideological confusion about a distorted self-knowledge that often generates undesirable suspicion about the Other. In today's context of the North-East India, dehistoricized communities often redescribe themselves in a totalitarian assumption of deterritorialized traces of identity that cannot be realized within their current habitat. The situation is further complicated when such dehistoricized and deterritorialized narratives of identity appropriate a sense of being authentic in various ways. It produces a set of disjointed discourses of contestation: national vs. local and regional; diasporic vs. transnational; settlers vs. indigenous etc. that simultaneously draw a line against a perceived Other as well as produce a blurring of lived experiences by a practice of insularity.

Social Change as an Experiential Category

A fragmentation of the collective and communitarian self stirs up a huge confusion between the past, the present and the future. All the time, there is a search for an appropriate subjectivity that can ensure rationalization of objectives and practices at the level of the collective, which is also public and global. A set of contrary phenomena arises at this juncture: national vs. local; state and market vs. indigenous polity, institutional representation vs. authenticity, insider vs. outsider and many other such dichotomies that essentializes and polarizes sensibilities. Examples galore such as conflict between church and indigenous faith, intra-tribal clashes, market driven economic activity vs. cultural niche in productive activity, only to name a few, produce a symptomatic fragmentation within the life-world of communities. Each of these elements of dichotomous development assumes a certain degree of rationality and irrationality to articulate itself. Exploration into these reasons reveal the movements beneath the social system/structure and it makes and un-makes some actors and agents significant in a specific historical conjuncture.

In this flow of developing situations that is so diverse and plural as forms of reality that any singular, coherentist and instrumental framework may prove to be just inadequate. The task before Social Sciences is neither an exploration into the tragicomic reality of the Commons nor it is an arrival at a prescriptive-altruist understanding of the 'emergent'. It should always give rise to a surplus of meanings such that Social Sciences explore meaning-constitutive processes in terms of ideas, reasons and ideologies that go into making of an event. For example, peace processes in a war-ravaged and insurgency ridden area of the North-East India need to involve the voices from within the people, rather than finding an expert solution. As people themselves take part in making their own history and deciding what is right and wrong, Social Sciences, in a true sense should make a return to its ground realities. This will require a careful interpretation of 'social facts', especially the possibilities of mutual implication between communities and cultures, a task so arduously generated within the liberal-democratic framework without initiatives of 'doing' it. Social Sciences have to do it, instead of merely representing and distancing itself as an 'objective' science. It has to unburden itself from its fatigued frames and throw itself in an open dynamics of social churning without pre-theoretical underpinnings.

The all important connection between economy and culture in the context of the North-East India often arises out of an intersubjectively shared life-world of communities. The shared life-world throws up issues of material, ideological and symbolic structuring of agency and power. Such an intersubjective sharing is based on an inclusion-exclusion dynamics that involves the experience of otherness and othering. Life-worlds of various communities present a dialectic between the self and the Other. The dialectic is concretized in a few foundational binary oppositions such as the native and the nation, civic and ethnic, underground and overground, and so on. Such oppositions are sustained by a structure of correspondence between the self and the Other without presenting a possibility of transformation. As an example of embeddedness of such a dialectic, one could locate in the language (i) the pre-ontic murmur, (ii) prior contact with the Other, and (iii) transformation of the natural world in an interpretative uses of language. But such a combined functioning of what we call embeddedness in language is based on the condition of operation of practices, in terms of how language accesses these practices. Access to these practices does not happen as something prior to language that lies out there in the world but as an available representation of a concept, which is accessed in language to exhibit the original intentional experiences that present the referent instantiating the concept. This assumes the knowledge of conditions of assertibility by which the application of a concept would either be true or false. Such knowledge obtains in the specific context of a community that anthropologists establish through an intuitive knowledge of the Other. The radical alterity of the Other, which is the subject without alterity, appears with differentiating, non-relational and non-universal generality that produces discrete notions and concepts within a culture, the value of which is contingent and undecidable. The undecidability of change figures from within the life-world through this dialectic of positioned objectivities.

Such positioned objectivities act independent of the will of the actor and it ensures the capitalist mode of production working in combination with bureaucratic-legal order within which attempts of self-preservation is also rendered superfluous by the state of productive forces. If we read the situation from a psychoanalytic point of view, it produces mutually contrary and yet multiply directed drives: the democratic mode of political authority is sustained by the fantasy of economic growth and the post-sovereign politics of self-preservation, while the desire of subjects for opportunity and development assumes a symbolic state of wish-fulfillment through the same political authority. The situation can be succinctly summed up in the words of Zizek, '[R]eduction of humans to bare life, to *homo sacer* as the malleable object of the expert caretaker of knowledge; and that of respect for the vulnerable Other carried to the extreme, the attitude of narcissistic subjectivity which experiences itself as vulnerable, constantly exposed to a multitude of potential 'harassments'. Is there a stronger contrast than the one between the respect for the Other's vulnerability and the reduction of the Other to 'mere life' regulated by administrative knowledge?' (2004: 399–400).

The question points at the reduction of self-reflection to a mere instrument of rationalization that provides a basis for law of value to operate and determine action of formally free individuals who execute them through desire, power and responses. Such responses abjure the demand for recognition in the face of rationalization followed by economy and technology. Abjuration of such a demand for recognition results into a violent and invasive transition in India's North-Eastern borderlands. The situation is far more dissatisfying than satisfying: the feeling of injustice that rationalization processes give rise to a society essentially based on an economic logic, which is struggle and competition, in which individuals are prevented from reaping the fruits of their own labour. What happens at the level of the group identity is a greater alienation that de-subjectivates the individual in her desire for self-actualization that leads to communities organized by the state in a uniform citizenship. Such a constitution, if individual along with her transition to citizenship via a group identity in the North-East India assumed a Janus face. It is a shape of reiterated, received and decalarative discourse of repression, as explained by Bhagat Oinam,'often, the language of violence is used as a response to any form of dissent. The room for self-reflection and self-critical enquiry to one's beliefs and knowledge is missing. It is not only the Indian State and its various parts that indulge in a declarative discourse, but also its counterparts (the non-state organizations) who equally or perhaps much more violently propagate their narratives through the same kind of discourse. (...) There is no room for dialogue, of questioning the basis of those declaratives' (Oinam, 2009: 175).

While one may not agree with Bhagat's ominous prediction of an impossibility of a dialogue, yet his philosophical concern in terms of absolute truth values assigned to 'declaratives' or better 'constatives' bring back the question of their iterability, which is conditioned by their unmediated circulating capacity. Narratives in their contextualized subjective surroundings are potential threats to any ethical response, as they forebear the function of the 'state', which, pace Schmitt, 'is already present in that which exceeds it as an exception. For the exception is merely the state in its negative form: it is above all a "*state* of exception," or more precisely, as the German word translated by *state* literally says, it involves a bringing "*to stand*" – a *Zu-stand* (cited in Weber, 2008: 108). Such exceptions assume the form of inchoate discourses plagued with narcissism and hysteric desire for dominance. The potential for self-conscious development is subverted in the disclosure of self-defeating discourses that reflect the suicidal autoimmunity of self-preservation. In such a politics of self-preservation, the 'self' needs to be creatively reconstructed on the condition of construing the life-force.[2]

In Lieu of a Conclusion

Transition in the North-East India is a peculiar one, seemingly from a democratic expansion of the space of articulation of the self to a space of self-actualization that is constrained by multiple forces of politics and economics. Such forces reduce the status of democratic actors from agents of self-conscious development to mere recipients of ideas, resources, plans and strategies. In terms of disciplinary bounds of understanding, such transitions require de-disciplining and deterritorializing the idea of the 'social' into 'social change' as an experiential category that discloses more than it declares. Such a shift in our disciplinary orientation could lead us to quite a few home truths that currently unsettles us in the realm of development as well as in our knowledge of the society in the context of the North-East. This unsettling experience is represented in conceptual contraries such as 'state of exception' and democratic practices.

Notes

1. Trust vote in support of UPA government was held on 22nd July 2008 in the Indian parliament. NPF is Nagaland Peoples' Front and BLT is Bodo Liberation Tigers.
2. Life-force is a Gandhian notion, while Derrida inverts it into 'force of life' in contrast to 'force of law'. Refer to Gandhi's *Hind Swaraj* and Derrida's *Rogues: Two Essays on Reason*, Stanford University Press, Stanford, 2005.

References

Althusser, L. 2003. *The Humanist Controversy and Other Writings*, edited by Francois Matheron and translated by G.M. Goshgarin. London: Verso.

—. 1970. *Lenin and Philosophy and Other Essays*, translated by B. Brewster. London: New Left Books.

Badiou, A. 2003. *Handbook of Inaesthetics*, translated by A. Toscano. Stanford: Stanford University Press.

Bourdieu, P. 1999. *The Weight of the World: Social Suffering in Contemporary Society*, translated by Priscilla Parkhurst Ferguson and Others. Stanford: Stanford University Press.

Brink, Bert van den. 2000. *The Tragedy of Liberalism: An Alternative Defense of a Political Tradition.* New York: SUNY Press.

Derrida, J. 2005. *Rogues: Two Essays on Reason.* Stanford: Stanford University Press.

Gerth, Hans H. and C. Wright Mills. 1946. *From Max Weber: Essays in Sociology.* Oxford: Oxford University Press.

Giddens, A. 1991. *Modernity and Self-Identity: The Self and Society in the Late Modern Age.* Stanford: Stanford University Press.

—. 1995. 'Living in a Post-Traditional Society', in U. Beck, A. Giddens and S. Lash (eds), *Reflexive Modernization.* Cambridge: Cambridge University Press, 56–109.

Habermas, J. 1984. *The Theory of Communicative Action. Vol. 1. Reason and the Rationalization of Society*, translated by T. McCarthy. Boston: Beacon Press.

Lukacs, Georg. 1971. 'Reification and the Consciousness of the Proletariat', in *History and Class Consciousness: Studies in Marxist Dialectics*, translated by R. Livingstone. Cambridge, Mass.: MIT Press, 83–84.

Marx, Karl. 1973. *Grundrisse*, translated by Martin Nicolaus. London: Pelican Books.

Oinam, Bhagat. 2009. 'Preparing for a Cohesive Northeast: Problems of Discourse', in Sanjib Baruah (ed.), *Beyond Counter-Insurgency: Breaking the Impasse in Northeast India.* New Delhi: Oxford University Press, 170–187.

Weber, S. 2008. 'Rogue Democracy', *Diacritics*, 38(1–2): 104–120.

Zizek, S. 2004. 'The Structure of Domination Today: A Lacanian View', *Studies in East European Thought*, 56(4): 383–403.

3

Social Change and Extraneous Interventions Among the Hill Communities of North-East India

A.C. SINHA

The doyen of the Indian sociology, M.N. Srinivas, published his book *Social Change in Modern India* way back in 1966. He states in the book that his analysis of the process of social change in India stops at the border of West Bengal. Thus, the North-East region, where massive social transformation has occurred encapsulating years into decades and decades into centuries, remained un-surveyed all these years for its social transformation. Conscious of its urgency, the Department of Sociology, North-Eastern Hill University, Shillong decided that "Social Change" will be its main concern of the academic thrust from its inception. I propose to undertake the same theme for my understanding: social change in the North-East India. Briefly speaking, social change arises when magnitude and dimension of the change are such as to result in significant alteration in the given social structure, interpersonal relations and social institutions. There may be a variety of stimulus for inducing social change: individual initiatives, social reforms, state sponsored welfare programmes, voluntary social engineering, ideology, revolutions, conflict, war, struggle for political objectives such as autonomy and the like. Similarly, it is not necessary that all components of the society in change operate at the same time, but may be the elite or a section of middle class or the traders, or the educated youth that take the initiative for social change. Indian society has changed in a big way since independence of the country, no doubt. However, the extent of social change in the North-East region has been massive in comparison to other parts of the country for a number of reasons and the region remained socially cut off from rest of the country. This change has also heightened the urge, expectations and endeavour among the people of the region to catch up fast with rest of the country, leading to a certain type of social conflict, which in itself deserves an urgent attention. And thus this endeavour to uncover aspects of social change in the region and for that, I propose to clarify two basic issues: one, there is a need to clarify the region, North-East India, and two, the baseline or bench line for uncovering the nuances of social change in the region has to be drawn in terms of its historicity.

The Region

The geographers would regard the region as comprising the Brahmputra and Barak Valleys and Eastern extension of the Himalayan mountain ranges. Historically, the plains in the region were variously known as Prayagjyotisha or Kamrupa/Kamakhya in the early period of the regional history. There are pre-historic and historic sites scattered all over the region right from Itanagar, Bhishmaknagar in Arunachal Pradesh, Garo Hills in Meghalaya, various locations in Assam, and elsewhere. It appears that at least the western part of the Brahmputra valley and southern slopes of Shillong plateau were in close political contacts with the kingdoms of Gaur, North Bengal, in the ancient period. Among the ruling dynasties of the region in the early medieval period, Koch, Dimasha, Kachari, Jaintiyas, Meiteis may be counted and many of them had ties with the various kingdoms in other parts of India. This was also the time, when upper Assam was visited by the Ahoms in 1228 A.D., who established their sway in the region and ruled over it for the next six hundred years. They were overrun by the Burmese in 1819, who were driven away by the combined Ahom and the British forces in 1824 leading to incorporation of the region in the British Indian Empire. With a view to securing their territories in the Brahmputra, Barak and Surma valleys, the British slowly and steadily extended their indirect rule in Khasi Hills, Garo Hills, Naga Hills, Lushai (Mizo)

Hills, Chittagong Hills, Hill Tipperah, and lastly Tuensang, Sadiya, Lakhimpur and Barlipara Frontier Tracts (Arunachal Pradesh). We hasten to add that among the many motives for doing that, there were two significant considerations for the British: one, search for suitable topography for tea cultivation and creation of forest reserves, and two, securing the administered territories against the chronic raids by the hill tribes.

In the wake of independence, the British India was divided into two states of India and Pakistan in the year 1947. East Pakistan was carved out of Bengal and parts of Silcher district of Assam province, which led to snapping the natural transport link to the rest of India and making the region a landlocked Indian territory. In the year, 1947, the North-East region consisted for Assam and two princely states of Manipur and Tripura. The state of Nagaland was created out of Naga Hills district and Tuensang Frontier Tract of the British province of Assam in 1963. The region was reorganized in the year 1972 and three new states of Meghalaya, Manipur and Tripura and two union territories of Arunachal Pradesh (known as NEFA – North-East Frontier Agency previously) and Mizoram (erstwhile Lushai Hills district) were created by an Act of Parliament. The North-East Reorganization Act also envisaged creation of North-Eastern Council (NEC) for the regional infrastructural development of the constituting seven units of five states of Assam, Nagaland, Manipur, Meghalaya and Tripura and two union territories. The two union territories of Mizoram and Arunachal Pradesh were elevated to statehood in the years 1985 and 1987 respectively. Purely from developmental and administrative point of view, Sikkim was integrated into North-Eastern Council in 1990s. In this way, there are two North-East regions: one, the formal one, for development and administrative points of view, and other, as the region in the North-Eastern part of the Indian Union, viewed from the point of view of the other parts the country. So, the North-East is a new creation, in which the relatively small states of the region are tagged together for the purpose of resource allocation from the Centre for developmental purposes.

Baseline or Bench Line for Social Change

With a view to measuring the phenomenon of change, it is significant that an imaginary line known as base or bench line in sociological literature is drawn from where the significant institutionalized social variations are recorded. Social change may be seen as recurrent, repetitive and relatively long term alteration in the human behaviour at personal, interpersonal, group and institutional levels. Societies pass through different phases of relative stability and relative dynamism in their histories. The pre-British traditional communities of the North-East India were marked by relative stability in their social relations. They were in relative isolation and stable at family, clan, village and community levels, they had simple tools and technology; a subsistence economy and there were chiefs or village elders' councils under strong social control at the community level to regulate their social behaviour. They also had extremely simple polities based on reciprocal obligations and exchange of commodities. They did trade in articles of rare necessities such as iron tools, threads, ivory, *agar*, etc. But volume of such commercial exchange was extremely small. Though long distance trade was not unknown, its prevalence was limited among some adventurous individuals.

The geographical extent, variation of the topography, settlement pattern in hills and plains, types of economy and its pattern and overall differential political development in the region suggest that there cannot be a single baseline for social change for the North-East region. For example, long history of political organizations in the Brahmputra, Barak, Imphal and Surma valleys suggest a complex historical process of social change. Further, relatively recent exposure of various communities in hills and plateaus of Arunachal Pradesh is recent enough to document satisfactorily. So, the point to consider is on what basis are we to draw the base line for examining the phenomenon of social change. The answer to this simple, but significant question, is not easy. However, a working solution may be identified in terms of uncovering the significant moments, movements, events, political interventions such as redrawing of the state boundaries, war, invasion, rebellion, inter-community feuds, etc. human migration, state sponsored programmes, acculturation and conversion to another faith. But it is imperative that before embarking on drawing the base line for charting social change in a particular community/society, as far as possible, a detailed and dispassionate ethnography of the particular society is recorded/is made available. To cut the long story short, as the incorporation of the various communities/territories in the British Indian Empire was accomplished at different points of time, there will be different base lines for different sub-regions/communities of the region. However, as a whole, the advent of the British rule in the region in 1825 after Anglo-Burmese war appears reasonably sound at least for the Brahmputra valley and Assam plains. Similarly, incorporation of many communities in Arunachal Pradesh was affected in 1950s and 1960s. So for Arunachal Pradesh bench line for examining social change may be Indian independence in 1947. Another factor for drawing the baseline especially for the hill states in the region may be the advent of Christianity, as in some cases, conversion to Christianity has been almost cent per cent resulting in total transformation of social style of life and the world view.

Social histories of established states such as Ahoms, Jaintias, Kochs, Dimasha Cacharis, Meiteis, etc. are available. Similarly, more than a dozen volumes of 'Ethnography of Assam' series of publications on Khasi, Garo, Cachari, Angami, Ao, Sema, Rengma, Lushai, Lakher and Powis, etc. provide a reliable base line for constructing social history of various communities. Similarly, the British rule worked through an organized officialdom, in which documentation, however limited and biased it was, played a pivotal role. These documents preserved at various administrative levels such as district, state, and central, first in Calcutta and then in New Delhi, may be invaluable to draw a reliable base line prior to introduction of British induced new practices. Church history, mission reports, proceedings of the annual conferences of the various Christian congregations, brotherhood associations, fellowship union reports are another source of base line for uncovering aspects of social change vis-à-vis organized religions in the region Then, there are travelogues, memoirs, adventure story, reports on the armed/military expeditions etc., which may be used as source materials in the absence of reliable ethnography for drawing baseline for charting the imminent social change in a sub-region/community. Folk literature, myths, legends, proverbs, etc. among the pre-literate communities and various forms of literary expressions in the vernaculars should be culled with a view to picturing the traditional forms of social institutions prior to initiation of significant social change.

The most significant landmark for initiation of social change in the North-East region was that of the creation of state of Assam in the British Indian Empire in 1825 after reorganizing the various sub-regions/communities in a centralized administration. The administration was headed by a lieutenant governor under the Viceroy of India, and the state was divided into districts and sub-divisions, which were again presided over by the British civil/military/police officials. The entire state was divided into Lakhimpur, Darang, Goalpara, Kamrup, Sibsagar, Nowgong, Silcher, Sylhet districts in the plains and United Khasi and Jaintia Hills, Garo Hills, Naga Hills, Mikir Hills and Lushai Hills districts in the hill areas. This territorial reorganization of the region was secured in seven decades starting from 1826 to 1895, when South Lushai Hills district was united with the North Lushai Hills with its headquarters at Aizawl. Apart from these directly and indirectly administered districts, there were un-administered territories on the fringe of Assam, such as Tuensang Frontier Tracts, Sadiya and Balipara Frontier Tracts which were administered by the Governor of state on behalf of the Viceroy as parts of the province of Assam. There were also two princely states of Manipur and Tripura with their resident British Agents and a number of zamindaris such as Bijni, Kalmalupur, etc., in the region. The point to be noted is that unlike the informal rule of a plethora of local rulers, the British introduced a formal centralized administration, which ran on formal orders duly recorded and such records were preserved as precedence.

In view of Nari K. Rustomji, one of last Indian Civil Service (ICS) officers, trained by the British colonial regime, it was 'the British policy – and herein lay its success – that of one of least possible interference' in the tribal affairs. It was the missionaries, and not the administrators, who were the main harbinger of change in the religious beliefs and ways of life of the tribal people (1983). The missionaries presented the momentous extraneous interventions in lives of a number of regional communities to begin with, and after that, the social scene in the region did not remain the same. Among these, the following may be enumerated:

Missionaries

With the opening of sea route to India from Europe by Vasco de Gama in 1498, not only the traders and adventurers, but also the Christian missionaries turned eastward to India with a view to spreading the gospel of Christ. Many of them turned to the courts of the various rulers in different parts of India and around. For example, two catholic fathers, Casella and Gabriel, travelled to the court of the

Bhutanese Dharamraja, Sabdrung Namgyal in 1626 and were honourably received and provided with hospitality. However, victory of the British East India Company over Nabob Sirajudaula of Bengal at Pallasey in 1757 provided an opportunity to the Christian missionaries to look for new openings under a more favourable regime. And for that they received occasional support from many of the zealot Company functionaries. Soon enough the missionaries realized that as they would not get desired response from the Hindus, Muslims, and Buddhists, so they naturally turned their attention to the preliterate communities in the hills, forests, and mountainous regions of India. The government used to issue license to the missionaries to operate in specific territories without competition from sister missions. The Serampore Baptist missionaries had earlier translated the Bible in Assamese, Khasi, and other regional languages. David Scott, the agent to the Governor General in the North-East region invited the Serampore missionaries to open schools in the region. But he expired in 1831 and his successor, Francis Jenkins, renewed the invitation to the missionaries to take up the literacy work in the region. Similarly, Charles A. Bruce, in-charge of the Chabua Experimental Tea Station, approached the Burma Field missionaries to work in upper Assam and for that his family set aside a certain amount of money. And that is how the Baptist missionaries first came to Guwahati and Jeypur in upper Assam, but within a few years, 'they discovered fertile fields in Garo Hills and Naga Hills'. Very soon, missionaries from other denominations like Presbyterians, Anglicans, and Catholics, etc. came to the region and took up literacy, medical and translation of scriptures in the local languages in the Roman script. These steps undertaken by the missionaries led to a total transformation of the tribal social life within a century and a half.

There was another problem: the American missionaries working in upper Assam and Goro Hills were known to be from the puritanical social background. They were teetotallers and were strictly against consumption of liquor among the converts. On the other hand, the tribes in the North-East India by tradition use home distilled liquor for consumption and ritual purposes, and in fact, liquor was part and parcel of their life. That was one of the reasons that the number of converts drastically fluctuated in the yearly decades of Christianity among the Aos. Another concern of the missionaries was that of the keeping a distance from articles and practices of the community considered immoral and heathen. One of such institutions was that of the Naga youth dormitory *(Morung)* in every village, which was not only the centre of the village communal activities, but it, was also the only shelter for the visitors to the villages. Considered as a centre of all immorality in the villages, the foreign missionaries avoided visiting it. Against the puritanical approach of some of the missionaries regarding the use of the *morung* and rice beer, Rev. Langri Ao made use of the *morung* as his night halting camps and preaching grounds in the Konyak villages and considered rice beer as part of his food and not an article of intoxicant beverage. His pragmatic and innovative approach to the Naga style of life endeared him to his brethren far and wide and he was one of the most popular and successful indigenous Naga missionaries (Sinha, 1993). Similar views were echoed in the expression of Dr Renthy Keizar, Professor of the Old Testament at the Eastern Theological College, Jorahat: 'I am an Ao, I eat as an Ao; I dress as an Ao; I live in an Ao manner; I am also a baptized Christian. In the same way, as I am baptized, so the culture is baptized' (Pruett, 1984).

Arunachal Pradesh, the former NEFA, was exposed to external religions like other social forces much later than other units in the region. However, S.K. Chaube noted much earlier: " A potent source of tension in NEFA is religion. When the Government of India decided to extend administration beyond the Inner Line, the early recruits to the service were mostly army officials and educated people from the advanced hill districts. Most of these recruits were zealous Christians, which made the government clamp down on semi-missionary activities. Local chiefs, as elsewhere, were at first opposed to missionary activities. But, the resources of the missions operating from the Brahmputra valley largely neutralized the administrative policies aimed at a 'cultural revival' and towards stalling proselytization. In 1967, when the government issued the quit order on some of the foreign missionaries (then totalling 299) in Assam, a virtual cold war started between the missions and the government. The reaction of the official circles produced a cultural parallelism with Hinduism. There is now a conscious effort among some officials to bring the indigenous religious faiths into a close proximity to Hinduism .... The temple of the gods, who in the Adi's pristine religion were not represented by images, was built with much fanfare in a more or less Hindu way. An absurd comparison has recently been drawn between the excavated site of a seventh century A.D. (?) civilization at Bhismaknagar and the legend of Lord Krishna and Rukmini. Buddhism is, of course, a well established religion in Kameng and Lohit, and is encouraged. Islam is absent. No proselytizing mission, Christian or Hindu, is allowed, through Christian officials and army personnel, some Adis and Daflas (Nyoshis), have their private churches ... but it is not allowed to preach" (Chaube, 1999: 196).

The Church

With the introduction of a new pantheon, which was also the religion of the new rulers, the white Englishmen, an alternative faith was made available. Unlike, the indigenous faith, the new religion was brought by missionaries, who tried to reach the common people with compassion, humility and persuasion. Unlike the aloof white British rulers, these new preachers, though White like the British rulers and who also spoke English language, mixed with the people, approached them with holy books, tried to diagnose their sickness, nursed their sick, played with the children and even had something for womenfolk like needle work. They used to dress differently, used furniture at home, lived in different type of buildings away from the habitation and used to pray in evening and morning regularly. The church building itself was a new and alternative symbol of other worldly approach to an unknown terrain of human faith. Christianity brought novelties like prayers, priests, and preachers, and a faith in the holy books, something entirely new to the tribal world in the region. It also brought new set of do's and don'ts; new taboos and still newer approach to old faith. It proposed a new concept of heathen, those, who did not believe in Christianity. It had conception of the Supreme Being, God, the Father, who created the universe.

"Church organizations also brought members of different villages and tribes within common structures for the first time. Villages of the same tribe that had previously been at war with each other were brought together in Associations and Presbyteries and Synods and Diocese. Different tribes were brought together in Conventions and Councils and Assemblies. Thus, evangelism and church structures fostered openness to others that in most cases had not existed before. This in turn, affected life-style" (Downs, 1994). Furthermore, Downs opines that whenever the communities faced a phase of crisis in life of the people, there was a phase of revival in faith of the Christianity, and the conversion of the heathen to Christianity increased appreciatively.

Schools

Christianity is the religion based on the holy book, the *Bible.* So literacy is a must for the believers to read the scriptures. That's the reason the Christian missionaries emphasize on universal schooling. With the schooling, reading, writing and arithmetic's (the 3R's) were introduced. In this way schools became integral part of the church activities. Another innovation was the introduction of written literature invariably on biblical themes in the Roman script, which was occasionally illustrated again on the scriptural themes. Very soon a situation emerged in which, youth dormitories versus West-oriented schools turned out to be the focal points for the young folk. The Missionaries also introduced new architecture of the buildings in the form of churches, schools, living quarters, different sets of furniture for various purposes such as cots to sleep, tables to write/eat on, chairs to sit, codes of dress and clothing on different occasions and seasons and also introduced a sense of proper dress and etiquettes to be followed in the company of variety of men and women.

The literacy programme of the missionaries had a cascading effect on the life style of the communities. American Baptist missionaries working among the Aos, Rev. Haggard and Perrine, reported on the occasion of 55th annual report: "The (Ao) Christians now have an increasing ambition to dress better, to live in better houses, and to be cleaner. They desire more to learn, how to read and write, and to use knowledge and powers they have for God's glory. For the past two years, the village schools have been self-supporting in the sense that they receive nothing from the mission. They are supported in part by the government and partly by themselves .... The village schools are also becoming self-managing and directing so that we feel that a good start is being made towards self-support ... a sort of Naga renaissance was brought about, and that too by very agency, namely the mere matter of a considerable number of Naga boys and girls learning to write. It would seem as if this alone would do more to show the Naga people the value of education ... *(Baptist Missionary Magazine,* Vol. 79, 1895). Furthermore, the Assam Baptist Mission Conference noted in the year 1907: "... Naga school books were especially desired by the government .... It fell to my (Rev. S.A. Perrine's) lot to do this, and I have prepared, by means of *pundits* (knowledgeable), primers and arithmetic's in Ao, Lhota, Sema and Mozunger Naga, also an English-Lhota vocabulary and gospel of Matthew in Lhota. The manuscripts of all these have gone to Shillong (capital of the Assam Province): the Government has passed of them and part of them are in (the printing) press. We have been assured by our Naga officials that they will all be approved though ... (Assam Baptist Mission Conference, 8th session 1907: 58).

The schooling for a different age group of the male pupils seating together for the same instruction in the same class room was an experience for the teachers. The students were taught the Roman alphabets on the biblical themes. These were the students, who were till the other day had been hunting in the woods, or working as the labour squads in the agricultural fields, or learning arts, crafts, games, handling weapons of war and defence and learning tribal folklore from their elders. In course of time, the girls joined the schools and apart from learning the alphabets, they began to learn needle work, stitching and tailoring. Note the satisfaction of Mary Clark, the wife of first American Baptist missionary among the Aos: "Instead of congregating promiscuously at different house to sleep at night, singing objectionable songs, telling doubtful stories and engaging in lewd conversations, these young reformers separated themselves and built a dormitory in which purity and holiness should reign. Here, at morning and evening time, the voice of prayer and songs of praise are heard" (Clark, 1978).

Healthcare

Against the traditional background, the missionaries cultivated a concept of causality as part of sickness against the traditional belief in sorcery, malevolent spirits, and evil eyes and so on. New ideas of pills against the illness, injections to cure a sick body fast and an idea of infection from a sore or certain diseases were introduced for the first time in the region. Similarly, medical doctors against the magicians and village medicine men were interposed and an idea of hospital for confinement of the sick people waiting for nursing to health was envisaged. Church historian Frederick Downs informs us about the American Baptist missionaries' medical efforts in the North-East region: "For whatever reasons, the Home Board began to appoint missionaries with professional medical training. In addition to wide-spread cholera during which they treated people at the roadside and in the villages, the missionary doctors and nurses established hospitals and nursing schools. The first Mission hospital (in the region) was at Tura, the first small building of which was completed with the help of an elephant for hauling timber in 1910. In 1925, a forty-five bed hospital for women was built at Guwahati, and construction of the twenty-five bed general hospital at Jorahat was completed in 1933. In 1934, the first nursing school was opened at Jorahat" (Downs, 1994).

Personal cleanliness and healthy living conditions were also stressed by the missionaries. The motto: "cleanliness is next to godliness" was emphasized for every Christian. It was not an easy task to convince the tribal people to keep their animals away from their living quarters. Similarly, disposal of the dead was another issue, which was hazardous from a point of view of healthy living condition. To convince the hill men/women to bath regularly in their villages situated at the top or higher slops of the hillocks was not an easy task. Again Dr Downs informs us the terms on which Mission Veng, Aizawl was established by D.E. Jones:

1. All houses must be at a distance of at least ten feet from one another (this was to obviate the danger of fire. Fires frequently occur and the over-crowding of houses in a small space often means that the whole village is consumed before fire can be put out).
2. Animals are to be kept in a separate building (this is never so in the average Lushai village. The cows and pigs are under the house at night between the supporting posts and hens and doves inside).
3. The beams of the houses must be at least six feet above the floor.
4. Each house must have a separate latrine.
5. Drinking water must be boiled.
6. Inhabitants are to go regularly to a place of worship (Downs, 1994).

Similarly, the newly converted tribals were constructing houses that would let in more air and light, village roads were improved, kitchen gardens introduced, as well as new forms of vegetables and poultry. There were occasionally conflicts between the indigenous faith and converts over contribution to the traditional village level worship, *genna* (taboo) days and propitiation to the spirits believed to add to fertility to earth, crops, animals and women. To begin with, as the converts were very few, they were made to shift their settlements away from the old ones to invariably a hunted location, known as 'mission compound'. As the conversion increased in course of time, both the settlements got combined, but the name mission compound continues for long time to come. Way back in 1899, the American Baptist missionary, S.A. Perrine reported on the Ao Nagas: 'They are building better houses for themselves, and with rooms … . Some of the Christians keep their person and homes and food comparatively clean, perhaps I should simply say, cleaner than the heathen. They do not eat rotten flesh, and the money they once spent for drinks, opium and false worship is making them prosperous. They have adopted a mode of burial and a more decent dress than the heathen' (cited in Downs, 1994). One of the sensitive points with the missionaries had been intoxication in form of rice beer and opium. Opium could be eliminated to a great extent with the help of the administration, but habit of drinking could not be contained to an appreciable extent.

Translation Work

The missionaries hired pandits to translate the holy *Bible* in Assamese, Khasi and other regional languages. After some hesitation, they decided to adopt the Roman script for translating the *Bible* in regional languages. Many of the tribal tongues had neither a script nor a written literature, though they were rich in oral literature. These languages did not have a sophisticated vocabulary to express abstract ideas, concepts and theological prepositions. The Christian missionaries provided such tribal communities with their first written literature in the form of basic alphabets and illustrated them on the biblical themes. Taking help from the knowledgeable tribal 'intellectuals' the missionaries tailored the Christian holy and related literature to the tribal languages in spite of the limited conceptual terms. In this way, the Christian missionaries are rightly credited for creating the first literature in many of the regional tribal languages. However, it goes without saying that they also introduced distortion in the tribal languages by usurping the indigenous tribal terms in the new Biblical context, which they were not intended to.

British Administration

British Tendency to Look for the 'Heads'

Many of the regional communities were near egalitarian in their simple life in good old days. Many a time, their politics evolved around regulation of sex relations, clan solidarity, hunting, collecting or harvesting forest products. Such communities regulated their lives through the institution of elders' councils, which could hold its sessions in an open square with all the adult members in attendance. However, with the exception of some communities such as the Konyaks, Lushais, and Semas, most of the regional communities were near democratic in their public spheres. Once the British stepped in, they began looking for the 'headmen', or chiefs of the communities for their convenience. As the British could not follow the local languages, they introduced a novel system of Dobhasis (those, who were apparently dominating tribesmen, and who could follow at least two languages and were well-versed in tribal customs), *dobhasi* courts; political jamadars (PJ: a type of semi-official messengers, who could run between community and the state functionaries), Gaon Buras (literally, the village elders or the Village Headmen) and political interpreters (PI: these were the semi-official local big-wigs, who interpreted the government decisions to the communities and local practices to the state functionaries). Unlike in the districts of the plains where elaborate arrangements were made for an effective land revenue administration, an indirect rule under an officer drawn either from the Army or the Police as the Political Officer or Deputy Commissioner of the hill districts was established. These Political Officers/Deputy Commissioners in the Hill Districts had relatively long innings such as P.R. Gordon among the Khasis, T. Hodgson among the Meiteis, J.H. Hutton among the Angamis, J.P. Mills among the Aos, Plaifaire among the Garos, etc. Many of them developed language skills and wrote monographers on the communities and even recorded the customary laws of the communities. These different political administrative arrangements from the districts in the plains created a gulf between the plains people and the hill communities, which was used by the British to their advantage.

There was another aspect of the tribal settlement in North-East region prior to the arrival of the British. The communities had been on move through wars, feuds, hunting expeditions, for a sheer sense of exploration, and at times, in search of better sites for a relative comfortable settlement through the centuries. The British froze this process, as if, by naming the territories after the communities such as the Khasi and Jaintia Hills, Garo Hills, Mikir Hills, Naga Hills and Lushai Hills districts and the like and fixing the capital tax and in course of time, even house tax on the tribesmen, and by appointing a British administrator for each of them. So much so that the village chiefs had to seek permission for establishing a new village from the Deputy Commissioner/Political Officers of the respective hill districts. Once the territories came to be known after a community, such as the Garo Hills or Lushai Hills, other communities residing within the boundaries of the hill districts began to be considered as the outsiders or the alien. This impression got further strengthened, when the administration sponsored volumes on the Assam tribes began to be written on a given format under the name of 'Ethnography of Assam' series of publications. These volumes, written invariably by scholar-administrators/missionaries with long years of experience in the district concerned, normally avoided the ethnographic details of inter-ethnic interactions, conflicts, long distance trade, and their contacts with the plains people.

Introduction of Cash as Medium of Transaction

The British insisted that the vanquished peoples from the hills must pay capital tax as a token of their subjugation, which was imposed on all male adults to begin with, which was changed to house tax later. But there was no locally available cash, as the communities followed barter system of economy. Thus, a novel concept of wages in cash was initiated for manual work in which the local people were engaged in cutting the village tracts, carrying officers' luggage on tours in the district, building Dak Bungalows by road sides, and offering their labour for building a little urban outpost in the tribal heartland. Consumer goods such as mill spun inexpensive cloth, iron tools, aluminum utensils, glass tumblers, coloured glass beads; tobacco, cheap cigarettes, and bottles of rum were made available to the communities even in the farthest corners of the region. With a view to making these consumer goods easily available even to the most isolated communities, the administration organized a chain of weekly markets on different days at nodal points in the bordering areas of the districts. The tribals were encouraged to bring their hill produce, such as fruits, roots, vegetables, honey, ivory, bark of the trees, hide and leather, natural rubber, birds, animals and the like in the markets for exchanging them with factory produce consumer goods. In this way, even the distant hill communities began to be linked with the market economy.

The British Efforts to Insulate the Communities

The British had termed their armed operations in hill areas as 'the task of pacifying and humanizing these primitive hill people' (Fuller, 1977), though their imperial designs were loud and clear. The British felt that regular administration in the hill districts was a costly affair and thus, they avoided regular administration in the hill districts. However, when hill communities mounted raids on tea plantations located on their former hunting and collecting grounds, the British were forced to extend their regular authorities in the hills region first by locating their district headquarters on the fringes such as Chumekedima for Naga Hills, Cherrapunji for Khasi Hills, Singimari in the Garo Hills and so on. As their administrative commitments in the hill areas increased, they were forced to move inside the tribal areas by creating administrative centres for each hill districts such as Shillong for Khasi Hills, Tura for Garo Hills, Kohima for Naga Hills and the like. These newly created district headquarters were invariably located on no man's land, away from local settlement. In fact, these administrative centres led to an intrusion of the European style of life in the tribal heartland by establishing civil lines, cantonments, the police and armed forces and new shops invariably run by a non-local *Kaian*, the Marwari retailers. Such activities in course of time did create new jobs such as those of coolies, blue coats, white collar, constables, soldiers and officers.

We may note social structure of the colonial hill cities in 1993: "To begin with, the hill cities had the Deputy Commissioner as the presiding deity with the Superintendent of Police, Civil Surgeon of the civil hospital, the post master of the post office, the Church Pastor and the Commandant of the Assam Rifles as the significant functionaries. Taxes were levied on houses and were collected by the village chiefs on commission. Entry of plainsmen to the hills was controlled and alienation of the tribal land was discouraged. The tribals were reluctantly induced to offer their manual labour on cash payment for various types of construction and porters' duties so that they could pay the house tax. The clerical staff of the small administration was invariably drawn from the plains and the domestic helpers were then Nepalese and the few shops available were owned by the plainsmen – the Kaians. In fact, these early urban centres were really 'non-tribal towns on tribal settings', functioning as the colonial administrative outposts, without much of urban amenities and style of life. "The station (of Tura) contains the bungalows of the few residents officials and of the missionaries, a small jail, the public offices, the lines of military police, a market place and a few shops, but it is nothing more than a village and in 1901 had a population of 1,370 souls … . It is a small, isolated and is generally thought to be unhealthy", wrote B.C. Allen in the District Gazetteer. And this statement might be applicable to most of hill districts towns of the British period with the possible exception of Shillong" (Sinha, 1993).

Paternalistic Indirect Rule by the Traditional Authorities

Unlike elsewhere in the plain districts, where an elaborate police administration was established under the piercing eyes of the ICS district officers, administration in the hill districts was considered a costly affair, as they did not generate revenue by paying taxes on the land. For that, drawing from their experiences gained from the Rajmahal Hills among the Santals, the British introduced an indirect administration in the hill districts of Assam by leaving the communities under the care of the traditional tribal leaders to govern themselves through their customary laws. Such administration was run under the benevolent gaze of the Political Officer, who was invariably drawn from the armed forces or police service. Apparently, their high handedness was silently noted by all and in a way, as they were answerable directly to the Governor of Assam, they were the lords of their job. These districts were variously termed as the Backward Frontier Tracts, then as the Excluded or Partially Excluded Districts and then Scheduled Districts under the Governor of the Province. With the exception of the Mikir Hills district of province of Assam, all the hill districts have been elevated to statehood in the Indian Union.

"The centre of the hill city was very much reminiscent of the quasi-feudal structure in the form of establishment of the Deputy Commissioner's office, residence, club, church, and his immediate associates (such as the Civil Surgeon, Superintend of Police, Post Master, Church pastor and the like). The barracks of the armed constabulary such as the Assam Rifles was a little away at a slight distance on a commanding hillock. In between the little shopping centre was located, which had establishments owned by the plainsmen on a crude model of contemporary departmental stores … The sites of hill cities were selected mainly because of the location, strategic and administrative vantage. As the hill districts were the British creation, similarly these administrative cities were all the more a British creation. They played significant roles as trend setters in life style of the communities among whom they were located. Thus, Shillong with Khasi, Jowai with Jaintia, Tura with Garo, Aizawl with the Mizo, Kohima with Angami and Mokokchung with Ao got inseparable identities of the above communities" (ibid.).

North-East India during World Wars

During the World War I, the British needed hard labour to carry heavy loads on their backs on difficult terrain and in trying circumstances. Naturally, they turned their eyes to the Assam hills and recruited sturdy hill men to the coolie corps. Once these simple and almost illiterate hill men were exposed to the societies outside, especially the quarters among the white men in Europe and defeated and suffering Europeans, the myth of the white racial supremacy came crashing to their mind. However, there was a much limited recruitment in the coolie corps during the First World War from the region, and it was limited to Khasis and Nagas. However, during the World War II, the region itself turned into a limited theatre of war, as the Japanese in league with the Azad Hind Fauz led by Subhas Chandra Bose mounted attack on the British Indian territories of Manipur, and Naga Hills. Prior to that they had vanquished the 'invincible British army' in Singapore, Malaya and Burma and caused a most disorganized evacuation overland leading to untold miseries to the deserting soldiers, civilian functionaries, and ordinary British subjects. The hill folk saw worst aspects of their white rulers for the first time, when the colonial rulers failed to provide basic security to their subjects. Moreover, they got exposed to the anti-British and the elements hostile to them for the first time in a big way. The defeat of the invincible British forces at the hands of the Asians such as the Japanese gave a lot of moral boost to the otherwise isolated and backward tribal folk. Furthermore, the retreat from Burma and brutalities by the retreating forces on equally suffering Japanese forces diminished the left-over trust and faith in the British claim of justice and rule of law in India. But these developments also caused immense anxieties among the literate and already converted Christian tribal folk for the forthcoming and uncertain political dispensation. Naturally, the collapse of the British rule led to rising of new aspirations among the exposed people of the region. The impending absence of the British colonial rulers made them face the fact that they had to negotiate with their country cousins for creating new a political space and future dispensations for themselves. This rising awareness of the new political possibilities made them assertive in their outlook. And that is how they opened negotiation for their future in independent India and their status as the tribesmen in the new dispensation.

The World War created new possibilities for the regional tribal elite to emerge as the effective spokesmen of the communities, as by then they were already exposed to a good doze of western education. How it created a new class of operators becomes apparent from Chaube's study: "The (World) War's greatest contribution was the creation of a tiny middle class among the Naga .... A rising middle class is the vanguard of the moderate solidarity movement in the hills. But the solidarity movement being in origin an elite ideology, it suffers from one weakness, the remoteness of the common people from its cause. In Khasi Hills for instance, where detribalization has gone a long way into the social set-up, the traditional leadership of the chiefs and headmen is still a formidable force having direct touch with the people. The emergence of the Naga National Council out of the Naga District Tribal Council heralded the rise of the middle class intellectuals. The NNC's resolution in June 1946 was integrationist and opposed to the 'grouping plan' of the (British) Cabinet Mission" (Chaube, 1999: 153–54). Amalendu Guha informs his readers that student leaders such as G.G. Swell (a Khasi) and T Aliba Imti Ao (an Ao Naga) and the like, who rose to prominence in ethnic, regional, state and national politics in course of time, had even flirted with the leftist politics as students in this period (Guha, 1988: 323).

Indian Independence and Acceptance of a Constitutional Welfare State

The British colonial administration began to treat various segments of Indian population at different levels. For example, followers of Islam were treated as the minorities, who needed protection against the alleged domination of the majority Hindus. Similarly, the British appeared to be especially worried for the future of the tribes on the North-Eastern frontiers and sought opinions of their administrators in the field such as J.H. Hutton, J.P. Mills, William Plaifare, Col

Shakespeare, and the like way back in 1928. Needless to say that many of those consulted were of the view that these hill communities were not part of Indian population and they should be treated differently. A proposal was mooted in 1942 by these administrators and supported by Governor of the province to create a 'Crown Colony under the British Empire' for the tribesmen from Garo Hills to the Upper Burma, which came to be known as Coupland plan. Prior to that, the administration had tried to organize Naga government officers in Naga Club in Kohima to raise their political demands. The Club had expressed its distinct views on the imminent Constitutional development in the British Indian Empire. There was another under-current going on that, if India was to be divided on religious ground among the Hindus and the Muslims, why the Christian tribes should not ask for separate dispensation for themselves. And for that there was a suspicion among the Indian nationalists that the White Christian missionaries did encourage such a move among certain tribes. There was a proposal to consider whether Lushai Hills District should be integrated with Chin Hills in Burma. However, credit goes to the sane elements among the tribal leaders and Mizo Union, who stood for a United India and saw their future safe in the Indian Union. It must be put on record that the Naga National Council did not agree to join Indian Union, and in fact, it declared independence for state of Nagaland a day before Indian independence on August 14, 1947. They did try to negotiate with the Indian Union for a satisfactory solution to the problem with the future Indian leaders. Having failed in their design, the NNC decided to boycott the first general elections conducted in 1952. The relation between the two sides deteriorated further; Naga Hills were declared as a disturbed area and full scale Naga insurgency erupted leading to imposition of Armed Forces Special Power Act in 1958 causing untold miseries to the masses. On the demand of the Naga leadership, state of Nagaland was created out of erstwhile Naga Hills district and Tuensang Frontier Tract in 1962 on ethnic consideration.

It is a fact that at least some of the Assamese leaders looked forward to the British departure from India as an occasion to create a greater cultural Assam by integrating the plains with that of the various hill districts. Though there were liberal leaders with different views from the above, the alleged chauvinists created apprehensions in the minds of the hill communities, especially on the issue of Assamese being made as the official language of the state. Diagnosing the transformation of the 'enchanted frontiers' to that of 'imperilled' one, Nari Rustomji with a long experience in Assam as an administrator records: "There was a lurking apprehension among the tribal people on attainment of Independence that India's teeming masses would overflow into their habitat, disrupting their traditional way of life and depriving them of their most precious possession, their land .... It is the land that provides him (the tribal) and his family, year after year, with their essential source of sustenance, and it is the land that supports the livestock upon which he depends. While, however, other communities accepted the safeguards enshrined in the Constitution for the protection of their culture and their land, it is significant that the tribes that had suffered most from the impact of the Japanese invasion, the Nagas, were not only dissatisfied with the statutory safeguards, but launched an armed rebellion to break away from the Indian Union" (Rustomji, 1983). The only ray of hope in such a chaotic situation was from that of the India's first Prime Minister, Jawaharlal Nehru. He was recognized as an internationalist, an idealist and a visionary; here was no hidebound bigot out to impose the blanket of Hindu orthodoxy upon the rich and varied tapestry of India's multifarious tribes with their freedom from the inhibitions of so-called more advanced societies.

The national leaders in free India were committed to provide constitutional support to 'socially and economically backward communities' in the country. Keeping that in mind, the Constituent Assembly of India constituted G.N. Bordolai Committee under the Chairmanship of Assam Premier, Gopi Nath Bordolai, to examine how best the special requirements of the North-Eastern tribes could be accommodated in the Indian Constitution. The Committee visited various districts in the hills and plains and filed its report to the Constituent Assembly after talking to a cross-section of the tribal spokesmen. The stipulations of the Bordolai Committee were incorporated in the Constitution of India as the provisions under the Sixth Schedule, especially dealing with the requirements of the North-East region. There was a commitment made by the national leaders during the freedom movement to create linguistic states in place of the loosely amalgamated British provinces. And, in course of time, such states were created on the basis of the recommendations of the States' Reorganization Commission (SRC) in 1956. It may be noted here that the North-East region in post-independence phase meant the British province of Assam, and the two princely states of Manipur and Tripura. Assam was conceived by the SRC as a multilingual state, in which Assamese and Bengali were the dominant languages. However, though the hill peoples in the hill districts of the state did use a type of pidgin Assamese, they desired to develop their own languages and create literature in the Roman script. Once, the Assamese language zealots tried to demand special role for their language in the state of Assam, the hill people rose in unison to oppose the move. And for that they created a joint political forum, All Party Hill Leaders Conference (APHLC), which organized protest meetings, processions, agitations and even demanded separation of the Hill Districts as a separate province away from Assam. Though APHLC had its branches in most of the hill districts except Naga Hills, its presence was strongest in the United Khasi and Jaintia Hills district and the Garo Hills district. On the other hand, the state of Assam had a bout of language agitations against linguistic minorities, which further worsened the already volatile situation in the hills. All these resulted in the Indian Parliament passing the North-East Reorganization Act, 1972, by which apart from Assam and Nagaland, three new states of Manipur, Meghalaya and Tripura and two Union Territories of Arunachal Pradesh and Mizoram were created. It was a matter the time that the two Union Territories were elevated to statehood in mid-1980.

The new independent Indian Union had inherited a divided country, devastated economy, and illiterate, poor and malnourished masses mainly residing in the rural areas engaged in basically a subsistence economy. There were very few heavy industries under Indian control and the ill-connected and inadequate infrastructure were owned by the expatriate British capitalists or their Indian counterparts. The newly established Indian Union was yet be integrated into a single Indian State; there was a tribal attack on Jammu and Kashmir; flood havoc and earthquakes in different parts of the country; and at the top of it all, there was scarcity of consumer goods, especially food items, and for that rationing had been introduced after the Second World War. The resources were limited and national commitment was gigantic. So, the problem was how to utilize the limited resources for the maximum benefit within the limited period of time. And for that the national leadership turned to the Soviet experience of planned development. The First Five-Year Plan was inaugurated in 1952 with an emphasis on agriculture, rural industries and basic education. The Second Five-Year Plan emphasized on heavy industries and so on. Since then, Indian Union had implemented ten Five-Year Plans and eleventh one is being finalized. In this context, the contributions of the first prime minister of free India, Jawaharlal Nehru, is memorable. He invariably emphasized the scientific temper in the place of the tradition bound religiosity. A number of centres of higher learning such as universities, engineering and medical colleges, Indian Institutes of Technology, Indian Institutes of Management, scientific laboratories, academies of arts and crafts, and scientific research were initiated. A series of heavy industries such as steel plants, machine building plants, machine tools factories, fertilizer factories, chemical factories, petroleum refineries, power houses and a strong industrial foundation for the national development was laid out.

On the side of the social sector, there was the component of social welfare schemes, especially tailored for the socio-economically backward tribal areas. The entire country was divided into various development blocks below the districts in the states under the Ministry of Community Development and Panchayati Raj and within that, there was a special provision for the Tribal Development Blocks for the predominantly tribal areas. These Blocks were envisaged especially to initiate steps for agriculture, handicraft, rural industry, literacy, health and hygiene, and over all improvement in the life style at the grassroots level. Though there was an emphasis on agricultural improvement, construction of the residential houses for the vulnerable segment of population, village roads, health centres with amenities and trained personnel, schools and training centres were established in a big way. As per national policy of not to overadminister the relatively isolated tribal areas of the North-East region, however, the entire country from village to the block, to the district, to the state and then to the national level was linked for the first time in the history so far as the planned development was concerned. It was a fact that the resources were limited in proportion to the task undertaken, but it was an effort not to leave any corner of India untouched from the purview of the development planning. In this context, two points need to be recorded: firstly, creation of a dedicated cadre of functionaries to work in the difficult frontier region in trying circumstance for the welfare of the Scheduled Tribes (IFAS: Indian Frontier Administrative Service: Elwin, 1964)), and secondly, conception of an especially tailored scheme known as five fundamental principles of tribal development enshrined as 'Tribal Panchsheel' in the publication of the NEFA administration, 'A Philosophy for NEFA' (Elwin, 1964A).

These developmental schemes opened new possibilities no doubt and a number of positive steps were initiated, in which benefits of the schemes reached to the target to an extent. However, among others, the far flung regions of the country was also linked to monetary economy in a systemic way, as there was provision for certain amount of money to be allocated for the various schemes. The availability of money in the region with limited avenues to absorb the cash flow led to spurious development causing exploitation of the people and region in an effective way. This process has been termed by a scholar not as development, but as 'decay of the local initiative' (Aier, 1986). With a view to human development, while the entire region was tagged to the Calcutta University for higher education till 1948, now all the states in the region has at least one Central University, funded by the federal government. Furthermore, apart from about a dozen of the universities, now the region has the centres of excellence such as the Indian Institute of Technology, Guwahati and the Indian Institute of Management, Shillong providing new avenues for human skills. However, ... 'where education spreads through the intervention of welfare state or voluntary philanthropic organizations, a contradiction arises between the economic goals of the educated and those of the larger society. The social distance between the tribal elite and the others keep increasing and this gets translated into social distance between educated tribals and educated non-tribals, a phenomenon that is seen even in the towns which have come into existence in North-East Hill areas. The opportunities for (social) mobility through education seem to be confined to small segments, if not some families' (Roy Burman, 1977: 417–18).

We have noted above how the North-East region was exposed to political upheaval in the aftermath of the Second World War, how that was the only region of India, on which the war was fought on the Indian soil. Naturally, the relatively small, politically insulated, westernized through Christianity and to an extent encouraged by the retreating English bureaucracy, some of the tribes in the region expressed the reservation to join the Indian Union. In this context, Naga National Council was the premier one, which came out with the plea that, as the Nagas and Nagaland had never been part of India in the past, so they would like to be independent of Indian Union after the British withdrawal. They opened a discussion with the Governor of Assam for a possible way out to work together and that led to an understanding between the two sides known as Sir Akbar Hydari's nine point agreement. However, there was a difference of opinion on the interpretation of the provision in the said agreement on the point, 'what happens to Nagaland after interim period of ten years?' (Rustomji, 1971). And, the agreement led to nowhere and the Nagas decided to boycott the Indian administration. Consequently, there was no general election in 1952 and 1957 in Nagaland and the Nagas took to arms in an open rebellion. The Assam Police having failed to curb the rebellion, the army was called in under Armed Forces Special Power Act, 1958 to fight against armed insurgency leading to untold misery to the people. A section of the Naga leadership pleaded for creation of a separate state of Nagaland by integrating the areas inhabited by the Nagas, which was accomplished in 1962. However, elevation of the Naga Hills district to statehood did not satisfy all sections of the Nagas and insurgency went on unabated, earning it the title of 'mother of all the regional insurgencies'. By then, other tribal areas such as United Khasi and Jaintia Hills, and Garo Hills districts were restive and had resorted to the various democratic steps for creation of a separate state for them, which came in being in 1972 as Meghalaya. Five years back, in February, 1967, old Lushai Hills district rose in open armed rebellion against the Indian Union and for that many of the 'disturbed villages' were 're-grouped by the side of the road with a view to providing security' against the Mizo National Front (MNF) insurgents. The MNF insurgency continued even in the next decade and ended with the signing of the peace accord with MNF leader Laldenga and creation of state of Mizoram in 1985. In the year 1962, China had mounted an armed attack on the Indian forces guarding the northern borders in NEFA (North East Frontier Agency) with Tibetan Region of People's Republic of China. The ill-equipped Indian forces were badly beaten in the armed conflict and once the

Chinese withdrew from the area, NEFA was first turned into a union territory of Arunachal Pradesh and then it was elevated to statehood in 1987. However, Nari Rustomji, notes insightfully, 'The constitution of the tribal districts into states on the pattern of the larger states of India may have been satisfying to the tribal ego, but it also resulted in the dislocation and disintegration of the vital fabric of the tribal communities, a fundamental shift in their value-judgements and ever-widening gap between the villagers and their leadership' (Rustomji, 1983).

The creation of new states of Nagaland, Meghalaya, Mizoram and Arunachal Pradesh was done on the plea that 17 Naga tribes of Naga Hills districts, three tribes of Khasi, Jaintia and Garo of United Khasi and Jaintia Hills district and Garo Hills district and various similar ethnic stocks of NEFA would develop themselves better 'as per their genius' in the new states of their own. Only the Mikir (now known as Karbi Anglong) hills district opted out of the statehood in 1972. However, the demands for creation of new states on ethnic consideration in the region did not stop. A number of ethnic groups Boros, Karbis, Dimasha and the like have raised similar demands and took up to arms. Many of the smaller ethnic groups came with all types of territorial demands. On the other hand, on the alleged 'colonization of Assam' by the outsiders, a segment of the Assamese youth organized themselves under the banner of United Liberation Front of Asom (ULFA) in 1980s and went on armed rebellion, which is still festering. The region has seen a plethora of ethnic formations: there have been ethnic fragmentations among some of the ethnic groups, while others have further amalgamated themselves in larger identities. Mizo, Zoro, Zomi group of communities provide one type of example. On the other hand, some combination of the communities such as Chakhesang, and Zelinangrong came in currency. Arunachal provides another type of example; a series of communities such as Galong, Padam, Minyong, Pasi, Panggi, Shimong, Boris, Ashing, Tangam, Ramo, Bokar, Pailibos etc. joined hand to form Adi group of communities as the most dominant social formation in Arunachal Pradesh. So, the region is ethnically speaking in turmoil, and formation of smaller states on the ethnic ground does appear to have brought prosperity, development, contentment and end of the ethnic conflict. One way to look at these phenomena is to view the ethnic ferment as small ethnics' efforts to come to terms with the process of the Indian nation-building. It appears that every ethnic group in its eagerness not to be left out in the onrush to the national efforts to march ahead with the time does not want to be left behind. And perhaps that is why, they evolve a variety of strategies in the garb of political demands to attract national attention and stake their claim of the national pie so to say.

Barring the Naga boycott of the first two general elections and the phase of the MNF insurgency in Mizo Hills district, there have been regular elections to the state assemblies and parliament in the region and the electorate have chosen their representatives for running their respective states and sent their nominees to the national parliament. The democratic process of incorporating the grassroots people's representatives to state level leadership though the electoral process is on since 1952, and the region has not only produced their own chief ministers and cabinet ministers to look after their charge, but also produced leaders at national levels as the federal ministers, state governors, ambassadors and even the high office of the Speaker of the Lok Sabha, the lower chamber of the Indian Parliament. People have formed their own political parties at the local, state, regional and national levels and took active parts in the electoral process. In principle, they run their affairs as per law of the land, but the demographic size of the states does matter in the Indian federal structure. After all, when states like Uttar Pradesh and Maharashtra send 80 and 48 members respectively to the Lok Sabha while states such as Mizoram, Nagaland and Sikkim choosing one representative each appears somewhat odd, but that is what is the counting of individual Indians, may be from Uttar Pradesh, may be from Nagaland. It is the democratic process, in which every body competes against every body for maximizing their benefits and no body is ranged against any body. The major problem is that of the denial of the people's democratic rights through means of violence and insurgency, which must not deny ordinary citizen's role to take part in the democratic process without fear and apprehension. However, the North-East region also represents the case of differential development of nationhood in the country. As the region was late in monetization of its economy, so was it late in social and political development in comparison to other regions. Naturally, politics of violence ingrained in the region for its being on the difficult frontiers with a long tradition of defiance of the established authority has turned into political insurgency. As many individuals come to believe in short cut through violence to success in their design, they not only take the law in their hands, but also usurp the rights of the ordinary people to make their choice. But it does not work in the long run and the perpetrators come grief at the end. However, the North-East region, of late, has emerged as the thriving theatre of insurgency, in which its perpetrators have turned insurgency into a money-making industry.

The Extent of Social Change in North-East India

Individual

Tribal people are known to be gregarious in nature in their traditional set-up. The individual tribal does not have a personal/private domain of social activity unknown to the community. They function in public domain from birth to death and all their social actions normally have a socially approved pattern of behaviour. There are various sets of actions beginning with a child's play, to training the teenagers to acquire skills, to the youth to choose their spouses, to the elders to guide the young to earn their living and to the old to instill traditional wisdom, customs, knowledge, faith in the supernatural and folk art, craft and literature among the members of the community. Thus, normally, a tribal moves in a socially approved pattern of actions all though his/her life. There are extremely few deviants among the tribals. Similarly, the harshest possible punishment inflicted on any body among Adis for burning granary or incest among the Konyaks was to banish the culprit from the community. And such harsh punishment was as good as bet in the woods for wild animals, as the banished individual would not be socially accepted by any body, even by the hostile enemy of the community. The traditional communities had age-set and sex-set division of labour for performing various actions leading to earning food and drinks, making shelters, weaving cloths, resorting to hunting, or entertaining the folk and the like. For example, it was invariably the adult male, who hunted in the jungles for games and it was the women, who could collect fruits and roots and cook meals. Similarly, it was the old, who instilled folk traditions, literatures, and myths of origin and stories of migration to the young ones. The average individual in the community followed the vocation, which was repeated by most of the people almost in the same way within the territory of the community and rarely a person would transgress the tradition bound actions. Normally, a tribal would be born and die while doing the same work all his/her life within the limited radius of the tribal territory.

It were the hunters, story tellers, chiefs, headmen, warriors, and the like, who guided the communities in coping with the crisis, when the white missionaries emerged among the tribes with their guides to preach a new faith or the British decided to invade/pass through the tribal territories. It was the marginal men/women in crisis, who turned to the missionaries; or terminally sick individuals, who had lost hope in life, who sought the white men's pills as a cure. Barring some specific cases, the chiefs and headmen were opposed to the British intrusion in the hills. Even among those of the tribals, who were attracted to the missionaries, they began to distance from the missions, when the missionaries insisted on prohibition of drinking country liquour, worship of native spirits, community dances and the like. Thus, the number of converts among the Aos kept on fluctuating in the first fifty years of the arrival of the American Baptist missionaries in 1876. The schools attached to the church did miracles by attracting pupils, who in turn joined blue collar jobs in the newly created district headquarters, or turned to be a teacher or a preacher in the mission structure. The British picked up such people or their progenies with some social standing in their communities as *dobhasis,* political interpreters or political jamadars as eyes and ears of the administration. A big boost to the conversion and church activities came, when the administration decided to assign educational budget in the hill districts to the missionaries for education work. With opening of the churches in more and more villages, more and more individuals began to flock to the mission activities, turning the Christian missions in the hills as an alternative organization to the traditional society. The colonial administration too got indirect assistance though the availability of the literate tribesmen as the potential collaborators/functionaries.

In February, 1941, Edna and B.I. Andersons, the American Baptist missionaries reported from their headquarters, Impur, Naga Hills district, two typical cases of conversion to Christianity from the Chang tribe, which influenced positively the spread of the Christianity among the Nagas. A powerful Chang village chief and the head interpreter at the Mokokchng court *(dobhashi),* who had been the chief proponent of the British power among the tribes for over 30 years. He ruined his health by excessive drinking and he was seriously ill in the year 1940. At the end of his life, he sought conversion to Christianity, and his example was followed by many in future. Similarly, there was another strong Chang tribal chief, who had saved the British officials from an attack in ambush and for that the King Emperor subsequently decorated him. At the fag end of his life, he was converted to Christianity along with the members of his family. He was an effective voice among the community whose opinion was honoured by the government officials. He had taken to the conversion of his flock to the Christian faith. In this context, the example of Rev. Langri Ao's innovative approach to the indigenous Naga institutions cited above may be remembered. How Rev. Ao succeeded as a native missionary among his fellow Nagas and while the foreign missionaries avoided them as heathens.

The educated tribesmen may not be educationally highly accomplished, but they appeared on the tribal scene as the effective and modern spokesmen of their communities in the fast changing first half of the 20th century North-East Frontier India. As the communities pass through various phases of crisis, they turned more and more to the Christian faith. Many of the newly educated tribesmen joined the administration on blue or white collar jobs, which proved very convenient to the colonial administration during the hours of political upheaval. Though these government officials were 'loyal to the colonial administration', they were first and last the tribesmen equally loyal to their tribal communities. Naturally, they had their own anxieties in the fast changing world around them. As the events began to unfold fast in the region in 1940s and the British began to signal that their days were numbered as the colonial masters in the region, the newly educated tribal elite appeared at a loss. They would have preferred to live in hills undisturbed, but with the departure of the British in hills that option was no more available. Now, they were administratively tagged to Assam province, which was further part of the British Indian Empire. Thus, indirectly, they would have to deal with the Indians, which to them meant the Hindu Assamese or the Bengalis. They had come to believe that the colonial administration was a filter against the Indian expansion to the hills. Now in their absence, the tribesmen were faced with an uncertain future, anxieties and personal helplessness. However, by the middle of 20th century, many of the tribesmen had become politicians, advocates, doctors, professors, church leaders, apart from low level employees and many of them had earned their names in their respective vocations. Such professionals came forward in the days of uncertainty as the effective spokesmen of their communities and negotiated with their counterparts for an honourable place in the new dispensation. Thus, new possibilities were opened for the tribesmen to play a larger role in the body politic of India as equal partners with constitutional guarantee for their special status. Naturally, many of them have worked as the ministers, governors, ambassadors, parliamentarians, educators, businessmen, advocates, bureaucrats and administrators like anyone else in the country. The regional insularity of the tribesmen was being broken day by day and the highly motivated youth of the region is moving fast anywhere in India and world to take up new opportunities and new challenges of life.

Family

The family in the traditional societies such as the North-East region is one of the most significant social units of an individual's identity. Barring the Khasi, Garo and Jaintias of Meghalaya, who happened to be matrilineal in descent, rest of the communities are strongly patriarchal, patrilineal and patrilocal. It is something abnormal for a tribe's man to remain unmarried. The family tradition is such that boys and girls seek their life partners freely from among the socially eligible clans/stocks. Free mixing of the sexes is the norm and there is a marked difference between the treatments accorded to maidens and married ladies in the communities. By tradition, there used be youth dormitories for the boys and girls under the care of the village authorities to train the youth in the art of life and prepare them for their potential roles as valued members of the community. As subsistence agriculture and hunting and collecting used to be the mainstay of the traditional activities, entire social life evolved around the annual cycle of events, festivals, seasons, and calendar. The elders were considered as the repositories of the tribal tradition, knowledge, literature and folklores. They were the models of behaviour as farmers, hunters, warriors, story tellers, soothsayers, medicine men, priests, and what not; all invariably rolled into one, and had, as if, multiple roles to play with. At the level of the family, the head of the family or the father had the last say in the affairs of the family. It was the father, who represented the family in the village assembly. He would settle the marital alliance of his sons and daughters; once the son would get married, he would make arrangement for his residential accommodation and may even apportion some of his land for his support. In short, the family functioned as a social unit through the father and rest of the members of the family did play their individual roles as mothers, sisters, sons, daughters-in-law, etc. as per tradition of the community in question. It was basically a folk society, where every act of an individual was open to social review. In other words, there was little room for private life as it is understood in urban/industrial societies. Naturally, as the guardians of the culture and repositories of the tribal traditions, they were conservative in their outlook and avoided changes as far as possible.

Against the above traditional setting, one finds now, broken families, deserted couples, uncared children, drunk and drugged individuals in many of the families. Rate of divorce is on the high; drug addiction among the children is turning alarming; and excessive drinking has reduced life expectancy among the promising young men/women in a big way. This has also led to family discord leading to divorce. Another alarming scene is demographic boom in the region. The reasons are not far to find out. Tradition wars, feuds, conflicts have been almost exterminated; chronic diseases such as malaria, cholera, plague, small pox, etc., have been eliminated; and Christianity has removed personal and social unhygienic practices such as burial of dead in the vicinity of residential accommodations. On the other hand, better eating habits, improved medical knowledge and facilities, spread of education, contacts with outside world, exposure to mass communication media, welfare measures adopted by the state, and improved means of transportation has made the life easier and comfortable. In such a situation, birth rate is high and the death rate has been drastically reduced, leading to an appreciable demographic increase in the region.

Family began to change, once Christianity came in a big way. Marital alliances were no more solemnized as per the traditions, but the couple travels to the church for a Christian marriage, which may even be registered as civil marriage. Similarly, the children are baptized by the Christian priest; death leads to a burial in the Christian cemetery, followed by a church service. Now, the *Holy Bible* has an important role unheard and unimagined by the indigenous traditions. Though the communities continue to speak in its tribal languages, the family life is turning to be formal through the intervention of the Christianity as a world religion. The ceremony in the church, music on various occasions, dress of the individuals, eating and drinking to an extent on festive occasions are turning westernized, of course, there is sprinkling of local flavour. Invariably, the confirmation to the Western style of good Christian behaviour is becoming the norm of the family behaviour, which has further been engendered by the children being sent to the English medium so-called 'public' or mission schools. However, one must add that the ethos of the tribal life is strong enough, which gets reflected through tribal languages, vigorous music and dances, strong kin ties among the siblings, and an abiding attachment to the land to which they belong. In this context, the legal provision of prevalence of the customary rights on the land and the property of the regional tribal communities has ensured the continuity of the traditions to an extent. A few words about the matrilineal Khasi would be in order over here. With conversion to Christianity, employments in the formal sector and exposure to the basically patriarchal societies all over, the Khasi sons tend to adopt fathers' clan titles, while girls go as per the tradition on the mothers' clan surname. There is also a feeble move by some male Khasis for a shift to patriarchy. Many of the Khasi women, who married ethnic Nepalis, Marwaris, Punjabis, and Muslims men, their children automatically, get absorbed among the mothers' clan. And thus, by the end of the second generation, any vestige of the inter-ethnic alliance gets almost obliterated. In spite of all the changes in the life style of Khasis, males are discriminated against at the domestic level.

Kinship

Traditional tribal communities were tied together through the network of kinship. As it is commonly understood, kinship is based on marital alliance and adoption of the individuals/families as the brothers/sisters and one has certain obligations to the kinsmen/women. With a view to avoiding the incestuous alliances within the siblings, every human settlement must have at least two clans of the same community: the wife-giver's clan and the wife takers' clan. As the population grows, the size and spread of the clans also grow leading to intricate system of kinship network. Most of the traditional communities have a system of ranking the clans in terms of their social status. Accordingly, there are preferred clans for the marital alliances and there are clans to be avoided or given last priority for such an alliance. The stable traditional communities of the North-East region had followed such indigenous practices over centuries uninterruptedly. There were a number of marital ties among the various communities of the region. However, boys and girls had relative freedom to choose their partners. Marriage ceremony was an easy affair in which bride-price was given and community feast was arranged. Subsequent marital affairs were simple and more of legitimatizing ceremony than social celebration. Separation by divorce was easy and children born out of wedlock did not suffer much social ostracism. The most important role of clan solidarity was reflected on the occasion of death. The clans own the bones of their male members and in case a member of the clan dies in a distant place, it is obligatory on the descendants of the deceased to return the bones of to the clan cemetery. With the advent of Christianity, marital practices have been altered. A young men's wedding has turned out very costly to the extent that some of the young men spend years earning and saving money to meet the heavy expenditure on the ceremony, party, and pomp and show.

Compared to the plains folk, the women among the hill tribes enjoyed an open space socially and otherwise. However, this statement needed to be qualified, as even among the matrilineal Khakis and Garos, it was the male relatives such as maternal uncles, who took the significant decisions on behalf of the matriarchs. In most of the tribes, the women had no role in public affairs. On the other hand, there are much repeated sayings decrying the women status, wisdom and dispensability: 'crabs and women never have religion'; 'a women's wisdom does not reach to the other side of the village'; 'a wife or a rotten fence can always be changed'. In such an atmosphere, education of the women was naturally considered as a waste of time and labour. The missionaries placed great emphasis on the education of the women with a view to putting the family relationships on a more egalitarian level. Most of the early missionaries came to the 'field' with their wives and when the husbands got busy with their formal mission work, it were their wives, who invariably volunteered to teach alphabets, health and hygiene, needle work and even rudiments of domestic healthcare to the women. Parallel primary education among the girls opened new possibilities of nursing, paramedic and evangelic works in course of time, which laid foundation to the higher and vocational education. It is a fact that women status did not change drastically in spite of the extensive conversion to the Christianity in many of the tribes. However, it goes without saying that Christianity opened new possibilities for the women beyond the limits of their tribal cultures and traditions. For example, now marital ties may be mediated through the mission sponsored activities among the boys and girls belong to different formerly hostile clans, feuding tribes or even between tribals and non-tribals. Today one finds educated tribal women of the region in every walk of life competing with their men folk with dignity and honour with the possible exception of politics.

Village

P.R. Gordon, the celebrated author of the monograph on the Khasis, the first authentic ethnography on any tribe written under the 'Ethnography of Assam' series of publications, found a Khasi village like this: 'Khasis build their houses fairly close together, ... Khasis seldom change the sites of their villages, to which they are very much attached, where as a rule, the family tombs are standing .... There is no such thing as a specially reserved area in the village for the Siem and the nobility, all the people, rich or poor, living together in one village, the houses being scattered about indiscriminately .... Generally up to the narrow village street, from house to house, there are rough steep stone steps, the upper portion of a village being frequently situated at as high an elevation as 200 to 300 feet above the lower. In a convenient spot a clear space is to be seen neatly swept and kept free from weeds, and surrounded with a stone wall, where village tribunals sit, and elders meet in solemn conclave. The dances are held here on festive occasion .... All the villages swarm with pigs, which run about the villages unchecked. The pigs feed on all kinds of filth, and in addition are fed upon the wort and spent wash of the brewings of the country spirit, or rice beer, the later being carefully collected and poured into wooden troughs' (1990: 33–35). This image of a traditional tribal village may broadly be applicable to most of the tribal villages inhabited by communities such as Aos, Angamis, Tangkhuls, Mizos, and so on. In many of the tribal villages in Naga Hills, Garo Hills, Lushai Hills districts and elsewhere, the most important landmark was the youth dormitory as the focal point of a series of activities. Furthermore, the Nagas, used to erect imposing village gates as a part of their defence device, and gates were constantly guarded against the attacks from the enemies. Thus, the village gate used to be some sort of garrison for the village defence force, consisting of the young men of the village.

Once Christianity came to be accepted as the faith of bulk of the villagers, youth dormitory was lebelled as immoral heathen practice. Furthermore, it was not only to be discouraged, but also to be replaced by the mission run schools for the boys and girls, where instead of folk traditions and folk literature, Christian hymns, prayers, religious songs and the *Bible* was taught. The new Mission Compound, consisting of pastor's quarters, little church or prayer hall, and school, was constructed at a distance in the beginning, as the followers of the indigenous faith objected many of the new practices. The new converts also refused to pay their contributions to the village festivals, terming it as irreligious practice. This act at times led to the court cases between the two parties. Once the number of the converts increased in the village, the foreign missionaries advised their followers to settle their villages in more systematic ways by constructing the individual houses at a distance from one another, keeping the animals away from the human residence, making separate arrangements for toilets away from kitchen and providing outlet for the smoke emanating from the kitchen. In course of time, the converts erected imposing churches, schools, seminaries made of reinforced cement concrete, changing the skyline of tribal landscape. Unlike the traditional living structures of thatch and bamboo, the church inspired houses were made of reinforced cement concrete, flattened kerosene tin sheets, and Galvanized Iron Sheets with the roof painted red. Inside the structures, there were separate living rooms, kitchens, toilets, stores at the back and animals kept away at a distance. Very soon, cots, chairs, tables, benches and stools, metal cooking wares, china crockery and iron cutlery were added to the tribal Christian family's proud possession. So was the change in the table manners: the tribesmen/women would offer prayers before their meals; would invite guests for tea and snacks. By then, there was a drastic change in their personal apparel, as the men began to dress in western style in trousers and shirts, coats, hats, shoes and ties. It took time for the women to adapt themselves completely to the western mode of dress.

Frederick Downs found ambiguity in the attitude towards the aesthetic components of life: "In the tribal areas this consisted essentially in weaving, dress and personal ornamentation, decoration of houses and village gates, as well as songs and dances. The missionary and subsequent local Christian attitude towards these depended on two tests to which they were subjected: (1) did they perpetuate the traditional religion? and (2) would they promote immoral practices? The moral question related to both sexual practices and warfare. Because the songs and dances were perceived to be either sexually suggestive or celebrations of war and head-hunting, they were condemned. Because of their association with the old religion, as well as the extensive dancing and drinking involved (and it must be born in mind that most of the early missionaries were opposed to the dancing and drinking that took place in their own culture), the missionaries and early Christians were almost all opposed to the observance of traditional festivals .... There is one area in which the Christians affirmed the traditional culture. That was in relation to language. ... Because of their Protestant and egalitarian backgrounds (both the Baptist and Presbyterian missionaries, the main Protestant groups, came from lower class backgrounds with strong democratic convictions) the pioneering missionaries in the hill regions were firm believers in use of the mother tongue for education, for worship and for literature" (Sangma and Syiemlieh, 1994: 234).

Tribal Solidarity

In view of S.K. Chaube, if the aspirations of the hill people are to be conceptualized on a single scale, the measurement would be called 'a quest for identity'. The steps initiated by the British led to the emergence of contemporary tribal identities in the region in most of the cases. For example, once a region was named as the Khasi or Naga or for that matter Lushai Hills districts, the varied communities residing within the respective districts tend to be addressed/assumed accordingly. The best example one may cite is that of the Naga Hills district. Till today, no community claims as the Naga, and the Naga as a tribe is a misnomer, but Ao, Angami, Chang, Lhota, Konyak, Mon, Sema, Tangkhul, and others all collectively call themselves 'Nagas'. Another example may be that of the Khasi or the Mizo, where varied communities were forced to coalesce to form the larger identity. Secondly, the efforts on the part of the missionaries to write the dominant local tongue in the Roman script further consolidated the given identity from linguistic point of view such as Khasi or Ao for that matter. Thirdly, the efforts to write ethnography on various tribes of Assam further carved a recorded image of a community, which turned out to be the recorded reference for the community in question for times to come. And lastly, the British decision to record the customary laws of the 'tribes' further gave shape to do's and don'ts as the future models of tribal behaviour. Tribal solidarity further emerged through the activities of the various Christian missions, which were issued license by the colonial regime to operate in a given territory. Thus, the American Baptists Missionaries could work among the Nagas and the Garos, and in course of time, the Nagas were mainly Baptist Christians to begin with and so were the Garos. Same was the case with the Khasi and the Lushai vis-à-vis the Presbyterian Mission, which helped to two communities to emerge as the Khasi Presbyterian Christians and the Lushai (Mizo) Presbyterian Christians. This may further be seen in the slogan of a section of the Naga dissenters, who called for "Nagaland for the Christ". Similarly, Chaube informs that Mizo church gave support to the Mizo Union against the MNF dictates necessitating them to warn the church that 'the Mizo National Front (rebel) Government will not tolerate any church organization which does not accept the present Government'.

Frederick Downs identifies four ways through which tribal solidarity was achieved by the missionaries: (1) through the creation of a standard language for the various tribes, (2) through its educational work among the tribes, the missionaries opened a much wider horizon to the tribal people, (3) through its ideology of a world-wide Christian theology, and (4) through its ecclesiastical structure (Sangma and Syiemlieh, 1994, 206–7). In course of time, the newly educated tribal elite found a common cause with the fellow tribesmen from far away hills in the region because of his English education and also acting on theological or missionary plank. Thus, in spite of all the diversity and ignorance of one another, they could constitute forums such as Synods of the Presbyterian Church of North-East India (PCNEI), Council of Baptist Church of North India (North-East India: CBCNI or CBCNEI), and similar councils for late comers such as the Catholics, Seven Day Adventists, and the like. No doubt, such forums turned out to be precursors of the later secular political forums for the region. Prior to proceeding on that line, it will be instructive to note that many of the tribal Christian leaders had been meeting each other through the mediation of the mission run institutions of the higher education in the region. Thus, formation of the tribal political forums such as Eastern India Tribal Union (EITU), All Party Hill Leaders' Conference (APHLC), Hill State Demand Party (HSDP) and various state specific political forums such as Naga National Council (NNC), Naga National Organization (NNO), NSCN, etc. for Nagaland; Mizo Union and MNF for Mizoram and KSU for Khasi Hills etc. may be added.

But even the mission inspired leadership had their limits in the secular domain. In spite of the preponderance of the Christianity in the life of the educated tribesmen, they remain hardcore tribal in their basic approach. Thus, records a perceptive observer of the hill politics: "... The Baptist Church of the Naga Hills was completely indianized by 1955. Most of the Naga pastors came from Ao community. Right from 1955, the Baptist Church threw its weight in favour of peace. The hardcore Phizo faction found the Church's gesture inconvenient and told it to keep aloof from politics. This necessitated the search for a secular foundation for the movement. China's hostility to India, if not its communism, was expected to supply this .... The persistence of the under-ground movement, in spite of the strong disapproval of the Church, showed that the movement was secular in character" (Chaube, 1999: 170). Again, it is the contention of Chaube that "like all-India politics, Naga politics was never based on any monolithic unity. The first Naga national Council of 1946 was expected to be an all-Naga platform. But it was very much an elite or middle class organization dominated by the advanced Ao. Phizo, with a middle class background but personally frustrated, was able to unify most of the Naga groups, through an appeal to tribalism and with the weight of the powerful Angami village Khonoma. His desperate bid to retain control led him to a major mistake, namely, the gradual alienation of the non-Angami Nagas" (Chaube, 1999: 166). Thus, in spite of the apparent racial and religious unity, region-wide tribal solidarity had never been achieved and the tribal remains and proudly retains his/her tribal diacritical marks.

We had organized a regional seminar on 'Youth and Youth Movements in North-East India' at Shillong in 1977. Unlike other parts of the country, where unemployment, illiteracy, lack of opportunity, regional backwardness, lack of infrastructure, absence of skilled opportunity, etc. were ranked as the most important problems faced by the youth, the youth in the North-East region verged unequivocally that identity crisis was the only problem confronted by them (Sinha, 1995: 216). This worry for the identity loss may be responsible at least partly for the rapid growth of Christianity in the region since independence. 'In India as a whole, the Christian population increased by 69 per cent between 1951 and 1971, compared to a general population increase of 52 per cent. In the North-East, the Christian population increased by 117 per cent, during the same period. Even these figures do not give the full picture .... North-Eastern Christians constituted 16.5 per cent of the total Christian population of in India in 1981, up from 12 per cent in 1971' (Downs, 1992: 8–9). Then Downs proceeds to provide conversion statistics for five states in the region from 1961 to 1981:

Table 3.1
Growth of Population in the North-Eastern States

States	*% growth of Xian's*	*% growth of population*
	1961–1971	*1971–1981*
Manipur	84% (38%)	51% (31%)
Nagaland	76% (40%)	80% (50%)
Meghalaya	75% (32%)	48% (32%)
Tripura	57% (36%)	58% (32%)
Arunachal Pradesh	641% (35%).	

The above table demonstrates that a big churning is on among the tribes of the region. The followers of indigenous faith nestled on the far-flung areas on the distant frontiers appear to be worried that perhaps their indigenous faith may be an obstacle to their search for a convenient passage to modernity, in which their neighbouring Christian tribal cousins were leading the way. As a pragmatic and dynamic community, they perhaps realize that the Christianity with its plethora of mission and NGO sponsored social service and packages of development facilitates their competitiveness vis-à-vis rest of the Indian society in their search for an honourable status in the Indian Union.

Lifestyle and World View

Though it is difficult to generalize for the individual tribes, but the tribal society in the region has seen a massive transformation at different levels since independence. Still some broad statements have to be made. At the face of it, average tribal man/women from some of communities such as the Naga, the Mizo, and the Khasi from the region appear highly westernized, modern, educated and competitive to accomplish any assignment given to them anywhere in the world. Again, in spite of all the turmoil, environment of violence, on going insurgency and infrastructural dislocations, they are found all over the country in appreciable numbers struggling with their country cousins in an effort to make a decent living. The casual observers fail to understand how such people/communities can be termed as the backward scheduled tribes. The state sponsored welfare schemes have, again in spite of their deficiencies have gone a big way to benefit the tribes. Naturally, the elite among them have competed in all India examinations successfully and occupy coveted positions in the state and federal governments. Numerically small, but their shares at the national levels in different spheres of life are visible. On the other hand, there are individuals and small communities in almost all states of the region, who are so ill-equipped educationally that they have apprehensions to be left out in the onrush of social transformation. Many a time, external observers get puzzled on the rapid march of Christianity in the region. Missionary historian, Frederick Downs identifies fast conversion of the tribes in the Christian fold as revival movements, which follow certain spell of crises in the lives of the communities in question. Fast conversion to Christianity in the post independence phase in the region suggests tribal anxieties and uncertainties for their future in the fast changing democratic India. And needless to add that Indian Union because of some historical reasons was identified by many of tribesmen as the Hindu rule, which meant their Hindu neighbours from Brahmaputra and Barak valleys in Assam. Though it looks simplistic, but it appears that with a view to buttressing their sagging morale, they appear to have rushed to the fold of the world-wide Christian religion.

In such a situation, Christianity provides them with a sense of alignment with a wider circle of human multitude on religious ground. The tribal may not be opting consciously, but this possibility is easily and locally available and it has certain amount of modern western outlook, which appeals to the educated tribesmen/women.

Unlike unknown distant 'Hindu' politicians representing Indian State for acclaimed welfare amenities, the Christian missionaries are invariably their own tribesmen/women from their neighbourhood looking like them, conversing in their languages, and providing even instant solace through a variety of church sponsored social services. It is something like a bird in hand is equal to two in bush situation. For a time, the newly converted tribal gets confused how to negotiate between his age old faith and the newly presented gospel of Christianity, but he/she is a die-hard practical person, who knows how to make his or her best of the choices in trying situations. Within no time, he picks up external western style of dress, material culture, English language, and a plethora of mission approved ways of doing things as the Christians do. Now, the die is cast and the former tribal is reborn, as if, as Christian tribal, who tries to imbibe world-wide Christian pattern of behaviour.

We have summarized the North-Eastern social scenario in the following broad generalizations: "Firstly, a number of hill communities such as Khasi, Mizo, Angami, Sema, Konyak, Wanchu, Apa-Tani, and Monpa had a tradition of social stratification, private property, individual ownership of land, forest, animal, etc. Such practices, which have the constitutional approval as part of the tribal customary rights, have of late eroded the claimed tribal solidarity as egalitarian systems and provided impetus to social inequality. Secondly, the progenies of the Khasi *Bakhraw*, Mizo *Sailos*, Apa-Tani patricians, Konyak, Sema, Wanchu chiefs and the Naga *dobhashis*, who emerged first as a rudimentary middle class and then provided their communities with an incipient upper strata. Thirdly, post-independence period in the lives of the hill communities brought in the concept of planned development and the welfare schemes resulting in flow of substantial cash effecting traditional barter system adversely. Since secondary sector of production is not available to the hill communities in an appreciable way, most of their savings are being invested in land, turning the communal control into private property. Fourthly, emergence of private property has resulted into a number of associated trends in lassaize faire economy. Among them mention may be made of absentee landlordism, wage labour, share cropping, landless labour, agrarian tensions and exploitation. Benefits of various welfare and rural development schemes do not reach the grass roots. Finally, in place of the traditional tribal 'notables', an aggressive set of neo-rich contractor-politician elite has emerged as the most significant power wielders among the hill communities. They have positioned themselves between their communities and the outside world as the most articulate spokesmen and mediators of the conflicting interests. The real underdog among the tribals have no spokesmen, as they are sandwiched between the fast vanishing traditional system and a new born welfare state" (Sinha, 1995: 113).

We have noted the human variety at the regional level in the North-East. We found that as the impetus to change was received differentially in different parts of the region, there cannot be a single base line for examining the nuances of social change in the region as a whole. Moreover, before the British colonial administrators emerged on the scene, they had already dispatched their advanced party in the form of the Christian missionaries in the region. These pioneering missionaries, with their preaching in the church, teaching in the village schools, literacy programmes for the women and adults male, healthcare and the *Bible* lessons they introduced momentous change in the tribal lives. The British colonial administrators recognized the chiefs, headmen, *dobhashis,* political interpreters, and political jamadars; introduced cash transaction; created tribal hill districts, urban centres and indirect rule of the tribal chiefs and *gaonburas.* During the First World War, the tribesmen from the region were recruited in the coolie corps and went overseas during the operation. The Second World War was fought in a limited way close at home in the region and when the tribesmen saw the 'invincible' British trounced by the Japanese and others and retreated in the most inhuman ways, they, as if, drew their own lessons of defiance. Lastly, with the coming of the independence, the regional society had a number of apprehensions, which were largely and formally taken care of by the constitutional guarantee of the tribal customary laws, provision of the welfare measures, creation of the tribal hill states and various effort to incorporate the tribal elite in the national fold and chalking out special programme for the distant small tribes. All these efforts, formal, the state sponsored welfare schemes, and voluntary ones by the plethora of non-governmental organizations inclusive of the Christian and other missionaries have played crucial roles to make the regional society adapt to the changing times more comfortably and retain their innate tribal ethos meaningfully. As a whole, the society in the region has totally transformed externally, but its inner core of tribal ethos is virile, resilient and flexible enough to withstand any challenge in its way to dynamism. It will be interesting to examine the nature of trends of social change in the region on the scale of modernization, westernization, urbanization, and industrialization, and at the same time, examine the empirical evidence how the indigenous institutions have coped with the on-rush of social change.

References

Aier, I.L. 1986. *Contemporary Naga Social Formations and Ethnic Identity: Development or Decay*. Ph.D. Thesis. Shillong: North-Eastern Hill University.

Chaube, S.K. 1999. *Hill Politics in Northeast India*. Hyderabad: Orient Longman.

Clark, M.M. 1978. *A Corner in India*. Guwahati: Christian Literature Centre.

Downs, F.S. 1971. *The Mighty Works of God: A Brief History of the Council of Baptist Churches in North East India: The Mission Period 1836–1950*. Guwahati: Christian Literary Centre.

—. 1992. *History of Christianity in India: North East India in the Nineteenth and Twentieth Centuries*. Vol. V. Part 5. Bangalore: The Church History Association of India.

Elwin, V. 1964. *A Philosophy for NEFA*. Shillong: Advisor to the Governor of Assam, 2nd Reprint.

—. 1964A. *Tribal World of Verrier Elwin*. Bombay: Oxford University Press.

Fuller, B. 1977. Foreword to *History of the Assam Rifles*, by Col. L.W. Shakespear. Calcutta: Firma KLM Pvt. Ltd. and Aizawl, Mizoram: Tribal Research Institute, 2nd Reprint.

Gait, E. 1990. *A History of Assam*. Guwahati: Lawyer's Book Stall.

Gordon, P.R. 1990. *The Khasis*. Delhi: Low Price Publications.

Guha, A. 1988. *Planter-Raj to Swaraj: Freedom Struggle and Electoral Politics in Assam, 1826–1947*. New Delhi: People's Publishing House.

Kedilezo, Kikhi. 2009. 'Change and Continuity in Naga Marriage: Case Study of Zounuo-Keyhonuo Group of Angami Naga', in T.B. Subba (ed.), *Christianity and Change in Northeast India*. New Delhi: Concept Publishing Company, 262–263.

Pruett, G.E. 1984. 'Christianity, History and Culture in Nagaland', *Contribution to Indian Sociology*, 64: 74–78.

Roy Burman, B.K. 1977. 'Social Process in the Hills of the North-East India: An Ecological Perspective', in M.N. Srinivas (ed.), *Dimensions of Social Change in India.* Bombay: Allied Publishers Pvt. Ltd., 405–418.

Rustomji, Nari. 1971. *Enchanted Frontiers: Sikkim, Bhutan, and India's North-Eastern Borderlands.* Bombay: Oxford University Press.

—. 1983. *Imperilled Frontiers: India's North-Eastern Borderlands.* Delhi: Oxford University Press.

Sangma, M.S. and D.R. Syiemlieh (eds) 1994. *Essays on Christianity in North-East India.* New Delhi: Indus Publishing Company.

Sinha, A.C. 1993. 'Christianity and Ethnic Identity among the Nagas', in M. Miri (ed.), *Continuity and Change in Tribal Society.* Shimla: Indian Institute of Advanced Study, 123–135.

—. 1994. *North-Eastern Frontier of India: Structural Imperatives and Aspects of Change.* New Delhi: Indus Publishing Company.

—. 1995. *Youth Movements in North-East India.* New Delhi: Har-Anand Publications.

—. et al. (eds) 1993. *Hill Cities of Eastern Himalayas.* New Delhi: Indus Publishing Company.

Srinivas, M.N. 1966. *Social Change in Modern India.* Bombay: Allied Publishers.

Subba, T.B. et al. (eds) 2008. *Christianity and Change in Northeast India.* New Delhi: Concept Publishing Company.

4

Social Change and Development

N. VIJAYLAKSHMI BRARA

The word 'development' has in itself certain inbuilt ideologies and presumptions. Those presumptions, when generalized and universalized, lead to certain problems. The epistemological constructs of 'development' have been embroiled in the unilinear, evolutionary path – from tradition to modernity. The concepts such as 'tradition' and 'modern' are given meanings and their definitions are presumed to be static. The first sociological account of development was modernization theory, which held that the 'less developed' countries would eventually catch up with the industrialized world, provided they emulated the economic and socio-political systems of Western capitalism *(www.highbeamencyclopedia: Dictionary of Sociology,* 1998). According to Devaki Jain, "The former colonies were called 'underdeveloped countries' as they arrived as free nations in the global space. This sounded demeaning as they had great and old civilizations and resources, so they were renamed as 'developing countries'. That word was also found not quite dignified and the word 'South' was coined because most of the countries belonged to the Southern Hemisphere. But this raised several questions – Australia and New Zealand, countries that belonged to the club of the rich, were in Southern Hemisphere. Another use of term emerged to denote the poor and underdeveloped, so there was a Global North and the Global South" (Jain, 2005: 5).

Lately, there has been a surge to create tangents to this unilineality. Scholars have shown that development is much more than copying the industrialized world. There has also been a renewed analytic emphasis on the interdependency and integration among nations, not just in terms of economic processes, but also at the level of culture and ideology. This is true not just between the nations but also within a nation.

The concept of 'Third World development' is rooted in specifically Western ideas. This leads to development policies, which destroy the cultures of non-Western populations. In particular, the drive towards global uniformity in cultures, lifestyles and mentalities has been responsible for bringing forth the identity assertions, emphasis on ethnicity, fear of marginalization, and territoriality and indigenous issues. Cultural uniqueness, economic self-sufficiency and indigenous developmental initiatives are deliberately marginalized in the dominant discourses of the modern global world.

An important reason for the current academic interest in ethnicity and nationalism is the fact that such phenomena have become so visible in many societies that it has become impossible to ignore them. In the early 20th century, many social theorists held that ethnicity and nationalism would decrease in importance and eventually vanish as a result of modernization, industrialization and individualism. This never came about. On the contrary, ethnicity and nationalism have grown in political importance in the world, particularly since the Second World War.

However, the recent academic discourses on 'modernity' understand it as a multiple phenomenon. This multiplicity is based on specific combinations of social and cultural patterns, divergent ideas and social uprisings. It is now being increasingly realized that societies are doing their own pick and choose and consequently making their own models of modernity.

The concept of development needs to have fluidity. Indeed, shifts are taking place, whereby, we are having plurality of components to measure development. Today, along with the per capita income, there are human development indices, happiness index, welfare index, etc., taking into account various dimensions of human development. According to Amartya Sen, "The initiation of the approach and the beginning of the annual series of Human Development Reports occurred under the remarkable leadership of Mahabub ul Haq, the great Pakistani economist. Even though Mahabub's primary focus was on the evaluative aspect of the human development approach (he questioned, in particular the commonly used measures of economic success, such as the gross domestic product, on which so much of the development literature had tended to concentrate), he also had deep interest in the agency aspect. Even as he was hammering home the need to judge progress differently, Mahabub was also scrutinizing the ways and means of enhancing – through commitment and determination – the 'life chances' that people enjoy in the miserable world in which we live" (Sen, 2003: vii-viii).

While ranking the countries on the basis of their human development, it revealed that the countries that had high and rapidly growing rates of growth of GDP often had a reverse trend in human development and in economic and other disparities.

Presuming that development is needed for those countries which are 'underdeveloped', the sociology of development became increasingly the study of the 'other'; specialized to analyse social phenomena in parts of the world that did not 'come up' to the level of the societies that had invented sociology as the central social science of modernity: urban, industrialized, highly differentiated societies with national economies of capitalist orientation and located in territories controlled by states where formal authority relied on a legitimacy founded on democratic control procedures. In comparison with the central topics of such mainstream sociology, development sociology frequently came up with the issues concerned with those that were too 'backward', too 'poor', too 'simple' and too far away to offer fields of real interest for sociological investigation.

Consequently, development sociology found itself predominantly measuring as to how much a society needs to do "catching up". It was forced to become specialists of the 'exotic' and 'primitive' societies. The studies in development sociology evaluated and suggested ways of interventions for the societies to build 'modern' 'democratic' institutions.

The crux of the problem lies in our (the academic clique) knowledge base. Our identification of sources, the narration of history, our underpinning of the ideas, according to Devaki Jain, is visibly Eurocentric (Jain, 2005: 3). Global waves, the great historical events, the thought process, the built up paradigms, the thinkers we look up to are all west derived. For instance, the events which lead to

World War II are more commonly used reference points than, say, our important anecdotes of independence movements. Therefore, we, as development practitioners, have to remind ourselves the comment by Linda Gordon, and that is, "Most historiographic progress – perhaps most intellectual progress – proceeds by rearranging relationships within old stories, not by writing new stories" (Gordon, 1991: 73). This author therefore sees development through re-arranging the old social processes rather than bringing in from the outside.

Social Change

"How can the sociologist be certain that a particular change is part of the process of modernization? Such a difficulty is not merely logico-philosophical, but is inescapable in the actual analysis of empirical process of change" (Srinivas, 1972: 54).

Studies on social change in India have also got wrapped up around the Eurocentric paradigms. But unlike in other Third World countries, Indian scholars were always conscious of their indigenous research establishment along with the ideology of the long-standing nationalist movement.

By the early 20th century these traditions had already produced a considerable body of works on the arts, sciences and cultural-religious practices of classical Hinduism, the cultural matrix of Indian as well as aboriginal communities and regional accounts of castes and tribes detailing their customs and manners.

With independence, the search for social change became an important theme. However, by the 20th century, the indologists' perspectives started to be sidelined and the study on social change moved around the Eurocentric paradigms. Nevertheless, there was a continuous debate involving questioning the western modernity. There was always a concern that tradition would be superseded.

Kenneth Pomeranz in his book *The Great Divergence* states that "... older literatures – from the late nineteenth century classics of social theory to the modernization theory of the 1950s and 1960s – stressed a fundamental opposition between the modern West and its past, and between the modern West and the non-West. As more recent literature has tended to narrow the first gap, it suggests that the second gap – European exceptionalism – goes back even further than we thought" (Pomeranz, 2000: 5). Even Wong outlined in his *China Transformed* that much of classic nineteenth century social theory has been rightly faulted for its Eurocentrism (Wong, 1997). According to him, "the assumption still made in much social science research that Europe provides a universal model of development is fundamentally mistaken. The solution is not, however, simply to reject Eurocentric norms but to build complementary perspectives, such as a Sinocentric one, to evaluate current understandings of European developments". A genuinely comparative perspective, he argues, will free China from wrong expectations and will allow those working on European problems to recognize the distinct character of Western development (*http://www.cornellpress.cornell.edu* cited on 18 November 2008).

M.N. Srinivas was among the first to have written exclusively on social change in his book *Social Change in Modern India.* For Srinivas, change takes two major forms: first, various forms of mobility within caste system and second, the wide ranging process of westernization. Today, neither tradition nor modernity is strong enough to completely erase the other. I have stated that in one of my works on Manipur, but it can also be said about the North-East in general; and that is that, "Even while opening up more and more to the outside world, these societies are returning to their roots, their culture and their belief systems, informed by an understanding that such a return to the past could help preserve the identity of their communities .... So, today, even as Manipuris adopt modern lifestyles they simultaneously maintain a deep-rooted faith in their tradition" (Brara, 1998: vi-vii). With the result today, as Madan has also pointed out, that developing societies have become 'deceived societies' as they have had their present transformed into a permanent transition, 'an endless pause'. Nevertheless, the search remains for modernity, democracy, capitalism or development.

The question now is, do we remain in this methodological limbo or do we understand development from the way it is perceived by the people. This paradigmatic shift requires a rigorous fieldworker's inquiry and bold methodological initiatives.

As suggested by Kenneth Pomeranz, it is first of all important to confront biased comparisons by trying to produce better ones. This can be done in part by viewing both sides of the comparisons as deviations when seen through the expectations of the other, rather than leaving one as always the norm (Pomeranz, 2000: 8).

Seen from this perspective, one can move out of the duality of development-underdevelopment, primitive-modern, North-South, etc., and rather concentrate on the comparatives without making one a norm for the other one to achieve for.

In Relation to the North-East India

A study in social change in the North-East India therefore needs a paradigmatic shift. When we study the North-East India from the above mentioned methodology, then, the whole perspective of North-East Region Vision 2020 goes astray.[1] Vision 2020 has in its focus that the North-East India needs to be 'mainstreamed' (sic) and it is only then it will be able to compete with the rest of India. As if the rest of India is a norm which the North-East has to achieve. I am here indicating a certain indi-centric theoretical fallacy in the line of what Wong called the Eurocentricism. Ironically, the same document also eulogizes the participatory models of NERCORMP project which is far from the mainstreaming idea and rather working towards indigenous models.

The methodology to study the North-East India therefore needs to be ethnocentric, with intensive comparative research, within and outside rather than judging it through the mainland perspective. For instance, gender is one such field in this area, which cannot be studied through the theoretical premise, empirical data and the measuring indices of the other parts of India. So are concepts such as social hierarchies, poverty and development.

We need to revert to monographs and village studies, the little traditions. We need to fade out the duality of universalism and particularism. The alternative theoretical paradigm needs to be built up on the ethnographic studies rather than the other way round.

Let me begin by citing some measuring indices:

1. *Social hierarchies:* The system of social stratification in the North-East tribal areas cannot be seen from a clear cut the perspective of caste (tradition) or class (modern). The societies are more or less egalitarian even if not based on equity. The hierarchies are horizontal rather than vertical.
2. *Poverty:* The poverty index in the North-East cannot be measured by taking into account the per capita income. Taken in this way the majority of the North-East will come below poverty line. We have to realize that these communities are self-sustaining and are not dependent on the market economy.

There are very few hunger deaths. At the same time, it cannot be wished out that there is poverty in the North-East.

3. *Gender:* In most of the South-East Asian societies, specially the Burmese, the Javanese and the Malaysian as well as in the North-East India, the collective strength of women offers material self-sufficiency and ensures a degree of co-operation with men in the social sphere. The South-East Asian women are visible. A woman's self-image in the North-East, just like her counterparts in the Javanese and the Burmese societies, generally speaking, is very much influenced by her role as a mother, which provides her a superior status and security as compared to her role as wife. The terrible horrors of widowhood as perceived in the other parts of India are absent here. There are no dowry deaths, female feticide, and to top it all, we have matrilineal structures. Yet we cannot say that we have gender equity (Brara, 2005: 87). Let me cite a horrific experience of mine: I visited Karbi Anglong, in Assam to access the gender mainstreaming in the project. With a preconceived notion that drunken men consequently beat their wives, I asked whether they have been beaten up? There was a total puzzled look on the faces of the women. On enquiry I came to understand that wife bashing is unheard of in this region. Not only did I a mistake of imposing my hegemonic ideas, but I also introduced an alien concept for them to wonder for the rest of the life. I would have done another mistake if I had presumed that due to the absence of the above-mentioned aspect we are achieving gender mainstreaming.

Participatory Development: The NERCORMP Experience

Along with interventions in methodological tools and contextual understanding of the concepts, the third area of our concern centres on the policy formulation of this region and their subsequent implementation. Here again, we need to be inclusive rather than exclusive, participatory rather than directorial and a grassroots planning rather than top-down.

A filtration of such a perspective has been initiated by North-East Community Resource Management Society,

As mentioned above, our central focus of the paper is that, social systems of exclusions, be it economic or political create a brittle society. Alienation leads to anomie and the centralization of ideas and planning create a vacuum in the periphery. NERCORMP tried to fill that vacuum.

Let me dwell upon it a little to put the point across that the development *analysts* should perhaps adopt similar perspectives (as stated above) as that of the development *practitioner* of this project.

Let me quote the *Vision 2020* document again from a different perspective: "However recent initiatives in communitization at the village level, aimed at harmonizing the 'village community with the traditional tribal body' have shown significant success. ... the NEC sponsored 'North East Community Resource Management Project' (NERCORMP) in Assam, Manipur and Meghalaya involving the International fund for Agricultural Development (IFAD). Such projects are worthy of emulation to accelerate participative village development. Examples from IFAD projects have shown that unlike government schemes, the IFAD funded projects have not been afflicted by the malaise of extortion primarily because they are community-driven and because people have shown a keen sense of ownership of the projects. This clearly indicates that many systems can co-exist if the delivery mechanisms work" (*Vision 2020,* chapter 2: 22).

North-East India is home to more than 250 different indigenous ethnic communities with very diverse cultural and socio-economic realities. The region presents a complex socio-cultural framework with a unique set of challenges. Agriculture is the primary occupation and most of the communities have strong dependency on forest and their resources.

The increasing asymmetrical symbiotic relations with the nature coupled with the political movements for self-determination has left the economy of the region in a stagnant form.

I am going to give a short background about this project, which is trying to improve the livelihood of the vulnerable groups. I do not want these initiatives to be known to the people *per se*, but because NERCORMP is trying and to some extent have been successful in initiating developmental programmes as according to what the people want, from their perspective of development.

This project is giving an alternative developmental model, especially with reference to the North-East India. It has been doing what the *Vision 2020* is now saying: "The participatory development as the new development strategy" and using terms such as "empowerment of people", "grass root plans", "prepared and implemented at the village level", "needs of the people" etc. (*Vision 2020,* chapter 1:1–35)

It is this bottom-up approach which through the democratic and gender-balanced and also women-centric institutions called the Natural Resource Management Groups and the Self-Help Groups (SHGs) is being implemented.

North-East, barring the plains and the whole of Arunachal Pradesh, does not have the likes of local self-governments, such as the panchayats. It is governed by the traditional institutions, which have sometimes have the statutory powers and again sometimes not. Some of the other limitations are that they tend to get elitist and have always been gender blind. Consequent to this, the land use pattern was also limited by a few and also governed by the few. Therefore, a need was felt whereby some institutions were created through the initiation of the NERCORMP, which are people-centric.

I am interested to showcase the interventions made by this project because, today when we are thinking of strategizing the development initiatives in the North-East and also envisioning a "Look East" policy, we have to understand the NERCORMP/IFAD model. Nearly all the agencies, which have to either evaluate this project or come for just studying it, have called it a successful and implementable programme.

Ushering in an all-encompassing institutional structure the NaRMGs and the SHGs have had the following pivotal roles to play.

Elitism as opposed to the all inclusive principles, in the sense of a coterie or even an individual deciding the affairs of the masses and gender blindness as opposed to gender equity, in the sense of complete exclusion of women as a rule and not merely as a norm are the areas of concern. The urgency to build people-centric institutions was compounded by the fact that in the project's areas of operation, Panchayati Raj Institutions (PRIs) has not come into fore. In Manipur, for instance, the elections to form village councils have not been able to take place. In the areas where there are councils, they have been able to maintain their status quo. In other words, women and the poor are continued to be excluded. For an all-inclusive development, therefore, the establishment of NaRMGs and SHGs are seen as ushering in a new era and a new paradigm of development. The institution of NaRMGs as a viable body of village governance, is a perspective into which the project is now trying to tread. Today, it can be said confidently that 'inclusivity' has been internalized and has become a process, the trend of which no body can stop. The NaRMGs have in their agenda the vision of developing their villages, in the sense of making roads, schools, electricity, availability of drinking water and lobbying the government departments for providing the facilities which is rightfully theirs. Along with this, they have, today, geared themselves for collective farming and collective marketing. They can today stand as an example of how a village should be governed. The SHGs, on the other hand, have consolidated women and provided strength in their collectivity. In the far-flung areas where the financial bodies are scarcely present, the use of the resources collectively has generated remarkable entrepreneurship among the women.

The Process or the Mobilization of Institution-Building

This is how it began. A team consisting of project staff, local NGOs and government line departments visited the villages a number of times to discuss various issues related to their day-to-day life. The team explained the project and its objectives. Several discussions were held with the village headmen, chiefs and other local leaders. After the initial visits, the community and the team jointly held a three-day camp at the villages. The village community usually provided a place to stay, cook food etc. During these camps, various tools of PRA on development and livelihood contexts were applied. These exercises helped the community to self-analyse their situation leading to a lot of debate amongst themselves.

Rapport-building between the team and the community was very important. It was necessary to state the objectives and purpose of the visit. Sensitivity remained a major concern. It was also very crucial to emphasize the importance of involvement of the women in voicing their opinions and decision-making. It was of utmost importance to discuss the relationship of the newly formed institution with the traditional institution. This was important since at no point the traditional bodies could have been made to feel threatened or ignored by the new institutions. This would have otherwise retarded the pace of the development of the new institutions and even hampered them to be formed.

Once the institutions were formed a lot of training input had to be given, specially in the field of capacity building, organizational management, accountability, transparency, vision building etc. The institutions were raw, with no precedence to set an example. The concepts of arranging their own priorities, self-management of finances with their own action plan and the actual implementation with their own hands were being treated like a newborn baby – with great caution and anxiety. From the project's side too, giving training to these newly formed Institutions was a hard master's task. Therefore NERCORMP kept giving trainings to these institutions till the time they started feeling confident. Today the Institutions by the name of NaRMG and the SHGs at the village level are firmly grounded.

The emphasis on the training is so much so that even today training is going on as a constant feature, now focusing more on a need-based and focused group training. The main aim of this project is not to give people the fish but to teach them how to fish.

SHGs, on the other hand, follow the classical SHGs lines of objectives and functioning namely savings, credits, thrift, meetings, account maintenance, livelihood/income generating activities and social mobilization. They have moved from rudimentary savings, thrift and credit to social issues and economic activities. They have regular meetings and take up various social and economic issues/activities. They maintain books of accounts, which are regularly supervised and audited. SHGs are successfully operating bank accounts untrained for in the past, and many of them have availed bank loans over and above their savings and revolving fund grant from the project, thereby building up a bigger capital base. Many of them are graduating into next higher level of entrepreneurship.

The SHG federations and NaRMG associations are taking up activities like micro-credits, collective farming, and collective weaving and are proud owners of pick-up trucks and inner-city buses. They have approached banks and other private funders for loans. The business out of these automobiles has been so good that they have been able to repay their loans before the stipulated period of time. Among the federations, which could not do it on their own have joined hands with their NaRMG associations. This has paved the way for better understanding between the two institutions and has enabled them to become a powerful block.

Although, the Government of India guidelines are very good and the money flowing towards rural economy is only next to the defense budget. However, implementation is the main problem. Therefore, utilization of these funds in proper way by increasing the capacity of the people is very important. In IFAD, the poorest gets the first chance and it trusts the people to be able to make their own decisions. This model particularly becomes relevant at the time when the gap is widening between policy makers and the people.

Concluding Remarks

The keyword is the 'sense of ownership'. The sense of ownership, on deciding their socio-economic status, on their role as the decision-makers, and policy formulations.

Next keyword is asking the communities as to "What do they want?" We cannot presume as to what they need and give to them. We need to ask them their own priorities.

In my previous studies on the panchayats in the North-East India, one of the major issues which came up was that unlike the rest of India, where the concept of panchayats as well as its etymology are very familiar cultural constructs; it remains outside the preview of the North-East concept and understanding of its authority system.

Secondly, the Hindi used in the government programmes to be implemented by these bodies is extremely elitist. In fact, now with some of the English terminology too this problem persists, although in a bit lesser degree. The issue therefore is to use simpler and people-friendly words. An effort can also be made to let the state governments translate the programmes in their own language.

Programmes designed for the diverse rural population all over India with different climatic conditions, culture, needs and demands are homogenized in the centre. Hence, they do not get the acceptability as they are considered not needed.

NERCORMP has passed through various stages and today has crossed many challenges successfully. It of course has still heights to attain. It has proved that it is possible to trust people to let them take up their own affairs and change their destinies. Also, they can be entrusted with responsibility and accountability. All they need is the crucial and initial support and handholding after which they can stand on their own feet. Appropriate role for development actors then, now and hereafter, is to be informed facilitators.

Next, we have to involve them in any planning. They need to be involved from the beginning, from plan outlay to the actual construction. They also need to chip-in certain contributions. That is how the sense of ownership will be perpetuated. Upon becoming active and dynamic they need to be constantly encouraged.

Therefore, this project's most important strategy had been the Bottom-up approach. Where they decide what do they want, who wants them more, how do they want, how will they implement it and how will they share the benefits of their fruits. The project was there to guide them in their process, encourage them and of course giving them options and opinions as a starting point to start their planning. All they need is a slight and honest push. This process needs constant trainings, awareness programmes, monitoring if they are laying dormant or moving in a different direction and capacity building.

The economy of the societies in which this project worked is at the subsistence level; somewhere they still have barter exchange. They are extremely tradition-bound. The women have never been vocal. Therefore, in the time period of 5–6 years, whatever change and betterment they have tried to bring is noticeable. It has had its fallouts, but the methodology of NERCORMP and also of the IFAD stands testimony of it being adoptable as a successful model in the development paradigm of our nation.

Development, especially social development, has to be ushered from the society. Neither the development practitioners nor the policy makers can define a path for the communities to tread. The villages in the North-East where this project has been implemented have created their own indigenous micro models of development. Each of these model is enmeshed in their own cultural mores with an inclusive principle. In other words, they are neither western nor indic but is 'development' nevertheless.

Note

1. *The North East India Vision 2020* is a Government of India's document brought out by The Ministry of Development of North-East Region and North-East Council. It has been brought out under the aegis of the Government's "Look East Policy" to ensure that the North-East Region plays the "arrow head role" in this policy implementation.

References

Brara, Vijaylakshmi. 1998. *Politics, Society and Cosmology in India's North-East.* New Delhi: Oxford University Press.

—. 2002. 'Breaking the Myth: The Social Status of Meitei Women', in Walter Fernandes and Sanjay Barbora (eds), *Changing Women's Status in India: Focus on the North East.* Guwahati: North Eastern Social Research Centre, 193–201.

—. 2005. *Situational Analysis of Women and Girls in Manipur.* New Delhi: Commissioned and Published by National Commission for Women.

—. 2009. 'Brushed under the Carpet: Inclusion and Exclusion in Manipur', in B.S. Baviskar and George Mathew (eds), *Inclusion and Exclusion in Local Governance: Field Studies of Rural India.* New Delhi: Sage, 285–315.

—. 2009. 'Paving the Way for the All Inclusive Institutions: Some Livelihood Alternatives', in *Livelihoods from Forestry in North East India.* Indonesia: CIFOR and India: NERCORMP and NEHU, 21–28.

Gordon, Linda. 1991. 'What's New in Women's History?', in Sneja Gunew (ed.), *A Reader in Feminist Knowledge.* London: Routledge, 73–75.

Jain, Devaki. 2005. *Women, Development and the UN.* Hyderabad: Orient Longman.

North-East Region Vision 2020. New Delhi: Ministry of Development of North East Region and North East Council.

Pomeranz, Kenneth. 2000. *The Great Divergence: China, Europe and the Making of the Modern World Economy.* Princeton: Princeton University Press.

Sen, Amartya. 2003. 'Forward', in Sakiko Fukuda-Parr and A.K. Shiva Kumar (eds), *Readings in Human Development: Concepts, Measures and Policies for a Development Paradigm.* New York: Oxford University Press, vii-viii.

Srinivas, M.N. 1962. *Caste in Modern India and Other Essays.* Bombay: Media Promoters and Publishers.

—. 1972. *Social Change in Modern India.* Bombay: Orient Longman.

Wong, R. Bin. 1997. *China Transformed: Historical Change and the Limits of European Experience.* Ithaca: Cornell University Press.

5

Social Change and Woman

Has She Acquired a New Identity in North-East India?

MANORAMA SHARMA

Heraclitus, the Greek philosopher had argued that the fundamental character of reality is change itself and in support of his argument had said, 'One cannot step twice into the same river' meaning that since the water in the river was constantly flowing the river even while remaining the river was undergoing constant change.[1] Even though Plato later questioned the very nature of reality being monistic he supported one part of Heraclitus' argument about the changing nature of the physical world although he believed that there was another reality which was universally true and unchanging.[2] Without going into the philosophical intricacies of these views the question that one would like to pose here is that in the process of its physical existence, to use the metaphor of Heraclitus' river again, does the river acquire a new identity? Perhaps it does if that change brings about a new environment and if those interacting with it change their perceptions in associating with it. The water remains water but the course, the size, the topography, its activity its utility might all change. It might be too abstract to try and find parallels between Heraclitus' view of change and identity, and change, women and identity; but it can perhaps be argued that while the water in a river remains water but perceptions about and attitudes to the river might be crucial for understanding the river so also women might remain women but change would require questioning whether she has acquired a new identity and whether societal perceptions about her has undergone any fundamental changes or not. It is to understand this that we need to delve into the concept of social change and the question of identity particularly the feminist perceptions of identity.

Piotr Sztompka would contend, 'the most striking feature of contemporary life is the revolutionary pace of social change. Never before have things changed so fast for so much of (hu)mankind. Everything is affected: art, science, religion, morality, education, politics, the economy, family, even inner aspects of our lives ... nothing has escaped' (1994: 4). When social change has been such a largely accepted phenomenon of society, there is no doubt that social scientists have debated very intensely over a century or more about the models that can be developed for studying this all important aspect of social reality. There have been those views which have looked at change within a *status-quoist* framework like the systems model 'which views social change as the change occurring within, or embracing the social system. More precisely it is the difference between the various states of the same system' (ibid.). Such a view therefore aims at maintaining the system rather than destabilizing it. The theoretical norms for this trend were set by Max Weber followed by the functionalists such as Emile Durkheim, Kingsley Davis, Wilbert Moore and Talcott Parsons.[3] There has also been what can be called a pro-change perceptions of change, the theoretical norms for which were set by Karl Marx and Friedrich Engels, which takes a more dialectical approach to the question of change and views change not just as internal to the system but as a holistic phenomenon which transforms the entire identity of the structure.[4] Such change also involves in it radical changes in social relations, in access to resources of various sections of the society and also perhaps societal values and norms. It is from this second perceptive that we would seek to view change in order to understand change in terms of women and the resulting gender relations in a society. Thus, when we talk about social change in North-East India, we need to ask ourselves the question whether the change that we perceive is a real change or a mere status-quo maintaining reorganization of the same system where social values and social norms, besides other societal aspects have remained the same particularly where perceptions regarding gender relations are concerned. We also need to enquire whether there have been any new realizations amongst both the sexes regarding the identity of the woman?

Why is the issue of identity so far as the woman is concerned so important in the context of change? To justify this a brief look into the dimensions of identity may be pertinent here. The concept of identity is perhaps one of the most hotly contested terrains in the field of the social sciences. There have been the critiques of identity who have sought to dismiss the idea of identity by arguing that 'identity as a basis for political action is theoretically incoherent and politically pernicious' (Moya and Hames-Garcia, 2000: 2). Many have pointed out that there is a tendency towards 'essentialism' in the entire concept of identity and such essential determinants are incompatible with socio-political realities. Countering this critique of identity Moya has argued that 'a theory of identity is inadequate unless it allows a social theorist to analyse the epistemic status and political salience of any given identity and provides her with the resources to ascertain and evaluate the possibilities and limits of different identities' (ibid.: 7). Following upon this line of thinking it is possible to argue that the process of identity construction is one upon which the realities of the surrounding social, cultural and political environment have a very strong impact. Identity thus has very deep political ramifications as well and history becomes the legitimiser for all these ramifications. Thus, if one were to begin from a definition of identity one could say that identity is 'what we are individually, as well as what we aspire to be, what determines and specifies us, as well as how we present our particularities to ourselves individually, and how we identify ourselves with groups and with the general norm' (Renault, 2004: 101). Who an individual is, that is how 'we perceive ourselves or are perceived by others' (Moya and Hames-Garcia, 2000: 8), are after all very political decisions determined not solely by the individual but by the society, or rather, by the dominant forces in the society. To quote Moya again, 'the significance of identity depends partly on the fact that goods and resources are still distributed according to identity categories' (ibid.: 8) and it is because of this that we can safely say that identity is a political category. However, like many other concepts like those of power and citizenship the concept of identity has largely remained within patriarchal constraints and only very recently has some writings begun to emerge which have sought to focus on gender as one of the important dimensions of identity.[5] In the debate amongst feminist scholars regarding the nature of essentialism in the gender dimension of identity some have sought to say that it is possible to argue that in this dimension there will always be in the last analysis a certain degree of essentialism because the basis for creating gender roles for men and women by society and history has been made possible by the reality of the biological difference. But here we must also remember that this essentialism has been the argument used by the defenders of patriarchy to justify gender roles and therefore it is necessary to question such notions of essentialism and reveal the androcentic notions inherent in such views.

Identity therefore remains a very political construct and the values of the socially dominant groups also create the essentials of identity – whether it will be race, language, caste, class or ethnicity. From that perspective the concept of the identity of the woman is also created by the dominant societal ideas, whether in a very early stage of the development of human society, or in a feudal system or in a developed capitalist system. In fact, women have very little autonomy to determine what they are individually, what they aspire to be, what determines and specifies them, as well as how they present their particularities to themselves individually, and how they identify themselves with groups and with the general norm. Thus, if the dominant forces in a society set the parameters of deciding what constitutes identity the question of the identity of the woman will also be decided within those norms which will therefore be basically patriarchal norms. It is from these perspectives that the gender dimensions of identity and social change in North-East India and in Assam in particular is sought to be analysed. To do this analysis the additive methodology of gender history will be used so that the available data can be used in a more gender sensitive manner.

There is no denying the fact that the entire North-Eastern region of India has witnessed a plethora of changes in society, economy and polity ever since the advent of colonial rule. These changes have had various kinds of impact on the society and social relations ranging from the positive and forward-looking to the negative and reactionary. But these changes have not really brought about such kinds of radical results which would have transformed the entire existing systems. The societal norms and values have remained more or less unchanged, particularly where gender relations are concerned. The changes therefore have not really touched the lives of women so far as their existence within patriarchal systems goes because these changes have not really engaged with patriarchy and the associated norms in any meaningful way. One very glaring example of this superficial aspect of what has been called change is the fact that when one looks into the official records, whether the official statistics or the official accounts, there is a stark invisibility of the women. For instance, even as late as 1994, the official *Statistical Handbook, Meghalaya* has no break up of its data by sex in crucial areas like employment, workers, labourers etc. Such blanket presentation of data clearly exposes the fact that the governments of the day are totally gender insensitive. There is no concept even of gender budgeting if you look at the budgets which the states prepare. Yet it is a known and also a generally apparent reality that whether during the pre-British period, the period under British rule, or during the post-1947 period the economic contribution of the women to the society has been substantial. Talking about the Khasi women, Tiplut Nongbri has very rightly pointed out that although the Khasi women contribute significantly to the economic processes, in the household or outside, their 'contribution remains a largely neglected area both in research and in policy' not only in the Khasi society but in the entire North-East as well (Nongbri, 2008). Elaborating on this point Nongbri has shown with a lot of statistical data how the census figures regarding women's work participation in the agricultural and non-agricultural sectors are 'in sharp contrast to the conditions on the ground where the presence of females in the workforce is particularly high' (ibid.: 44). The apathy of the powers that be regarding women and the fact that nothing really has changed for the women so far as societal attitudes go is reflected in these very gender biased presentation of official figures. But even if we consider these very figures and try to extricate the women's experiences from them certain interesting realities emerge. For instance, if we look into the statistics of small scale entrepreneurs amongst the Khasi we find that the gender roles determined by patriarchal norms in the private sphere influence the economic roles in the public sphere as well (even in a matrilineal society). Small-scale industrial activities like tailoring, bakery, embroidery, knitting and weaving have large number of female entrepreneurs and workers while activities like furniture making are dominated by men. This information which can be gathered from official statistics and ground realities of the period 1997–1999 (ibid.: 51–53) as has been presented by Nongbri, is very revealing because it shows that the identity of the woman whether in the 19th century or in the 20th century has remained the same despite all the talk of social change. Such changes have not really touched the lives of women so far as attitudes and social norms are concerned.

Moving out of the Khasi matrilineal society if you look into nearby Assam we see that there too the situation has been very similar. By the end of the 19th century the Assamese middle class had begun to establish its hegemony over the society and as such the values, norms and preferences of that class came to permeate all the other sections of the society.[6] It was this middle class that also was the forerunner in creating dominant value systems which have come to be reflected through various social institutions including the literary culture developed by this middle class through its conscious attempts at developing the Asomiya language.[7] Through the Asomiya language a new Asomiya identity began to develop and this identity was to a large extent the construct of the Assamese middle class. The economic and social conditions in Assam in the second half of the 19th and 20th century were such that there were practically no possibilities of the emergence of any other dominant class and therefore the middle class was able to exercise its hegemony over the society.[8] Thus, its views and values were reflected in the various institutions – social, political and cultural – that it created and an Asomiya identity begins to take shape through that culture. The views of the middle class regarding gender relations also get reflected in this new culture and thus there is a construct of the identity of the woman too. These middle class perceptions regarding women can be seen very well reflected if we make a gender interpretation of some of the contemporary literature.

The last decades of the 19th century saw a rapid and rich development of Asomiya literature. There were also organizations which came up during this period which aimed at not only preserving the Asomiya language but also worked towards developing the language. One such important literary personality of the time was Lakshminath Bezbaroa. He was amongst that small group of Assamese students in Calcutta, who, in the last decade of the nineteenth century established the "*Asomiya Bhasa Unnati Sadhani Sabha*" for the development and preservation of the Asomiya language.[9] It was this young group under the leadership of men like Lakshminath Bezbaroa which began publishing a magazine called

"*Jonaki*". The *Jonaki* became so famous that the entire period has come to be known in the *Asomiya* literary culture as the *Jonaki* era (1889–1895) (Saikia, 1984). Bezbaroa's writings, both his short stories and his satirical pieces under the pseudonym Kripabor Borboruah called "*Kripabor Borboruahar Kakotor Tupula*" reflect not only the complexities of the development of a literary culture but more importantly they are a reflection of societal values as well. As Maheswar Neog has very rightly pointed out, under this pseudonym 'Bezbarua laid bare the idiosyncrasies of individuals of society, and even of the nation' (Neog, 2004: 318). The fictional writings of Bezbaroa, as presented through many of his short stories, shows a projection of the man-woman relationship in a manner that clearly reflects the very Victorian idea of the woman that the Assamese middle class upheld and Bezbaroa seems to accept this as the most natural concept of the woman.[10] The perception of Asomiya identity at this point of time thus does not seem to give any place to the woman as an individual entity and how she perceives herself and what she aspires to be, and what determines and specifies her. All these decisions have been taken for her by the patriarchal society and she is represented as accepting that position without a murmur and without any consciousness of her own self. She is presented as completely submerged in the identity of the man. Yet the man who has presented this view of the woman has, in his satirical writings mentioned earlier, actually laughs at the men for considering themselves to be very superior to the women and showing their heroics only in front of their wives at home while outside they are actually cowards. At the same time, in another satirical piece on 'Rights of Women'[11], he presents a very derisive view of women asking for their equal rights with men and in a very subtle satire presents the general male perception of women standing forth for their own rights. This ambiguity in Bezbaroa's ideas is interesting and can perhaps be understood if placed against the backdrop of the ideas on gender relations that were developing in Bengal at that point of time because Bezbaroa and his group were at that point of time all working from Calcutta (Kolkata) and were therefore no doubt highly influenced by the ideas that were prevalent in Bengal amongst sections of the educated 'bhadralok'. Here, we see Bezbaroa's awareness about those ideas and yet a hesitancy in accepting them all easily and also perhaps conscious of the fact that very radical ideas about women would not be very acceptable to the middle class Asomiya society. So, his awareness of the rising new consciousness he expressed in the form of satire while the more dominant societal perceptions on gender relations, which he may have generally subscribed too also, are presented in the form of fiction and sometimes also through satire.

Literary works of the 20th century too present very interesting pictures of women. In a work like the Gyanpeeth award winning novel of litterateur Birendra Kumar Bhattacharyya, *Mrityunjay* (Bhattarcharyya, 1970), one sees two kinds of women being portrayed. One is the 'respectable' woman in whose case there is no concept of autonomy or independent identity outside the fold of the men's identity and most of the women have been presented in their political roles because of the involvement of their husbands except one woman, Koli Baideo. This woman is presented as an independent fearless woman, but she is depicted as a widow whose husband died while she was quite young, and having no family support she was brought to the Congress camp. The other is the woman who has autonomy and self-determination but such qualities are presented in women who are either not considered 'respectable' by the Asomiya middle class or are outside the parameters of that society. An example of such a woman is seen in the character of Dimi who belongs, as Bhattacharyya writes, to the Mikir tribe,[12] and married to a Garo. She is presented as a fearless independent character having the courage to defy even her husband and other men in her society to help the revolutionaries because of her attachment to and trust in a man (Dhanpur) she had known before her marriage. The significant aspect of Dimi's relationships are that these are her decisions There are also works by women litterateurs of the end of the last century who depict in their works a far sensitive approach to women and the question of their identity. Mention can be made here of the writings of Nirupoma Borgohain and Tilottama Misra (Borgohain, 1991). The novels of these writers, both historical novels, present women and the issues of their identity from a completely different perspective. They try to portray the fact that women in nineteenth and early 20th century Assam, despite all disadvantages faced in a patriarchal society, were still able to make a stand to assert their independent existence and this is the reality which most historical and other works of the time have sought to play down. The identity of the woman that emerges through this middle class created social milieu from the last decades of the 19th century to the end of the twentieth century was by and large one where the identity of the woman was neither acknowledged nor given expression to. But running as an undercurrent in this situation we find the ideas of the identity of the woman beginning to take shape which the dominant culture was unwilling to give expression to. The ideas regarding the emancipation of women which came to be expressed through the nationalist movement as a follow-up of the religious reform movements of the 19th century begin to have some influence on the more progressive sections of the Asomiya middle class and this dimension of middle class ideology also can be seen emerging in the developing social ideas. However, these 19th century ideas were also very much within the structures of the patriarchal world views and the concept of an independent identity of the woman as an individual entity did not form a part of that world view. But outside of these ideas we do see an independent consciousness beginning to emerge from amongst the women. The Asomiya middle class still retained its hegemony even at the end of the 20th century because the social and economic conditions in Assam had not undergone the kind of changes that might give rise to new class alignments and emergence of another hegemonic class. As a result of this, middle class values regarding women still basically remained what it was at the end of the 19th century although it came to be expressed in a much more refined and cautious manner. Women themselves also became more articulate in expressing their experiences and aspirations for identity.

However, despite all these developments that can be extricated by using the various tools of gender history, the basic reality still remained that societal attitudes still remained dominantly patriarchal and this gets reflected in policies and programmes of the various government institutions. For instance, today, on paper there are various schemes like the *Vande Mataram Scheme*, *Rastriya Jayanti Suraksha Yojana* and so on. The *Vande Mataram Scheme* is a nationwide programme aimed at improving ante and post-natal care, which was launched on February 9, 2004. The scheme envisages free ante and post-natal check-ups, tips to avoid nutritional problems and anaemia and counselling on small family norm and is a major initiative in public-private partnerships during emergency. In fact, while launching the scheme in the Ganeshdas Hospital in Shillong, the

Deputy Commissioner appealed for public-private cooperation so that the scheme could be successful.[13] But, the question that one may ask here is that in a society hegemonized by patriarchal values will this kind of an appeal really work towards a gender sensitive functioning of such schemes? So far as poor women are concerned, there are several other schemes like the *Rastriya Jayanti Suraksha Yojana* for the betterment of the poor women's health. But it is a matter of concern that a large number of poor women of Assam are still totally ignorant of these benefits provided by the government. Although the government's Integrated Child Development Services (ICDS) scheme is supposed to cover children and pregnant mothers, yet there are several rural as well as poor urban women who are unaware of it. Thus women who are not literate and who live below the poverty line are not enjoying their rights in the truest sense of the term. So, the education of girls should be made compulsory and free up to elementary level and reproductive health system should be accepted as human rights issues. All policies relating to the development and betterment of women must touch the grass roots level where the real scenario is to be found (North-East News Agency, 2006). Thus, despite some attempts being made, the majority of the women remain where they are with little awareness of their rights and even knowledge of schemes that are available for them.

All these schemes are for the betterment of the poor women's health but there has been so much social and governmental apathy regarding the question of women's education or raising social awareness amongst them that the poor urban and rural women are unaware of these schemes made for them. The reasons for this situation are not far to seek. The societal attitudes towards educating the women is still one of general indifference and if there has to be a choice between educating a boy or a girl, or providing better facilities and exposures, the choice will go in favour of the boy. According to the latest census figures women's literacy rate in Assam is 43 per cent and only 2.4 per cent women are graduates. In the matter of literacy alone, the gender gap in Assam for instance is 16 per cent and in other areas like employment etc., it is even bigger. Perhaps the societal attitudes toward women get reflected very specifically in issues like rape and witch hunts. In the five months ending July 2008 there were 500 rape cases. Witch hunts against women are increasing and women are the first victims in the ethnic clashes that have been on the rise in Assam.[14] These have been mentioned here as indicators of the fact that so far as change is concerned it has been only the status-quoist kind which only keeps the system stable but does not fundamentally change social values and norms and gender relations therefore have remained where they were a century or more back.

The most telltale evidence of the above argument stares us in the face if we look at the question of women in decision-making which actually reveals the power relations in a society and whether there have been the kind of social changes which have made power relations more gender friendly. The pages of history provide us with very interesting insights into women's lives and particularly their relation to power and power structures over the centuries. The debates on the concept of power may have had no concern for the women because that was the insensitivity created by patriarchy and was for the convenience of patriarchy. But women's history tells a different tale. Scholars researching into the area of women and power in history hold that a matriarchal society had never existed in history. Matriarchy has to be seen as a mirror image of patriarchy, i.e., women having power over men and not alongside men and that power has to be exercised in the public sphere where women take decisions about foreign relations, about their whole community and not just their families or relations and where women also take decisions and also control the sexual behaviour of men (Lerner, 1986: 31). It is in such a context that historians have said that matriarchy as the reverse of patriarchy has never existed. But, as Gerda Lerner points out with sufficient empirical evidence that there have existed societies 'where women shared power with men in many or several aspects of life and societies in which women in groups have considerable power to influence or check the power of men' (ibid.). Evidences from archaeology tell us of the existence of societies in the Neolithic and the Bronze ages where women commanded a lot of respect and this may indicate that they held some amount of power and control in the society. The 'urban revolution which took place in history'[15], saw the gradual transformation from kinship based societies to class based societies. This transformation brought along with it important changes in the societal structures which begins the subordination of women. The various archaeological and other remnants of the Mesopotamian civilization, for instance, support the conclusion that 'elite women were respected and accorded dignity ....'[16]

Such women also actively participated in political, social and religious life of the society but they derived their power 'entirely from the male on whom they depended'.[17] They also wielded power over men and women of the lower ranks but this power depended entirely on their sexuality. If they failed to please their men they also lost their political and economic power.[18] So, historical evidence shows that from about 3000 B.C. the subordination of women had begun although they were not yet fully relegated to the private sphere. This divide was achieved through the gradual process of the strengthening of patriarchy and the greater subordination of the women, not merely by brute force but also by, what Antonio Gramsci has called consensual power where women were made to believe that dependence on the male was not only natural but also advantageous for them. As Gerda Lerner has pointed out, 'the earlier societies were often matrilineal and matrilocal, while the latter surviving societies were predominantly patrilineal and patrilocal. Nowhere is there a reverse process, going from patriliny to matriliny'.[19] From this point of history it is easy to trace the subsequent developments in power relations in society where social structures evolved which marginalized the women and thus created a set of gender relations where the values and norms of the dominant (the men) pushed women out of the power structures.

Even in matrilineal societies like the Khasi-Jaintia and Garo in India's North-East women are still marginalized in the decision-making process. Here, very often, tradition is cited for the exclusion of the women from power. The reference is made to the Khasi *Dorbar* which has traditionally debarred women from taking part in public parleys and from decision-making in the *Dorbar*. This idea of women's exclusion from power has not only been internalized by the women but has become a convenient tool in the hands of the men to keep political power in their hands and to relegate women to the private sphere of the domestic world. Thus, even in a matrilineal society the societal norms are patriarchal and thus the basic concepts and values in the socialization process are the patriarchal ones (Sharma and Baruah, 1999).

A proof of the exclusion of women from power lies in the composition of the sixty-member Meghalaya Assembly. Since its inception in 1972 the House has not had more than two or three women members in the House (Malngiangn, 1996). The situation in a highly patriarchal society like Mizoram is even worse. Traditionally, women there had no societal power because the chiefs controlled the politics, economy and society till the coming of the British. However, the abolition of the chieftainship did not bring about any changes in the power relations in the society and women continued to remain in the fringes of those relations. The traditional patriarchal norms were further reinforced by the Church because Christianity, like all other established religions, upheld highly patriarchal societal norms (Lalrinchhani, 1998).

These values have become so deeply embedded in the society that women in Mizoram fare even worse than the Khasi women in terms of their participation in politics and decision making. The representation of women in the Mizoram Assembly is negligible even today. Thus, whether in patriarchal societies or in matrilineal societies the values and norms of patriarchy are so strong that the social hierarchies which are created are highly unjust in the sense that they are highly gender biased and exclude women from the realms of power. One must agree however that women in places like Meghalaya, Mizoram, Nagaland and to some extent even Assam fare better in social relations than their sisters in other more deeply feudal and thus more male dominated states in many other parts of the country. Yet their exclusion from decision-making and political power is almost at par with rest of the country and despite all the 'change' one talks about today this major societal reality has not changed. In a state like Kerala the gradual dissolution of matriliny and the spread of male dominated monogamous households marked a retrograde step for women. But, even then women in Kerala have been able to get access to literacy and salaried jobs which have made crucial differences to family incomes and household management. However, despite all these advantages, women have not been able to play any major role in politics or public decision making and thus here too the power equations remain unfriendly to women (Jeffrey, 1992). This perhaps is best represented as an all-India phenomena in the Indian Parliament where women account for not more than 8 per cent representation.

Women's role in decision-making in Assam beginning from the colonial times till that has also been nominal. The number of women members in the legislative assemblies bears proof of this which has never been more than 8 per cent (Guha, 1977). This lack of women in decision-making bodies is also responsible for the fact that policies undertaken for development are very insensitive towards the interests and welfare of women. What women need for themselves is decided by others who are least knowledgeable about the experiences of women. The fact that women need to be a part of the developmental programmes and not mere add-ons for political niceties is still not a part of developmental thinking in this part of the country as in many other parts of India and also other countries. As mentioned earlier, changes have definitely taken place in the societies of North-East India but these changes have not changed systems rather merely reorganized them for better performance. In the process the questions about gender relations have remained unattended to. Societal attitudes towards women have remained totally unchanged and values and norms have remained very much within the earlier existing patriarchal frameworks. Women have therefore found it very difficult to establish an identity of their own, an identity that is not constructed by male value systems and which provides women the dignity of existing as independent entities. All talks about social change will therefore remain only at very superficial levels if that change does not aim at challenging existing dominant value systems in the society and does not facilitate the acceptance of women as equal partners in social production. It is only such an approach to change that will enable any society to be a gender just society, will change attitudes of both men and women towards gender roles and gender relations and will ultimately bring about the social environment where women will have an independent identity of their own.

Notes

1. The readings from Heraclitus are taken from T.Z. Lavine, *From Socrates to Sartre: The Philosophic Quest* (Bantam Books, New York, 1989[rep.]), pp. 24–26.
2. Ibid.
3. These views have been discussed by us in detail in Manorama Sharma, *Social and Economic Change in Assam: Middle Class Hegemony* (Ajanta Publications, Delhi, 1990), Chapter I.
4. For a detailed discussion on these perceptions of change see V.I. Allen, *Social Analysis: A Marxist Alternative* (Longman, London, 1975).
5. There has been extensive discussion on this issue by Simone de Beauvoir, *The Second Sex* (Vintage Books, New York, 1989); Judith Butler, 'Subjects of Sex/Gender/Desire', in Sandra Kemp and Judith Squires (eds), *Feminisms* (OUP, Oxford, 1977), pp. 278–285 amongst others.

6. The issue of the hegemony of the middle class in Assam has been discussed by us in Manorama Sharma, op. cit.
7. The term *Asomiya* is used here to refer to that identity which is created by the language as distinct from the word *Assamese* which is used to refer to all those who have accepted Assam as their homeland but may have separate identities. This distinction was first made in A.K. Baruah and Manorama Sharma, 'Promises to Keep', *North East Quarterly*, Vol. 2, No. 2, 1987. Subsequently this has been accepted by a number of other scholars working on Assam.
8. See Manorama Sharma, op. cit., for a detailed discussion. The issue of the hegemony of the middle class in Assam has been discussed by us in it.
9. See *Bezbaroa Granthawali*, Vol. II (Sahitya Prakash, Guwahati, 1988, 2nd edn.), p. 3.
10. In this connection one can refer to his short story *Bhodori*. See *Bezbaroa Granthawali*, op. cit., p. 644.
11. Ibid., p. 1597 (*Tirutar Adhikar*).
12. Today they are all called Miri.
13. Press release No. 102/04 by the Govt. of Meghalaya, issued on 9 February, 2004.
14. Reports in the local vernacular and English newspapers have carried almost regular information on cases of witch hunting and killing of women and even their entire families at times name of witch hunting.
15. This refers to the process through which Neolithic villages gradually evolved into agricultural communities to urban centres and finally to states. See ibid., pp. 54–75.
16. Ibid., p. 74.
17. Ibid.
18. Ibid., pp.74–75.
19. Ibid., p. 53.

References

Allen, V.I. 1975. *Social Analysis: A Marxist Alternative.* London: Longman.

Baruah, A.K. and M. Sharma. 1987. 'Promises to Keep', *North East Quarterly*, 2(2): 30–46.

Beauvoir, Simon de. 1989. *The Second Sex.* New York: Vintage Books.

Bhattacharyya, B.K. 1970. *Mrityunjay.* Calcutta: Assam Book Depot.

Borgohain, N. 1993. *Abhjatri.* Nalbari: Journal Emporium.

Butler, J. 1977. 'Subjects of Sex/Gender/Desire', in Sandra Kemp and Judith Squires (eds), *Feminisms*. Oxford: Oxford University Press, 278–285.

Guha, A. 1977. *Planter-Raj to Swaraj: Freedom Struggle and Electoral Politics in Assam 1826–1947*. New Delhi: Indian Council of Historical Research.

Jeffrey, R. 1992. *Politics, Women and Well-Being: How Kerala Became 'A Model'*. New Delhi: Oxford University Press.

Lalrinchhani, B. 1998. *Impact of Christianity on Women in Mizoram*. Unpublished M.Phil. Dissertation. Shillong: North-Eastern Hill University.

Lavine, T.Z. 1989. *From Socrates to Sartre: The Philosophic Quest*. New York: Bantam Books.

Lerner, G. 1986. *The Creation of Patriarchy*. New York: Oxford University Press.

Moya, P.M. and M.R. Hames-Garcia. 2000. *Reclaiming Identity*. Hyderabad: Orient Longman.

Neog, M. 2004. *Essays on Assamese Literatures*. New Delhi: Omsons Publications.

Nongbri, T. 2008. *Gender, Matriliny and Entrepreneurship: The Khasis of North East*. New Delhi: Zubaan.

North-East News Agency 2006. *Major Events*, 2(19): January 16–31.

Renault, E. 2004. 'European Conceptions of Identity', in Nadia Tazi (ed.), *Keywords/Identity*. New Delhi: Vistaar Publications.

Saikia, N. (ed.) 1984. *Asam Bandhu*. Guwahati: Assam Publication Board.

Sharma, M. 1990. *Social and Economic Change in Assam: Middle Class Hegemony*. Delhi: Ajanta Publications.

Sharma, M. and A.K. Baruah. 1999. 'Matriliny, Land Rights and Political Power in Khasi Society', *Indian Journal of Human Rights*, 3(1 and 2): 210–228.

Sztompka, P. 1994. *The Sociology of Change*. Massachusetts: Blackwell Publishers.

6

Construction of Tribal Identity from a Socio-Historical Perspective

C.L. IMCHEN

Sociologists agree that today there are around 6,000 discrete ethnic/tribal or nationality groupings in the world, and that each of these groups is defined – and defines itself – in significant part with reference to history. But writing about these peoples, particularly about their identities, has its limitations. The available writings have so far tended towards distortion in the face of the contingency of the dominant thinking of a particular point in time. This paper proposes to dwell at length on the Western world's legal and politico-religious interpretations of the rights of the "other". The first part of this paper will be concerned with tracing the roots of the European idea of natural law and the doctrine of *Terra nullius*.[1] Thereafter, it will deal with matters of trusteeship and what constituted "civilized behaviour" during the colonial period. The discussion is not intended as a compendium on the history of colonial or post-colonial policies towards indigenous and tribal peoples. Rather, it is an attempt to give a contextual backdrop for assessing policies of the nation-states pertaining to contemporary tribal peoples, which will be the main concern of the last part of this paper, with particular reference to Nagas.

I

The Rights and Status of non-Christian People in the 13th Century under Natural Law

The Western world's colonizing system in the fifteenth century revived legal debates on the rights and statuses of the non-Christian peoples that Europeans wanted to dominate. The debates that had receded to the background after the Crusades in the late thirteenth century were rekindled during the era of 'discovery' of 'strange lands' in the non-European world. The Roman Catholic Church took the lead in this discussion, particularly on the question of legitimacy of secular power outside the jurisdiction of the Church. Reference to the rights and duties of pagan nations under what they called ' natural law' occurred in Pope Innocent IV's legal commentary on Pope Innocent III's Papal decretal *Quod super his.* Pope Innocent IV held that all 'rational creatures,' whether Christians or non-Christians, had the right to own property and exercise political authority under natural law. In this case, the 'infidels' (Saracen, Moor, etc.,) could enjoy this right as long as they maintained the peace and did not provoke the Christians. But the Cardinal of Ostia, Henrico de Sequisia in his *Hostiensis* rejected the idea that non-Christians could govern Christians in Palestine, especially in Jerusalem. He cited St. Peter's stand against the practice of Christians appearing before non-Christian judges. In this understanding, 'lordship' was a divine gift, based on justice and it could be obtained only through grace; as such, non-believers could not qualify for *dominium* (lordship and property). Moreover, the Cardinal maintained that only those 'infidels' who recognized the lordship of the Church should be tolerated by the Church. In any case, the Church could wield both the 'two swords', i.e., the spiritual and temporal for protection of Christians under 'infidel' rule. Coming back to Pope Innocent IV, he argued that Roman jurisdiction over the area called the Holy Land had been inherited by the Emperor, one of whose titles was 'King of Jerusalem', and he had been unjustly deprived of it by the Muslims. Therefore, the Christians had not only a right but a duty to re-conquer the area for reinstating its rightful ruler as long as it was done with proper authorization. While conceding that non-Christian peoples possessed the same rights under natural law as Christians to exercise *dominium*, Pope Innocent IV argued that these rights were qualified by the Roman Papacy's divinely instituted Peterine mandate (i.e., the mandate of St. Peter). His position was as follows: As the Vicar of "Christ's universal Christian commonwealth on earth", the Pope had been entrusted by Christ through St. Peter, the first Pope, with the care and well-being of the souls of the Christian flock, including heathens. It necessarily included Pagans. According to Pope Innocent IV, these non-Christian peoples belonged to the flock by virtue of their creation by the same 'Creator-God', although the infidels did not belong to the fold of the Church. Thus, the Pope claimed jurisdiction over the pagan nations in law, but not in fact and he was responsible for them even though they might not recognize his authority. Furthermore, it was understood that the 'infidels' could not be attacked merely because of their non-belief in the Christian God. Only specific violations of the natural law would justify papal sanctions imposed through intermediaries such as the Christian princes. The Pope reasoned that sexual perversion or polygamy, to cite just one example, would necessitate papal intervention and punishment. The worship of idols would also constitute a violation of natural law, because it was natural for human beings to worship only God. The Pope could order 'infidels' to admit preachers of the Gospel in the lands that they administered. The Pope could also declare a Crusade against the 'infidels' and that Christian missionaries were to accompany these crusading secular armies to 'infidel' lands. Pope Innocent IV pointed out that 'infidels' such as Muslim missionaries could not be accorded reciprocal rights to preach in Europe 'because they are in error and [Christians] are on the righteous path'. These papal decretals profoundly influenced subsequent developments in legal theories concerning the treatment of non-Christians. The decrees focused on the central legal problem raised by the medieval Crusades and Christian warfare against non-Christian societies: Under what circumstances might Christians legitimately dispossess pagan ('savage' and 'barbaric') peoples of their *dominium*? The legal discourse initiated by the colonizing regimes of Portugal and Spain as the principal instruments of their empires was essentially built up upon the canonically approved Christian 'humanist' foundations of Pope Innocent IV's earlier medieval ideas on the rights and obligations of 'infidel' nations as defined under 'natural law'. Thus, the legal formula that emerged out of the Iberian colonization of the Americas eventually became the cornerstone of European enthusiasm for colonization of the non-European world.

Development of the Doctrine of Trusteeship

As is well known, the invasion of the Americas by the Spaniards resulted in unimaginable demographic imbalances. Responsible European theorists questioned the legality and morality of the subjugation of the indigenous people, especially in the Americas.[2] Among the most vocal were the Dominican clerics, Bartholomé de Las Casas (1474–1566) and Francisco de Vitoria (1486–1547). Bartholome de Las Casas, Bishop of the Indies, sent as a Roman Catholic Missionary to the native Americans, bitterly wrote about the Spanish massacres and enslavement of the indigenous people in the early sixteenth century. He expressed particular detestation for the Spanish *encomienda* system that had granted plots of land along with inhabitants to the Spanish conquerors and colonists. Appalled by the atrocities of the conquerors, De Las Casas compelled Charles V of Spain to summon a council of fourteen leading theologians at Valladolid to debate on the justifications for the Spanish treatment of the Indians. The debate dragged on through 1550 and 1551. Charles V asked them to address the question of whether or not the indigenous peoples were part of the same human race or species as the Europeans; and, depending on the answer to this fundamental question, the council was to provide suggestions on how the European colonial powers should treat the 'natives' of the colonized world. The king particularly asked a philosopher, Juan Gines de Sepulveda, and De Las Casas, to answer the question: "How can conquests, discoveries and settlements in the King's name be made to accord with justice and reason?" Both De Sepulveda and De Las Casas agreed that all human beings, including the indigenous peoples, were of one species. Both also agreed that it was the duty of the Europeans to convert the people of the entire world to Christianity. They disagreed only on matters of method and rationale. Relying on Aristotle, De Sepulveda argued that some races were inferior to others, and that some people were born to slavery. By this reasoning, Europeans, as a superior race, were justified in subjugating the indigenous peoples, an inferior race. De Las Casas reasoned, on the other hand, that the American Indians possessed an evolved culture, with social, economic and religious institutions. He argued that Indigenous peoples were rational beings, fit to be compared with the ancient Greeks and Romans. De Las Casas did not argue that Spain should not conquer the indigenous peoples of the Americas, but rather that Spain's only justification for doing so should be to

Christianise them. Francisco de Vitoria, Primary Professor of Theology at the University of Salamanca, concurred with De Las Casas to 'establish' the essential human attributes of the native Americans. But here De Vitoria emphasized more on the development of a legal regime that would recognize the original autonomous powers and land rights of the natives that the Europeans were bound to acknowledge. He spelled out the terms under which the Europeans could acquire lands and assert authority over the natives. Subsequently, De Vitoria's viewpoint formed the basis of the principles and rules governing encounters among all peoples.

The early European jurisprudence concerned with indigenous peoples and associated with the early development of international law was thus built upon the legacy of medieval European ecclesiastical 'humanism'. This jurisprudence perceived a normative order independent of and higher than positive law or temporal authority. There were variants of conceptions about the source of higher authority, characterized as natural or divine law. For Francisco de Vitoria (de Vitoria, 1917) and other theorists of the Spanish School, God figured prominently as the source of legal authority, and law merged with theology. It is to be noted that De Vitoria rejected the view that Papal donation to the Spanish monarchs provided sufficient and legitimate basis for establishing the primacy of Spanish rule over American Indians in the Western Hemisphere. Spanish monarchs claimed that Pope Alexander VI had granted to them all territories discovered by their envoys that were not already under the jurisdiction of Christian rulers. Furthermore, the Spanish monarchy considered this donation as entitlement to establishing legal title to New World lands, in addition to entrusting the Spanish crown with the mission of converting its inhabitants to Christianity. While not accepting the Spanish claim to title by discovery or papal grant, De Vitoria found it more acceptable to argue that the Spaniards could legitimately assume a benevolent wardship over the natives. De Vitoria's stand exerted considerable influence on the works of Hugo Grotius, who was the leading systematiser of seventeenth century European-centric International Law. On a comparative note, however, Grotius (Grotius, 1633) moved towards a secular characterization of the law of nature. The philosophical foundation of trusteeship (or mandated territories) that was formulated a few centuries later is attributed to the ideas propounded by De Vitoria. As colonizing states consolidated power over indigenous and tribal lands, many such states adopted the notion of trusteeship similar to those advocated earlier by De Vitoria. Although representing an element of humanistic thought toward the "other", nineteenth- and early twentieth-century trusteeship doctrine was rooted in the same Western philosophy that underlay the positivist construct of International Law, which viewed non-European tribal peoples and their cultures as 'inferior'. It was undoubtedly an extension of the notorious School identified as that of "scientific racism". In that sense the main objective of trusteeship was to pull away the native peoples from their "backward" ways and bring them within the ambit of modern "civilization".

It was the emergence of the modern "nation-states" in Europe that prompted a revision of the framework within Western legal discourse for the treatment of indigenous and tribal peoples. The era of the independent territorial states began in earnest with the conclusion of the Treaty of Westphalia in 1648, which ended the Thirty Years' War and the political hegemony hitherto asserted by the Roman Catholic Church. Along with the rise of the modern state came a marked evolution in naturalist thinking. European theorists transformed the concept of natural law from a universal moral code of humankind into that of a bifurcated regime comprising the natural rights of individuals and the natural rights of states. The post-Westphalia concept of the law of nations attained its full expression in the works of the Swiss diplomat, Emmerich de Vattel (de Vattel, 1758). Vattel's construct, particularly the individual-state dichotomy profoundly affected Western liberal thought on the idea of the state. This idea of the individual-state dichotomy maintains that the state is the mainspring of human associations and aspirations. statehood and nationhood became conterminus, hence the term "nation-state". Vattel thus articulated the foundation for the doctrine of state sovereignty. The doctrine invariably included exclusive jurisdiction, territorial integrity, and nonintervention in domestic affairs, which became inbuilt into International Law. For Vattel the state was free, independent, and ensured equality for all, as a result of its commitment to protect the natural rights of its individual constituents. The very construct of the nation-state would thus prevent non-European indigenous or tribal people to qualify for equality of rights. Moreover, Vattel's idea of "nation-state" and "civilized states" were mutually reinforcing concepts. This point was spelled out in I.L. Oppenheim's *International Law*,[3] which spoke of the existence of "civilized states". Oppenheim's contention was as follows: "there are three conditions for the admission of new members into the circle of Family of Nations. A state to be admitted must, first, be a civilized state which is in constant intercourse with members of the Family of Nations. Such state must, secondly, expressly or tacitly consent to be bound for its future international conduct by the rules of international law. And, thirdly, those states which have hitherto formed the Family of Nations must expressly or tacitly consent to the reception of the new member" (Oppenheim, 1920: 134–35). Furthermore, statehood does not exist in international law until the moment of recognition. It means two things: tribal nations or other indigenous peoples not qualifying as states could not participate in the shaping of international law nor could they look to it to affirm the rights that had once been deemed to inhere in them by natural and divine law. States could create doctrines to affirm and perfect their claims over indigenous inhabitants according to domestic policies shielded from uninvited outside scrutiny by International Law. The law itself was limiting the parameters of international concern over the ongoing colonization or reckless adventurisms if colonial powers were not held in check. It is to be noted that tribal people, at least prior to European contact, typically had been organized primarily by tribal or kinship ties, had decentralized political structures often linked in confederations, and had enjoyed shared or overlapping spheres of territorial control.

By the early part of the nineteenth century, international law desisted from considering indigenous peoples as political bodies with rights under international law. It began to respond favourably to Western colonizers craving for legitimacy of their consolidation over indigenous lands within their respective spheres of political hegemony and control. The major premises of the nineteenth century and early twentieth century Positivist School ensured that the law of nations, or international law, would become a legitimizing force for colonization and empire building. By deeming indigenous peoples incapable of enjoying sovereign status or rights in international law, international law was thus able to govern the patterns of colonization and ultimately to legitimate the colonial order. Henceforth, the presence of the indigenous people became inconsequential. The late nineteenth – and early twentieth century – Positivist School highlighted certain 'main premises of International Law'. The first premise was to uphold the rights and duties of states. The second premise, derived from Vattel's position, was to uphold the exclusive sovereignty of states, which are regarded as equal and independent, and to secure the exercise of that sovereignty from outside intervention. The positivist formulation, however, parted company with Vattel's view that a third premise was that international law is law between and not above states. This particular premise marked a break from Vattel's position that the natural law necessarily governs the law of nations and therefore is universally applicable to all states. The fourth premise was that states that drew on international law and obtain rights and duties under it are within the limited confines of European civilization. Positivism ensured that attainment of statehood for international law purposes depended upon recognition by the nineteenth century European and European-derived states. These premises meant that indigenous and tribal political organizations peoples not qualifying as states and embedded within states would not be able to seek redressal outside those confines whatsoever. The British publicist Westlake (Westlake, 1894) offered the positivist justification for the categorical exclusion of the indigenous and tribal peoples as subjects of international law. He made a distinction between 'civilized and uncivilized humanity' and declared the idea of "international society" as limited to the civilized. In no uncertain terms he deemed the European-style government and sedentary lifestyle as the hallmark of "civilization". The Positivist doctrines of effective occupation of territory and recognition of such occupation by the Family of Nations provided the legal mechanism for consolidating territorial sovereignty over indigenous lands by the colonizing states. Through this recognition only and exclusively a state becomes an international entity and a subject of International Law. It is based on the constitutive theory of recognition of statehood, by which statehood does not exist in international law until the moment of recognition (Brownlie, 1990).

British Colonial Imperialism: Social Theory and Law

When Britain became engaged in the colonization of the world British legal rules were already in place that addressed several major questions which arose subsequently. The "non-Christian" enough rationale, developed to cope with the Irish situation, became codified in law in 1608, when Britain's Chief Justice Coke articulated what is known as 'infidel rule': "if a Christian King should conquer a kingdom of an infidel, and bring them under his subjection, there *ipso facto* the laws of the infidels are abrogated, for that they be not only against Christianity, but against the law of God and of nature".[4] The British imperial policy rested on archaic legitimating principles of the superior rights of Christian Europeans over the non-Christians. It also utilized the feudalistic idea of state derived from the Norman discursive practices and latter day developments called the Law of Nations. A memorandum of the Privy Council of Great Britain in 1722 consolidated imperial law by setting out rules for establishing British sovereignty in two possible situations. The first option, alternatively referred to as the doctrine of discovery, or the doctrine of occupation, or the doctrine of settlement, was to be applied in circumstances where the land discovered was *Terra nullius* – literally, uninhabited by human beings. The second option, the doctrine of conquest, was to be applied where tribal peoples were encountered. Of course, Britain never had colonized and never would colonize any uninhabited land. Therefore, the doctrine of discovery/occupation/s ettlement based on the notion of *Terra nullius* was never concretely applied "on the ground". Rather, already inhabited territories were simply legally deemed to be uninhabited if the people were not Christian, not agricultural, not commercial, not "sufficiently evolved" or if simply in the way.

It bears noting that British imperialism and colonial law differed from Spanish colonial history in some significant ways. British imperial law could be traced to the common law tradition that emerged in the fifth century A.D. when the Anglo-Saxons took over the area corresponding to what is now England after having conquered the indigenous Britons. The Anglo-Saxon eventually assimilated the immigrant Danes and Gauls and they were in turn conquered by the Normans in 1066. This event marked the origins and development of a feudal social order and subsequently the emergence of a centralized state and church, and the unrestrained power of the king. Under this Norman-derived legal regime, referred to as the "Norman Yoke", the king or sovereign embodied the "underlying title to all land" and was said to "hover over the land". Almost at the same time that De Sepulveda and De Las Casas were debating in Valladolid, English jurists were wrestling with problems regarding colonization in Ireland. In this instance their debate was not necessitated by the "discovery" of alien peoples. Their problem was centred on the re-classification of the Irish neighbours who were earlier undoubtedly similar and familiar. Ireland comprised fertile land whose 'wild and barbarous people' were touched by 'papistry' and potential agents of Catholic Spain. Besides, according to the English, the Irish were 'not Christian enough' to be a civilized people. Ireland claimed by England since the medieval crusading era but not fully conquered, was a testing ground for Elizabeth I's Protestant *conquistadors* for practising Spanish style colonizing techniques on "savage people." That the Irish were Christians was never doubted by the Normans or their successors, but Christianity in Gaelic Ireland did not fully conform to Roman liturgical practices, and many pre-Christian traditions and customs had been slightly veneered in these territories by Christianity. For these reasons, the Irish were classified by British imperial law as 'atheists' or 'infidels'. Unlike certain "savage tribes", the Irish were rarely accused of cannibalism, but they were described as "little better than cannibals". Moreover, the English took the Irish practice of *transhumance* as proof that the Irish were nomads, hence 'barbarians'. The English colonists thus developed a social theory, to the effect that the Irish had evolved to a level of cultural development analogous to the stage the ancient Britons had attained before they were 'civilized' by the Romans. It was thought fitting that the Irish should be made subservient to the English (the true inheritors of Roman civilization) so that, through subjugation, the Irish could come to appreciate civility and thus eventually achieve freedom as the former Britons had done. It was believed that meting out punishment to subordinated peoples and individuals "for their own good" would result in their eventual emancipation. Queen Elizabeth's Irish wars were testing grounds for development of her colonial doctrines. England refined her colonial praxis under Lord Humphrey Gilbert, the decorated veteran of Spanish wars. Gilbert, who had been commissioned to help the French Huguenots against the Spanish, got a few ideas from the French Protestant filibusters and their piratical harassment of their enemies. Gilbert's ventures led to the encounters with Native Americans. It was followed up by another explorer, Hayes, who advocated the obligation of the English to establish Christian colonies in North America. Hayes was profoundly influenced by the Cambridge Calvinists. The English Puritanism represented an extreme self-righteous theology that developed from the doctrines of John Calvin on 'pre-destination' and the state of grace. In the late 16th century, William Perkins, Fellow of Christ College, wrote and preached that faith was a tiny seed planted in the soul by God's spirit. It was then the duty of the soul to nourish it into growth. Hayes metaphorically applied Perkin's discourse to the English farmers' establishment of colonies in North America. It meant planting seeds of civility and Christian religion in the wild. In Hayes's appropriated Puritan-inspired discourse of conquest, the English will to extend the British Empire fulfilled in the New World wilderness was regarded as a predestined event.

It is important to note that, among the colonial powers of the nineteenth century, Great Britain was a leader in devising special administrative regimes over native peoples with the objective of 're-engineering' their social and cultural patterns in line with European conceptions of civilized behaviour. In the field of British jurisprudence, Sir Henry S. Maine's 1861 volume, *Ancient Law*, set out a conjectural history of the evolution of law from "primitive custom" that "mingled religious, civil and merely moral ordinances without any regard to differences in their essential character" to "civilized law," which "severs law from morality, and religion from law." The purported independence of law from the social conditions of its emergence, the law's professed autonomy from the society in which it is practised, were evidence for Maine that Western law "belongs very distinctly to the later stages of mental progress". Another common idea that arose from the same social evolutionary premises was the analogy drawn between the stages of individual psychological development hypothesized by Western developmental psychology, and the social organization of non-Western societies. In this framework, adults were to children as Europeans were to Aborigines. Within the framework of historical analyses, contemporary tribal societies, imagined as being "frozen" at "stages of development" believed to be "antecedent" to the present, were seen as resembling ancient European ones. The Dutch anthropologist, Johannes Fabian (Fabian, 1983), likened this notion to what " they" are now, as "we" were then, a "denial of coevalness" that he identified as the most enduring obstacle to mutually respectful dialogue between Europeans and the " other."

The authors of the grand theories of European Enlightenment Era usually began with an evocation of the so-called "primitive life in the New World," meant to illustrate "raw human nature" and "original human society". For romantics like Jean Jacques Rousseau, the "state of nature" was to be found in a simple Garden of Eden, the indigenous peoples in America, imagined to be "noble savages". At the opposite extreme, for philosophers like Thomas Hobbes, the "state of nature" was an instinct driven war of all against all. The establishment of society and collective survival depended upon the imposition of a sovereign's power and government to contain and control an essentially competitive and aggressive human nature. The Hobbesian "state of nature" that he, too, claimed was being lived in 18th century American indigenous societies, was one of constant warfare, an absence of law or government, and a life that was "nasty, brutish and short." Whatever the Western rendition of "primitive life", tribal peoples occupied one or the other of these "savage slots" in the European imagination: the noble child of harmonious nature, or dangerous child with animal instinct. John Locke (1970), usually identified as the most significant political theorist of this imperial era in Britain, gathered together arguments circulating during the early seventeenth century and set them out in theories that would serve many of the legal and political justifications of European seizure of property in North America. Locke argued, in the fashion of the times, that the aboriginal peoples lived in a pre-political state of nature which represented the first stage in universal human evolutionary development. Important characteristics of this early developmental phase included a foraging and hunting economy without an idea of established systems of property or governance. Locke further argued that aboriginal peoples could have property rights only "in the products of their labour: the fruits they gather, the deer they catch and the corn they pick". Locke rationalized that only Europeans could increase the productivity of the land through settled agriculture. Since this process was governed by the "natural law" of evolutionary development, Europeans were therefore justified in taking away tribal lands without consent. This would allow them to appropriate land under the dubious doctrine of *Vacuum domicilum* all across the colonial empires.

II

Post-colonial Conditions in India: The Case of the Nagas

During the colonial period, tribal groups in the Indian subcontinent were basically considered as insignificant quasi-juridical entities, i.e., primitive tribes, swidden agriculturists, who were numerically small, geographically remote and without valuable economic resources. In the 19th and during the first quarter of the 20th centuries they were generally ignored since they were considered not worth the cost of administering seriously. Earlier, the highlanders in India's North-East region, though subjected to stimulation of the Buddhist and Hindu early state systems, remained largely outside their orbit. This implied various forms of jural sanctions and administrative promulgations, but by and large did not make for a total disintegration of their polity. The hill tribes remained unencapsulated by the geo-political environment of the plains, and retained their 'traditional' forms of social organization. The forms of social formation evolved within their cosmological basis without the need for an intrinsic legitimizing accorded by Buddhist, Hindu and Islamic models. Encapsulation in the anthropological sense would mean either the absorption of smaller systems by the larger system or total transfer of value system from the latter to the former. In this case, the former may also be considered as evolving archaic entities. It continued to be an essential framework in spite of the rigours of an encapsulating situation, which is more marked today than during the Brahmanization process in the valley.

In the 18th century, the extent of the early state control was determined by whether a local lord or chief paid tribute and acknowledged the overlordship of a particular king. Frontiers constantly shifted in accordance with the relative strengths of particular courts. The 'traditional' polities were not defined with reference to precise territorial boundaries as they were to be in the nineteenth century. This observation holds good for most of the tribal communities in both the South-East and South Asian highlands. The unencapsulated condition of the tribal groups, especially the Naga polities, emerged as disparate units each functioning independently, yet coalescing together in particular ways during the eighteenth and nineteenth centuries. The Naga relationship with the British power was determined by the principle of 'immemorial possession'.[5] This doctrine acknowledged the rights of those who had occupied territories over prolonged periods of time. It entailed recognition of the inherent freedom and proprietary rights of the Nagas. This we find expressed in the *inner line*. This doctrine of the colonial era was drawn on the earlier legal theorists of the Middle Ages as had been derived from the Romans before them. But it was implemented only after the British appropriated huge tracts of land and forest from the Nagas for cultivation of tea, extracting coal, and logging (now in Assam) under the dubious principle of *Vacuum domicilium,* i.e., lands the natives ostensibly never "subdued" for farming. It is obvious that the British assumed paramountcy over Naga Hills only for strategic reasons, that is, to establish a viable sphere of influence that was thought imperative to check uneasiness in the 'eastern frontier'. Though the Nagas did not really enter into a treaty with the British, they were nonetheless encapsulated within this broad framework under two types of jurisdictions as follows: (a) the Naga Hills district was declared an excluded district outside the purview of the provincial autonomy under the Government of India Order (Excluded and Partially Excluded Areas), 1936 (this has been misinterpreted as bifurcation of a pre-existing Assam with reference also to the Treaty of Yandabo, which is actually not the case); (b) the Naga Tribal Areas referred to the area along the eastern frontier of India, which were not a part of British India or Burma or any other foreign state (such as China or a Western colonial power). The situation begs the question: What prevented the British from entering into treaty relations with the Nagas? One may assume by using an archaic definition that the village and clan confederacies of the Angami, Ao, Lotha, Rengma and Sumi tribes did not constitute a 'political society' at that time. Then, what about the case of the tribal areas where large chiefdoms of Konyak, Wanchu and Nocte developed? These polities approximated the Khasi *Syiemships,* and the British had treaty relations with the *Syiemships* and classified them as native states. It is pertinent to note that the Government of India Act added and defined the tribal areas as the 'areas along the frontiers of India or in Baluchistan which were not a part of British India or Burma or any foreign state [Section 311 (1)]. 'India' was defined in the same section as British India together with all territories under the suzerainty of such an Indian ruler, *the tribal areas, and any other territory which His Majesty in council may from time to time declare to be part of India …*' (italics mine).

In the 'settled district' a special administrative parlance and style was introduced to secure control over the territory. For instance, the Nagas in this area by a Regulation of 1880 were declared 'excluded'. That is to say, 'unsophisticated' tribes did not entail administration of a complex nature; thereby native traditional laws were recognized as more effective for the purpose of handling both civil and criminal cases. From April 1, 1937, the Naga Hills district was declared 'excluded area' of the province of Assam, while leaving the eastern and northern lands unadministered. The Naga tribes in the south were confined to the 'native state' of Manipur, which was later annexed. The British toyed with the idea of extending the boundary of the 'excluded area' upto the westernmost watershed of the Patkoi range. But before a semblance of authority could be exercised over the remaining eastern territories (occupied by Nagas on either slope of Patkoi), the separation of Burma from British-India in 1937 saw the need for a proper boundary. Subsequently, the 'watershed theory' of the Brahmaputra and Chindwin was found to be a convenient demarcation point between British Burma and India. This inter-colonial boundary was laid down on what was essentially a buffer zone, and eventually became an international boundary when India and Burma got their Independence in 1947 and 1948 respectively. Before the colonial rulers departed, they defined tribal peoples as subjects of particular states with reference to their relations to a territorial boundary, and not as peoples with territories of their own. As Reverend Michael Scott (1966) tellingly put it, 'the origins of the misunderstanding must be traced back to the time when the British Imperial Government first extended its sway over the area of the Naga Hills – until that time the Nagas had never regarded themselves as part of India or, indeed, as part of Assam or under any form of permanent suzerainty to the Ahom kings. I have not been able to trace any agreement with the Nagas or any submission to, or acceptance of, protectorate obligations by the British or the Nagas. There are many treaties and agreements with other tribes such as Abors, Singpos and Khampti chiefs in which undertakings regarding headhunting and settlement of disputes are specified. But it appears to have been a matter of decided policy not to raise the question of sovereignty with the Nagas, or to undertake protective responsibilities.' In fact, C.U. Aitchinson in his *Treaties, Engagements and Sanads* (Vol. XII, Calcutta, 1931, p. 91) categorically says: 'No written treaties or engagements have been made with any of the Naga tribes'. There are references to parts of the Naga Hills becoming a British district in 1881. Sir Robert Reid in his *History of the Frontier Area Bordering on Assam* (p. 99) refers to the policy adopted towards the Nagas and traces a gradual process of penetration with the object of protecting the border of Assam. But by what instrument were the Naga Hills formally annexed or possession of their territory claimed by consent or by conquest? The answers to these questions still elude me.

The Indian State argued that India represents an initial condition of sovereignty over its landmass. Therefore, rights of tribal groups can exist only in a constitutionally entrenched sense through explicit acts of legislation, as is the case of Article 371A for the Naga. The Naga hold that the British aggrandizing thematic was based on a "pragmatic management" of frontiers solely to safeguard tea and forest economy; and that neither the Crown had ever formally conquered their land nor any treaty had been arrived at. The Naga posed the question: Did not India and Burma claim political and legal legitimacy directly from the British Crown's fictitiously maintained prerogative rights of conquest of erstwhile excluded district of Naga Hills or jurisdictional claims of inchoate rights to conquest of unadministered Naga lands? India answered this question herself during the "re-conquest" of Goa from Portugal. During the decolonization era, anti-colonial states tended to deny in principle the validity of the right of conquest as it was historically asserted by the European states in their relations with Afro-Asian societies. India asserted a form of re-conquest to deny Portugal's title to Goa in the 1960s based on her interpretation of the definition of conquest. In the Security Council debate on this issue, the Indian delegate defended India's action on the ground that Goa was:[6] 'a colonial question, in the sense that part of our country is illegally occupied – occupied by right of conquest by the Portuguese ... Portugal has no sovereign right over this territory ... if any narrow-minded, legalistic considerations – considerations arising from international law as written by European law writers should arise, those writers were, after all, brought up in the atmosphere of colonialism. I pay all respects due to Grotius, who is supposed to be the father of International law, and we accept many tenets of International law. They are certainly regulating international life today. But the tenet ... quoted in support of colonial powers having sovereign rights over territories they won by conquest in Asia and Africa is no longer acceptable ... we cannot accept the position that there is any legal frontier in our country or, for that matter, any country, India is one, Goa is an integral part of India.'

India's justification of her invasion and annexation of Goa was that Goa was ethnically an integral part of Indian territory and there was no question of aggression against your own people, whom you want to bring into freedom.[7]

India also claimed a right of self-defence in Goa on grounds that Portugal commenced aggression 450 years before and was continuing to do so, besides stating that we cannot in the twentieth century accept that part of International Law ... specifying that colonies in Asia and Africa which were acquired by conquest conferred sovereignty on the colonial power.

In an analogous way, the obvious – if curious – implication is that India and Burma inherited Naga territory sustained earlier by a colonial legal fiction. By the same argument, India was obviously referring to her *pre-colonial* geography and people. The political separation of the enclave of Goa from the rest of India was held to be an arbitrary disruption of the national unity and territorial integrity of India by a colonial power in the 16th century. One cannot deny the fact that an Indian civilization did exist before the advent of British paramountcy, but neither the Hindu texts nor history books suggest that the Naga were ever part of that civilization. While this is not to say that a common colonial condition did not engulf the sub-continent, what it does suggest is that the outcome of India's struggle for freedom was generally considered to be in accordance with the requirements of a right to self-determination of a people – claiming a 6,000 year-old civilization. Or, to put it another way, the right to self-determination of 'one Indian people' is not necessarily co-terminus with an imagined unity within a colonial boundary – based on British definition of what constitutes India. This definition is given in the Interpretation Act of 1889, which defined India as British India together with any territories of any native prince or chiefs under the suzerainty of Her Majesty. Later on, the Government of India Act added and defined the tribal areas as the, 'areas along the frontiers of India or in Baluchistan which were not a part of British India or Burma or any foreign state [Section 311 (1)]. 'India' was defined in the same section as British India together with all territories under the suzerainty of such an Indian ruler, *the tribal areas, and any other territories which His Majesty in council may from time to time declare to be part of India* ...' (italics mine)

The last point refers to the Crown's prerogative to declare *any* new territory a part of India. It was the British equivalent of the Spanish fiats in the Americas. The Nagas hold that their right of self-determination to decide whether or not they wished to continue the association with India after a period of ten years was recognized by India.[8] In one of their statements on this subject, they maintained that an identical proposal for the political future of Eritrea was submitted by B.B. Rao, India's chief delegate to the United Nations (UN) in 1949 which proposed that at the end of a ten-year period under the trusteeship of the UN it should be left to the people of Eritrea to decide whether they wished to become independent or join Ethiopia. State policies toward tribal peoples all over the world stress the need to "bring them into the 21st century". At the core of the prejudice against tribal societies are the dual issues of modernization and development. States feel they cannot modernize effectively if they tolerate tribal culture in their midst. This asymmetric relationship has led to the continued antipathy between the Naga and the Indian State.

Notes

1. During the colonial era, territory of the so-called 'discovered' peoples (in Asia and Africa) who were unwilling to accept Christianity was subject to "conquest" or "re-conquest". Justification came from the Roman legal principle, the *Territorium Nullius*. Essentially, any territory inhabited by non-Europeans was considered "backward" and *terra nullius*. Thus in the European context, it meant a territory which was 'no man's land' until the first European power chose to occupy or earmark it for future assumption of sovereignty over it. This was one of the controversial colonial doctrines that legitimized their aggrandizing pursuits. To clarify this point, it is pertinent to refer to the Advisory opinion of the International Court of Justice given in October 1975 in response to a United Nations query as to whether Western Sahara belonged to no one at the time of colonization by Spain in 1884. The legal fiction broke when it became clear that this doctrine was not part of International Law. See, *Western Sahara*, Advisory Opinion, ICJ Reports (1975), p. 12.
2. See, David Maybury-Lewis. 1992. *Indigenous Peoples, Ethnic Groups, and the State.* Needham Heights: Allyn & Bacon, p. 13.
3. The Family of Nations constituted by the old Christian States of Western Europe and the body of Christian states that grew up outside Europe includes "the American States which arose out of the colonies of European states". Oppenheim further included in the 'Family of Nations' the two "non-Christian" states of Turkey and Japan, while excluding "such states as Persia, Siam, China, Abyssinia, and the like" Oppenheim added that the Law of Nations does not apply to "organised wandering tribes."
4. Calvin's Case 1608 referred to in Mark Walters. 1993. 'British Imperial Constitutional Law and Aboriginal Rights: A Comment on Delgamuukw v. British Columbia'. *Queen's Law Journal*, 17: 350–413.

5. For a discussion on the English phrase "Time immemorial" as an established legal expression, see Dara Culhane. 1998. *The Pleasure of the Crown: Anthropology, Law and First Nations*. Burnaby, BC: Talonbooks, p. 37.
6. SCOR, 16th year, 987th meeting, 18 December, 1961, pp. 46–47 and p. 60.
7. SCOR, 16th year, 988th meeting, 18 December, 1961.
8. On the question of Trusteeship, the Nagas thought that the Naga National Council and Akbar Hydari (Governor of Assam) agreement of 1947 meant entitlement to a pre-existing inherent right, i.e., allegiance and collective identity would be vested in their own institution: the Naga National Council. It was also linked with the doctrine of Trusteeship under a guardian power. The implication here was that a 'Naga status' would approximate the second possibility, which was spelled out during the Decolonization process in the UN system. Roger Clark and Sue Rabbit Roff summed the relevant models:

   > In 1960 the UN General Assembly had codified, in Resolution 1541 (XV), the outcomes of the decolonization process that were acceptable to the evolving international community. Three possibilities were mentioned: Independence, Free Association with an Independent State, or Integration with an Independent State ... *the second option entails self-government for the entity concerned in internal affairs and some sharing or delegation of power in the field of foreign affairs and security. It envisages the right of the associated entity to terminate its relationship unilaterally*... [italics mine]

   See: Roger Clarke et al. 1984. 'Micronesia: The Problem of Palau', in *The Minority Rights Group Report*, No. 63, London.

References

Anaya, James. 1989. 'The Rights of Indigenous Peoples and International Law in Historical and Contemporary Perspective', in *Harvard Indian Law Symposium*. Cambridge: Harvard Law School Publication Center, 192–225.

Bartholomé, De las Casas. 1971. *History of the Indies: Selections*. Edited and translated by Andre Collard, New York: Harper & Row.

Brownlie, Ian. 1990. *Principles of Public International Law*. 4th edn. Oxford: Clarendon Press.

Culhane, Dara. 1998. *The Pleasure of the Crown: Anthropology, Law and First Nations*. Burnaby, BC: Talonbooks.

de Vitoria, Franciscus. 1917. *De Indis et de Jure Belli Reflectiones.* Translated by J.P. Bate. Washington, DC: Carnegie Institution of Washington.

Emmerich de, Vattel. 1916. *The Law of Nations or the Principles of Natural Law.* Translation of 1758 edition by Clarks G. Fenwick. Classics of International Law Series. Washington, DC: Carnegie Institution of Washington.

Fabian, Johannes. 1983. *Time and the Other: How Anthropology Makes its Objects.* New York: Columbia University Press.

Gross, Leo et al. (eds) 1969. *International Law in the Twentieth Century.* New York: Appleton-Century-Crofts.

Grotius, Hugo. *Freedom of the Seas.* Translation of 1633 [1916 edition] by Ralph van Deman Magoffin. Carnegie Endowment for International Peace Edition. New York: Oxford University Press.

—. *The Law of War and Peace.* Translation of 1848 [1929 edition] by Francis W. Kelsey. Classics of International Law Series. Oxford: Clarendon Press.

Hobbes, T. 1651. *Leviathan.* Edited by Richard Tuck [1991]. Cambridge and New York: Cambridge University Press.

Lindley, Mark F. 1926 [1969 Rep.]. *The Acquisition and Government of Backward Territory in International Law.* London and New York: Longmans Green & Co.

Locke, John. 1970. *Two Treatises of Government.* Edited by Peter Laslett [1991]. 2nd edn. London: Cambridge University Press.

Maine, Henry Sumner. 1961. *Ancient Law: Its Connections with the Early History of Society and its Relations to Modern Ideas.* Edited by Raymond Firth. Gloucester, Mass.: Beacon Press.

Maybury-Lewis, David. 1992. *Indigenous Peoples, Ethnic Groups, and the State.* Needham Heights: Allyn & Bacon.

Oppenheim, Lassa F.L. 1920. *International Law.* Edited by Ronald F. Roxyburgh. 3rd edn. London and New York: Longmans.

Richardson, Boyce. 1993. *Terra Nullius.* Toronto: Macmillan.

Rousseau, Jean-Jacques. 1762. *The Social Contract and Discourses.* Translated by G.D.H. Cole. London: Dent.

Scott, Rev. Michael. 1966. *The Nagas: India's Problem or the Worlds?* Chatham, Kent: W & J Mackay.

Tully, James (ed.) 1993. *An Approach to Political Philosophy: Locke in Context.* Cambridge: Cambridge University Press.

Westlake, John. 1894. *Chapters on the Principals of International Law.* Cambridge: Cambridge University Press.

Prepared by: Chubawati Longchar, Department of Geography, NEHU, Shillong

7

Ethnicity and Social Change

The Context of Mizos

D.V. KUMAR

Study of Social Change

The study of social change has been a central concern with sociology. As a matter of fact, the very birth and growth of sociology in Europe has often been looked at in terms of its engagement with making sense of the nature of social changes occurring there. In this context, the contribution of events of momentous significance such as Industrial Revolution and French Revolution to social changes in Europe has widely been acknowledged. These revolutions led to immense changes in the social, economic and political fabric of the European society. Sociology as a field of enquiry emerged to make sense of these changes that were sweeping there. It distinguished itself by engaging with the social consequences of modernity (Mudimbe, 1996: 19). Though modernity has emerged a dominant category in social sciences, its precise meaning remains ambiguous. The nature and character of modernity and the different possible ways of dealing with it have been dealt with elsewhere (Kumar, 2008). We would not therefore proceed on this further. It was during the occurrence of these changes that the most brilliant minds such as Marx, Durkheim and Weber came up with illuminating ideas about the nature of societies they were living in and social changes taking place. Though there were profound differences among them in terms of the way they looked at the social reality, one thing which was common to them was their deep engagement with social change. Marx had looked at changes in societies in terms of changes taking place in the mode of production and how these led to changes at the level of societies whereas Durkheim looked at the transformation of societies characterized by mechanical solidarity into societies characterized by organic solidarity in terms of the changes in the material and moral density. Max Weber looked at the growth of capitalism (a change of momentous significance) in terms of the motivational framework embedded in the Protestant ethic. Thus, one can see social change has always been a central preoccupation with sociology. It engaged the attention of the classical figures in sociology and continues to occupy a prominent place in the sociological writings. Given this context, it is only in the fitness of things that we are looking at social changes taking place in the north-east, their processes and responses. In this paper I would try and look at one such response, i.e., the emergence of the Mizo ethnicity and ethnic movement in Mizoram in the 1960s and 1970s.

Ethnic Group and Ethnicity

Some working definitions of ethnic group and ethnicity would be in order to proceed further. Paul Brass defines an ethnic group as 'any group of people dissimilar from other people in terms of objective cultural criteria and containing within its membership, either in principle or practice, the elements of complete division of labour and for reproduction forms an ethnic category' (Brass, 1991: 19). As far as ethnicity is concerned, George de Vos defines it as 'subjective, symbolic or emblematic use by a group of people – of any aspect of culture, in order to differentiate themselves from other groups' (1975: 16). Paul Brass, however, modifies the last phrase to read 'in order to create internal cohesion and differentiate themselves from other groups' (1991: 19). Though there are quite a few understandings of ethnic group which have become powerful at different points of time (Barth, 1969; Bromley, 1974; Cohen, 1974; Glazer and Moynihan, 1975; Oommen, 1997; Smith, 1981), we keep the above definitions in view as we proceed along.

Ethnic Movements and Social Change

It would be meaningful to look at ethnicity and its manifestation as an ethnic movement as a response to social changes, in terms of changes in the social reality followed by changes in the perception of that reality and self-ascription of a group. One needs to firmly locate them in the context of changes in the social, economic and political institutions and perception of changes in these spheres. As all of us know, ethnic/nationalist movements do not take place in a vacuum. They invariably take place in a sociological context and it is needless to add, no context is static. One needs to look at the context and the changes taking place therein in order to have an adequate understanding of an ethnic movement and ethnicity. Some scholars (Bromley, 1974; Geertz, 1963; Issacs, 1975, Shils 1957, to mention a few) have sought to look at them as a primordial phenomenon thereby implying that they have nothing much to do with what is happening in the society. For this they have had to answer, which they are still not able to do quite satisfactorily, the question how the intensity of ethnic mobilization/movement changes. This is a major failure of the primordial approach and this is primarily a result of their reluctance to relate ethnicity to changes taking place in the society. For an adequate appreciation of ethnicity and an ethnic movement, there is a strong need to relate them to the changes taking place in the society. Further, one needs to keep in mind that the argument that ethnic identities would be dissolved in the context of deepening of the process of modernization stands discredited as one has seen the resurgence of ethnicity in the recent past (Kumar, 2006a) and in fact the relationship between modernization and ethnicity has been the subject of considerable social science literature (see Kumar, 2006b). It may be pertinent to mention here that among the different approaches which have taken a serious look at the resurgence of ethnicity, the oppositional approach has recently gained a lot of credibility (Kumar, 2009).

What we propose to do here is to look at Mizo ethnicity and its manifestation in an ethnic movement in the 1960s and 1970s which finally culminated in the acquisition of Statehood for Mizoram. This is an attempt to relate a historical phenomenon to the sociological context in which it occurred and the changes taking place therein.

While looking at the Mizo ethnicity, we make use of two central concepts, *imago* and correlative space, which were made extensive use of by Dipankar Gupta in his work (1997) on the growth of Sikh ethnic movement. It would be in the fitness of things if we briefly recapitulate Gupta's arguments about the Sikh movement which made use of these two central concepts. While dealing with the Sikh ethnic mobilization in Punjab, Dipankar Gupta employed the concepts *imago* and correlative space (which he derived from Jacques Lacan). *Imago* refers to self-ascription/image during the times of tension and correlative space refers to the accompanying perceptions of the social reality. These two need to be comprehended together and we can not understand one without understanding the other. Imagos are determined by the perception of reality and at the same time our self-image also determines the way we perceive the reality. There is thus a dialectical relationship between the two.

As Gupta would argue, the Sikh *imago* (its self-image) began to change in response to the changing context from the early 1980s. That was roughly the period from when the Hindus began to be viewed as an oppositional group bent upon deeply hurting the sentiments of Sikhs by not treating them with respect, inflicting considerable wrong on them and not recognizing their contribution to the strengthening of the Indian nation. Further, their self-respect had been repeatedly violated by the Indian State by refusing to make Chandigarh the only capital of Punjab and intervene in the territorial dispute between Punjab and its neighbour. Chandigarh was regarded by many Sikhs to be an incontrovertible part of Punjab and this was consistently denied by the Indian State (107). In the eyes of an average Sikh, the state was increasingly losing its legitimacy as it was seen as being partial toward Hindus and their interests. Questions such as whose state it is began to figure quite prominently in the ordinary discourse of an average Sikh. The Indian State was being increasingly perceived as a Hindu Sarkar. As a result, the self-image *(imago)* of a Sikh, as he would argue, began to change. Till some time back the self-image of a average Sikh was that of a sword-arm of Hinduism, as a trustworthy bulwark against Pakistan intrusion etc. But in the 1980s, he began to see himself as somebody who was pushed to the wall and whose self-respect had been subjected to repeated mutilations. He began to see himself as a person deeply wronged. Hindus too began to perceive him as a murderous wrecker of the Indian nation-state (1997: 96). The only way of getting back the lost glory was by acquiring political autonomy in the form of Khalistan. In the context of the change of imago, this led to a situation whereby Sikhs in general, though they did not support the demand for Khalistan *en masse,* felt humiliated when militants surrendered before the security forces. The spectacle of militants surrendering clashed with their *imago* of brave, hot-blooded and aggressive Sikhs. The important point to be noted is that by employing these two notions *imago* and correlative space, he made a meaningful attempt to make sense of the Sikh ethnic mobilization in Punjab.

One problem that, however, remains in his analytic exercise is his insistence that there has to be a triadic framework (two separate ethnic groups and the state) to understand the sociology of ethnic mobilization. While such a framework would be useful in the context of Sikh ethnic mobilization where Hindus, Sikhs and the Indian State were the principal actors, such a framework would not be useful in the context of Mizo ethnic mobilization as we shall see a little later. At this juncture, a brief point could be made. The principal actors in the case of Mizo ethnic mobilization were the Mizos and the Indian State. The Indian State acting through the then Assam government was considered the principal adversary and responsible for their social, cultural, economic and political deprivation. The question of another ethnic group coming in their way of achieving their social, economic and political advancement did not exist as there was no clearly identifiable group with which it was in confrontation. Contractors, businessmen, defense personal with whom they came in contact were seen more as agents of the Indian State rather than any clearly identifiable group. Thus, the Mizo situation also poses a serious challenge to the existing scholarship on ethnicity which primarily views ethnicity and ethnic movement as a product of changing social relations between ethnic groups. The dyadic framework can still exist but the actors are Mizos and the Indian State rather then any two ethnic groups as in the case of Punjab when Hindus and Sikhs were the principal actors along with the state. We leave it at that for now, and look at the significance of the changing context for the construction of *imago* and correlative spaces which have implications for ethnicity and an ethnic movement. We do this in the context of Mizo ethnicity and ethnic mobilization in Mizoram. Before we do so, however, we need to take a brief look at the history of Mizos.

A Brief History of the Mizos

The term 'Mizo' has two parts: Mi and Zo. Mi means 'man' and zo means 'highland'. Therefore, Mizo literally means people living in highland (Verghese and Thanzawna, 1997: 45). There are different theories which explain the origin of Mizos. One of the most widely accepted theories is that Mizos were said to have originated from 'Chhinlung' in South-West China (Nunthara, 1996: 39). From there they were said to have migrated to Burma where they lived for a long time. Acute poverty caused by the famine called *thingpui tam* forced them to move towards the present-day Mizoram (Vanlawma, 1972).

In terms of their racial roots, they are said to be the Assamese-Burman sub-group that had branched off from the Tibeto-Burman group of the main Tibeto-Chinese race. Some authors have classified them as Tibeto-Burman, because of the affinity of the language, even though they have described them as people who once lived in Chhinlung (as stated above). However, it needs to be stated quite clearly that in view of the absence of the records or documentary evidence regarding any contacts between this group and the people of other countries or states or areas, it is quite difficult to trace the exact history of the Mizos.

Mizo is a generic term which refers to various groups such as Lushai, Lakhers, Pawi, Chakma, Hmars etc. who claim to possess distinct cultural traditions and identity from each other. Lushais (the most dominant among Mizos) constitute about 68.89 per cent and they inhabit the major portion of the heartland of Mizoram. Pawis, Lakhers, Chakmas and Hmars constitute about 6.9 per cent, 5.1 per cent, 7.14 per cent and 2.65 per cent respectively and mainly made the periphery either in the north or the south of Mizoram as their homeland (Singh, 1994: 124).

When the Mizos came and settled in Mizoram, they were scattered all over the Lushai Hills, as Mizoram was previously known as. The dominant tribe, i.e., the Lushai tribe occupied the main heartland and other groups occupied peripheral areas of the hills. These different groups lived in relative isolation as there were hardly any transport and communication facilities. Village was the basic unit of living. Chieftainship was the form of political rule which prevailed. Each village was ruled by a chief. The Mizo chiefs were the real source of authority. The chief was called 'Lai' meaning Lord. The chief was the supreme administrative authority. He maintained his position more through his personal qualities than through statutory authority (Verghese and Thanzawna, 1997: 38). It is said that the people adopted this system as they felt secure and well taken care of in the system. In due course of time, the office of the chief became hereditary and the benefits of becoming a chief went to the youngest one. However, the elder son of the chief, soon after attaining maturity were transferred to new villages. These sons, in turn, were the chiefs of those new villages, but they were not supposed to pay any tribute to their father – a chief and were left to establish their position as chiefs through their own personal ability. The chiefs were the protectors of village life and property. The entire lands and village belonged to the chief and it was he who distributed the 'jhum' land to the village for cultivation. The chief also administered justice, according to the Mizo customary law.

This kind of rule continued even after the British formally annexed the Lushai Hills in 1852 after a series of raids. For many years there were frequent clashes between the British and the Mizos who were trying hard to occupy the adjoining parts of the Lushai Hills. Their attempts were foiled by the British government.

The Britishers even after annexing the Lushai Hills did not want to disturb the chieftainship as they realized that without the cooperation of the chief, they would not be able to adminster the Lushai Hills. Effective and profitable administration of the Lushai Hills could only be carried out with the active co-operation of the chiefs. They went ahead with the chieftainship despite the fact that they were aware that the chiefs were becoming increasingly autocratic and indifferent towards the plight of common men and women. The villagers were forced to render various forms of services to the village chief such as payment of paddy, physical labour for the construction of chief's house and other household works of the chief. Even then the British decided to continue the indigenous system of village administration through the chiefs in view of their continued relevance for the British rule. Vacant houses were allotted to them as a reward for their services.

Beginning of the Process of Unification of Mizos

It was the arrival of the missionaries into the Lushai Hills which proved extremely consequential for the Mizos. Rev. Lorrain and Rev. Savidge were the first to arrive in there (Buragohain, 1994). Through their untiring efforts, despite some initial setbacks, most of the Mizos were converted to Christianity. Till then they practiced animistic beliefs. The arrival of Christianity proved to be a huge unifying factor for the Mizos as most of them were converted to Christianity, they began to feel a great sense of unity, a feeling which was clearly absent when they subscribed to animistic beliefs. Each group had its own notion of God and spirit and followed its own system of animistic ideas. Another most important thing which created a great unifying factor was the reduction of the language of the Lushais called Duhlian to writing. The missionaries also took upon themselves the responsibility of developing the Duhlian dialect into the present-day Mizo language with Roman script (Hminga, 1994: 106). This made communication among different groups much easier. These two important developments, entry of Christianity and development of writing, had greatly contributed to the evolution of new *imago,* i.e., that of a homogenous and unified group. The strong sense of 'we-feeling' was not there in the past. Different groups of Mizos were scattered all over the Lushai Hills without any great unifying features. With these new developments a strong sense of being a homogenous and unified group began to emerge. This process was aided by another development. From the early 1940s a large number of Mizos went out to participate in the Second World War and they were exposed to English education and modern political ideals. They observed what was happening outside in terms of growing democratization and increasing number of instances of achieving political autonomy. After the war they returned and impressed upon other Mizos about the need to assert their identity and demand political autonomy (Burgohain, 1994: 66). They began to look at themselves (change in *imago*) as a group fully deserving of political autonomy. They began to demand that Mizos should be given the freedom to determine the kind of life they would like to lead. Only in this way they would be able to ensure their political and economic interests were not only protected but also promoted. They would also be able to develop their socio-cultural traditions. Mizos, in general, began to realize they were living like slaves without any autonomy whatsoever. Therefore the time had come to assert their distinct identity and fight for their socio-economic and political rights. But the stringency with which they would argue out their case was missing.

Critical Events that Led to Changes in *Imago* and Correlative Space

It was precisely at this point of time that some critical events took place in Mizoram which greatly intensified the feeling of being neglected and deprived leading to a process of change in their *imago* and correlative space. These events made them realize that their social, economic and political interests could never be served effectively as long as they did not have sufficient political autonomy. As a result they began to feel a strong sense of opposition toward the Indian State, the Assam government and 'outsiders' in general accentuating their sense of dissatisfaction leading to a powerful assertion of Mizo ethnicity finally culminating into one of the most successful ethnic-based autonomy movements in India.

The first critical event which unambiguously and effectively conveyed to the Mizos that they were indeed a neglected group took place in the form of a famine called the *Mautam* in the Mizo Hills district in 1958 (Verghese and Thanzawna, 1997). The *Mautam* famine that occurred in 1958 was one variety of famine which caused considerable loss of life (about 15,000 Mizos died). This was the result of flowering of the Mau variety of bamboo that led to the substantial multiplication of rats. These rats would invade the agricultural field and eat away all the crops resulting in a huge loss of food for the Mizos. The shortage of food and the consequent starvation led to the death of a large number of Mizos. Famines are not new to the Mizo society. They have been a recurrent feature of the Mizo society, the first recorded case being the famine which occurred in 1881 and later it occurred in 1913. In fact, famines have been a regular feature of many of the countries located in South Asia. What was striking about the famine which occurred in Mizoram was the *nature* of the famine (the flowering of bamboos leading to increased number of rats and subsequent destruction of crops) and the extent of damage it caused.

Looking at the nature of the famine, what was intriguing to many people right from the days of British rule was the connection between the flowering of bamboo plants and the increase in rat population. This set the British officers and missionaries to explore reasons for the substantial increase in rat population following the flowering of bamboos. The Baptist Mission Report states that, 'the periodical flowering, seeding and dying down of certain species of bamboo all over these hills was followed last autumn by an enormous increase in the number of jungle rats – the connection between the flowering of bamboos and the invasion of rats is a disputed point, but the theory which seems to be most satisfactory is that the bamboo fruits have the property of making the rats, which eat them, extraordinarily fertile' (quoted in Nag, 2001: 1031). In a letter to the administration, the Reverend Lorrain wrote, ' it appears that the rats began to get more than extraordinarily troublesome years before the simultaneous seeding of mau-thing bamboos but as soon as the seeding was over, they increased to such an extent no human power could save the crops from their depredation' (ibid.).

When the famine took place in 1958 Mizos looked to the Assam government for timely help. But they were disillusioned to see that no help of any consequence was forthcoming despite the fact that the then Assam government was duly informed about the impending famine. Instead of taking appropriate measures, it took a nonchalant view of the matter and questioned the very wisdom of predicting a famine like this. But, when the famine finally happened, the government was taken by surprise by the enormity of the situation. When it finally decided to send the relief team and the required supplies to help out the Mizos, it realized that there was hardly any motorable road (by which trucks could travel). The delay in sending of food samples resulted in a great loss of lives among the Mizos. Mizos were deeply disturbed about the fact that no assistance was forthcoming either from the Assam government and/or Centre. They began to perceive this indifference as a clear reflection of the fact that they were treated as second-class citizens in the country. This led to the gradual development of negative *imago* and correlative space among the Mizos.

When the similar famines occurred in the past, during the British rule (1881 and 1913), the then British government had extended timely and proper help for the Mizos. This is despite the fact that the initial contact between the Mizos and British officers was not one of cordiality. There were many uprisings from the Mizos who were trying to come to the plains and engage in kidnapping of the British officers and headhunting, and there were counter attacks and invasions from the British Army. The British could annex the Lushai Hills (as Mizo Hills were then known as) only after a series of invasions of the hills. But, the striking thing which was noticed by the Mizos was that the missionaries and the British officers took all possible steps to render timely help when the famines occurred.

The Mizos had to move towards the plains in search of food and shelter following the occurrence of the famines and shortage of food. That was the time when the British officers extended employment opportunities rehabilitating all those who were affected by the famine. There was an attempt to extend timely help in terms of food, shelter and other necessary items. Not only that effective steps were taken to ensure that there was no growth in the number of rats. Rat traps were developed along the French model and they were provided to the people. This enabled them to trap rats easily. The other initiative taken by them was to inculcate the habit of saving among the Mizos. Though they had nothing much to save, as it was a subsistence economy, whatever they had they were encouraged to save the food grains and share with those who had nothing with them.

This contributed to a great extent towards the development of a positive image about the British rule which incidentally, as stated above, had to confront the Mizos who were invading the plains and indulging in headhunting and kidnapping. The unpalatable memories they had about their initial contact with the British began to give way to the feelings of gratitude towards the British with the extension of timely help. The British rule began to be seen as kind and merciful willing to extend help in times of distress (Nag, 2001: 1032).

The situation in 1958 was in complete contrast and it was quite harrowing. Unlike the British government which came to the rescue of the Mizos promptly, the Indian government and the then Assam government remained indifferent to the plight of the Mizos. That was the time when under the leadership of Laldenga, the Mizo National Famine Front was formed. It began to work in right earnest and rendered invaluable assistance to the needy. The sense of neglect and alienation nurtured by the Mizos consequent upon the indifferent attitude of the Assam government and the Centre provided a fertile ground for the transformation of the Mizo National Famine Front (MNFF) into the Mizo National Front (MNF) when the famine was over. The MNF which constantly harped on a feeling of being neglected which was prevalent among the Mizos became a progressively strong organization (Ray, 1982). It was being viewed as an authentic expression of the desire on the part of Mizos for greater autonomy. The MNF became a symbol of their identity and their main instrument for demanding self-determination. It began to command huge support from the Mizos in general. Though they were other organizations like the Mizo Union (which wanted the Mizo Hills to be part of India) and United Mizo Freedom Organisation (UMFO) (which wanted the hills to join Burma and was in favour of continuation of chieftainship), the MNF became an extremely powerful political party as it was seen the only political party that understood the needs and aspirations of the Mizos. It became the main instrument around which Mizo ethnicity began to crystallize.

The original objectives of the MNF were moderate as it were. However, some extremists in the MNF took over and by harping on the ethnic consciousness of the Mizos which by that time became fairly intense began to demand 'Sovereign Independent State of Mizoram'. The perception that their interests and those of other (dominant groups from outside) were fundamentally irreconcilable became increasingly stronger. Simultaneously dissatisfaction with the malfunctioning of the District Council (introduced in 1952) grew by leaps and bounds. They wanted total autonomy but it was not possible through the District Council. In 1972 union territory status was granted to Mizoram. Though this marginalized the MNF to some extent and proved to be a boon to the sagging morale of the Mizo Union, it did not materially alter the ground reality. The economic conditions of the Mizos became progressively worse. Outsiders were infesting Mizoram and getting prosperous, in the perception of an average Mizo.

Apart from building on the sense of agony which the Mizos suffered in the wake of famine, what the MNF also took advantage of was implications arising out of the ill-conceived policies of the Central Government towards the Mizo Hills. The successive policies followed by the government essentially had two components: the first, a military strategy of economic suppression and the second one was the political strategy to divide and rule which really did not help matters (Rangasami, 1976: 654). They contributed to the accentuation of feelings of neglect and deprivation which in turn had a great impact on their *imago*. Some of the Acts which were passed under the first component were the Assam Maintenance of Public Order Act 1953, Assam Disturbance Act of 1955, Armed Forces (Special powers) Act of 1958 etc. These Acts set out to impose severe restrictions on their habitation. They set out to severe links of the tribals with their main source of livelihood, i.e., forests. Whatever traditional rights they had over the forests were taken away from them. With the imposition of curfew from dawn to dusk for a period of seven years, they had nothing much to do and could not engage themselves in agriculture throughout the day. They had to return home early as curfew would be operational. There was frequent searching of houses and anybody suspected of having arms would be taken away to army barracks. Army had full control over the source of food supplies too.

Due to certain steps taken by the Indian Army under these Acts, agricultural production suffered immensely in Mizoram. For example, the tribal institutions of *tlawbawk,* the huts built near the jhum for camping during harvesting and weeding period – were abolished (Rangasami, 1976). Further, agriculture was primarily dependent on male labour and the number of workers was reduced drastically due to the arrest of a large number of males. This resulted in a great reduction of food supply which in turn led to food scarcity and starvation. The draconian Armed Forces Special Powers Act of

1958 gave enormous powers to the Army. It authorized them to enter and search any premises without warrant on flimsy grounds. It also imposed severe restraints. These included restriction of the movement of people, their access to employment and/or business, their communication or business with other persons and their activities in relation to the dissemination of news or propagation of opinion.

To be able to effectively control the underground and the violent activities of the MNF activities, the Central Government embarked upon the regrouping of villages in Mizoram (Nunthara, 1996). The regrouping of villages meant the whole population of some villages was lifted and physically relocated at another place. With the regrouping of villages they were forced to build barricades around their villages and were not allowed to move outside. They were also not supposed to carry food to the fields as it was feared that they would supply the food to the rebels. The regrouping of villages was yet another critical event in the post-independent history of the Mizos which accentuated the sense of opposition among the Mizos towards the Indian State and had a deep impact on their *imago* and correlative space. Though the declared objectives of the regrouping of villages were to provide protection to the villages, facilitate economic development and improve communication facilities, the real objective of that step was to exercise greater control over the activities of the underground elements of the MNF. What happened in the process was that considerable amount of hardship was inflicted on them. The shifting of the villagers was compulsory and the people suffered both physically and psychologically. They were forced to leave their villages where they lived for a number of years. The scars of a such forceful eviction are still evident in the lives of the Mizos. Many of them suffered from severe destitution from which they never really recovered.

Adding fuel to the fire was another critical event in the form of the Assam Official Language Act 1961 (Chakraborty, 1994: 116). It made Assamese the official language of the state. Mizos began to fear that their traditional and cultural life would be destroyed if they were forced to learn the Assamese language. A language holds extremely affective significance for its users. Any attempt to deny the right to learn one's language would always be resisted. This is what happened in the case of Mizoram too. When Assamese was made the official language, the disillusionment they began to feel following the *Mautam* famine became more acute. It was like adding fuel to the fire.

They became increasingly convinced about the fact that unless they fought for their autonomy and acquired it their distinctiveness as Mizos would be gradually eroded.

Following these developments there was an accentuation of an unpalatable *imago* and perception of reality, the MNF was increasingly becoming popular and powerful by harping on the issues such as above (*Mautam* famine, imposition of the Assamese language etc.) and exploiting the ethnic sentiments of the Mizos. It also began to muster the resources for an armed revolt to achieve what it termed as total autonomy. It recruited and trained a large number of people and motivated them to engage themselves in a violent struggle. It finally succeeded in issuing the Declaration of Independence. It is worth reproducing it at length, 'in the course of history, it becomes invariably necessary for mankind to assume their social, economic and political status to which the laws of Nature's God entitle them. We hold this truth to be self-evident that all men are created equal and that they are endowed with inalienable fundamental human rights and dignity of human persons and to recover these rights, governments are instituted among men deriving their just powers from the consensus of the governed, and whenever any form of the government becomes destructive of them, it is the right of the people to alter, change, modify and abolish it and institute a new government laying its foundation on such form as to them shall seem most likely to effect their rights and dignity. The Mizos created and formed into a nation and nurtured as such by Nature's God have been intolerably dominated by the people of India in contravention to the laws of nature' (quoted in Kumar, 1996: 63).

A careful look at the above quotation would tell us something about the great emphasis placed on the rights of every group of people to determine their own social, political and economic future. Secondly, the MNF also began to prepare the ground for the evolution of the Mizos as a 'nation'. It was able to issue such a strongly-worded declaration because it knew that the Mizos in general were becoming absolutely intolerant of the indifferent attitude of the government both at the state and the Centre. The distinct ethnic identity of the Mizos was sought to be invoked in the context of the situation which the Mizos perceived as being inimical to their interests. Ethnicity became the essential material around which their opposition towards the Indian State was sought to be articulated.

The important point to be noted is that events mentioned above resulted in a change in their imago and correlative space. They began to sees themselves as people deeply wronged. These events accentuated the sense of opposition among the Mizos towards the Indian State, Assam government and 'outsiders'. This led to intensification of ethnic sentiments, a clear crystallization of ethnicity and finally one of the most successful ethnic-based autonomy movements in the North-East. The distinctiveness of the Mizos was constantly stressed. In fact, Mr Laldenga was reported to have commented sometime in 1982 that the 'crux of the problem was the different racial origin of the Mizos and their struggle to maintain their distinct identity' (Chakraborty, 1994: 119). As one can see, the change in the *imago* and correlative space need to be factored in any understanding of ethnicity and ethnic movement. This is what has been attempted in the present paper in the context of the Mizo ethnicity and ethnic movement. Changes which took place in Mizoram led to changes in the *imago* and correlative space of the Mizos contributing to a very powerful assertion of ethnicity and launching one of the most successful ethnic movements in the North-East.

References

Barth, F. 1969. 'Introduction', in F. Barth (ed.), *Ethnic Groups and Boundaries.* Boston: Brown and Co., 9–38.

Brass, P. 1991. *Ethnicity and Nationalism: Theory and Comparison.* New Delhi: Sage.

Bromley, Y. 1974. 'The Term Ethnos and Its Definition', in Yulian Bromley (ed.), *Soviet Ethnology and Anthropology Today.* The Hague: Mouton, 14–24.

Burgohain, R. 1994. 'Autonomy Movements in Mizoram: A Study in Historical Perspective', in R.N. Prasad (ed.), *Autonomy Movements in Mizoram.* New Delhi. Vikas Publishing House, 62–71.

Chakraborty, P. 1994. 'Autonomy Movements: A Case Study of the Mizos', in R.N. Prasad (ed.), op. cit., 109–122.

Cohen, A. 1974. 'Introduction', in A. Cohen (ed.), *Urban Ethnicity.* London: Tavistock, 9–35.

de Vos, George. 1975. 'Ethnic Pluralism', in George de Vos and Lola Romanucci-Rovi (eds), *Ethnic Identity: Cultural Continuities and Change.* California: Mayfield Publishing Co., 12–24.

Geertz, C. 1975. 'Thick Description: Towards an Interpretive Theory of Culture', in Clifford Geertz (ed.), *The Interpretation of Culture*. London: Hutchinson, 5–23.

Glazer, N. and D.P. Moynihan. 1975. 'Introduction', in N. Glazer and D.P. Moynihan (eds), *Ethnicity: Theory Experience*. Cambridge: Harvard University Press, 1–26.

Gupta, D. 1997. *The Context of Ethnicity*. Delhi: Oxford University Press.

Hminga, C.L. 1994. 'Basis of Autonomy Movements in Mizoram', in R.N. Prasad (ed.), op. cit., 103–108.

Issacs, H.R. 1975. 'Basic Group Identity: The Idols of the Tribe', in N. Glazer and D.P. Moynihan (eds), op. cit., 45–72.

Kumar, B.B. 1996. *Re-organisation of North-East India (Facts and Documents)*. New Delhi: Omsons Publications.

Kumar, D.V. 2006a. *Modernisation and Ethnicity*. New Delhi: Mittal Publications.

—. 2006b. 'Modernisation and Ethnicity: Interrogating Theoretical Perspectives', *The Eastern Anthropologist*, 59(3–4): 340–356.

—. 2008. 'Engaging with Modernity: Need for a Critical Negotiation', *Sociological Bulletin*, 57(2): 240–254.

—. 2009. 'Explaining Mizo Ethnicity: The Relevance of Oppositional Approach', *Man in India*, 89(1–2) (January–June): 37–49.

Mudimbe, V.Y. 1996. *Open the Social Sciences: Report of the Gulbenkian Commission on the Restructuring of the Social Sciences*. Stanford: Stanford University Press.

Nag, S. 2001. 'Tribals, Rats, Famine, State and the Nation', *Economic and Political Weekly*, 36(12): 1029–1033.

Nunthara, C. 1996. *Mizoram: Society and Polity*. New Delhi: Indus Publishing Company.

Oommen, T.K. 1997. *Citizenship, Nationality and Ethnicity*. Cambridge: Polity Press.

Rangasami, A. 1976. 'Mizoram: Tragedy of Our Own Making', *Economic and Political Weekly*, 13(15): 653–662.

Ray, Animesh. 1982. *Mizoram: Dynamics of Change*. Kolkata: Pearl Publishers.

Shils, E. 1957. 'Primordial, Personal, Sacred and Civil Ties', in *Centre and Periphery: Essays in Macro Sociology of Edward Shils*. Vol. 2. Chicago: University of Chicago Press, 111–126.

Singh, S.N. 1994. 'Hmar Autonomy Movement', in R.N. Prasad (ed.), op. cit., 123–132.

Smith, A.D. 1981. *The Ethnic Revival in the Modern World*. Cambridge: Cambridge University Press.

Vanlawma, R. 1972. *My Country and I*. Aizawl: Zoram Printing Press.

Verghese, C.G. and R.L. Thanzawna. 1997. *A History of the Mizos*. Vol. 1. New Delhi: Vikas Publishing House.

8

Identity Politics, Social Exclusion and Dissolution of Culture Change

Issues of Re-distributive Justice in the North-East India

N.K. DAS

Studies on cultural revivalism have been shaped by theoretical developments in three major areas: ethnicity, nationalism, and modernity. Right since 1960s with appearance of work of Nathan Glazer and Daniel Patrick Moynihan (1963), ethnic groups are regarded as interest groups: ethnic identity is proposed and solidified in multiple frames, as the native customs, and cultural heritage cannot be abandoned. Rather the subnational communities seek access to material resources and a bid for access to the benefits of development with 'culture' operating as their symbolic legitimation and means of solidifying group loyalty. In more recent years, the postmodernist interpretations of cultural revivalism are premised on the axiom that 'culture' is a text, which, like all texts, is an assemblage of signifiers from the sign systems of cultural discourse at large. The cultural elements sought to be reclaimed by reviving groups prove to be the basic standard to fight for the justice from the dominant culture against which the revivalists stake their claim.

This paper examines how various brands of identity politics since the colonial days have served to create the basis of exclusion of groups, resulting in various forms of rifts, often envisaged in binary terms: majority-minority; sons of the soil-immigrants; local-outsiders;

tribal-non-tribal; hills-plains; inter-tribal; and intra-tribal. Given the strategic and sensitive border areas, low level of development, immense cultural diversity, and participatory democratic processes, social exclusion has resulted in perceptions of marginalization, deprivation, and identity losses, all adding to the strong basis of brands of separatist movements in the garb of regionalism, sub-nationalism, and ethnic politics, most often verging on extremism and secession. Until the independence and for a while afterwards the tribespeople did not worry about slow adoption and internalization of the elements of the foreign language and religion in their cultures. Introduction of non-tribal languages in education and administration created a sense of rupture slowly in tribal minds. The Ahom, Meitei, Zeliangrong, Seng Khasi and Zomi communities, among others, were foremost to start revivalist movements in order to reverse the process of unilateral culture change process. It is argued that local people's anxiety for preservation of culture and language, often appearing as 'narcissist self-awareness', and their demand of autonomy, cannot be seen unilaterally as dysfunctional for a healthy civil society. Their aspirations should be seen rather as prerequisites for distributive justice, to which no nation state can neglect.

Colonial Impact and Genesis of Early Ethnic Consciousness

The North-East India is a politically vital and strategically vulnerable region of India. Surrounded by five countries, it is connected with the rest of India through a narrow, thirty-kilometre corridor. The region, then called Assam, is divided into Arunachal Pradesh, Assam, Manipur, Meghalaya, Mizoram, Nagaland and Tripura. Diversities in terms of Mongoloid ethnic origins, linguistic variation and religious pluralism characterize the region. This ethnic-linguistic-ecological historical heritage characterizes the pervasiveness of the ethnic populations and Tibeto-Burman languages in the North-East. The North-Eastern mountain ranges and river valleys indeed divide up South-East Asia from South Asia. This predominantly tribal region, replete with protracted records of isolation, difficult terrain, and lack of intense inter-ethnic contacts, had witnessed formation of three types of society and polity such as 'tribe', 'chiefdom' and 'state' (Das, 1989). The clans and age-set systems within them had often functioned hierarchically-involving unequal statuses (Das, 1993). Full-fledged state-formation took place in the 4th century A.D. Hinduism remained confined to some pockets, including the royal families, among the Kachari, Ahom, Jaintia, Koch, Tripuri, and Meitei. Penetration of *Sarania dharma* of Shankar Dev was felt in some plains tribal societies, who became followers of *Sarania* even while simultaneously pursuing tribal religions often involving 'animal sacrifices' (Das, 2003).

The British colonization process of Assam started in 1826 and ended in 1898. The colonial regime, at the beginning, resorted to the policy of non-intervention in most of the larger Assam. Two administrators J.H. Hutton and N.E. Parry advocated for separation of hill areas from general administrative scheme. In 1873 was introduced "The Inner Line" in hill areas, beyond which no person could pass without a license. Local tribes-people resisted colonial interference in their midst, and thus they often attacked the British. Their resistances were depicted as 'raids' and 'uprisings' (Das, 1989, 1993: 28). There is long chronology of such resistance. In 1860 and 1862 entire Jaintia tribe and the Garos (1852–57, 1872) rose against imposition of taxes. The Lushai-Kuki, Manipuri and many plains – Assam tribes raided British posts in 1860–90, 1891 and 1892–1894 respectively. There are records of Aka/Khamti resistances – 1835–1839; Naga resistances – 1835–1852, and even an agrarian movement in 1893–94.The Sonaram (1902), Kuki (1917) and Jadonang-Gaidinliu movements (Singh, 1982; Das, 1989) symbolized early ethnic struggles. Consequent upon the visit of the Statutory Commission in 1920s, further apprehension of marginalization, had grown among the tribespeople and minority communities. Colonial rulers allowed missionary activities. Association with the Christian missionaries and gradual spread of education amongst the tribes and other communities infused a sense of self-esteem. This factor is crucial to understand the birth of ethnonationalism eventually among the Nagas, the Mizos, and the Manipuris. In some hill areas and the Brahmaputra valley, there was simultaneous revulsion for Assamese linguistic-cultural domination. This perception alienated a few tribes and thus there grew discontentment among the Bodos, the Karbis, the Ahoms and many others. Under the relatively peaceful period of 1930s, which may be called 'the silent phase of identity consciousness'; the tribespeople had demanded 'participative representation' in the principal Legislative Assembly. The Khasi, Ahom, Naga, Mizo, Bodo-Kachari, Miri and Deuri tribes were the first to demand "ethnic representation". The Lalungs established a Durbar in 1967, and the Koch people had similarly been conscious about their minority status. In a memorandum submitted to Assam Government the Assam-Koch-Rajbanshi-Khatriya Sammilani demanded proper representation in all bodies, quota in employment, scholarships to students and publication of their history and culture. The All Assam Garo Union was established in 1983. The Hajongs in Assam urged the Government to recognize them as a scheduled tribe.

In the long history of this region the feelings of in-group/out-group, perceived marginalization, and 'minority-consciousness' have variously surfaced as key factors causing ethnic unrest. Depending on varied influences of marginality and ethnicity some movements remained more explicit and specific than others, in articulating and defining their objectives. Strategies of operation have correspondingly varied. Ethnic conflicts in the North-East originally grew essentially through primordial affiliations. The distinctive ethnicity factor amongst communities led to steady expansion of aggressive binary categories of in-group and out-group (Das, 1989: 1994, 2004, 2007).

Invalidating the Culture Change: Linguistic and Religious Revivalist Movements

Language has always been in the centre stage of ethnic turmoil in the North-East. Making Assamese the compulsory language from class VIII onwards led to massive agitation in the Barak valley, reminiscent of the agitation launched earlier over the issue of the medium of instruction. In 1972 the Bodo led plains tribes council of Assam (PTCA) complained that the plains tribes have been "uprooted in a systematic and planned way from their own soil" and that the "step motherly" treatment of the administration, dominated by the Assamese-speaking people has reduced them as "second class citizens" of the state. The Bodo Sahitya Sabha (established in 1952) and PTCA however ultimately succeeded in making the Bodo language the medium of instruction (up to the secondary level). In doing so the Bodo-leaders opted for the Roman script – though they were ultimately convinced to accept the Devanagari script. The Mishing Agom Kebang (Mishing Sahitya Sabha) formed in 1972 and several other Mishing organizations had also worked consistently and succeeded in 1987 to introduce Mishing language as a subject of study in primary schools. The rejection of the Assamese script by the Miris, the Bodos and others dismayed the Assamese, who thought, without their tribal counterparts they may become minority, overwhelmed by the Bengali-speaking population (Miri, 1993: 71). Following the recognition of native languages at primary level in Bodo-Kachari and the Karbi areas, the Mishing perception of marginalization sharpened. This led to the formation of Mishing Literary Association in 1972. In order to maintain a distinct minority linguistic identity vis-à-vis the majority Assamese, the Mishing were in favour of the Roman script. The Assam Sahitya Sabha insisted that the Assamese script should be retained for 'Mishing language'. The Mishings were ultimately facilitated to use Roman script, and their text books came to be printed in the Roman Script, so also some newspapers and journals. The Bishnupriya Manipuri language issue, particularly in Assam, has also acquired the shape of an ethnic movement.

The Ahom, Meitei, Zeliangrong, Seng Khasi, and Zomi communities had all felt threatened by the near extinction of their original language and religion (Das and Gupta, 1982; Das, 1989). In Manipur Valley the Meitei revivalist leaders (before the formal inclusion of Manipur-Meitei in the Eighth schedule to the Constitution), had demanded that the Manipuri language be named "Meiteilon'. The Zeliangrong movement grew as a religious-cultural movement, originally against the spread of Christianity, but it assumed an anti-colonial political overtone. It actually came out to be the only tribal movement of the North-East which maintained links with the national freedom struggle (Das, 1989). The Zeliangrong People's Conference (ZPC), demanded the recognition of ethnic nomenclature 'Zeliangrong', an acronym (Ze-Liang-Rong), who are spread in the contiguous areas of Manipur, Nagaland and Assam. In our report submitted to the government through the Director General of the Anthropological Survey of India, we had suggested recognition of common nomenclature as ethnographic facts supported the claims. It was recommended that an inter-state autonomous regional council for the Zeliangrong areas will be best suited to protect the cultural and economic interests of these tribes. In 1905, when the spread of Christianity was widely felt in Meghalaya, the Seng Khasi organization took upon itself the responsibility of defending the Khasi religion. The members of the association called themselves the 'Khasi-Khasis' so as to distinguish themselves from those 'Khasis' who had adopted Christianity. Having initiated the process of revivalism and reformation of the Khasi religion, the Seng Khasi encouraged the people to abide by the matrilineal system of descent, to respect the kith and kin on the maternal and paternal side, to believe in God, and to serve God through service of humankind. The Seng Khasi flag came to depict a crowing cock in white and red setting. The red signifies courage and white represents the world. The Seng Khasi started organizing archery competitions and traditional dance performances such as 'Ka Shad Suk Mynsiem' and 'the Nongkrem Dance'.

Ethnic Conflict and Militancy

On the eve of the independence of India, several ethnic groups had variously made effective use of the factors of ethnicity and regionalism as basis of ethnic rage, and democratic struggle for self-rule, greater autonomy and militant actions. Other factors such as frontier location, development process, rise of Christianity and democratic process, partition of country, influx of 'infiltrators' and minority syndrome variously led to claims of separatism among the communities. The more assertive tribes who consistently rebelled against their incorporation within the new Indian nation-state such as the Nagas and the Mizos who ultimately succeeded in attaining status of 'statehood' and greater autonomy. Thereby they also succeeded in changing their minority status to that of a majority status in respective hilly states. Even after the formation of Nagaland, however, the Naga movement had not died, as A.Z. Phizo, who had originally given the call for a 'long Naga struggle' in 1953, continued to occupy centre-stage later also (Das, 1982, 1994, 2004, 2007). The Naga movement, in which both 'ethnicity' and 'extreme nationalism' were used as operational strategies, is regarded as the mother of all movements in the North-East India. The origin of ethnicity among the Nagas may be traced first in the formation of a Naga Club in 1918, which consisted of the Naga headmen and members of English educated Naga middle class (Das, 1982). The Nagas formed the Naga Hills District Tribal Council in 1945, which was renamed as Naga National Council in 1946 (Das, 1993: 33). NNC had gradually articulated the sense of 'Naga nationalism' (Das, 1982: 2001). It also emphasized the theme of Naga oneness as 'a moral category' (Imchen, 1993), NSCN (IM) led the Naga movement in its modern phase. In order to globalize the Naga cause, NSCN (IM) took a delegation to the UN Conference of 'Indigenous Peoples', held in

July 1994. Muivah established links with the Asia Indigenous People's Pact and the Belgium-based Flemish Support for Indigenous People. The Nagaland Assembly also passed a resolution in 1994, extending support to the demand of the greater Nagaland: Nagalim. Outside the hills, the Ahoms (who formed the Ahom League, in the wake of 1935 Act) and the Bodos (by forming PTCA) had consistently raised the questions of 'tribal self-rule' right from the colonial era. The All Assam Ahom Association (formed originally in 1893) was perhaps the earliest ethnic association of its kind (Das, 2001). From the 1980's onwards, virtually the entire North-East was plagued with various ethnic movements. Most of the movements were non-violent in earlier stages, but gradually assumed severe militant nature. In the seven states of the North-East India reportedly more than 30 'insurgent' groups operated, carrying on protracted armed-struggle.[1] Among them the National Socialist Council of Nagaland (NSCN-IM, NSCN-K) and the United Liberation Front of Asom (ULFA) remained the prominent ones. Even though some scholars have tried to apply typology of class – formation to describe the ethnic conflict in the region, it may be argued that there are innumerable ethnic – regional factors buttressed by typical tribal features, which seem to influence the escalation of unrest.

The larger inventory provided highlights the severity of the ethnic dissent prevalent in the region. Amongst the outfits, some are non-operational; some are actually active, and some are no more active, as they used to be. It is amazing to note that at one point, more than 120 militant groups operated in India's North-East. Their demands ranged from autonomy to outright secession. In recent years, the Indian state has had considerable success in achieving stability in the region, using tactics from negotiations to military operations to root out the militants. Militant outfits also used various tactics. They even joined hands as early as 1989 forming the Indo-Burmese Revolutionary Front (IBRF), which consisted of NSCN, ULFA, KNF (from India) and Chin National Front (Myanmar). The influence of IBRF diminished gradually. Until recently, the NSCN (IM), NSCN (K), Bodo Security Force (BSF), National Democratic Front of Bodoland (NDFB), United Liberation Front of Assam (ULFA) and Kamtapur Liberation Organisation (KLO) have remained the most forceful and assertive groups. In the meantime quite a few Muslim extremist outfits too became active in the region (Das, 1994). In the Manipur Hills, the most powerful defiant groups, besides the NSCN, are UNLF – (Meghen), PLA, KNO, KNF, KNA, KDF and KFC. The Kuki-Naga conflict rocked the state of Manipur in the mid-nineties. When the Naga claim of 'proprietorship' over the vast hilly region of Manipur was endangered by demands for a 'Kuki Homeland', the NSCN quickly asserted its dominion. The Kuki Impi and the Zomi Council had worked tirelessly to bring about a permanent settlement. In Mizoram, the Reangs came to form Bru National Liberation Front whose leaders held talks with the Mizo Chief Minister. The population of displaced Reangs rose to 40,000 in camps in Tripura. The Mizos were specially perturbed when the Bru National union, formed in 1994 to protect the rights and privileges of the Reang minorities called for Autonomous District Council under the Sixth schedule of the Constitution. What gives strength to the demand of the Reangs (Brus) is their position as the second largest ethnic group in Mizoram. Both in pre-Independence and post-Independence eras, Tripura witnessed regular inflow of emigrants, and land alienation of tribals was rampant. The tribespeople thus became a minority in their own homeland. Tripura National Volunteers therefore did not target the state, but it opposed a community. In this respect, Bhaumik, says, "The TNV's anti-Bengali violence created a general climate of ethnic hatred, which were sharpened by large-scale alienation of the tribal lands and actual marginalization in jobs, professions and politics (1996). Prior to TNV, the Seng-krak (Clenched Fist) surfaced as a tribal insurgent group in 1967. It maintained close links with the Mizo National Front (MNF). Tribal leaders of Tripura, right from 1974, voiced demands of reservation, restoration of tribal land, and specially the restoration of native Kok-Borok as one of the official languages, and lastly the Autonomous District Council. The language and script issue, which engulfed Tripura for a long time, has hardly been addressed in right earnest.

Illegal Émigré, "Anti-Infiltrator Movement" and Terrorism

There is a long history of incursion of outsiders, emigration and resettlement in Assam. One can see this broadly in four spheres; tea plantation related manual labour, Bengali Muslim emigration (mostly occupying agriculture), Hindu Bengali migration (mostly occupying service sector), and Marwari migration in trading sector. Bangladesh war resulted in over 10,00,000 'refugees' taking shelter, who never returned. Modern Bangladeshi "infiltration" is however said to be a more severe phenomenon. It was alleged that Bangladesh Char area dialects spoken by the migrant Muslims, were declared as Assamese dialect to the census enumerators. Politicians too encouraged the Bangladeshi Muslims and other minorities into Assam, giving them voting rights. This was a narrow exercise in electoral politics (Dixit, 1998, 2003). This last wave of illegal-exodus from Bangladesh is a more dangerous phenomenon, as some among these infiltrators got involved in terrorist activities in parts of urban India. It is said, fear within the native Assamese community of being overwhelmed by the unabated influx of illegal Bangladeshi migrants from across the porous border triggered off the long-drawn "Anti-Foreigner mass uprising – 1979–1985", spearheaded by the All Assam Students' Union (AASU). It ended by arriving at an agreement, the Assam Accord on 15, August 1985. The Accord fixed 25 March 1971 as the cut-off date for detection and expulsion of the illegal foreign migrants. The Assam movement was led by AASU. All Assam Gana Sangram Parishad-AAGSP, which was umbrella organization of several outfits, including Asom Sahitya Sabha, emerged as the political forum the AASU. In 1985, AAGSP swept the elections on the wave of anti-foreigner sentiments. The ULFA'a inception dates back to the frenzied years of the Assam Movement when a section of the militant youth lost faith in peaceful programmes of AASU and the AAGSP. According to Baruah (1992) ULFA combined Naxalism, with a strong dose of "sub-nationalism". In 1990, the ULFA had forged links with various insurgent outfits inside and outside the country, including the PLA, NSCN and even JKLF in Kashmir. In 1986, ULFA first established contacts with the then unified National Socialist Council of Nagaland (NSCN) and the Kachin Independence Army (KIA) of Myanmar for training and arms. Subsequently, links were established with Pakistan's Inter Services Intelligence (ISI). The ULFA, according to Gohain, 'advocated a line of "de-nationalization" or "divesting oneself of ethnic identities except that of Assamese identity". It characterized India as a "colonial state" and the North-East as the 'colony', though no serious economic analysis substantiating this assertion had come to light.

Identity Politics of 'Small Ethnicities' and 'Minority Syndrome'

After its partitions, Assam was left with 23 tribes, comprising of 14 hill tribes of Karbi Anglong and North Cachar Hills; and nine plains tribes inhabiting the plains of the Brahmaputra Valley. Seeing development in the hills, some tribes became conscious to develop their sub-regions. Some tribes who had earlier launched movements rushed to renew their agitations. Thus the Ahom renewed the demand for the re-scheduling their scheduled tribe status. In order to push forward demand of a separate Ahom State, the 'Tai-Ahom Land Committee" was formed, by merging old organizations. In 1995 the Ahoms placed a 17–point charter of demands. Showing his concern for the Ahoms, the then Ahom Chief Minister of Assam, Hiteshwar Saikia, highlighted the unique cultural heritage of the Ahom people. The Karbis have been conscious about their minority status vis-à-vis the majority: the Assamese. Notwithstanding the gradual incorporation of the Karbis into the Assamese society, culturally and linguistically, the cultural incorporation was never conceded. What is more, the kinship based tribal political system, territorial affiliation (Mikir Hills), survival of Karbi folksongs and fable of their distinct origin, tribal mortuary rituals, and tribal costumes which survive in vibrant manner helped the Karbis to put forward their autonomy demand (Das, 1989: 188–90). Though the Karbi National Council demanded in 1986 only an autonomous district, but last two decades have seen the growth of the Karbi Students Association and the Autonomous State Demand Committee (ASDC) spearheading a movement for creation of a separate Karbi state. Seeing the ever growing demands of the minority tribes the administration had granted the Sixth Schedule status to some plains tribes, such as the Mising, Rabha and Tiwa.

The Bodo movement is the longest social movement in the plains of Assam. The first two phases of the Bodo movement were concerned with social reforms (1947–1967) and consolidation of the Bodo identity vis-à-vis the Assamese community (1967–1987). Earlier phase of the Brahma movement (1907 onwards) was a short-lived 'Sanskritization movement' led by the Mech-Bodos. The early cultural awakenings had led to birth of the Bodo Sahitya Sabha in 1952, which demanded Bodo language as the medium of instruction at secondary level. In its modern phase (1967 onwards) a new section of Bodo elite emerged which demanded a greater share in political power. A call was given for carving a separate region called Udayachal. After second phase of mass protests, there was a Bodo Accord signed in February 1993 that had led to the creation of the Bodoland Autonomous Council (BAC). The BAC was a non-starter, as the territorial boundary issue remained unresolved. The movement for maximum autonomy by the Bodos, succeeded ultimately in securing a new politico-administrative structure within the existing state of Assam following a memorandum of understanding with the Government of India on 10 February 2003. The Bodo-majority areas have now come under the new Bodoland Territorial Council (BTC), an elective body. The BTC Accord is seen as a fulfilment of the sub-national aspirations of the Bodos of Assam. Under the BTC understanding, the Government of India provides financial assistance of ₹ 100 crores per annum for five years for projects to develop the socio-economic infrastructure.

The North-East Indigenous and Tribal Peoples Forum, comprising fifteen diverse tribal organizations in its meeting in October 1994 resolved that "the entire region has been swamped by alien people migrating from neighbouring countries and also from other parts of India" (*The Telegraph,* 6 October 1994). Similarly Tribal Students Federation (TSF) was constituted by several tribal students' organizations such as Karabi Students Union, All Tiwa Students Union, Takam Miashing Porin Kebang, All Assam Deuri Students Union, Maan-Tai Students Union, Sonwal Kachaari Students Union, Dimasa Students Federation, and All Assam Tribal Students Union. The main objective of the TSF was to provide coherent direction to the various tribal movements of the region for "the right of self-determination". An important aspect of TSF was its abhorrence to militant-armed actions. TSF failed to achieve its goals.

In view of extensive demand of Chakma and Hajong for Indian citizenship, the Arunachal Pradesh Legislative Assembly passed a unanimous resolution to deport these émigrés settled in the state. To protect the cultures of indigenous tribes the Legislative Assembly passed the Bill called "The Arunachal Pradesh Protection of Customary Laws and Socials Practices Bill, 1994" for protection of the native tribal institutions. The All Arunachal Pradesh Students Union (AAPSU) also opposed such demands of citizenship. The Nepalese of Assamese origin demanded 'special protected status' under the Constitution. They aimed to thwart attempts at branding them as 'foreigners'/illegal infiltrators. Fact remains that the Nepalese did face the Khasi anger manifested in the 'ethnic cleansing' of the sort in late 1980s, and which had triggered the larger Nepalese demand of the Gorkhaland (Das, 1989, *The Statesman,* 18 July 2002). In September 1994 the North-East Students Organization (NESO) alleged that the Illegal Migrants (Determination of Tribunal) Act 1993, was full of loopholes and which had made detection and expulsion of illegal migrants in North-East difficult. There have been strong reactions to the threat of infiltration of outsiders in varied manners. Thus, the National Socialist Council of Nagalim (Isak-Muivah) made it mandatory for non-Nagas living "all over Nagalim" to make identity cards for themselves and their families.

In Assam, the Adivasis today can broadly be divided into two communities, the tea garden workers and those who came out of the tea gardens at the end of their contracts and settled in and around the tea gardens after procuring some land. Through gradual expansion these Adivasis, form nearly 20 per cent of the state population, but their representation in the legislative assembly is said to be markedly lesser (Other Backward Class, 5 May 2008, India Together News Service). Hiren Gohain has discussed the Adivasi Militancy in Assam. The All Assam Adivasi Students' Association along with Assam Tea Tribal Students' Association (strong in Sibsagar, Dibrugarh and Laximpur districts of upper Assam) have been agitating for years demanding recognition of tea tribals and Adivasis as scheduled tribes. The Adivasis have been neglected by the state. Only special measures, like the campaign against poverty, can win their hearts. The state Congress leaders failed to muster political will to fulfil that demand. The latest response from the Registrar General is that some relatively homogeneous groups among this population may be considered for inclusion under this list if the state government agrees.

Reconciliation for Self-Rule and Autonomy: Ceasefire and Peace Accords

Noteworthy peace initiatives were undertaken during the 1960s and 1970s involving several militant outfits of the region. However, it was during 1994 that several underground organizations came 'over-ground' and surrendered before the government authorities, particularly in Assam, Meghalaya and Mizoram. These organizations were the Dimasa National Security Force (DNSF), Achik Liberation Matgrik Army (ALMA) and Hmar People's Convention (HPC). The Dimasa Kachari generally live in North Cachar Hills, Cachar, Karbi-Anglong, Nowgong (all in Assam) and Dhansiri region of Nagaland. Prior to 1961 Census they were identified as a 'Sub-tribe' of Kachari. In the 1971 census and afterwards they projected themselves as a distinct tribe. The 'Dimasa Jalairaoni Hosoma' was established in 1972 to promote their distinct cultural identity. The Dimasa National Organisation (DNO) was born in 1979. In March 1979 the Dimasa demanded the proper preservation of ancient Dimasa monuments and relics. In 1980, Nikhil Hidimba Barman Samity, Cachar, demanded reorganization of the Dimasa speaking areas of North-East India. Even though the Dimasa National Security Force (DNSP) had close ties with the NSCN its leaders realized the futility of their actions and thus they had surrendered before the Assam State government authorities in 1994. A breakthrough achieved during 1994 was the signing of the Hmar Peace Pact. An accord was signed at Aizal on 27 July, 1994 between the Hmar People's Convention (HPC) and the Mizoram Government, bringing to an end the seven years old Hmar insurgency. The accord envisaged the setting up of a Hill Development Council in Hmar inhabited north Mizoram. In Meghalaya also the Achik Liberation Magrik Army (ALMA), trained by the NSCN, and inspired by the ULFA, surrendered before the Meghalaya Chief Minister at Tura, on 25 October 1994. The Garo Baptist Convention (GBP) played a major rule in bringing the militants to the negotiating table. In Assam, Hiteswar Saikia (Congress)-led government declared "grant of total autonomy to several major ethnic tribes". Besides the Bodo Accord (1993), his government signed accords with the Karbi and Dimasa tribals. Self ruling bodies were provided to Rabhas, Mishings and Lalung (Tiwas). In Assam, many organizations have ceasefire agreements with the government: UPDS since January 1, 2004, the UPDS since May 23, 2002 and the NDFB since May 25, 2005. Similarly, in the state of Meghalaya, the Achik National Volunteer Council has had a ceasefire agreement with the government since July 23, 2004. ULFA in Assam in 2005, too, has appointed a People's Consultative Group to prepare the groundwork for eventual dialogue with the government.

The Naga peace initiative has a long tradition. Diverse perceptions surrounded the earlier 19–point Agreement of 1960 and the Shillong Accord of 1975. In recent times the Naga Hoho convened a series of meetings of Church leaders and NGOs from all Naga areas culminating in a call for "journey of conscience" to seek reconciliation and to rebuild the Naga society. A Declaration was adopted in 2001 to pursue the cause of peace. Since 1998–99 peace parleys particularly with the NSCN (IM) has been generally successful. The NSCN (IM) has been demanding a homeland for all Nagas living in the North-East, which will be called 'Nagalim'. These peace initiatives have led to what is termed as bilateral cease-fire, whereby belligerence and hostility is halted. Even during cease-fire the cause for worry has been the fratricidal schisms between the different factions of the Naga National Council, the Isak-Muivah group and Khaplang faction of the National Socialist Council of Nagaland. There has been success of peace talks with the Khaplang faction too. It is also a matter of satisfaction that 'substantive issues' have been discussed. At the same time in a statement titled "Journey for Peace" the NSCN (I-M) has recognized the 'legitimate aspirations of all neighbouring people including the Meiteis, the Assamese and others', and appealed to them to 'let us end tension between us' (Navalakha, 2003). NSCN (I-M) has appreciated the government of India's understanding of the "unique history of the Naga people". The Kamtapur movement, initiated by the Kamtapur People's Party (KPP), involves the Koch and Rajbanshi communities, who call themselves Kamtapuris. The Kamtapuri ethnicity and language question gave birth to this movement, which started as a peaceful movement, but turned violent after the movement came in contact of the some Assam based militant outfits such as ULFA in 1999–2000.Apart from the demand for a separate state to be carved out from five north Bengal districts, the Eleven – point charter of the KPP includes the recognition of the Kamtapuri language, introduction of Kamtapuri programmes in TV., and 're-settlement' of the people who arrived after 1971. The KPP supporters, mostly of Rajbanshi origin consider themselves indigenous to the region, and they feel they have the right to self-determination. Today, the situations mainly in Manipur, Assam and Tripura remain indeed disturbing. The Manipuri militants have shown no inclination for peace talks. All Tripura Tiger Force and the National Liberation Front of Tripura, which operate from camps in Bangladesh, will be weakened by the Naga peace accord, if reached (*The Statesman,* 23 November 2002). The NLFT has a link with the NSCN and the ATTF has links with the ULFA. Though the NLFT talks of secession, the state is not their enemy. Their targets are the settlers who have migrated from former East Pakistan after partition and subsequent settlers who have reduced the indigenous tribes of Tripura into minority (Chakraborty, *The Statesman,* 23 November 2002).

A Recapitulation

In North-East India cultural differences and incongruity sharpened the ethnic boundaries and generated cleavages along ethnic conceit, leading to inter-ethnic discord. Ethnic unrest in the North-East is as old as the country's independence. The Indian independence along with the partition, influx of émigrés, suspected fear of linguis-tic-cultural subjugation, economic negligence, and failure to value approaching political institutions variously infused in the minds of the ethnic communities a 'sense of narcissistic self-awareness'. The spectre of social exclusion, minority-syndrome and ethnic rivalry remained the driving force for protests demanding autonomy in the shape of homeland/state/or autonomous district council, within constitutional framework. Some of the movements followed the violent paths. While the former opted for constitutional path, the later sought an extra-constitutional/secessionist ideational path. Ever increasing evidence, however, now indicates that most of the militant outfits in the North-East have now transformed themselves into terrorist entities, empty of their original objectives and ideology. For example, ULFA in Assam, since 1990s, has repudiated its earlier anti-Bangladeshi position. Vested interests and quarrel over them led militant groups to clash among themselves. It will be incorrect to attach terrorist label to NSCN, but the media reports suggest that most fatalities in Nagaland are the result of the infighting between the two factions of the NSCN, rather than with government forces. Despite several successful peace initiatives, the security force operations are in place by utilizing the army, state police forces and the paramilitary forces to contain militancy.

Poor governance has been a major problem in the region. Wasbir Hussain says the region is caught in a vicious cycle of lack of economic development and then militancy, and the resultant violence further retard economic growth. Under the circumstances, it is natural to find the people of the region harbouring a sense of alienation from the Indian mainstream and feel neglected. We have noted above how the state of Assam is under siege with the aspirations of different communities and groups showing no signs of a decline despite attempts at devolution of power to the grassroots level. B.P. Routray of the Institute for Conflict Management, has rightly observed that 'this is primarily a governance issue. Poor governance is the main trigger factor for ethnic groups clamouring for autonomy.

Such demands from newer groups are here to stay'. Special provisions for self-governance and autonomy are provided for people of the North-East within the Constitution of India, particularly through such Acts as the Sixth Schedule, NEC and Department of North-Eastern Region (DONER). The DONER and the North-Eastern Council, under the central control need more effectively to tackle the problems of unemployment, underemployment, and economic backwardness of the region. Let the people's representatives monitor the activities of these institutions. The DONER has an annual budget of ₹ 550 crores. The NEC has another ₹ 500 crores earmarked for the region. These are apart from the enormous amount of funding available to the states through different central schemes, one-time packages announced by successive Prime Ministers, 'peace packages' provided to states like Nagaland and Mizoram, grants by international development agencies like the World Bank, and the Asian Development Bank (ADB), which in 2003 approved a master project of ₹ 2, 000 crores for the North-East. These institutional arrangements and provisions need to be appropriately regulated to assuage ethnic misgivings. In more recent years the peace initiatives, such as the bilateral ceasefire, and the peace talks held between militant leaders and government representatives, symbolize the determination of the nation-state to resort to a broad -spectrum consensus on vital issues by adhering to flexibility and extendibility. These are basic foundations aimed at the national-consolidation, which should be strengthened. Peace, development and proper linkages are bound together and are intrinsic to achieving harmony in the region. Gradually, the region has increasingly witnessed not only naturalization of electoral politics, but also slow adaptation of national political parties.

Resurgence of ethnic identity and persistence of ethnicized politics does not indicate repudiation of the political state. Their concern for variously perceived threats to their distinct ethnic identities and their anxiety for preservation of culture and language and their demand of autonomy can not be seen as dysfunctional for a healthy civil society. Their aspirations should be seen rather as prerequisites for distributive justice, to which no nation state can neglect. Indian path of institutional adjustments aimed at wining over and changing the opinion of hostile ethnic groups and extending special safeguards to hill states have helped solve ethnic problems to a great extent. These need to be endured.

Notes

1. The following list provides names of the outfits, some of which are no more active, as they used to be.

   Arunachal Pradesh:
   United Liberation Volunteers of Arunachal Pradesh (ULVA)
   United People's Volunteers of Arunachal Pradesh (UPVA)
   United Liberation Movement of Arunachal Pradesh (ULMA)
   National Liberation Front of Arunachal: Koj Tara Dragon Force (ADF)

   Assam:
   United Liberation Front of Asom (ULFA)
   Bodo Security Force (BDSF)
   National Democratic Front of Bodoland (NDFB)
   Dimasa National Security Force (DNSF)
   Bodo Liberation Tiger Force (BLTF)
   Dima Halim Daogah (DHD)
   Karbi National Volunteers (KNV)
   Rabha National Security Force (RNSF)
   Koch-Rajbongshi Liberation Organisation (KRLO)
   Hmar People's Convention-Democracy (HPC-D)
   Karbi People's Front (KPF)
   Barak Valley Youth Liberation Front (BVYLF)
   Birsa Commando Force
   Adivasi United Liberation Front of Assam
   Cobra Force
   United Liberation Front of Barak Valley
   Muslim United Liberation Front of Assam (MULFA)
   Muslim Liberation Tigers of Assam (MULTA)
   United Social Reform Army of Assam (USRAA)
   United People's Democratic Solidarity (UPDS)

   Manipur:
   National Socialist Council of Nagaland (NSCN-IM)
   People's Liberation Army (PLA)
   Revolutionary People's Front (RPF)
   United National Liberation Front (UNLF)
   People's Revolutionary Party of Kangleilpak (PREPAK)
   Kuki National Organisation (KNO)
   Kuki National Front (KNF), Kuki National Army (KNA)

Kuki Revolutionary Army (KRA), Kuki Defense Force (KDF)
Kuki Front Council (KFC), Manipur People's Liberation Front (MPLF)
People's Republican Army (PRA)
Kangleipak Communist Party (KCP)
Kanglei Yawol Kanna Lup (KYKL)
Manipur Liberation Tiger Army (MLTA)
Iripak Kanba Lup (IKL)
Kangleipak Kanba Kanglup (KKK)
North-East Minority Front (NEMF)

Mizoram:

Hmar People's Convention (HPC)
Hmar People's Convention-Democracy (HPC-D)
Hmar Revolutionary Front (HRF)
Zomi Revolutionary Army (ZRA)
Zomi Revolutionary Volunteers (ZRV)
Indigenous People's Revolutionary Alliance (IRPA)
Kom Rem People's Convention (KRPC)
Chin Kuki Revolutionary Front (CKRF)
Bru National Liberation Front
Bru National Front (BNFM) of Mizoram
Bru Welfare Association of Mizoram (BWAM)

Meghalaya:

Hynniewtrep Volunteer Council (HVC)
Hynniewtrep Achik Liberation Council (HALC
Hynniewtrep National Liberation Council (HNLC)
Achick Liberation Matgrik Army (ALMA)
A'chik National Volunteers Council (ANVC)
People's Liberation Front of Meghalaya (PLF-M)
Hajong United Liberation Army (HULA)

Nagaland:

National Socialist Council of Nagaland (Isak-Muivah) – NSCN (IM)
National Socialist Council of Nagaland (Khaplang) – NSCN (K)
Naga National Council-NNC (Adino), Naga Federal Government (NFG)
Naga National Council (Khodao) – NNC (K)

Tripura:

TRIPURA: National Liberation Front of Tripura (NLFT), All Tripura Tigers Force (ATTF)

Bru National Liberation Front (BNLF)
National Liberation Front of Tripura (NLFT): Biswamohan Debbarma
Nayanbashi Jamatia
All Tripura Tiger Force (ATTF): Ranjit Debbarma
Tripura Tribal Volunteer Force (TTVF)
Tripura Liberation Force (TLF)
All Tripura Volunteer Force (ATVF)
Tripura National Army (TNA)
Borok National Council of Tripura (BNCT)

North Bengal:

Kamtapuri Liberation Organisation (KLO)

References

Baruah, S. 1992. 'Symbolism and Statesmanship', *The Telegraph*, 11 June: 9.

Bhaumik, S. 1996. Patterns of Minority Violence in North-East India. Paper presented at a *National Seminar on Minorities in North-East India*, 13–14 January, Calcutta: Department of Political Science, Calcutta University.

Chakraborty, K. 2002. 'Tripura Turmoil', *The Statesman*, 23 November: 4.

Das, N.K. 1982. 'The Naga Movement', in K.S. Singh (ed.), *Tribal Movements in India*. Vol. I. Delhi: Manohar, 39–52.

—. 1989. *Ethnic Identity, Ethnicity and Social Stratification in Northeast India*. New Delhi: Inter-India Publications.

—. 1993. *Kinship, Politics and Law in Naga Society*. Memoir No. 96. Calcutta: Anthropological Survey of India.

—. 1994. 'Ethno-Historical Processes and Ethnicity in North-East India', *Journal of Indian Anthropological Society*, 29(1–2): 3–35.

—. 2001. 'Regionalism and Ethnicity in Northeast', *J.Anthrop. Surv.India*, 50: 1–16.

—. 2002. 'Dalit Women, Dalit Literature and Anthropology', in R. Chauabe and K. Saini (eds), *Status of Women in Rural Societies*. Bina: Aditya Publishers.

Das, N.K. and P. Gupta. 1982. 'Ahom Movement', in K.S. Singh (ed.), *Tribal Movements in India*. Vol. I. New Delhi: Manohar.

—. 2003. 'Religious Syncretism and Cultural Homogenisation on Northeast India', in N.K. Das (ed.), *Culture, Religion and Philosophy: Critical Studies in Syncretism and Inter-Faith Harmony*. New Delhi: Rawat Publications.

—. 2004. 'Regionalism, Ethnicity and Nationalism in Northeast India', in A. Basu, B.K. Das Gupta and J. Sarkar (eds), *Anthropology for Northeast India: A Reader*. Calcutta: Indian National Confederation and Academy of Anthropologists, 39–72.

—. 2007. 'Ethnicity, Nationalism and Regionalism in North-East India', in R.K. Bhadra and Mita Bhadra (eds), *Ethnicity, Movement and Social Structure: Contested Cultural Identity.* Jaipur: Rawat Publications, 133–169.

Dixit, J.N. 1998. 'No Suitors for Seven Sisters', *The Telegraph*, 26 October.

—. 2003. 'Back to Square One', *The Telegraph*, 12 March.

Gohain, H. 2007. 'A Question of Identity: Adivasi Militancy', *Economic and Political Weekly*, 14(3): 334–338.

Hussain, W. 1998. 'Contemporary North-East India: Problems and Prospects', in J.P. Singh (ed.), *Trends in Social Sciences and Humanities in North-East India.* Delhi: Regency Publications, 129–136.

Imchen, C.L. 1993. 'Naga Politics: Regionalism or Non-State Nation', in B. Pakem (ed.), *Regionalism in India.* New Delhi: Har-Anand Publications, 103–122.

Miri, S. 1993. *Communalism in Assam: A Civilizational Approach.* New Delhi: Har-Anand Publications.

Navalakha, G. 2003. 'Naga Peace Process', *Economic and Political Weekly*, 13(2): 234–242.

Routray, B.P. 2003. *Neglected North-East: Whose Responsibility?* http://www.ipcs.org/article_details.php?article No. 1145 (10–03–09).

9

Migration and Settlement of Nepalis in North-East India

A Historical Perspective

TEJIMALA GURUNG

Migration, which is a major symptom of social change, has emerged as an important theme and an issue of major concern in national politics in South Asian countries for a variety of reasons. Cross-border population movements are regarded as issues that affect internal security, political stability and international relations, not simply the structure and composition of the labour market, or the permission of services to new comers (Weiner, 1993). As a phenomenon human migration dates back to the pre-historic period. The rapidity with which the *Homo sapiens* occupied all the continents (except Antarctica) in about 50,000 years, breaking through climatic and geographical barriers attests the propensity of humans to migrate. The development of agriculture, pastoral nomadry (about 3000 B.C.), emergence of seafaring populations, creation of civiliza tions with its occupational specializations and social diversity has structured subsequent patterns of human migration. In modern times, the colonial period has witnessed large-scale migration and settlement of people resulting in the transfer and distribution of diverse population groups in different parts of the world. The commercialization and industrialization of the economy under the aegis of the post-industrial colonial state also served to stimulate the migratory movement of the people. As a concept, migration is applicable to various forms of human movement which may be voluntary or forced, brought about either by socio-political or ecological reasons. It implies a definite move from one geographical area to another by a collectivity called migrants either for a temporary or permanent period preceded by decision making on the part of the migrants and resulting in changes in the interactional systems of the migrants (Mangalam, 1968: 8). Migration thus involves not only physical shifts in population but also change, political, economic and cultural, in both the places of origin and destination.

The Historical Antecedents

One of the important migratory movements that took place in the South Asian subcontinent during the nineteenth and twentieth centuries was from Nepal to India. Both these countries have historical and cultural ties which dates back to the ancient period. Lumbini, the birth place of Buddha is located in Nepal and until recently Nepal was the only remaining Hindu monarchy in the world. During the eighteenth century, the establishment of British rule in India and the rise to power of the Shah dynasty in Nepal brought the two expanding powers into conflict with each other. Till 1815 there was no clearly demarcated Indo-Nepal border; only a roughly defined land dividing the Terai region of Nepal from India. The Indo-Nepal boundary is of comparative recent origin which took place after the Anglo-Nepal war. By the Treaty of Segowli (1815–1816) the British not only formally demarcated the boundaries and effectively curtailed the southwards territorial expansion of Nepal; it also virtually annexed all its foothill territory of about 105,000 sq km which included Darjeeling, then a small settlement of 100 people in the east (later restored by the British to Sikkim by the Treaty of Titalaya, 1817). The treaty also paved the way for the recruitment of the Nepalis into the British force as Gurkha soldiers. However, the unrestricted movement of people of both countries continued even after the Indo-Nepal border was demarcated. From the early nineteenth century the North-East region of India came to be an important destination for the migratory movement of the Nepalis. This migration itself was a consequence of the change in the political, economic and social scenario in both the sending and receiving destinations. The positive factors encouraging Nepali migration to the geographically contiguous the North-East 'frontier' were not only a sparsely inhabited Himalayan ecology suitable to their economic subsistence and need, but also the scope for employment in the colonial army, as well as the conscious patronage extended by the colonial state to such migration and settlements (Gurung, 2003: 173). People, small producers in particular, who migrated from the hills of Nepal to India during the nineteenth century, did so because of their inability to subsist. In the hill regions agricultural production failed to keep pace with population growth, subsistence was difficult and emigration soon became a common alternative to declining yields and deteriorating living standards (Rengmi, 1971). The repression of the autocratic Rana regime, increasing taxation and rising rents, indebtedness to local money lenders and absence of employment in non-agricultural sectors pushed the people to migrate to neighbouring India where prospects of living appeared brighter.

Historically, from very early times, the region now known as North-East India has been one of the important highways of human movement and cultural interaction (Chatterjee, 1970). After the first Anglo-Burmese war (1824–26) the British occupied Assam and most of the hill areas by the close of the nineteenth century and which was integrated to British India. The political consolidation of the region and the exploitation of the vast resources for commercial purposes like tea industry, mining, oil and construction of railways etc, under the British colonial state created favourable conditions for the migration of people from other parts of India including Nepal. The nature of migration thus saw a visible change during this period in terms of its magnitude and features.

The migration of the Nepalis to North-East India thus took place in this broad historical and social context. At present, they are found permanently settled in almost all the seven states of the region pursuing diverse occupations. The colonial state which created the basis for the migration induced and sponsored different typologies of Nepali migration in North-East India. Such migration to the region was from two sources: Nepal, and from Darjeeling and Sikkim. With the leasehold annexation of Darjeeling from Sikkim by the British in 1835, the British encouraged the migration of the Nepalese to Sikkim and Darjeeling as part of British imperial strategy and to develop the nascent tea industry (Gurung, 2008: 150). In 1901 the Nepalis comprised more than 50 per cent of the total population of Darjeeling district (O'Malley, 1907: 41). Outside West Bengal, the

North-East has the largest concentration of Nepalis in India. Known also as Gorkhas or Gurkhas, they form a minority community in all the North-Eastern states. As per the 1991 Census the Nepali population in the region was 6, 53, 281or less than a million.

Table 9.1

Nepali Population in North-East India (1991)

States	*Nepali Population*	*Percentage to total population*
Arunachal Pradesh	81,176	9.39
Assam	4,32,519	1.93
Manipur	46,498	2.53
Meghalaya	49,486	2.77
Mizoram	8,246	1.20
Nagaland	32,274	2.67
Tripura	3,082	0.11

Source: Census of India, 1991–Part IV B (1) (A), (C) Series, Language Table C-7.

A migrant community which came initially during the British colonial period, and settled down here; the Nepalis have been very much a part of the historical experience and change witnessed and undergone from the nineteenth century onwards. In spite of their long presence and settlement, the Nepalis residing in the North-East and elsewhere in India are perceived to be the 'reciprocal migrants' of the 1950 Indo-Nepal Treaty. The issue of 'migrants' continues to be a live issue and has dominated the politics of North-East India during the last eighty years. When anti-outsider and foreign national sentiments are being widely expressed, it becomes socially imperative to undertake a historical study of Nepali migration and settlement in the North-East in order to situate their current presence and changing status in the region. The scope of this paper necessarily limits it to making an analytical study at the macro level. Primary sources for the paper include archival and British official records. For the post-colonial period data has been collected from the Census Reports and State Gazetteers. Secondary works both in English and the vernacular are available about the Nepalis. As a minority and marginalized people scholarly studies of the community in the North-East have been inadequate. With few exceptions (H.K. Barpujari, ed., *The Comprehensive History of Assam,* 1992 and Amalendu Guha's *Planter Raj to Swaraj,*

1977) the community does not find space even in the history of the region. But even in these works they are not dealt as people but as 'migrants' (Nag, 2003: 185). As Sajal Nag has perceptively observed, 'the difference between the history of 'the people' and the 'migrant's is immense. While 'people' are dealt with as embodiment of emotions, hopes, aspirations, 'migrant's are dealt as 'things' whose movements and actions are just recorded and not seen as struggles and aspirations. While people are central to history, migrants are appendages' (2003: 186). The emergence of nationalist historiography, and subsequently, the development of regional history which focused on the dominant indigenous nationality or majority community meant that along with the Nepalis the histories of the other migrant groups like the Marwaris, Sikhs and ex-tea garden labourers have been excluded from the history of the region. A proper understanding of the processes of social change in the region has to incorporate also the histories of the excluded others who have been overlooked by the nationalist historiography. A recently published work (Sinha and Subba, eds., 2003, *The Nepalis in Northeast India: A Community in Search of an Indian Identity*) has sought to uncover various historical and social aspects of the settled Indian Nepalis in the region and their contribution in the consolidation of North-East India.

Colonial Rule and Nepali Migration

The extension of British colonial rule into the North-East region, laid the basis for the migration and settlement of Nepalis. In the early period, the Nepalis came as Gurkha soldiers with the British and as part of the Military Police (Assam Rifles). The significance of the soldier pioneer migration was not large but in the example it set. It helped to pave the way for later migration, which subsequently came to include other categories of people like the herders, cultivators etc. The experiences of the pioneer migrants opened up the horizon of the people back home and of opportunities that lay beyond the confines of their world. The settled Gurkhas helped to bring other families and friends. Once a network of Nepali settlements had been established migration tended to flow towards the areas where the kins or friends of the migrants were located. Migration during the colonial period was of two kinds – sponsored as well as natural. While the soldier and labour migration in industries was sponsored by the colonial state, the natural migration consisted of grazier/herdsman and marginal farmers, sawyers, labourers etc. By the 1940s Nepali migration to India and the North-East had become an established social process. As a result, at the time of Indian independence there was already a considerable Nepali presence and settlement in the North-East. The Indo-Nepal Treaty of Peace and Friendship 1950, the tripartite Delhi Agreement of 1951 and The Revised Indo-Nepal Treaty of 1956 recognized what was a de-facto situation existing from the British time (even earlier) by providing for a free and unrestricted reciprocal flow of nationals and goods of both countries. Migration of the Nepalese to the region therefore, continued even in the post-colonial period. In 1979, The All Assam Students Union (AASU) was the first to raise the issue of large scale migration of Nepalese and of being demographically overwhelmed by the 'foreigners'. The effect of the anti foreigners movement had repercussions throughout the North-East where the unorganized minority Nepalis settled in various states were subjected to hostile treatment. The Indian Nepalis were very often identified as being Nepalese citizens. This led to forcible displacement of many Nepalis from their homes (Gurung, 2002: 154). The century-old process of integration and social assimilation of the Nepalis within the society received a setback due to the post-1979 developments. Whereas earlier the Nepalis were confident of their status and role in the host society and regarded themselves an integral part and parcel of the land they had inhabited and called it their home, at present a sense of insecurity about their future pervades the community. One way of responding to this has been a reassertion of their political identity as Indian Nepalis separate from the Nepalese nationals of Nepal.

The Settlement of Nepalis during the Colonial Period

The Gurkha recruitment into the Assam Light Infantry (earlier Cuttack Legion raised in 1817) and the Sylhet Light Infantry (1824), which were the two local corps connected with the defence of the Eastern Frontier; the local Military Police (1835), and the events of 1857–58 which established the foundations of Gurkha recruitment in the military and police forces in Assam on a firm footing paved the way for Nepali migration and settlement in different parts of the region. Initial settlement of the Nepalis began with that of the ex-Gurkha soldiers who on retirement settled down with their families in the nearby headquarters, district towns and other strategic areas where the military posts were located. The capacity of the

Gurkhas for colonization was recognized by the British very early. The Moamaria rebellion against the Ahom state (later half of 18th century) and the Burmese invasions had devastated the economy and depopulated the region. As such for increasing cultivation and villages for productive purposes Gorkhas who had brought their families were granted lands at very moderate rate (Pemberton, 1835). Retired Gurkha soldiers have been rehabilitated in at least forty sites by the Assam Rifles alone (Sinha, 2003: 44). After World War 1 many retired Gurkha personnel were allotted settlement land by the Cantonment Authority at Jhalupara (Singh, 1980: 82) which is the oldest Nepali settlement in Shillong then the administrative headquarters of Assam. Gurkha soldiers were also allotted land by the colonial state for settlement. In the erstwhile Lushai Hills district (present Mizoram) a few retired military policemen or Gorkhas were allowed in the first decade of the twentieth century to settle in Aizawl, which had became the district headquarters in 1898. For about two decades the Gurkhas were the main inhabitants of Aizawl (Chatterjee, 1990). The Hindu temple of the Gorkhas in Aizawl is the oldest public place of worship. Such settlements were encouraged by the colonial state in what was then a hostile, unfamiliar and sparsely inhabited territory. As a result, many such settlements of retired Gurkha soldiers came up in the administrative headquarters and districts in Assam and in Manipur, then a princely state under British suzerainty.

From the later part of the nineteenth century, Nepali herdsmen began to settle in the *Chapari or* riverine *areas* of Assam as graziers and dairy farmers. Most of the graziers were Jaisis and Upadhyay Brahmins or Chettris. The demand for milk created by the growth of urban centres and coming of colonial functionaries led the Nepalis to rearing cattle in the Brahmaputra plains and hilly peripheries of the region. Many areas in the sparsely inhabited Brahmaputra Valley were declared as professional grazing reserves by the British for whom grazing fees constituted an expanding source of revenue. The Burachapari of Tezpur was recognized as a professional grazing reserve as early as in 1881 facilitating dairying by the Nepalis. In 1933 the Nepali community had organized the *Tezpur Graziers Association* (later the Assam Graziers Association) at Singri in Assam under Chhabilal Upadhyaya, a Nepali Mahajan and a prominent member of the Assam Pradesh Congress to preserve the grazing reserves and the interests of the Nepali graziers from the threat posed by migrant agriculturists from Bengal. The term '*dhudhwala*' became synonymous with a Nepali. The contribution of the Nepalis to the rise of dairy farming industry in the region has been significant and until recently till the1980's they had continued to monopolize this section both in the plains and hills (Gurung, 2008).

From dairy farmers, the Nepalis also increasingly began to settle as agriculturists and take up land in several districts of Assam (Assam Administrative Reports). In Lakhimpur and in the east of Sibsagar and Darrang districts sugarcane cultivation was mainly in the hands of the Nepalese who also specialized in the manufacture of an improvized jaggery. After the ex-tea garden labourers and immigrant peasant cultivators from East Bengal, the Nepalis constituted the third largest single immigrant group during the colonial period to take up land for settlement and cultivation. In the year 1939–40, the total area of land, settled direct with the ex-tea garden labourers and other immigrants in the Assam Valley division, was 10,70,761 acres of which 1,04,773 acres (9.8%) were settled by the Nepalis. The break up of land held by the Nepalis is indicated in the table below:

Table 9.2

Break-up of the Land held by the Nepalis

Districts	*Goalpara*	*Kamrup*	*Darrang*	*Nowgong*	*Sibsagar*	*Lakhimpur*	*Garo Hills*
Area (acres)	9,790	11,386	57,186	5,491	6,896	13,987	37

Source: Report on the Land Revenue Administration of Assam Valley Division, 1939–40.

In Manipur the migration and settlement of the Nepalis began during the nineteenth century when the princely state of Manipur came under British control. During and after the revolt of 1891–92, the 42nd (raised 1817 as the Cuttack Legion, renamed 6th Gurkha Rifles in 1903), the 43rd and the 44th Gurkha Rifles (raised 1824 as the 16th Sylhet Local Battalion, renamed 8th Gurkha Rifles in 1903) were posted in Manipur at various times. In 1917 the 4th battalion of the Assam Rifles in which 80 per cent of the soldiers were Gurkhas, was transferred to Manipur with it's headquarter at Imphal. After retirement many of these ex-soldiers were allowed to settle down in Manipur by the British. Settlement colonies were opened for them. Subsequently an increasing number of graziers belonging to the

Upadhyay and Jaisi castes began to come and settle down. Many Nepali settlements came up particularly on the then Manipur-Mao cart road which connected Imphal with Kohima and Dimapur. By the early period of the twentieth century there were a number of Nepali settlements at Koirengi, Keithenmanbi, Sapermeina, Kanglatongbi, Kangpokpi, and Maram (Gurung, 2003: 272).

In 1901 Census the total percentage of Nepali speaking population in the North-East to the total population was 0.35 per cent. The census figures of 1911, 1921 and 1931 recorded the percentage of total population rising to 0.67; 0.94; and 1.02 respectively. The number of Nepali-speaking population (as per the 1931 Census) in the hill districts was 3,000 in the Naga Hills, 2,000 in the Lushai Hills and 3,000 in Manipur. By far the largest number was found in the Khasi and Jaintia Hills district. The large number of Nepalis in Khasi-Jaintia and Naga Hills was due to the Gurkha regiments stationed there. The Nepali migrants during this period were either temporary or seasonal migrants (those who came during the winter months to work as sawyers, miners, and returned home for agricultural work during the rainy season); those who were semi-permanent and those who settled down permanently.

Post-colonial Migration

So at the time of Indian independence in 1947 there was already a large number of Nepalis who were permanently settled and living for at least two or three generations in various parts of the North-East India. They were either serving in the Gurkha Regiments and Military Police Battalions or were earning a living as herdsmen, as cultivators and in small time trade and artisan services. Indeed, at the time of Indian independence 'the Nepalis were the quietly dominant element in the lower hills around Assam except for NEFA (present Arunachal Pradesh) and Tripura and this continued to be the case after Independence' (Rose, cited in Baruah, 2001: 63). Every Nepali by virtue of his/her domicile in the territory of India at the commencement of the Constitution of India (26 January 1950), under Article 5 of the Constitution was a citizen of India (Gazette Notification on the Issue of Citizenship of Gorkhas, Government of India Ministry of Home Affairs, New Delhi, 23rd August, 1988). In November 1947, under the *Tripartite Agreement* signed between Nepal, Britain and, India the original ten Gurkha Brigade of the colonial army was divided between India and

Britain. Six regiments (twelve battalions) passed to the post independence Indian army, which recruited an additional regiment for a total of seven Gurkha Rifles. (1st, 3rd, 4th, 5th, 8th, 9th, 11th,) The Gurkha personnel at independence was as high as 4 per cent. The *Indo-Nepal Treaty of Peace and Friendship*, 1950 allowed reciprocal movement and settlement of nationals of both countries. As a result the recruitment of Gurkhas to the Indian army and also to the Assam Rifles continued alongside the migration of herdsmen. In 1951 there were 1,22,823 Nepali speakers in the North-East or 1.39 per cent of the total population. Nepali herdsmen began to migrate in great numbers to the hill districts of Assam, particularly into the Khasi and Jaintia Hills. In the Khasi Hills, the entry of Nepali graziers was even encouraged by the Khasi *syiems* or chiefs who derived additional revenue from grazing fees collected from them. In the 1960s every village below 4,000 feet in the Khasi-Jaintia Hills were inhabited by Nepali speakers, with little evidence of tribal authority being exercised in these tribal areas. In the erstwhile United Mikir Hill and North Cachar Hill districts (Assam), the Nepali graziers 'who keep large herds of cows and buffaloes' were reported to have penetrated deep into the interior of the district and established *Khuties (herdsmen sheds)* (United Mikir Hills and North Cachar Hills District Gazetteer, 1979) The graziers continued to be one of the major components of post-colonial Nepali migration to the North-East region.

The *Indo-Nepal Treaty of Peace and Friendship 1950*, the tripartite *Delhi Agreement of 1951* and *The Revised Indo-Nepal Treaty of 1956* recognized what was a de-facto situation existing from the British time (even earlier) by providing for a free and unrestricted reciprocal flow of nationals and goods of both countries with privileges to reside, own property and participate in economic activities. By mid-twentieth century, one in every ten Nepalis had migrated. In Nepal the migratory waves were caused by increasing fragmentation of landholding, indebtedness, ecological crisis through intense cultivation and deforestation, rising population without further land to cultivate and chronic deficits in food production in the hill areas of Central Nepal (Dutt, 1981). The annual rate of migration from Nepal in 1961 was 82,000 a year of whom 20,000 remained permanently per year in India. In the United East Khasi and Jaintia Hills districts the Nepalis numbered 19,721 or 5.42 per cent of the total population of the district. In the Naga Hills they formed 4.29 per cent (numbering 4,649) of the total population in the 1961 census. During 1951–1971 the Nepalis became demographically a significant group in Assam. Many Nepali leaders contested in the state electoral politics and were also elected to the Assam Legislature (Thapa, 1998). Construction of border roads inside NEFA (North Eastern Frontier Agency) led many Nepalis to migrate to Assam and NEFA. Many later settled down in Assam (Hussain, 1993).

Forging a "Nepali Identity" in the North-East

In North-East India the Nepali language which belongs to the Indo-Aryan family came to forge a sense of common ethnic identity amongst the various *jats* (then used to mean either ethnic groups or caste) who had migrated from Nepal during the colonial period. From the eighteenth century the Shah dynasty of Nepal tried to establish their rule based on the caste system and incorporated many ethnic groups mainly into the middle ranks of their caste hierarchy. This was reinforced and formalized under the Rana regime (1845–1951) which deliberately and consciously sought to mould its subjects by means of Hindu law leading to caste based social hierarchies and inequalities. In their social practices the higher castes, i.e., the Brahmins, Chettris and Thakurs were socially differentiated from the so-called *Matwalis* like the Magars, Gurung, Rai, Limboo who were more liberal as far as their eating habits and social relationships were concerned. In the initial stage the migrant Nepalis, however, identified themselves by their tribal identity as Magars, Gurung, Thapa, Limbu, Rais, etc., or caste identity in case of the Bahuns, Chettris etc. Each group had its own tribal language (*kura*) belonging mainly to the Tibeto-Burman family. In the early twentieth century, it was only the high caste Brahmin, Thakurs, Chettris and the other lower castes who identified themselves as Nepalis and spoke *Khaskura*. The early census reports of Assam identified the Nepalese migrants on the basis of their *jat* (here ethnic group within Nepal) as Gurung and Magars (these were then categorized as minor languages of Nepal) and only those who spoke *Khaskura* or Nepali were listed as Nepalis. The 1901 Census of Assam indicates that the migrants had begun identifying themselves as Nepali by 'caste' (sic) and language. Only if 'probed' (by census people) would they give their *jat* (ethnic identity). This happened due to the changed social context and necessity. As soldiers under the British a common identity as Gurkhas (this generic term was applied to the recruits from Nepal in the British Indian Army) came to develop amongst these various ethnic tribes. Nepali language was the *sine qua non* for the recruits in the Gurkha regiments. In Nepal *Khaskura* language had remained confined to the upper caste of Brahmin-Chettris and it could not easily form the link for linguistic and cultural affinity with the other groups of Nepalese who spoke Tibeto-Burman languages. In India the Tibeto-Burman speakers of Nepal, also picked up Nepali or *Khaskura.* In Darjeeling district of Bengal it was around the Nepali language that an identity as Nepalis/Gorkhas came to develop during the colonial period. In 1901 Census out of 53.8 per cent listed as Nepalese in Darjeeling district only 20 per cent returned as Khas or Nepali; the rest were recorded by their tribal languages (O'Malley, 1907: 47). The use of Nepali as the medium of instruction in the missionary schools and publication of texts and newspapers in Nepali and its use in 1918 as a vernacular by the University of Calcutta popularized and standardized the language. Nepali developed as the *linqua franca* and an important agency for constructing a common ethnic identity amongst the disparate people belonging to various caste and ethnic groups settled in Darjeeling. At present, the Nepalis settled in the North-East have almost completely forgotten their tribal dialects. The Nepali identification was probably given to them by the others who identified them by a generic term as Nepalis or Gorkhas who came from Nepal. Here, it was the larger social identification as a community known as Nepalis which was more apparent and predominant than their caste or separate ethnic identities. The long years of settlement in a distant land also relaxed strict observance of caste and social practices and impracticability of maintaining strict ethnic differentiation. The use of Nepali for communication between the various groups led to their being identified and identifying themselves as Nepalis on the basis of a common language. In the process, despite the social diversity of the Nepalis existing in terms of caste and ethnic composition, Nepali language became an important agency for the growth and consolidation of a wider, single ethnic identity as Nepalis. (The 71st Constitutional Amendment Act, 31st August, 1992 has included Nepali/Gorkha in the Eighth Schedule as one of the national languages of India).

In Assam the majority of the Nepalis (as distinct from the post-1950 settlers) due to their long settlement since the colonial period have integrated into the larger Assamese society and were identified as the Nepali *Asamiya.* During the freedom struggle, the

Nepalis supported the Assamese nationality in their struggle against the perceived threats to their existence posed by the increasing number of Bengali Muslims in Assam and the fear of being included in the proposed state of Pakistan. It is reported that a large number of Nepalis complied with the requests of the Assamese leaders and recorded their mother tongue as Assamese in the 1941 census. The first Annual conference of the Assam Pradeshik Gurkha Leaque held at Guwahati in January 1947, representing the Gurkhas of Assam confirmed its solidarity with the Assamese to oppose the Cabinet Mission Plan proposal to tag Assam with Bengal. The Nepalis have not only supported Assamese as the state language but also accepted it as a vernacular in the schools. Many Nepali litterateurs and writers have contributed to Assamese language and literature. Sri Hari Prasad Gorkha Rai of Kohima and D.B. Sonar of Shillong were associated with the Assam Sahitya Sabha from its early days. In the pre-independence period Dalbirsingh Lohar, a prominent Nepali leader in Assam was elected to the Assam Legislative Assembly in 1946 as a Congress candidate from Tinsukia constituency. While retaining their cultural identity, the Nepalis have contributed to the growth and development of a composite Assamese culture (Upadhyay, 1998: VII). The Nepalis also have adopted many Assamese social practices and customs. Many Assamese terms have entered into the vocabulary of the Nepali language in Assam. For the *Asamiya Nepalis*, their home or *basai* is Assam. The majority of old settlers inhabiting Manipur and other hill areas in Meghalaya, Mizoram and Nagaland got assimilated within the host community. Various aspects of assimilation included adoption of food habits, costumes, languages, intermarriages and participating in the activities taking place in the community. The occupations which they then chose did not clash with the interest and livelihood of the dominant host community. In various capacities as soldiers, dairy farmers, cultivators etc, they contributed to the economic development and consolidation of the region during the colonial period.

Political Fallout of Nepali Migration in Post-colonial Period

The year 1979 witnessed an important shift in the ongoing process of migration and socio-cultural assimilation that had been going on for more than a century. Cross-border migration came to be viewed as a threat and a security issue. It was the 1979–1985 Anti-Foreigners

National Movement in Assam initially directed against the Bangladeshis that drew attention to the fact that there was a large number of people of Nepalese origin in Assam. From illegal immigrants from Bangladesh the term foreign national was then widened to include the Nepalese migrants too. The All Assam Students Union (AASU) was the first to raise the cry of large-scale migration of Nepalese nationals into Assam and of being demographically overwhelmed in the near future.

Table 9.3

Nepali Population in Assam (1901–1991)

Year	*Nepalis in Assam*	*Percentage in Assam*
1901	21.347	0.35
1911	47.654	0.67
1921	70,344	0.94
1931	88,306	1.02
1951	1,01.338	1.26
1961	2,15,213	1.98
1971	3,49.116	2.38
1991	4,32,519	1.93

Source: Census of India, 1901–1971, 1991; M. Hussain, 1993: 258.

Mass demonstrations, collective threats and sporadic assaults were some of the means used to force the Nepalis out of Assam during the movement. No distinction was made between the Nepalis of Indian origin and the migrants coming from Nepal. As a result of this, a slow out-migration of frightened Nepalis from Assam was witnessed. Some of the families were forced to leave. An analyst of the movement observed, 'notwithstanding its popular character, the leadership of the movement failed to contain the anti-democratic, non-secular and violent tendencies generated by the movement itself particularly against the Hindu-Bengalis, Na-Asamiya Muslims and in some cases Nepalis living in the Brahmaputra Valley' (Hussain, 2000). There is no official record of how many Nepalis left Assam in the wake of the Assam movement but the Nepali intellectuals of Assam who have been observing the situation feel about five hundred families emigrated from different parts of Assam during the movement especially after the Nellie massacre (1983). These families mostly went back to Nepal while some dispersed to other states of the region where they had friends and relatives.

The Foreign National Movement of Assam had its repercussions in other states of the region, mainly Manipur and Meghalaya. In the princely state of Manipur there was a substantial settled Nepali population, descendants of graziers and of retired Gurkha soldiers who had been settled by the British in various colonies in the valley. Considering the contribution of the Gurkhas in the developmental process of the state and their long period of association, the Gurkhas were made the domiciled community in 1947 by the Manipur State Council. The total number of Nepalis in Manipur was 36,604 in 1971. As many as 100 Nepali Villages were spread over ten Assembly constituencies in the hills and plains of Manipur (Chettry, 2003: 315). Nepali candidates have been elected to the State Assembly from Kangpokpi and in the Sadar Hills Autonomous District Councils. Encouraged by the Assam Movement, the Meithei or Manipuri's also started a Foreign National Movement targeting the Nepalis. The Student Union took the onus of driving the 'foreigners' out of Manipur themselves. Several Nepali villages were burnt down in 1980, compelling a number of Nepalis to leave their settlement and flee to safer places. The riots of 1980 created fear and insecurity which led to the shifting of a few Gurkha houses from Pukhao to Kanglatombi, Kalapahar, Serou, etc. Again, there is no official record of the displaced Nepalis but estimates put it at 60–100 families. Some of the families who had temporarily settled in other neighbouring states like Nagaland returned as the situation cooled down.

In Mizoram, the permanent Nepali settlers, who are called Gorkhas, enjoyed certain benefits in the state with regard to employment, land settlement, trade, higher education etc. (the Census of 1951 listed 3,468 Nepalis in the then erstwhile Lushai Hills). But from the early 1980s situation began to change. An important reason for this was the migration into the state of Nepalese from Nepal and other states who were engaged as labourers, cow-herds and lumber-jacks. Since there were no specific criteria to distinguish the permanent settlers from the newcomers, the Government of Mizoram categorized all Nepalis as foreigners (Pradhan, 2003: 300). The State Government has accepted the figure of 4,453 as the number of Gorkhas who were in Mizoram before January 26, 1950 (Pradhan, 2009: 231). Total population of Mizoram as per 1991 Census is 6, 89,756. The state-wide Gorkha Census of Mizoram approved by the government in 1993 showed that there was 4,471 Gorkhas (0.64% of the total population). The growth rate of population of the Nepalis in Mizoram is thus negligible. Certain benefits that had been extended to permanent Nepali settlers and their descendants who were residing in Mizoram prior to 26 January 1950, on matters of education facilities, land settlement certificates, employment, trade, etc. were withdrawn by the government by a notification on 15 November 1992, succumbing to the pressure put by the Students Joint Action Committee. Confronted by this entire situation and feeling insecure a number of families are reported to have left Mizoram, though no official data are available. The Gorkhas, who were earlier categorized as Other Backward Classes (OBCs) when Mizo district was a part of Assam, is presently not recognized as such. Though the Gorkha community has been identified as OBC, by the Mandal Commission and the Government of India has approved it, the State Government has refused to extend this category to them thereby depriving them of reservation facilities arising out of such recognition.

The Nepalis and their direct descendants who have settled in Nagaland (erstwhile Naga Hills District) permanently prior to 31st December 1940, are treated as local non-Naga Gorkhas. They are included in the list of "educationally backward communities" and enjoy facilities similar to that of the Nagas. They are mainly settled in the urban towns especially in Kohima and Dimapur and employed in white-collar jobs and services. Those settled in rural areas work as cow herders and as sawyers. But here too the phenomenon of extortion and anti-outsider feelings has forced a number of families to leave the state. In the railway town of Dimapur, which had become a prime area from the 1980's, extortion was used as a means to terrorize the Nepalis, who had substantial landed property, to resort to distress sale. A number of such families who were thus displaced mostly went back to Nepal as well as Darjeeling. A large number of Nepalis settled at places near the Assam-Nagaland border have also been displaced due to the border clashes at Merapani, Bokajan, etc.

In Meghalaya, after the Bengalis the Nepalis constitute the second largest speaking minority. From the 1980's coal mining operations started in the Jaintia Hills on a large scale, which necessitated a huge labour force. Since the local people were mostly mine owners themselves or agriculturists, the supply of labour had to come from outside. The coal mines attracted a large number of immigrant Nepalese from Nepal as well as Nepalis from Darjeeling, where several tea gardens had just been shut down. The Nepalese formed a significant portion of this labour force and their immigration to Jaintia Hills became conspicuous. The 1987, Foreign National Movement in Meghalaya targeted the Nepali speakers. The Khasi students led agitation against the 'outsiders' led to large-scale violence against them and their deportment by the state outside its border. In a significant move the Government of Meghalaya sided with the demands of the student leaders for the expulsion of Nepalis from the state. The Government of Meghalaya detected 12,000 Nepali 'foreigners' of whom 7,000 to 10,000 were expelled in February-March 1987.

Construction of a 'Gorkha' Identity

Within the region "all" the Nepalis residing here are suspected of being Nepalese citizens and looked upon as 'foreigners'. The treaty of 1950 further compounds their problem. That their presence and settlement in the region is the outcome of a historical process predating the Indian independence is not widely known. In consequence, whether it is in Assam, Manipur or Meghalaya, the small community of Indian Nepalis have off and on become targets of hostile attacks from the dominant local population. Such reaction from the host community has to be seen in the global perspective where tribalism, ethnicity, xenophobia and ethnic conflicts have become widespread. In 1988 the Government of India, Ministry of Home Affairs had to issue a notification clearing the misconception of the citizenship of the Gorkhas settled in India. Since the AASU movement a definite process of constructing a separate identity as Indian Nepalis to distinguish them from the legal Nepalese citizen of Nepal is noticeable. A trend towards this can be seen in the demands being made to abrogate Clause VI and Clause VII of the 1950 Indo-Nepal Treaty to stop the unrestricted flow of nationals of both countries. A conscious change in the nomenclature of Nepali Associations to Gorkha is also noticeable. Within Nagaland, Manipur, Meghalaya and Mizoram the nomenclature "Gorkha" had been used for Nepali associations and organizations set up during the colonial period. Since 2002 the All Assam Nepali Students Union (set up in

1976) has been renamed as All Assam Gorkha Students Union. To secure constitutional identity and all round development of the settled Gorkhas in Assam, from 2002 the Gorkha Students Union has raised a popular demand for a Gorkha Autonomous Council within Assam. In January 2009, the Government of Assam has announced the setting up of autonomous councils for seven ethnic groups including the Gorkhas. The present political assertion of the Nepalis reflects the concern of the community for establishing a distinct Indian Nepali identity and for a recognized social and political space within Assam. The issue of Nepali displacement in the North-East in the nineteen eighties was one of the major issues leading to the Gorkha National Liberation Front (GNLF) movement for a separate state for the Indian Nepalis in Darjeeling. A Gorkhaland state it was felt would clear the general misconception about the political identity of the Indian Nepalis as Indian nationals. The support for a separate state of the Gorkhas in Darjeeling by the Nepalis in North-East India has to be located within this socio-historic context. However, there is insinuation by detractors of the Gorkhaland State, of a political conspiracy on the part of Indian Nepalis to establish a Greater Nepal. Politics is thus continued to be played on what is a *legitimate constitutional* demand of the Indian Nepalis of Darjeeling for a separate state of Gorkhaland within the Indian Union. The support for Gorkhaland by the Nepalis outside West Bengal is largely due to the perceived implication and necessity to carve out a separate identity as Indian nationals distinct from the Nepalese nationals of Nepal. The process towards establishing and consolidation of such an identity can be seen in the various organizations and associations to set them up at the state, regional and national levels.

Shifting Trend in Nepalese Migration to the North-East

The North-East is no more a favourite destination for Nepalese migrants. From the 1950s onwards the malaria infested Terai frontier in the plains stretching from the east-westward along the Indo-Nepal border has accounted for nearly 80 per cent of hill migration from Nepal. The Nepal Census of 1981 showed an increase in internal migration from 4, 45,000 in 1971 to almost 9, 30,000 in 1981.This would have certainly reduced the scale of migration to the North-East. Migration from Nepal to India has also been declining. Increasing trend was observed for the periods 1901–11, 1921–31 and

1951–61; and decreasing trend for the period 1911–21, 1931–51, 1971–81 and 1981–1991 During 1971–81 and 1981–1991 the volume of immigrants to India has fallen significantly (Datta, 2002). In the 1961 Census of India the Nepal-born population in India constituted 0.11 per cent, in 1971 0.9 per cent, in 1981 0.07 per cent and in 1991 about.06 per cent. Emigration to India has generally been temporary involving poor people who migrate seasonally to India in search of jobs and for trade to supplement the family income (UN, ESCAP, 1980). The prospects of employment in India as manual labourers for Nepalese migrants who are generally uneducated and unskilled; as well as recruitment in the Indian Army for Nepalese are becoming increasingly limited (Ghimire, 1992: 182). Recruitment of men from Nepal into the Indian Army has also declined. Within Nepal there is an increasing opposition to the Gurkha recruitment which "is being viewed as an affront to the national honour of Nepal" by its detractors. The Gurkhas from Nepal constitute nearly 5 per cent of the strength of the Indian Army (Sinha, 1986: 83). The Census of 1991(Nepal) shows that during 1981–1991, 3.6 per cent (6,58,337) of its total population emigrated out of which 89.2 per cent went to India. About 3.05 and 0.96 per cent emigrated to other Asian countries and South Arabia respectively. The 2001 census of Nepal revealed that during 1991–2001 the number of Nepal emigrants to India have declined to 68 per cent, while emigration to South Arabia had increased up to 8.9 per cent. Nepalese labour is presently shifting to the Gulf and other South Asian countries which are more lucrative financially. An analysis of Nepali migrant workers in 2001 by the Nepal Institute for Development Studies for UNIFEM, the women's fund at the United Nations, revealed that two-thirds of Nepalese working overseas were employed in the Gulf, mainly in South Arabia (42%), Qatar (11.5%) and UAE (9%) (Seddon, 2005: 4). Since the nineteen eighties the social forces generating Nepalese emigration and the political and economic situation in the North-East have undergone a change. Insurgency and separatist movement has affected internal security and economic development of the region discouraging the Nepalese poor. The likelihood of outward migration of Indian Nepalis from the North-East in search of better economic prospects is bound to grow as they find themselves increasingly marginalized and their mobility limited in terms of employment in state services and participation in political and economic opportunities in a polity where numbers and protective discrimination like reservations matter.

In the ultimate analysis, the Nepali migration and their subsequent settlement in the North-East was part of the historical process fostered by the colonial situation and specific conditions existing and operating in Nepal and North-East India. Beginning with the occupation of Lower Assam (1828), the British colonial state tried to develop the productive forces of the region, then dense and thinly inhabited, by bringing wastelands under agriculture, encouraging cash crop production like tea, commercial activity and developing communication through railways etc. As a result of all these Assam had become a receiving economy. The human movement to the North-East in the form of migration had taken place under these colonial conditions (Gurung, 2003: 81). Like many of the challenges post-colonial India faces the issues relating to the migration and settlement of Nepalis also originated in the colonial period. The British colonial state used the physical resources, the resilience and sentiment of loyalty of the Nepalis in consolidating the empire in the North-East then a frontier region. It was the British political dispensation which provided opportunities to these hardy people to come here for a living and subsequently to settle down. In the process along with the other migrant communities, the Nepalis have contributed significantly towards the political consolidation and socio-economic development of the region. However, in the post-colonial period, the political, social and economic forces operating in the South Asian region and in the global context have changed. The phenomenon of the creation of modern nation-states in South Asia has contributed to the present-day conflictual nature of migration in a region where earlier people have moved freely with little or no regard for boundaries or legal conception of citizenship.

References

Baruah, S. 2001. *India against Itself: Assam and the Politics of Nationality.* New Delhi: Oxford University Press.

Census of India. 1961. Part-1. *A General Report.* Vol. 3. Assam.

Chatterjee, S. 1990. *Mizoram Encyclopaedia.* Bombay: Jaico Publishing House.

Chatterjee, S.K. 1970. *The Place of Assam in the History and Civilization of India.* Gauhati: Gauhati University.

Chettry, G.K.N. 2003. 'The Nepalis in Manipur: Movement and Settlement', in A.C. Sinha and T.B. Subba (eds), *The Nepalis in India: A Community in Search of Indian Identity*. Delhi: Indus Publication, 304–318.

Chhetry, D.B. 2009. 'Nepalis and Bangladeshis: A Comparative Study', in T.B. Subba et al. (eds), *Indian Nepalis: Issues and Perspectives*. New Delhi: Concept Publishing, 351–361.

Datta, P. 2002. Nepali Migration to India. Paper presented at the IUSSP Conference on *Southeast Asia's Population in a Changing Asian Context*. Bangkok, Thailand.

Dutt, S. 1981. 'Migration and Development: Nepalis in North-East India', *Economic and Political Weekly*, 13(24): 1053–1054.

Gazetteer of India: Assam State. 1979. United Mikir and Cachar Hills District. Guwahati: Government of Assam.

Ghimire, K. 1992. *Forest or Farm? The Politics of Poverty and Land Hunger in Nepal*. Delhi:

Guha, A. 1977. *Planter-Raj to Swaraj: Freedom Struggle and Electoral Politics in Assam, 1847–1947*. New Delhi: Indian Council of Historical Research.

Gurung, T. 2002. 'Displacing the Displaced: The Nepalis in Northeast India', in C.J. Thomas (ed.), *Dimensions of Displaced People in Northeast India*. New Delhi: Regency Publications, 149–158.

—. 2003. 'Colonial State and Nepali Grazier Migration in Manipur', in *Northeast India Historical Association Proceedings*, Shillong: Guwahati Session, 271–278.

—. 2003. 'Human Movement and Colonial State: A Study of the Nepalis in North-East India under the British Empire', in A.C. Sinha and T.B. Subba (eds), op. cit., 172–183.

—. 2008. 'Nepali Grazier Migration and the Rise of Dairy Farming in Northeast India', in D.R. Syiemlieh and M. Sharma (eds), *Society and Economy in Northeast India during the Nineteenth and Twentieth Century*. New Delhi: Regency Publications, 159–171.

Hussain, M. 1993. *The Assam Movement: Class, Ideology and Identity*. Delhi: Manak Publications.

Mangalam, J. 1968. *Human Migration*. Lexington: University of Kentucky Press.

Nag, S. 2003. 'The Fei-isation of the Nepalis in Northeast India', in A.C. Sinha and T.B. Subba (eds), op. cit., 184–193.

O'Malley, L.S.S. 1907. *Bengal District Gazetteers: Darjeeling*. 2nd edn. Calcutta: Bengal Secretariat Book Depot.

Pemberton, R.B. 1835. *Report on the Eastern Frontier of Bengal*. Gauhati: DHAS.

Pradhan, K.L. 2003. 'The Gorkhas of Mizoram', in A.C. Sinha and T.B. Subba (eds), op. cit., 300–301.

—. 2009. 'Mizoram Gorkhas: Issues and Problems', in T.B. Subba et al. (eds), op. cit., 225–236.

Rengmi, M.C. 1971. *A Study of Nepali Economic History, 1768–1847.* New Delhi: Manjushri Publishing House.

Rose, E. Leo. 1973. *Nepal Strategy for Survival.* Delhi: Rawat Publications.

Seddon, D. 2005. Nepal's Dependence on Exporting Labour, available online: http://migration information.org/Feature/display.cfm?id=277.

Singh, J.P. 1980. *Urban Land Use Planning in Hill Areas.* Delhi: Inter-India Publications.

Sinha, A.C. 2003. 'The Indian North East Frontier and the Nepali Immigration', in A.C. Sinha and T.B. Subba (eds), op. cit., 31–53.

Sinha, S.K. 1986. 'Class Composition of the Army', *Indian Defense Review*, 1: 48–62.

Thapa, R. 1998. 'Nepalese Participation in Electoral Politics of Assam', in Girin Phukon and Adil-ul-Yasin (eds), *Working of Parliamentary Democracy and Electoral Politics in North-East India.* New Delhi: South Asian Publishers, 139–149.

Upadhyay, K.P. 1998. *The Nepalese in Assam.* Guwahati: Offset Printers.

Weiner, M. 1993. 'Rejected Peoples and Unwanted Migrants in South Asia', *Economic and Political Weekly*, 28(3): 1737–1746.

—. 2003. "Nepali Participation in the Electoral Politics of Assam', in A.C. Sinha and T.B. Subba (eds), op. cit., 250–261.

10

The Ongoing Naga Traditional Authority Under State Structure

I.L. AIER

By 'Naga traditional authority,' we simply mean the politico-administrative institutions which are moored upon primordial sentiments, traditional values and practices and based on unwritten code of law, power and rule. These traditional authority institutions are identified with the village councils and chiefdoms of the Naga tribals. Here, 'the Naga tribals' refer to those of Nagaland state. In response to the exercise of traditional authority, as stated by elders about those traditional times and also as observed today, *obedience* or *adherence* to a command is a natural reflex, similar to Weber's "imperative coordination". That such coordinated obedience in the case of the Naga tribesmen then and now to the centre of authority echos Weber's analysis of traditional authority (1947: 56). In the case of the Naga tribals, traditional authority rests on the *beliefs, sanctity, and therefore legitimacy* of what is understood to be traditional.

From the above, certain aspects become clearer on analysis and comparison. Weber's type of authority is described to be autocratic and which in comparison with the Naga tribal's case finds similarity with the chiefdoms of the Angh of the Konyak tribe (Haimendorf, 1969: 38) and the *Akekao* of the Sema tribe (Hutton, 1921: 180–181). These two chiefdoms are described to be highly autocratic. With both the tribes, succession to be the chief is determined by birth, the rule of primogeniture being the basis. Thus with the Sema tribe the eldest son succeeds the chief. The Konyak Angh chiefdoms consist of multiple villages and succession is determined by the eldest male born. The Lotha tribe in each village possesses a chief called *Pvuti* assisted by a clan representative council called *Tongti.* The *Pvuti* generally is identified as overbearing and arrogant (Aier, 2006: 39).

Of other Naga tribes and their village councils (a loose English translation from vernacular term), for the Ao tribe it is called *Putu Menden* (seat of a generation). This seat of a generation is represented by elder members of each clan in a village with a modern day equivalent of a chairman called Tsunger/Onger. They were responsible for all matters of policy, administration and justice. With the Sangtam tribe, they have the *Yangpumji* (village council) constituted by the *Lakhimru* (council of elders) representing each clan in the village and its function share similarity with that of the Ao tribe (Aier, 2006: 37). With the Angami tribe, the village is organized simply to reflect an image of unity of the community: the reality being that within the village each locality represented a particular clan exhibiting independent existence from that of other locality/clans (Capt. Butler's Report, 1873). However, for general convenience of all, a council of elders operates representing all the localities/clans. The Angami village also maintains a chief of sorts called *Pehuma* whose sole role is to lead the village warriors during war or in a raid and thus with no privileges or continuity of line as with the Sema, Konyak and Lotha chiefs (Gundevia, 1975: 25).

Here, in identifying Naga traditional authority of the various tribal groups, we are presented with two fundamentally different structures. One is that of autocratic seats of authority as is the case with the Sema, Konyak and Lotha tribes. The other is that of representative type of authority as it is found among the Ao, Sangtam and the Angami tribes. These tribes mentioned here are just a few representative samples out of 17 major tribes in Nagaland state. Also, it is to be noted that in spite of the variations in the structure of the traditional authority seats, what is common among them is that they are all based on their *beliefs, sanctity* and therefore *legitimacy* of what they understand to be traditional. We have refrained from discussing the function, powers and jurisdictions of these traditional institutions except for some passing mention of their activities, as the focus of this paper is to do with a different issue.

Gait (1967) states that through the Treaty of Yandabao of 1826, the British colonial power established itself in the Ahom period of rule in Assam, which eventually encompassed the entire region that today is the North-East India. Inevitably, the Naga tribes and their habitat as stated earlier were brought under British colonial control in 1878. Colonial control and policies then laid the seeds of many consequences which went a long way as to determine and establish the predicament of the seeds of traditional authority now under discussion.

The control over the hills started in gradual stages. In 1866, the British made the hills inhabited by the Angami, Ao, Lotha, Rengma and Sema into the Naga Hills District under the control of a Deputy Commissioner, based at Sibsagar, Assam. At this stage, the British pursued the policy of non-interference or 'mere political control' from afar (Yaden, 1970: 14). However, tribal aggressiveness, occasioned by raids into British administered plains of Assam and Manipur, affected a change in British policy: a proposal for gradual physical occupation of the hills and control of the tribals was formulated (Ao, 1958: 55).

The Lotha tribal area was annexed by the British in 1875. In the same year, through the permission of the British Secretary of State, London, the policy of physical occupation/control materialized. Accordingly, Kohima (presently the state capital) was occupied in 1878 as the headquarters of the Political Officer of the Naga Hills. In the same year, Wokha in the Lotha area was occupied *(Nagaland Gazetteer* Wokha 1973: 6). The Sema tribe and area were brought under control in 1884, marked by the capture of Lungtang village. Again this was followed by the eventual control of the Ao tribe, with the area headquarter established at Mokokchung in 1888 (Ao, 1958: 74–75).

Prior to the above, it is pertinent to state here that in the absence of documented records and therefore, resorting to oral history, the different Naga tribes existed in their respective ecological niches. Oral history informs us that most of these tribal groups knew only those immediate neighbouring tribes and were unaware of the existence of other tribesmen on the hilly expanse. Of this, Elwin's edited book (1967) is a lone ready reference, which provides images of hill tribesmen existing in isolation and ignorance of others. Besides this, there are some more documented reports of Naga tribesmen, of the Ao and Konyak in particular, of having an ambivalent relationship with the Ahom kingdom and subjects of Assam, as recorded in the Ahom Buranji (Baruah, 1985).

The colonial presence on the hills meant political and administrative control of the tribesmen, who hitherto had never known control of their lives and activities by anybody, much less an alien people. The colonial power pursued a policy of "non-interference" in so far as local customary practices and internal power arrangements were concerned. However, in exertion of their superordinate power, colonial control meant that the traditional Naga villages lost its age-old practice of independent self-governance as a compact unit. Realistically, traditional Naga village chiefs and village councils lost their independent existence and unfettered way of life that they enjoyed since time immemorial. Here, *monetization* of the hitherto moneyless barter-exchange economy, by levy of house tax upon the tribesmen meant acceptance and recognition of a superordinate power on the part of the tribal population and their now subdued local chief and the village council authority. Further, monetization also meant economic, political and social control.

A levy of annual house tax in 1877 formalized the monetization of the then barter economy which for the Angami and Ao tribes was ₹ 2 while for the others it was ₹ 5 depending on expenditure incurred in running the administrative/military affairs (Yonou, 1974: 110). The consequence of monetization was to usher in a form of *economic control* in the sense that the tribesmen slowly had to regulate their agricultural activities into a tight time schedule so that immediately after the harvest, able males of each household would flock to the plains of Assam to sell their physical labour for money by clearing jungles for the expanding tea gardens and work in the administrative and military camps clearing land for housing developments. What was earned was not for personal/family gain but to be paid to a foreign ruler to enable them to administer more effectively over the tribesmen! It further ushered in a form of new social control of proscribing inter-village and tribal hostilities and violence, so far a characteristic of their daily existence. What is peculiarly amusing in this is that the tribesmen's submission to colonial power and to work to earn cash to pay their rulers (in the name of house tax) to enable them to militarily and administratively control the subject population gains much irony. Consequently, what emerged out of all this was a collective tribal consciousness of sharing a common master and by identification, a common foreign enemy.

As a further measure of losing their stature and power for that of the traditional authority, *dobashis* (language interpreters) were appointed from among the various tribes by the new dispensation to assist them in matters of communication of administration and adjudication (*Assam Secretariat Report,* 1866). This represented another level of authority to the traditional village authority to contend with; wherein their attempt to contact the colonial super ordinate authority could only be done through the dobashis. The *dobashi* seats were institutionalized when its role and status was provided formal sanction in 1914. This rendered the *dobashi* institution into a semi-judicial body based on Naga customary law. Consequently, being a *dobashi* and a paid functionary meant rising above the traditional village polity and authority of chiefs and councils; a new form of mobility. Practically, they proved to be the real executors of colonial government policy aside from the duty of interpretation and collection of revenue.

The semi-judicial function of the *dobashis* eventually led to forming the *dobashi court* where any type litigation between individuals, parties and villages was tried by it. Such courts emerged to serve each tribe respectively, on the basis of customary law which may be understood as those customary beliefs, norms and practices through time to regulate and control society, besides passing judgement to provide justice and punishment. These laws were all oral and even contemporarily, most Naga tribes' customary laws are still to be compiled. These courts from the early days were understood at large to serve the needs of the community. Consequently, the orders, decree and judgements of Naga tribal chiefs and village council traditional authority began to meet defiance from aggrieved parties; in that they would not comply, show obedience or adherence as traditionally expected and ignoring the judgements made, seek review, redressal and revocation from the *dobashi court* which to the tribal common man was seen and accepted as higher and more powerful.

If colonial control demolished the Naga traditional authority of chiefs and councils as the highest arbiter and decision-maker in the villages, the *dobashi* institution further weakened them. That is to say, the *dobashis* being empowered could on the basis of their respective tribal customary laws try and arbitrate in any matter of litigation involving tribal individuals. Inevitably the *dobashi court* became the chief arbiter of what once was the omnipotent function of the traditional chiefs and councils. The *dobashis* were chosen out of the tribal rank and file in a way overriding and surpassing the dignity of the traditional seats of authority directly. Then, for the new appointees *(dobashis)* it proved to be matter of social mobility and consequently, a change of fortune for kith and kin by gaining emancipation from past lowly status and a doorway found to better and newer prospects. These *dobashis,* during the colonial period were located at Kohima as the district headquarters and Mokokchung as sub-divisional headquarter. In Kohima, the dobashis represented the tribes known today as Angami, Chakhesang, Rengma, Zeliangs while in Mokokchung, they represented the Ao, Lotha, Sema, Sangtam & Chang.

The above arrangement continued till the achievement of Indian independence and the creation of the state of Nagaland in 1963. It would not be wrong to state here that through these years, the *dobashi* institution rendered yeoman's services to state authority. It would also be correct to spell out that the traditional seats of authority, although having much of their stature and functional strength diminished, sustained as repositories and carriers of what are traditional life and ways.

In 1973, the Government of Nagaland realizing the role and importance of traditional seats of authority in relation to state policies of development and change enacted the Nagaland Village and Area Council Act (Ao, 1993). In short, this act gave legal recognition and formal sanction of the traditional seats of authority which were reorganized as *Naga village councils,* wherein all the council clan representatives are recognized as formal members representing the traditional structure and ways. Into it are embedded government representatives called *gaonburas* (village elders), which is seen as the state trying to exercise greater influence over the traditional institutions. The *gaonburas* as an institution was historically formalized by colonial office in 1895 (Sub Divisional Office Record, Mokokchung). In the early years, they served as messengers and heralds, generally supervized by the *dobashis.* Presently, the *gaonbura* presence in the village council side by side with the traditionally based representatives means further diffusion of traditional authority of a process begun with the invention of the *dobashi* institution in the 19th century. Thus from 1973 onwards, Naga traditional authority has slid into a strata and position within a colonial invented structure of having the *dobashis* and furthermore, the state structure above it as in a stratified syndrome.

The Nagaland Village and Area Council Act of 1973, it is said, was a well meaning step and an expression of concern on the part of the state government. It was ostensibly intended to strengthen and preserve the traditional seats of authority as significant aspects of Naga culture and traditional practices. It was also envisaged as a measure of change (of continuity) by linking it to state authority by the infusion of *gaonburas* (government representatives) into the village council. In the process, the status and function of the *chiefs* (Angh Akikao, Puvuti) as it would appear, were not provided adequate study and concern as what would be their exact position, particularly under the structures of state authority. We would conjecture that out of democratic concern and principles as opposed to the autocratic nature of the traditional state of Naga chiefs, they were summarily reduced in status and function, to that of the clan representatives in the village council. That is to say in effect, they were reduced to being nothing more than common men.

Consequently and under ongoing perspective, the seat of the traditional *chiefs* are still evident in its function of being a repository of traditional knowledge, customs and practices. The seat of the *chief* still enjoys respect and is accorded public services to a certain extent although they are not exactly reflective and reproduction of past prestige. Those chiefs with personal merit and personality do manage to be in the village public eye and thus for ceremonial purposes during various cultural celebrations manage to be invited as the chief guests and have their past glory recreated, however temporarily.

It is further noted that in spite of the 1973 Nagaland Village and Area Council Act in revamping and strengthening the Naga village councils as traditional authority, there are other new entities of state creation, such as the *Village Development Board* (VDB) which in many cases compromises traditional authority. These boards are generally constituted as per government rules, by village school teachers and other free individuals who are, to a degree, considered knowledgeable. Thus, to do with village development schemes under state funding, by virtue of their position of being more knowledgeable than that of the village council, most developmental projects results in favouring members of the VDB directly or indirectly side-lining decisions of traditional authority. The acts of manipulation here are not overruled.

The role of state politics, political parties and politicians is an important factor that severely retards traditional authority. For instance, in those matters of village developmental projects funded by state for agriculture, soil conservation, forestry, water supply et.al, the village community involvement through provision of physical labour and earn wages is a common feature. However, if a section of the village community feels slighted, ignored or feel under-represented – and who has allegiance to the ruling political party in the government, will practically see to it that the village councils are compelled to cancel or change or rearrange the work programmes. Such interferences further weaken the role and functions of traditional authority.

In matters of litigation within the villages, politicians and political parties most often bear upon village council judgements and decisions. That is if the person or party has been ruled against and who happen to provide support to the dominant political party easily has the rulings revised or altered by state intervention. Here too, the traditional authority gets severely marginalized, if not sidelined altogether.

Further illustrations of contemporary predicament of the Naga traditional seats of authority are that any litigation in the villages that come under the purview of the village council and its pronouncement of judgement does not conclude the case therein: but further recourse taken to by dissatisfied parties to appeal to higher courts that are permitted by the judiciary structure of contemporary state authority which very much compromises the position of traditional authority. This practice and pattern does not reflect nor establish weakness and deficiency of the efficacy of traditional customary law and sanction. However, the modern democratic state authority and its superordinate position as higher proves to be another avenue to seek justice above the sanction of the village councils, that renders them to be irrelevant, inadequate and thus an oddity under contemporary settings.

The role of modern lawyers in towns and district headquarters prove to be another factor that significantly marginalizes the role of the traditional authority. Disgruntled parties from the villages in the hope that state courts would upturn verdicts passed upon them take recourse to hiring the services of lawyers. The lawyers virtually represent, the Constitution of India and what it entails in the various structure and levels of the Indian judicial system. These are aspects that members of traditional authority are only remotely aware of and least prepared to contend with. Most of all, the traditional seats of authority do not enjoy or have any superordinate state authority arrangements or provisions that qualify their judgements/decisions as final, conclusive and non-revocable and therefore non-transferrable. The absence of this provision is the biggest loophole, it is felt, that marginalizes traditional authority. In these ways the role and function of lawyers end up compromising and negating the seats of Naga traditional authority, in addition to the action of disgruntled parties who are also not far from blame.

The ideals of democracy simply speaking provide every man much latitude of freedom, liberty and justice in established as well as perceived ways. In many ways, it is true of India at large and also that of the Naga tribesmen in Nagaland state. Thus, in spite of the *beliefs, sanctity and legitimacy* thereof of Naga traditional authority in addition to the provisions of Article 371 (A) of the Indian Constitution (an omnibus that establishes, ratifies and justifies the role and function of Naga traditional authority by interpretation), it is seen that it is the so described democratized Naga individual and groups that negates the status and role of Naga traditional authority to begin with. How democratized they are intrinsically is a matter of speculation. However, it would appear that democratic spirit and practice in the present context of Naga society have lost respect for traditional authority. Into this, comes in the role of the *dobashis,* politicians, political parties and lawyers that ultimately reduces the role, function and status of Naga traditional authority. Most of all, as stated earlier, there are no legislations from the national to the state level that specifically provides that all village litigants are conclusively bound and subject to the decision and judgement of the seats of Naga traditional authority, and therefore non-transferrable anywhere, even as a measure of respect to village territorial jurisdiction and that of the traditional aspects that it represents.

By all the above, Naga traditional authority contemporarily is observed to be a neutralized entity, notwithstanding the cultural role of perpetuating tradition, customs and its practices. Questions abound as to how long Naga traditional authority can sustain just as it applies to Polynesian islanders about which Goldman's (1955) framework of study has been amply applicable here in addition to mentioning certain similarities of inner dynamics of power in the two divergent communities. Finally beginning from traditional/pre-colonial to contemporary situations, Naga tribal attitudinal position to authority as such also brings to focus Navajo ways and authority system (Shepardson, 1963). These far flung apart communities in comparison are ongoing examples of marginalized entities overshadowed by greater state structure and authority, while like many others, pitted against globalization process simply pale into insignificance. However, by a process of comparison and drawing out patterns and features of similarity and providing it magnification in the proper fora hopefully would draw attention and place these institutions in their proper settings.

References

Aier, I.L. 2006. *Contemporary Naga Social Formulations and Ethnic Identity*. New Delhi: Akansha Publishing House.

Ao, A.L. 1993. *Rural Development in Nagaland*. New Delhi: Har-Anand Publications.

Ao, Tajenyuba. 1958. *A History of Anglo-Naga Affairs*. Gauhati: Eastern Printers.

Baruah, B.S. 1985. *Ahom Buranji*. Guwahati: Spectrum Publications, Reprint.

Butler, Capt. J. 1875. 'Rough Notes on the Angami', *Journal of Asiatic Society*, 25(4): 53–55.

Elwin, Verrier. 1967. *Nagas in the Nineteenth Century*. Delhi: Oxford University Press.

Fuhrer-Haimendorf, C.V. 1969. *The Konyak Nagas*. London: Holt and Rinehart.

Gait, E.A. 1967. *History of Assam*. 3rd rev edn. Calcutta: Thacker & Spink.

Goldman, Irving. 1955. 'Status Rivalry and Cultural Evolution in Polynesia', in Ronald Cohen and John Middleton (eds), *Comparative Political Systems: Studies in Politics of Pre-industrial Societies*. New York: The American Natural History Press, 375–395.

Gundevia, Y. 1975. *War and Peace in Nagaland*. Dehradun: Palit & Palit Publications.

Hutton, J.H. 1921. *The Sema Nagas*. London: Oxford University Press.

Shepardson, M. 1963. 'The Navajo Ways in Government: A Study in Political Process', *American Anthropologist*, 65(3): 46–72.

Weber, Max. 1947. *The Theory of Social and Economic Organization*. Glencoe, Ill.: Free Press.

Yaden, L.L. 1970. *Nagaland*. New Delhi: Laxmi Press.

Yonou, Asoso. 1974. *The Rising Nagas*. New Delhi: Vikas Publications.

Select Official Sources

1. *Assam Secretariat Report* No. 4728, File No. 305, Dt. 29/10/1866.
2. *Sub-Divisional Officer Record* Mokokchung, 1895.
3. *Nagaland Gazetteer* Wokha, 1967. Government of Nagaland, Kohim.

11

Entrepreneurial Development in the North-East India

PARIYARAM M. CHACKO

Economic Development

After the World War II, some economists admitted that "really fundamental problems of economic development are non-economic" (Buchanan and Ellis, 1955: 9). Many developmental plans depend for their success on religious beliefs, values, kinship, education and politics. Polanyi says that "the human economy is embedded and enmeshed in institutions, economic and non-economic. The inclusion of the non-economic is vital" (Polanyi et al., 1957: 250). For Hoselitz, economic growth can take off when traditional culture changes from a system of particularism, diffused economic activity and ascription to a system of universalism, achievement orientation and functional specificity (Hoselitz, 1960: 19). Max Weber was one of the first to systematically examine the relationship between religion and economic development. He posited a positive relationship between the rise of the spirit of capitalism and the Protestant ethic (Weber, 1950). He also argued that Hinduism hindered economic growth (Weber, 1960).

Entrepreneurship

Entrepreneurship is an important component of economic growth. To study the entrepreneur is to study the central figures in modern economic history (Cole, 1946: 8).

Defining the concept of entrepreneurship is problematic. The term has been used to refer not only to industrial owners and managers, but also to cultivators (Sayigh, 1962: 26) and educationists (Young, 1971: 147). Milton Singer (1972: 283) calls even a Minister of Industries in a state government as an entrepreneur. The entrepreneur as a unique risk-bearer was identified by Richard Cantillon in the beginning of the 18th century (Cochran, 1968: 88). Joseph Schumpeter stressed innovation as the distinguishing mark of entrepreneurship, which is simply doing of new things or the doing of things that are done in a new way (1947: 51). He names the carrying out new combinations as enterprises and the individuals whose function it is to run them as entrepreneurs (1961: 74–75). Everett Hagen (1962) introduced the concept of creative personality who is characterized by a high need for achievement. An element that brings about development is an historical shift in the status of certain groups within the society. Individuals from the victimized and marginalized groups suffering from status withdrawal (Ibid.: 185) become leading businessmen. Satish Saberwal (1972) has applied this concept to an Indian case study. Ramgarhias, a Sikh occupational group, traditionally in a low level of economic progress, achieved significant success in business activities. The withdrawal of status with conditional conferral of status respect played a great part in their transformation as leading businessmen. David McClelland (1961) introduces a psychological factor, the need for achievement. Child-rearing practices which emphasize high standard of excellence, material growth and self-reliance produce a high need for motivation for success. McClelland collaborated with the Small Industry Extension Training (SIET) Institute in Hyderabad to carry out research and training in entrepreneurship in Andhra Pradesh and Tamil Nadu The finding pointed out that entrepreneurial capacity could be developed through training and follow-up interventions (Nagayya, 2000: 34).

As per Global Entrepreneurship Monitor, there are two classes of entrepreneurial activities. Opportunity entrepreneurship is manifest among those who have taken up business as an opportunity to increase their income. The necessity-driven entrepreneurship includes all those who have been pushed into it for lack of any other useful profession (Bhattacharya, 2008: 86–87). Most of these latter firms are based on low technology and are not very innovative. Most of the businesses in India are necessity-driven. However, it should be borne in mind that the small businesses in the unorganized sector provide 79 per cent of India's non-agricultural employment (Sundaram, 2008: 4). According to Bhattacharya (2008: 94), "India has a large number of micro and small enterprises who account for about 90 per cent of the total employment in the country".

Business Communities

Specialization of economic roles by certain caste group in India helped the growth of trading and business. "An analysis of entrepreneurship can thus be viewed in terms of social community and caste of entrepreneurs in various regions", says Nafziger (1971: 293). In northern India, the term *banya* is used to denote any merchant. Gadgil (1959) has given a broad outline of the castes that were responsible for trading activities in the various parts of India in the 16th century. According to him, the Marwaris played a predominant role in the trading business activities in the North-East India (Ibid.: 19). Kinship and family system have positive influence on the development of entrepreneurship. Kinship networks consolidated the French businessmen (Smelser, 1965: 59). Medhora (1965) discusses the leading business communities and concludes that the Indian family system affects favourably the rise of industrialists. Agarwala (1955) pointed out that the joint family was the backbone of the Marwari community. Singer (1972) finds structural and organizational parallelism, between joint family and business management among the Madras industrialists.

Entrepreneurship in North-East India

The beginning of entrepreneurship development programmes in the North-East was made by the Assam government in 1973 by starting Entrepreneurial Motivation Training Centres (EMTC) and with the establishment of the North-East Regional Centre of SIET Institute in Guwahati in 1979. This centre later became the Indian Institute of Entrepreneurship in 1994. The North-Eastern Industrial and Technical Consultancy Organization (NEITCO) and North-Eastern Consultancy Organization (NEICON) carry out entrepreneurial development programmes. Apart from North-Eastern Council, other institutions such as Small Industries Service Institute (SISI), Industrial Development Bank of India (IDBI) offer assistance to entrepreneurs.

Centrally-sponsored Growth Centres Scheme has been in operation since 1988 for helping set up industrial units in the North-East India.

As per a survey carried out in 1996 by the Ministry of Industry, the North-East India had 37770 small scale industrial units. Out of these 49.3 per cent were found in Assam, Arunachal had 3.2 per cent, Manipur, 13.3 per cent, Meghalaya, 5.2 per cent, Mizoram, 7.6 per cent, Nagaland, 2 per cent and Tripura had 19.4 per cent (Nagayya, 2000: 47).

D.D. Mali shows that an area approach was successful for the small-scale business ventures. Out of 169 persons trained by the Indian Institute of Entrepreneurship (Guwahati), 137 prepared project reports, 104 applied for loans and 76 units were established during 1996–98. These consist of manufacturing, fruit processing, *supari* making, automobile servicing and small transport operations. Out of these 76 establishments, women owned 15 of them. Roughly 50 per cent of the owners were below the age of 30. The majority of the entrepreneurs were educated up to school level, though there were some degree holders and professionally trained people. Atul Bora (2000: 70) suggests establishing ancillary industries for Oil India Ltd, Oil and Natural Gas Corporation and Railways. However, such contract arrangement in the public sector is not very successful on account of low technology used by ancillary unit owners. Maruti Suzuki Udyog Ltd. has achieved great a success in sub-contracting (Odaka and Kiyokawa, 2008).

Gautam Dutta (2000: 72–88) thinks that entrepreneurial development programme is an effective intervention. Out of 5375 persons trained in such programmes in the North-East India during the years from 1990 to 1996, data about 3713 were collected through interviews and questionnaire. It was revealed that 935 (25.2%) trainees set up establishments in industrial (wooden products, metal fabrication, weaving and bamboo works), commercial and service activities. Among them 161 were women. The majority of these business people were unemployed before starting their enterprises. It was also noticed that 63 per cent of the enterprises were self-financed. S.S. Khanka (2000: 103–112) says that the entrepreneurship programme should not confine itself to training and motivating, but also should be engaged in supporting and sustaining their new ventures. G.P. Prasin (2000: 139–145) made a survey of 50 tribal entrepreneurs of Charchandpur District of Manipur. It was found that the majority were unemployed before taking up business. Twenty-four, out of 50, were women. Choudhury (2000: 175) finds that Assam has 18 per cent women entrepreneurs as against 7.7 per cent in India as a whole. In a survey of 250 women entrepreneurs, 127 of them were in textile-based industries. In the North-East, 12.5 per cent of the small enterprises were controlled by women as against 7.7 per cent in India as a whole. There are markets such as Ka Iewduh in Shillong (Jala, 2002: 6) and Kairanband in Imphal (S.C. Sinha, 2000: 179) that are mostly run by women.

Magreeta Jala (2002) examines the economic and social organization of 70 Khasi entrepreneurs in Shillong. According to her, the matrilineal system of the Khasis does not encourage entrepreneurial activities in the community. She writes, "The main reason for the failure of business among the Khasis is that the sons who get experience from their fathers have no right of inheritance (ibid.: 9). When they marry, they have to leave their natal household and the businesses have to be run by their sisters' husbands. She also thinks the Khasis loathe investing in productive enterprises with a long term perspective" (ibid.).

Entrepreneurial Activities in the North-East India: Issues and Challenges

There are many reasons why the seven states of the North-East India are now economically backward. It transpires that at the time of Indian independence the erstwhile state of Assam had one of the highest (if not the highest) per capita income among all the states of India (discussion, broadcast on Lok Sabha Channel, 2008). A number of causes are cited, some real and some exaggerated, for the economic backwardness of the region. A few of the impediments to development discussed by the participants in the above-mentioned broadcast programme (Sanjoy Hazarika, Falguni Rajkumar and Guha Thakurta) were the following. The North-East India is a land-locked region; the erstwhile Assam is fragmented into many states with the result that the political leadership does not think of the region as a whole for its development. Because of the militancy and illegal immigration, the region is politically unstable. Devastation by flood is a usual feature of Assam for 3–5 months in a year. The people are reluctant to invest in industries and in cash crops. The amount of money earmarked for the region remains unspent and there is a lack of expertise in using the money for useful purposes. An overdependence on the Central Government funds has bred powerful elites and enormous corruption.

Low and behold, the region has fallen behind in terms economic growth despite a lot of inputs in terms of infrastructural and educational development. The Assam movement which started in the early eighties is still active going through a violent phase. A similar movement, the Khalistan, started in Punjab in the early eighties mercifully came to an end because of the sagacity of the Punjab people and its political leadership. The political leaders of the North-Eastern states do not seem to think of the region or their state as a whole; the region's various movements, secessionist or otherwise, perpetually fight against the Central Government and also against their own sister groups. Not only is the North-East a divided house, but also some of the small states themselves are embedded in factional fights on account of social and tribal identities. Unfortunately, the international boundaries of the region bordering several independent countries are baneful instead of serving as a boon, because of the underdevelopment and poverty prevailing in some of these surrounding countries.

Geographical isolation and a lack of infrastructural assets are supposed to create hurdles for economic growth. But are they? The so-called BIMARU states (Bihar, MP, Rajasthan and UP) are not at all land-locked and they do not suffer from locational disadvantages. On the other hand, they are well-placed with more than adequate rail, road and air transport facilities. They have also well-developed industries and universities. The territorial region of some of these states has undergone periodic ravages of war and the rise and fall of kingdoms and empires. Besides, in today's context, some of the most powerful politicians come from these states. Yet, these states remain backward. Let us look at the state of Punjab, which borders Pakistan, a country with which we are always at odds. The state of Punjab was completely ravaged by the vicissitudes and onslaught of foreign powers and most recently by the post-partition communal conflagration. And yet, this state has become the richest in India in terms of per capita income. Punjab is industrially well advanced. Most of the woollen clothes the Indians wear come from Ludhiana. It is said that the Punjabis buy raw rubber from Kerala and manufacture *Hawai Chappals* and other goods in Jallunder and sell the finished products back in Kerala at a cheaper rate than that of the local manufacturers there. This may be true to some of the products manufactured in the North-East India. The local products may not have many takers if they are costlier than that of the goods brought from the outside. The influx of Chinese goods marketed in the North-East reinforces this view. We are forced to concede that the Punjabis are very hard working and they have good business acumen. One of India's largest foundry industries is found in Batala, a sleepy village bordering Pakistan. The examples cited above debunk the theory that the unfavourable geographical location of the North-Eastern states greatly hampers their economic advancement. The evidence suggests that the cultural environment rather than the locational disadvantage has a significant influence in the course of economic prosperity. We do need to research on these human factors that impact social and economic development.

Sarat Chandra Sinha, the former Chief Minister of Assam, says that easy money lures the youth in Assam. He wrote (2000: 164) that "most of the youth are averse to hard work, facing any risk that may be involved in the enterprise and reluctant to pursue. Most of the youth are running after easy money and earning unearned money". This danger of easy money might kill entrepreneurial initiative. The state governments are happy to have Central Universities than to set up their own universities. Lavish Central funds to the North-Eastern states make them more *dependent*; however they want to be *independent* as far the governance is concerned. The tribal states are not used to outside political power. They are more comfortable in their own separate tribal and village autonomies. There is no doubt about the fact that some of the tribal-inhabited villages are little kingdoms and this constraints developmental plans for the region as a whole. Lack of cooperation and interaction between tribes or between the villages of the same tribe is a conspicuous aspect of the tribal culture. The importance of the Parsonian (Hoselitz, 1960) variables cannot be overlooked as the modernization process is concerned.

A few students of Sociology from the North-Eastern Hill University have gone to Bangalore to work in the BPOs. Can we not have BPO centres, which are not constrained by time and space, in the hill cities of the North-East where salubrious climate and adequate human resources exist? The moot question is whether these cities can offer security environment even for such centres.

India has an immense diversity in terms of castes, tribes and communities. If we were to provide some insights into the relationship between entrepreneurship and the group values, it might help policy-makers in promoting entrepreneurial activities in the North-Eastern states without which economic development cannot make much progress.

References

Agarwala, B.R. 1955. 'In a Mobile Business Community: Symposium on Caste and Joint Family', *Sociological Bulletin*, 4(2): 139–145.

Bhattacharya, Abhijit. 2008. 'Bringing Academic Rigour in the Field of Entrepreneurship in India', *Economic and Political Weekly*, XLIII (39): 87–95.

Bora, Atul. 2008. 'Entrepreneurship Development in the North East: An Appraisal', in D.D. Mali (ed.), *Entrepreneurship Development in the North East*. Guwahati: Indian Institute of Entrepreneurship, 67–72.

Buchanan, N.S. and H.S. Ellis. 1955. *Approaches to Economic Development*. New York: Frank Cass and Co.

Chacko, P.M. 1976. *A Sociological Study of a Business Community in a Kerala Town*.

—. 1991. *Caste, Business and Entrepreneurship in South India*. Delhi: Kanishka Publishing House.

Choudhury, Hira Neog. 2000. 'Women Entrepreneurship in Assam: Problems and Prospects', in D.D. Mali (ed.), op. cit., 167–176.

Cochran, T.C. 1968. 'Entrepreneurship', in David L. Sills (ed.), *International Encyclopedia of Social Sciences*. New York: The Macmillan and Free Press, 87–91.

Cole, Arthur H. 1946. 'An Approach to the Study of Entrepreneurship: A Tribute to Edwin F. Gay', *The Journal of Economic History*, 6(Supplement): 1–15.

Discussion, Broadcast in Lok Sabha T.V. Channel. 2008 (18th October).

Dutta, Gautam. 2000. 'Developing Entrepreneurship in North East through Training Intervention: A Critical Analysis', in D.D. Mali (ed.), op. cit., 73–88.

Gadgil, D.R. 1959. With the assistance of M.V. Namjoshi. *Origins of the Modern Business Class*. New York: Institute of Public Relations.

Hagen, E.E. 1962. *On the Theory of Social Change: How Economic Growth Begins*. Homewood, Ill.: Dorsey Press.

Hoselitz, Bert F. 1960. *Sociological Aspects of Economic Growth: An Adaptation.* New York: Free Press.

Jala, Magreeta. 2000. *A Social Background of the Khasi Entrepreneurs.* M.Phil. Dissertation. Shillong: Department of Sociology, North-Eastern Hill University.

Khanka, S.S. 2000. 'Making the Entrepreneurial Society with Reference to the North East India', in D.D. Mali (ed.), op. cit., 103–112.

Kilby, Peter (ed.) 1971. *Entrepreneurship and Economic Development.* New York: The Free Press.

Mali, D.D. (ed.) 2000. *Entrepreneurship Development in the North East.* Guwahati: Indian Institute of Entrepreneurship.

McClelland, David C. 1961. *Achieving Society.* New York: The Free Press.

Medhora, Phira B. 1965. 'Entrepreneurship in India', *Political Science Quarterly,*

Nafziger, E.W. 1971. 'Indian Entrepreneurship: A Survey', in Peter Kilby (ed.), op. cit., 287–316.

Nagayya, D. 2000. 'Entrepreneurship Development in the North Eastern Region: Retrospect and Prospect', in D.D. Mali (ed.), op. cit., 31–50.

Odaka, Konosuke and Yukihiko Kiyokawa (eds) 2008. *Small and Medium Scale Industry in India and the Model of Japan.* New Delhi: Allied Publishers.

Polanyi, Karl, C.M. Arensberg and H.W. Pearson. 1957. *Trade and Markets in the Early Empires.* Glencoe, Ill.: Free Press.

Prasin, G.P. 2000. 'Entrepreneurship among the Scheduled Tribes of Manipur: A Case Study of Churachandpur District', in D.D. Mali (ed.), op. cit., 139–148.

Renascence. 2008. *The Quarterly Newsletter of Indian Institute of Entrepreneurship* (April-June), Guwahati.

Saberwal, Satish. 1972. On Entrepreneurship, Everett Hagen and the Ramgarhias (mimeo). Paper presented in the National Seminar on Social Change, Bangalore.

Sayigh, Yusif A. 1962. *The Role of a Business Leader in the Developing Economy.* Cambridge: Harvard University Press.

Schumpeter, Joseph A. 1947. 'Creative Response in Economic History', *The Journal of Economic History,* 7(2): 149–159.

—. 1961. *The Theory of Economic Development.* New York: Oxford University Press.

Singer, Milton. 1972. *When a Great Tradition Modernizes.* London: Pall Mall Press.

Sinha, Poonam. 2000. 'Women Empowerment through Entrepreneurship Development in the North East', in D.D. Mali (ed.), op. cit., 177–184.

Sinha, Sarat Chandra. 2000. 'EMTCS: Strengths and Weaknesses', in D.D. Mali (ed.), op. cit., 163–164.

Smelser, Neil J. 1965. *The Sociology of Economic Life.* New Delhi: Prentice Hall of India.

Sundaram, K. 2008. 'Employment, Wages and Poverty in the Non-Agricultural Sector: All India 2000–05', *Economic and Political Weekly*, 43(24): 14–20.

Weber, Max. 1950. *The Protestant Ethic and the Spirit of Capitalism.* London: Allen and Unwin.

—. 1960. *The Religion of India.* Glencoe, Ill.: Free Press.

Young, Frank W. 1971. 'A Macro-Sociological Interpretation of Entrepreneurship and Economic Development', in Peter Kilby (ed.), op. cit., 141–159.

12

Structural Change in Meghalaya

Theory and Evidence

P. NAYAK AND S.K. MISHRA

Theoretical Issues on Structural Change

Structure is defined as the fundamental condition that is assumed as invariant for purposes of analysis and modeling, regardless of the nature of the model (Machlup, 1967). It was also viewed by Machulp as synonymous with 'composition that does not change easily', referring mostly to the composition of basic macro-economic magnitudes, such as national product, investment, employment, exports, imports, etc. This feature of structure as composition is also evident in Ishikawa's (1987) definition of structural change, in which it is seen as 'a change in the relative weight of significant components of the aggregative indicators of the economy, such as national product and expenditure, exports and imports, and the population and labor force'. The structural change of an economy is thus understood as a long-term widespread change of the fundamental structure, rather than micro-scale or short-term change in output and employment. Short-term economic challenges that are managed with fiscal or monetary policies do not form part of the structural change. Structural change takes place when a subsistence economy is transformed into a manufacturing economy, or a regulated mixed economy is liberalized. It can also be initiated by policy decisions or through permanent changes in resources, population or the societal relationship. Structural change involves obsolescence of skills, vocations, and permanent changes in spending patterns and mode of production. A current structural change in the world economy is globalization. The breakdown of communism, for example, was a political change that had had far-reaching implications for the economies dependent on the state-run Soviet economy.

Study on structural change has been an important tradition in the literature on economic theory. Though the phenomenon of structural change is as old as the very problems of economic development, the term 'economics of structural change' was until recently practically unknown (Silva and Teixeira, 2008). Some of the oldest important literature on structural change that deserve mention are of Fisher (1939) and Clark (1940). Both of them looked at the patterns of the changes in sectoral employment. They put forward the idea that an economy passes through three stages of production: In the first stage the low-income countries are assumed to be dominated by primary production/extraction of raw materials through agriculture, mining, fishing, and forestry. After the first phase is over, the economy passes through the stage of industrial production in the form of manufacturing and construction. The final stage, which is the sign of economic maturity in the development process, is the stage of generation of high income through a large tertiary sector with the provision of services such as education and tourism. However, their thesis of the sequence of movement of economy from primary to secondary and then to tertiary sector may be more natural to relatively closed economies.

In the initial stage of development of economic theory, the literature could not provide a unified approach to the issue because of the complexities involved in it. But in the last decade Baranzini and Scazzieri (1990) and Landesmann and Scazzieri (1996) made some contributions in this regard. The latest contribution in this line is the work of Silva and Teixeira who made a compilation of most of the important works based on a review of 910 research papers comprising theoretical and empirical works by combining 9,703 citations indexed in *Econlit* over the past four decades. Their work provided a basic framework in dividing the entire literature under four different categories: (i) Foundations of Structural Change (Classical Economists (1700–1870) and The Legacy of Schumpeter), (ii) Formal Approaches to Structural Change and Economic Growth, (iii) Empirical and Historical Processes of Structural Change, and (iv) Recent Trends in Structural Change.

Foundations of Structural Change

Perhaps the earliest treatment to the study of the structure of a market-oriented economy is due to Sir William Petty who, in 1691, concluded that there is much more to be gained by manufacture than husbandry; and by merchandise than manufacture (Clark, 1940). Although classical economists did not use the term 'structure' in any significant way, many authors like Turgot (1766), Steuart (1767) and Smith (1776) contended that the progress of wealth was intimately related to changes in the pattern of interaction among a few critical variables, which can be seen as distinct representations of the economic structure. Smith discussed relationship between the sectoral composition of the economy and the stage of development. Quesnay while doing an analysis on the structure of the economy explored the general interdependence between economic sectors (1758). The study on the structure of an economy as the characteristic feature and interrelationship among various classes (labourers, farmers, landlords, manufacturers etc.) became more prominent in the works of Ricardo (1817) and subsequently in Marx (1885). The importance of non-producible resources in the enhancement of wealth was emphasized by Ricardo, while Marx considered structural dynamics through its schemes of extended reproduction. Veblen (1899) elaborately addressed and analysed the changes in socioeconomic modalities, institutions, people's mindset and their habits of thought and action when a primitive (pre-industrial) economy evolves into an industrial and market-based economy. Schumpeter (1934) believed that structure of an economy had to change if there were to be long-term shifts in economic well-being. When there is technological competition among firms, innovation brings out structural change in the economy and helps in the formation of business cycles. In the middle of the 20th century the importance of the growth of primary, secondary and tertiary industries, and of the shifts among them, were given prominence by Clark (1940). The basic methodology of national accounting as outlined by Marshall in 1879 is based on the sectoral composition of the economy (Kenessey, 2004).

Formal Approaches to Structural Change and Economic Growth

Even though growth brings out fundamental changes in the structure of an economy and the composition of its main aggregates, the theories on economic growth, especially in the mainstream economics, were developed without having any reference to it. Both von Neumann (1945) and Sraffa (1960) viewed that production is a circular process in which commodities are produced by means of commodities. While describing economic system, Leontief (1941, 1991) explored the idea of general interdependence and circularity of production. Leontief (1953, 1970) in his model while discussing horizontal-flow, supplemented his analysis with the specification of construction and delivery lags that incorporate the time structure of inter-sectoral flows. Boeke (1953) conceptualized the structure of an economy in the socio-economic dualism. Lewis (1954) analysed the process of economic expansion in a dual economy where both the capitalistic and the subsistence sectors have interrelations. Sraffa (1960) demonstrated the possibility of the progress of an economy from a circular to a vertical one. Pasinetti (1973) also made analysis on vertically integrated sectors in the usual input-output scheme and examined meticulously the logical properties of the process of vertical integration. Richard Goodwin (1976, 1983) and Goodwin and Punzo (1987) provided a different approach to remove horizontal interdependencies in the Sraffa-Leontief system. A number of seminal works on structural change also dealt with horizontal and vertical representations of the economic structure (Hicks 1973; Pasinetti, 1981, 1993). Andersen (2001) made an effort to endogenize demand and technology factors in Pasinetti's (1993) model, by transforming it into an evolutionary model with explicit micro-foundations. Similar effort to endogenize demand has been made by Gualerzi (2001). However, explicitly Baumol (1967) did not take demand into account in his seminal work but emphasized on unequal impact of technology among sectors leading to unbalanced economic growth.

Empirical and Historical Processes of Structural Change

In order to explain the observed processes of structural transformation the early literature on development economics was devoted to exploration of theoretical arguments which were based on appreciative strands rather than on formal reasoning. Rostow (1960) in his growth theory mentioned the existence of structural discontinuities. The dual-economy model and big-push theory stressed the importance of sectoral differences in the growth process. Lewis (1954) made a distinction between traditional and modern sectors. Sectoral differences as a requirement for balanced growth were emphasized in the works of Rosenstein-Rodan (1943, 1961) and Nurkse (1953). While Rosenstein-Rodan argued on the complementarities among different industries for large-scale planned industrialization Nurkse was in favour of mutually supporting demand for the promotion of a diversified increase in output. Fisher (1939) made an analysis by decomposing the economy into primary, secondary and tertiary sectors. Similarly Kuznets (1961, 1971) in his empirical analysis of the theory of economic growth decomposed the economy by making classification into agriculture, industry and services. He found an association between growth of per capita income and shift in production structure (structural change). According to him the relationship so established was due to combined effect of changes in the (i) structure of consumer demand, (ii) comparative advantage, and (iii) technology. Among these three, technology played a major role. Rosenberg (1963) tried to establish the link between investment and economic growth and highlighted the crucial role of capital goods in the stimulation of technological innovation. A number of studies using both cross-section and time series data were undertaken to examine the relationship between growth and changes in the economic structure (Chenery 1960, Chenery and Taylor, 1968 and Chenery and Syrquin, 1975). North, 1981 opined that the structure of an economy is determined by the resource base, technology and institutions. The substantial content of a socio-economic system lies in its resource base in the short run and the natural endowments in the long run. Guntqr (1998) provided an exhaustive review of the literature on the measurement aspects of structural analysis. Branson et al. (1998) while studying the patterns of development of 93 countries over the period from 1970 to 1994 used 45 macro-economic indicators such as sectoral shares of GDP, trade intensity, financial market development, etc., to measure economic structure.

Recent Trends in Structural Change

The emergence of the *new economy* and the controversy regarding the impact of information and communication technologies on growth further provided stimulus to the debate on technical change and its impact on growth. A growing body of literature was developed as 'neo-Schumpeterian' or 'evolutionary' economics and has been accepted as an alternative approach to mainstream economics (Lucas, 1988, 1993; Romer, 1990; Grossman and Helpman, 1991; Aghion and Howitt, 1992). These economists have been putting stress on the idea of disharmony and competition in the growth process unlike mainstream economic theories based on the assumption of rational human behaviour. Analysis on structural change have come to the fore as a powerful analytical tool that is capable of establishing links between changes at the level of micro-structures and higher-level changes, while providing, at the same time, a more realistic account of the process of technology adoption and its effects on the economy, by emphasizing the sequential and path-dependent nature of economic change. In particular, it provides a useful foundation for the study of the problems of adjustment and inter-temporal coordination brought on by technical progress that is totally neglected and taken for granted by the mainstream equilibrium approach. The strong connection between major technological breakthroughs, structural change and economic growth is analysed in terms of technological systems, trajectories of technology and technological paradigms (Amendola and Gaffard, 1998). Perez (1983, 1985) explored the relationship between technological trajectories and structural change introducing the concept of 'techno-economic paradigm'. David (1975, 1985) and Arthur (1988, 1989, 1994) showed that the occurrence of random events or 'historical accidents', particularly in the early phases of the introduction of a technology, might have a decisive influence on the long-run outcomes of the economy. Goodwin (1987) presented a model in which the impact of technology on the economy is transformed by the internal dynamics of the economic system, which reshapes the non-cyclical rate of emergence of a major innovation cluster into both business cycles and long waves. Assuming a capital stock 'vintage' structure Silverberg and Lehnert (1993) developed a Schumpeterian dynamic model (based on the Goodwin growth cycle) to conclude that 'clustering' of innovations is not necessary for generating long-waves but necessary for the process of arrival of new technologies to be stochastic. Silverberg (2002) presented a 'mosaic-avalanche' model based on percolation theory that illustrates the emergence of macro-innovations from a stream of incremental innovations, which are then transmitted to changes in sectoral structures and macro-economic performance. The conceptual framework of 'technology gaps' was also formalized by Verspagen (1991), Amable (1993), and more recently by Los and Verspagen (2006). Los and Verspagen developed a dynamic model in which the impact of innovation, learning and technology spillovers on output growth, convergence and structural change was analysed.

In the recent past there have been some attempts to combine both supply-side and demand-side factors within the micro-to-macro approach to the process of economic development. Saviotti and Pyka (2004a, 2004b) presented a model in which changes in the composition of the economic system accompanying the emergence of pervasive innovations are seen in connection with changes in the demand side of the economy. Montobbio (2002) also took into account the role of demand in his evolutionary model of structural change. At the same time, the role of technology as a source of productivity growth and structural transformation was examined in a large number of studies using input-output analysis (Peneder et al., 2003; Franke and Kalmbach, 2005; Sánchez Chóliz and Duarte, 2006). The empirical literature on the role of technologically leading industries on economic growth has led furthermore to a changing image of the services sector, with several studies pointing out the impact of the new technological paradigm on the creation of new and improved services (Petit and Soete, 2001; Petit, 2002; Peneder et al., 2003). The high productivity growth rates found in these sectors, together with evidence showing the declining role of manufacturing in economic growth in the more recent period (Fagerberg and Verspagen, 1999, 2002) has led to the abandonment of the traditional view regarding manufacturing as the major producer and user of technology, and as the sector providing the major stimulus for growth (Kaldor, 1966, 1970; Cornwall, 1976, 1977). The new evidence on the service sectors has inclusively led to a change of focus in the services literature, as the debate on the consequences of de-industrialization and on the impact of rising services in productivity slowdown is to some extent replaced by a far more optimistic view, which emphasizes the role of technological factors in the tertiarization process (Andersen et al., 2000; Miles and Tomlinson, 2000; Peneder et al., 2003). Dopfer, Foster and Potts (2004) and Dopfer and Potts (2008) theoretically address the issue of structural change and economic dynamics in the micro-meso-macro framework, especially highlighting the transformations at the 'meso' level. However, much of the empirical literature have failed to address the fundamental issues of the change in patterns of demand associated with the spread of new technologies that is suffering to some extent from 'technological determinism'.

Empirical Issues of Structural Change in Meghalaya

Before we discuss the issues of structural change in the context of Meghalaya let us first introduce the Meghalaya state. It is one of the eight states in North-East India and is one of the smallest states of the country. The state attained full statehood on 21st January 1972 after having been carved out from Assam. It has an area of 22,429 sq kms which is about 0.7 per cent of the total area of the country. The state is surrounded in the west and south by Bangladesh and in the east and north by the state of Assam. It lies between 85°49' and 92°53' East Longitude and between 20°1' and 20°5' North Latitude. The state has an undulating topography. Most of the area of the state is hilly plateau with deep gorges and valleys. The southern fringes are steep and abrupt whereas the northern and western edges have gentler slopes. It is predominantly a tribal state and majority of her population reside in rural areas.

Since the present study is severely constrained by availability of relevant data for analysis we decided to choose those few demographic and socioeconomic indicators for which data are available. The indicator variables that are analysed in the following paragraphs are sex ratio, natural growth rate of population, literacy, work force participation, infrastructure and finally output/income and its sectoral composition.

Change in Sex Ratio

As per 2001 Census, the state had a population of 2.31 million, which was about 0.2 per cent of the total population of the country (see Appendix Table 1). Though populations of both the sexes are increasing over time, the rates of increase are observed to be different in Meghalaya at different point of time whereas the same is not true in case of India. In 1901 for every 1,000 males there were 1,036 females. This was reduced to 1,013 in 1911 and this tendency continued till 1971 after which the trend has been reversed. Thus, we find that from 1901 to 1911, the sex ratio was favourable to females in the state but became unfavourable from 1921 onwards. However, from 1991 onwards, the rate of increase of females again has started picking up. It is likely that in the process of attaining the statehood of Meghalaya in 1972, the male immigrant population in Meghalaya reverted back to its source regions and since then the amelioration of imbalance in the sex ratio began showing up. It is also likely that since 1980s out-migration of male population from Meghalaya to the other parts of the country increased.

Changes in Birth, Death and Natural Growth Rates of Population

The data on the birth, death and natural growth rate of population reveal a significant structural change in the demography of Meghalaya (see Appendix Table 2). Until 1995, the natural growth rate of population, measured as the difference in the birth and death rates, has an increasing trend (see Figures 1 to 3). The trend was reversed since 1985 and the natural growth rate began declining. When looked in the background of an increasing trend in the sex ratio in favour of the female population, declining birth rates after the mid 1980s indicate several changes that might have occurred in the socio-economic sphere. There are no statistics to support our conjecture, but it is likely that the age of marriage, especially of the women might have gone up. It is indirectly indicated by the appearance of matrimonial advertisements earlier unheard of in the Meghalaya society. It is also likely that economic participation of women in the non-traditional economic activities might have increased that demand more time from them leaving less time available for childbearing and rearing.

Changes in Economic Participation

Changes in the demographic features indicated above are partially explained by the proportion of total workers in the population (see Appendix Table 3). In 1991, 42.38 per cent of the total workers in the rural areas were female which increased to 43.04 per cent in 2001. For the urban areas, these figures were 25.41 and 33.05. These changes are more consistent for the urban areas. Among the main workers in the urban areas in 1991, about 24.24 per cent were female which increased to 30.03 in 2001. Thus the proportion of main female workers increased substantially. In the rural areas, however, these figures were 39.38 for 1991 and 37.64 for 2001. Thus, the participation of the womenfolk as the main workers in rural areas showed a decline in the period 1991–2001, while it increased in the urban areas. It is reflected in the relatively sharper rate of decline in natural growth rate of population in the urban areas vis-à-vis the rural areas. In comparison to 1991, dependency ratio of population on the female workers, especially in the urban areas, increased substantially as depicted in Figure 4. The overall economic participation rate of women is increasing; but the increase is more pronounced in the urban areas (see Figure 5).

The occupational structure of a state also indicates the degree of structural change in an economy. Appendix Table 4 provides an in depth view of the occupational pattern of the state of Meghalaya. Despite the changes in the definition of workers in various Censuses, some broad inferences on the trend of occupational distribution may be made. During 1971–91 the proportion of main workers engaged in the primary sector decreased from 82 per cent to 63 per cent. The 2001 figures stated in Primary Census Abstract (PCA) for the state provide work force data only under four categories, namely, cultivators, agricultural labourers, household industry and other services. Thus comparison between the shares of main workers in primary sectors in previous years with 2001 is not possible. The share of cultivators and agricultural labourers taken together, there has been decline in share from about 79 per cent in 1971 to about 63 per cent in 2001. However, the share of agricultural labourers increased from 9.88 per cent to 12.54 per cent during same period. Although statistical information is lacking, perceptible changes could be seen in the structure of land ownership – from the communal to the private – and these changes could have affected the occupational structure, albeit the incomplete census data do not help in comparing the sectoral change in the occupational pattern. However, it can be concluded that there was no perceptible change in the employment in secondary sector and the decrease in the employment in agricultural sector has been neutralized mainly by the corresponding increase in tertiary sector. This type of sectoral shift actually indicates a growth of informal sector particularly in the urban fringe.

Changes in Literacy Rate and in Favour of Women

Increased economic participation rate of women in the decade 1991–2001 is partly explicable by spread of literacy among the womenfolk. Appendix Table 5 and the associated Figure 6 present these changes. There has been impressive change in the literacy rate of women in the rural areas enhancing their human development status.

Changes in Per Capita Net State Domestic Product

Since the financial year ending March 31, the per capita net state domestic product (₹ per year at constant prices 1993–94) has been growing consistently, as presented in Appendix Table 6, Appendix Table 7 (a, b and c) and Figure 7. As presented in Appendix Table 8, the share of agriculture and forestry in the NSDP is on a decline while the share of mining and quarrying is constantly increasing. The share of unregistered or informal manufacturing sector is on a decline and the share of the registered manufacturing sector is increasing. Decline in the role of unregistered or informal manufacturing sector has serious implications with regard to employment, income distribution, rural development, gender-based inequality and self-dependence. Fast increasing share of mining has considerable implications with regard to income inequality, environmental hazards, fragility of the economy subsequent to resource depletion and changes in the demographic composition.

Infrastructural Changes

Along with changes in the structure of the economy leaning towards mining and manufacturing, the number of vehicles on the roads is increasing very fast (see Appendix Table 9). Road length is increasing over the years, and the traffic and the vehicles on the roads are increasing much faster. During 1979–1998, the surface road length increased a little over 2.5 times but heavy vehicles (trucks and buses) on the road increased about nine times. Light vehicle increased over 5 times. As reported in Appendix Table 9, the per capita power consumption in the state increased six-fold during 1978–1999.

Concluding Remarks

Some aspects of structural changes in Meghalaya are worth noting. First, the sex ratio is gradually going in favour of the women. The female participation in the economy is increasing and the dependency ratio on the women is on the increase. There has been a decrease in the employment in agricultural sector which has been neutralized mainly by the corresponding increase in tertiary sector particularly in the urban fringe. Manufacturing and mining sectors are gradually becoming more prominent. Per capita income is rising. Infrastructure is improving, and the vehicles on the roads are increasing faster. Per capita power consumption is increasing. At the meso-level, several shifts are perceptible – the changes in the ownership of land drifting from the communal control to the private domain being very prominent. These changes clearly indicate that Meghalaya is undergoing a change; it is gradually moving from the traditional economy to the industrial economy. These changes have their own social implications, treatment of which would require a separate paper.

References

Aghion, P. and P. Howitt. 1992. 'A Model of Growth through Creative Destruction', *Econometrica*, 60(2): 323–351.

Amable, B. 1993. 'Catch-up and Convergence: A Model of Cumulative Growth', *International Review of Applied Economics*, 7(1): 1–25.

Amendola, M. and J.L. Gaffard. 1998. *Out of Equilibrium*. Oxford: Clarendon Press.

Andersen, B., J. Howells, R. Hull, I. Miles and J. Roberts (eds), 2000. *Knowledge and Innovation in the New Service Economy*. Cheltenham, UK: Edward Elgar.

Andersen, E.S. 2001. 'Satiation in an Evolutionary Model of Structural Economic Dynamics', *Journal of Evolutionary Economics*, 11(1): 143–164.

Arrow, K.J. 1962. 'The Economic Implications of Learning by Doing', *The Review of Economic Studies*, 29(3): 155–173.

Arthur, W.B. 1988. 'Self-reinforcing Mechanisms in Economics', in P.W. Anderson, K.J. Arrow and D. Pines (eds), *The Economy as an Evolving Complex System*. New York: Addison-Wesley, 9–31.

—. 1989. 'Competing Technologies, Increasing Returns, and Lock-in by Historical Events', *Economic Journal*, 99(394): 116–131.

—. 1994. *Increasing Returns and Path Dependency in the Economy*. Ann Arbor: The University of Michigan Press.

Baranzini, M. and R. Scazzieri (eds) 1990. *The Economic Theory of Structure and Change*. Cambridge: Cambridge University Press.

Baumol, W.J. 1967. 'Macroeconomics of Unbalanced Growth: The Anatomy of Urban Crisis', *American Economic Review*, 57(3): 415–426.

Boeke, Julius H. 1953. *Economics and Economic Policy of Dual Societies, as Exemplified by Indonesia*. New York: International Secretariat, Institute of Pacific Relations.

Branson, W.H., G. Isabel and B.G. Guntor. 1998. *Patterns of Development, 1970-94.* Washington, DC: World Bank.

Chenery, H.B. 1960. 'Patterns of Industrial Growth', *American Economic Review*, 50(4): 624–654.

Chenery, H.B. and L. Taylor. 1968. 'Development Patterns: Among Countries and Over Time', *Review of Economics and Statistics*, 50(4): 391–416.

Chenery, H.B. and M. Syrquin. 1975. *Patterns of Development, 1957–1970.* London: Oxford University Press.

Clark, C. 1940. *The Conditions of Economic Progress.* London: The Macmillan & Co. Ltd.

Cornwall, J. 1976. 'Diffusion, Convergence and Kaldor's Laws', *Economic Journal*, 86(342): 307–314.

—. 1977. *Modern Capitalism: Its Growth and Transformation.* London: Martin Robertson.

David, P. 1975. *Technical Choice, Innovative and Economic Growth: Essays on American and British Experience in the Nineteenth Century.* Cambridge: Cambridge University Press.

—. 1985. 'Clio and the Economics of QWERTY', *The American Economic Review*, 75(2): 332–337.

Dopfer, K. and J. Potts. 2008. *The General Theory of Economic Evolution.* New York: Routledge.

Dopfer, K., J. Foster and J. Potts. 2004. 'Micro-meso-macro', *Journal of Evolutionary Economics*, 14(3): 263–279.

Dosi, G. 1982. 'Technological Paradigms and Technological Trajectories', *Research Policy*, 22(2): 102–103.

—. 1988. 'Sources, Procedures and Micro-economic Effects of Innovation', *Journal of Economic Literature*, 26(3): 1120–1171.

—. 2002. 'Technology-gaps, Innovation Diffusion and Transformation: An Evolutionary Approach', *Research Policy*, 31(8 and 9): 1291–1304.

Fisher, A. 1939. 'Production: Primary, Secondary and Tertiary', *Economic Record*, June, 24–38

Franke, R. and P. Kalmbach. 2005. 'Structural Change in the Manufacturing Sector and Its Impact on Business-related Services: An Input-Output Study for Germany', *Structural Change and Economic Dynamics*, 16(4): 467–488.

Freeman, C. and C. Perez. 1988. *Structural Crisis of Adjustment: Business Cycles and Investment Behaviour.* London: Routledge.

Freeman, C. and L. Soete. 1997. *The Economics of Industrial Innovation.* Cambridge, Mass.: MIT Press.

Georgescu-Roegen, N. 1971. *The Entropy Law and the Economic Process*. Cambridge: Harvard University Press.

Goodwin, R.M. 1967. 'A Growth Cycle', in C.H. Feinstein (ed.), *Socialism, Capitalism and Economic Growth*. Cambridge: Cambridge University Press, 54–58.

—. 1976. 'Use of Normalized General Coordinates in Linear Value and Distribution Theory', in K.R. Polenske and J.V. Skolka (eds), *Advances in Input-Output Analysis*. Cambridge: Ballinger Publishing Co., 581–602.

—. 1983. *Essays in Linear Economic Structures*. London: Macmillan.

—. 1987. 'The Economy as an Evolutionary Pulsator', in T. Vasko (ed.), *The Long-Wave Debate*. Berlin: Springer-Verlag.

Goodwin, R.M. and L.F. Punzo 1987. *The Dynamics of a Capitalist Society*. Cambridge: Polity Press in association with Basil Blackwell.

Grossman, G. and H. Helpman. 1991. *Innovation and Growth in the Global Economy*. Cambridge, Mass.: MIT Press.

Gualerzi, D. 2001. *Consumption and Growth: Recovery and Structural. Change in the US Economy*. Cheltenham, UK: Edward Elgar.

Guntor, Bernhard G. 1998. *Economic Structure and Investment under Uncertainty*. Unpublished Doctoral Dissertation, Washington, DC: American University.

Hicks, J. 1973. *Capital and Time: A Neo-Austrian Theory*. Oxford: Clarendon Press.

Ishikawa, S. 1987. 'Structural Change', in *The New Palgrave: A Dictionary of Economics*. Vol. IV. London: Macmillan, 523–525.

Kaldor, N. 1966. *Causes of the Slow Rate of Economic Growth in the United Kingdom*. Cambridge: Cambridge University Press.

—. 1970. 'The Case for Regional Policies', *Scottish Journal of Political Economy*, 27(3): 337–348.

Kenessey, Z. 2004. *The Primary, Secondary, Tertiary and Quarternary Sectors of the Economy*. USA: Federal Reserve System, 359–385.

Keynes, J.M. 1936. *The General Theory of Employment, Interest and Money*. London: Macmillan.

Kuznets, S. 1961. 'Quantitative Aspects of the Economic Growth of Nations: IV. Long Term Trends in Capital Formation Proportions', *Economic Development and Cultural Change*, 9(2): 1–80.

Kuznets, S. 1971. *Economic Growth of Nations: Total Output and Production Structure*. Cambridge: Harvard University Press.

Landesmann and R. Scazzieri (eds), *The Economics of Structural Change. Vol. III. International Library of Critical Writings*. Aldershot: Edward Elgar, 3–37.

Landesmann, M. and R. Scazzieri (eds) 1996. *Production and Economic Dynamics*. Cambridge: Cambridge University Press.

Leontief, W. (ed.) 1953. 'Dynamic Analysis', in *Studies in the Structure of the American Economy*. New York: Oxford University Press, 53–90.

Leontief, W. 1941. *The Structure of the American Economy, 1919–1929*. Cambridge: Harvard University Press.

—. 1970. 'The Dynamic Inverse', in A.P. Carter and A. Brody (eds), *Contributions to Input-Output Analysis*. Amsterdam: North-Holland Publishing Company.

—. 1987. 'Input-Output Analysis', *The New Palgrave: A Dictionary of Economics*. London: Macmillan, 860–864.

—. 1991. 'The Economy as a Circular Flow', *Structural Change and Economic Dynamics*, 2(1): 181–212.

—. 1954. 'Economic Development with Unlimited Supplies of Labour', *The Manchester School*, 22(2): 139–191.

Los, B. and B. Verspagen. 2006. 'The Evolution of Productivity Gaps and Specialization Patterns', *Metroeconomica*, 57(4): 464–493.

Lucas, R. 1988. 'On the Mechanics of Economic Development', *Journal of Monetary Economics*, 22(1): 3–42.

—. 1993. 'Making a Miracle', *Econometrica*, 61(2): 251–272.

M. Setterfield (ed.), *Growth, Employment and Inflation*. London: Macmillan, 113–126.

Machlup, F. (ed.) 1991. *Economic Semantics*. New York: Norton.

Marx, K. 1867. *Das Kapital*. http://www.econ.utah.edu/~ehrbar/cap1.pdf

Miles, I. and M. Tomlinson. 2000. 'Intangible Assets and Service Sectors: The Challenges of Service Industries', in P. Buiges, A. Jacquemin and J. Marchipont (eds), *Competitiveness and the Value of Intangible Assets*. Aldershot: Edward Elgar, 154–186.

Montobbio, F. 2002. 'An Evolutionary Model of Industrial Growth and Structural Change', *Structural Change and Economic Dynamics*, 13(4): 387–414.

Nelson, R. and S. Winter. 1982. *An Evolutionary Theory of Economic Change*. Cambridge: Harvard University Press.

North, Douglass C. 1981. *Structure and Change in Economic History*. New York: W.W. Norton & Co.

Nurkse, R. 1953. *Problems of Capital Formation in Underdeveloped Countries*. Oxford: Basil Blackwell.

Pasinetti, L. 1973. 'The Notion of Vertical Integration on Economic Analysis', *Metroeconomica*, 25(1): 1–29.

—. 1981. *Structural Change and Economic Growth: A Theoretical Essay on the Dynamics of the Wealth of Nations.* Cambridge: Cambridge University Press.

—. 1993. *Structural Economic Dynamics: A Theory of the Consequences of Human Learning.* Cambridge: Cambridge University Press.

Peneder, M., S. Kaniovski and B. Dachs. 2003. 'What Follows Tertiarisation? Structural Change and the Role of Knowledge Based Services', *The Service Industry Journal*, 23(2): 47–66.

Perez, C. 1983. 'Structural Change and Assimilation of New Technologies in the Economic and Social Systems', *Futures*, 15(5): 357–375.

—. 1985. 'Microelectronics, Long Waves and World Structural Change: New Perspectives for Developing Countries', *World Development*, 13(3): 441–463.

Petit, P. 2002. 'The Roots of the New Economy: An Institutional Perspective', *International Productivity Monitor*, 4: 39–54.

Petit, P. and L. Soete. 2000. 'Technical Change and Employment Growth in Services: Analytical and Policy Challenges', in P. Petit and L. Soete (eds), *Technology and the Future of European Employment.* Aldershot: Edward Elgar, 166–203.

Quesnay, F. 1758. 'Tableau Économique', in H. Hagemann, M. Landesmann and R. Scazzieri (eds), op. cit., 29–41.

Ricardo, D. 1817. *The Principles of Political Economy and Taxation.* Paris: Traduction chez Calman-Levy.

Romer, P.M. 1990. 'Romer, Endogenous Technical Change', *Journal of Political Economy*, 98(5): 71–102.

Rosenberg, N. 1963. 'Capital Goods, Technology, and Economic Growth', in H. Hagemann, M. Landesmann and R. Scazzieri (eds), op. cit., 118–128.

Rosenberg, N. 1982. *Inside the Black Box: Technology and Economics.* Cambridge: Cambridge University Press.

Rosensetein-Rodan, P. 1943. 'Problems of Industrialization in Eastern and South-Eastern Europe', *Economic Journal*, 53(210): 202–211.

—. 1961. 'Notes on the Theory of the Big-Push', in H.S. Ellis and H.C. Wallich (eds), *Economic Development for Latin America.* London: Macmillan.

Rostow, W.W. 1960. *The Stages of Economic Growth: A Non-communist Manifesto.* Cambridge: Cambridge University Press.

Sánchez Chóliz, J. and R. Duarte. 2006. 'The Effect of Structural Change on the Self-Reliance and Interdependence of Aggregate Sectors: The Case of Spain, 1980–1994', *Structural Change and Economic Dynamics*, 17(1): 27–45.

Saviotti, P. and A. Pyka. 2004a. 'Economic Development by the Creation of New Sectors', *Journal of Evolutionary Economics*, 14(1): 1–35.

Saviotti, P. and A. Pyka. 2004b. 'Economic Development, Qualitative Change and Employment Creation', *Structural Change and Economic Dynamics*, 15: 265–287.

Scazzieri, R. (eds) 2003. *The Economics of Structural Change. Vol. I. International Library of Critical Writings.* Aldershot: Edward Elgar.

Schumpeter, J.A. 1934. *Theory of Economic Development.* Cambridge: Cambridge University Press.

Schumpeter, J.A. 1942. *Capitalism, Socialism and Democracy.* http://boccard.free.fr/iocb/1942-Schumpeter.pdf

Silva, E.G. and Aurora A.C. Teixeira. 2008. 'Surveying Structural Change: Seminal Contributions and a Bibliometric Account', *Structural Change and Economic Dynamics*, 19(4): 273–300.

Silverberg, G. 2002. 'The Discrete Charm of the Bourgeoisie: Quantum and Continuous Perspectives on Innovation and Growth', *Research Policy*, 31 (8 and 9): 1275–1289.

Silverberg, G. and D. Lehnert. 1993. 'Long Waves and Evolutionary Chaos in a Simple Schumpeterian Model of Embodied Technical Change', *Structural Change and Economic Dynamics*, 4(1): 9–37.

Smith, A. 1776. *An Inquiry into the Nature and Causes of the Wealth of Nations.* https://www.blackwellpublishing.com/content/BPL_Images/Content_store/Sample_chapter/0631228616%5C001.pdf

Sraffa, P. 1960. *Production of Commodities by Means of Commodities.* Cambridge: Cambridge University Press.

Turgot, A.R.J. 1766. 'Reflections on the Formation and the Distribution of Wealth', in R.L. Meek (ed.), *Turgot on Progress, Sociology and Economics.* Cambridge: Cambridge University Press, 119–134.

Veblen, T.B. 1899. *The Theory of the Leisure Class: An Economic Study in the Evolution of Institutions.* New York: Macmillan.

Verspagen, B. 1991. 'A New Empirical Approach to Catching Up or Falling Behind', *Structural Change and Economic Dynamics*, 2(2): 359–380.

Von Neuman, J. 1945. 'A Model of General Economic Equilibrium', *Review of Economic Studies*, 13(1): 1–9.

Appendix

Table 1

Population and Sex Ratio in Meghalaya

Census Year	*Population in Meghalaya*			*Sex Ratio*	
	Male	*Female*	*Total*	*Meghalaya*	*India*
1901	167,256	173,268	340,524	1036.9	972
1911	195,706	198,299	394,005	1013.3	964
1921	211,216	211,187	422,403	999.9	955
1931	243,993	236,844	480,837	970.7	950
1941	282,666	273,154	555,820	966.3	945
1951	310,706	294,968	605,674	949.4	946
1961	397,288	372,092	769,380	936.6	941
1971	520,967	490,732	1,011,699	941.9	930
1981	683,710	652,109	1,335,819	953.8	934
1991	907,687	867,091	1,774,778	955.3	927
2001	1,176,087	1,142,735	2,306,069	971.6	932.9

Source: Census Reports, Government of India.

Table 2

Birth, Death and Natural Growth Rate of Population (per 1,000 persons) in Meghalaya

Year	Birth Rate			Death Rate			Natural Growth Rate		
	Total	Rural	Urban	Total	Rural	Urban	Total	Rural	Urban
1976	33.5	36.1	20.6	15.5	17.6	5.1	18.0	18.5	15.5
1977	32.5	35.8	15.9	14.1	16.0	4.6	18.4	19.8	11.3
1978	32.0	34.7	17.8	10.2	11.3	5.0	21.8	23.4	12.8
1979	33.2	36.7	15.3	12.1	13.2	6.4	21.1	23.5	8.9
1980	31.2	33.6	18.8	11.1	12.3	4.7	20.1	21.3	14.1
1981	32.6	35.0	18.5	8.2	8.9	4.3	24.4	26.1	14.2
1982	31.1	32.9	23.1	8.9	9.9	4.4	22.2	23.0	18.7
1983	30.0	32.8	17.2	8.3	9.2	4.4	21.7	23.6	12.8
1984	38.3	41.9	20.9	11.8	13.2	5.5	26.5	28.7	15.4
1985	39.1	42.4	24.1	12.7	14.3	5.6	26.4	28.1	18.5
1986	35.4	38.3	21.7	10.1	11.2	5.3	25.3	27.1	16.4
1987	34.9	38.6	17.6	9.1	10.2	3.6	25.8	28.4	14.0
1988	36.4	40.5	17.7	9.1	10.6	2.7	27.3	29.9	15.0
1989	31.9	37.3	19.0	11.9	12.6	4.7	20.0	24.7	14.3
1990	31.8	35.4	15.5	7.8	8.7	3.4	24.0	26.7	12.1
1991	32.4	35.4	18.7	8.8	9.9	4.0	23.6	25.5	14.7
1992	29.8	33.1	15.0	8.5	9.7	2.7	21.3	23.4	12.3
1993	28.5	30.7	17.6	6.8	7.7	2.7	21.7	23.0	14.9
1994	29.5	32.1	16.7	7.1	7.6	4.3	22.4	24.5	12.4
1995	29.0	31.8	14.8	8.9	9.7	5.1	20.1	22.1	9.7
1996	30.4	33.2	16.3	8.9	9.9	4.1	21.5	23.3	12.2
1997	30.2	32.9	16.6	8.8	9.7	4.4	21.4	23.2	12.2
1998	29.2	–	–	9.0	–	–	20.2	–	–
1999	28.7	–	–	9.1	–	–	19.6	–	–
2000	28.5	31.0	15.3	9.2	10.1	4.6	19.3	20.9	10.7

Table 3

Changes in the Rate of Economic Participation of Work Force in Meghalaya

Area	Sex	2001					1991				
		Total Popn.	Total Workers	Main Workers	Marginal Workers	Non Workers	Total Popn.	Total Workers	Main Workers	Marginal Workers	Non Workers
Total	P	2306069	956425	742762	213663	1349644	1774778	757322	715587	41735	1017456
	M	1167840	557807	471830	85977	610033	907687	454469	449625	4844	453218
	F	1138229	398618	270932	127686	739611	867091	302853	265962	36891	564238
Rural	P	1853457	826334	629401	196933	1027123	1444731	650731	611164	39567	794000
	M	939803	470712	392511	78201	469091	734865	374958	370511	4447	359907
	F	913654	355622	236890	118732	558032	709866	275773	240653	35120	434093
Urban	P	452612	130091	113361	16730	322521	330047	106591	104423	2168	223456
	M	228037	87095	79319	7776	140942	172822	79511	79114	397	93311
	F	224575	42996	34042	8954	181579	157225	27080	25309	1771	130145

Note: P: Person, M: Male, F: Female

Table 4
Sectoral Distribution of Main Workers (%)

Sector	*Category*	*Census Year*			
		1971	*1981*	*1991*	*2001*
Primary Sector	i. Cultivators	69.15	62.56	55.31	50.23
	ii. Agricultural labourers	9.88	9.98	12.51	12.54
	iii. Livestock, fishing etc	2.66	6.53	6.39	–
	iv. Mining and quarrying	0.15	0.69	0.60	–
	***Total* (i to iv)**	***81.84***	***79.76***	***74.81***	***62.77***
Secondary Sector	v. Household industry	1.09	0.84	0.40	1.75
	vi. Other than HH industry	1.26	1.64	1.75	–
	vii. Construction	0.95	1.75	1.59	–
	***Total* (v to vii)**	***3.30***	***4.23***	***3.74***	***1.75***
Tertiary Sector	viii. Trade and commerce	2.98	3.52	5.26	–
	ix. Transport, storage etc	1.25	1.23	1.45	–
	x. Other services	10.63	11.27	14.75	35.38
	***Total* (viii to x)**	***14.86***	***16.02***	***21.46***	***35.38***
Total Main Workers (i to x)		**100.00**	**100.00**	**100.00**	**100.00**

Source: Compiled from Primary Census Abstracts of Different Years.

Table 5
Literacy Rate in Meghalaya

Category	*1991*	*2001*
Total Population	49.10	63.31
Total Male	53.12	66.14
Total Female	44.85	60.41
Rural Population	41.05	57.00
Rural Male	44.83	59.90
Rural Female	37.12	54.02
Urban Population	81.74	87.12
Urban Male	85.72	89.90
Urban Female	77.32	84.30

Table 6
Growth of NSDP in Meghalaya

Year	*NSDP*	*Year*	*NSDP*
1981	5441	1992	7052
1982	5513	1993	6464
1983	5441	1994	6720
1984	5413	1995	6705
1985	5537	1996	7221
1986	5645	1997	7225
1987	5585	1998	7413
1988	5936	1999	7935
1989	6052	2000	8333
1990	6056	2001	8460
1991	6928	2002	8827

Table 7(a)

Net State Domestic Product at Factor Cost by Industry of Origin, Meghalaya (At 1980–81 Constant Prices)

Sl. No.	Industry	1980	1981	1982	1983	1984	1985	1986	1987	1988	1989	1990	1991	1992
1.	Agriculture	6781	6758	7054	6988	7326	7603	7115	7613	6277	7641	8178	8244	6514
2.	Forestry and Logging	380	530	217	177	147	114	98	279	312	311	339	259	193
3.	Fishing	63	64	62	57	44	47	42	51	28	52	78	183	216
4.	Mining and Quarrying	299	432	438	541	688	641	747	692	585	1290	2088	1910	1552
5.	Manufacturing	579	759	613	547	574	709	749	878	799	1037	1262	1418	1506
5.1	Registered	158	209	219	152	157	229	270	321	291	413	471	490	622
5.2	Unregistered	421	550	394	395	417	480	479	557	508	624	791	928	884
6.	Construction	2096	1899	2009	2120	2061	2046	2127	2172	2245	2198	2572	2795	2924
7.	Ele., Gas and Water Supply	–61	–90	–94	–153	–250	–198	–383	–275	–353	–519	–569	–618	–697
8.	Trans. Stor and Comm.	419	574	632	867	948	845	1008	992	1385	1436	1627	2080	2241
8.1	Railways	0	0	0	0	0	0	0	0	0	0	0	0	0
8.2	Tran. by other Means and Storage	308	454	513	732	796	694	857	813	1223	1269	1452	1617	1730
8.3	Communication	111	120	119	135	152	151	151	179	162	167	175	463	511
9.	Trade, Hotels and Restaurants	1922	1960	1974	1906	2082	2163	2107	2336	2552	2844	3770	4243	3542
10.	Banking and Insurance	310	359	360	392	548	605	834	964	1080	1210	1101	1158	1183
11	Real Estate, Own. of Dwels. and Bus. Se	1524	1574	1624	1681	1734	1796	1858	1992	2061	2133	2208	2286	2370
12.	Public Administration	2147	2242	2415	2481	2757	3190	3452	3848	4391	4608	4488	4515	5183
13.	Other Services	1503	1667	1710	1853	1800	1871	2013	2183	2371	3214	3286	3332	3191
14.	Net State Domestic Product	17962	18728	19014	19457	20459	21432	21767	23725	23956	27455	30428	31805	29918
15.	Population ('000)	1320	1358	1397	1437	1477	1518	1558	1598	1646	1720	1754	1808	1856
16.	Per Capita Income (₹)	1361	1379	1361	1354	1385	1412	1397	1485	1455	1596	1735	1759	1612

Source: National Account Statistics, Government of India, New Delhi.

Table 7(b)

NSDP at Factor Cost by Industry of Origin, Meghalaya (At 1999–2000 Constant Prices)

Sl. No.	*Industry*	*1999–2000*	*2000–2001*	*2001–2002*	*2002–2003*	*2003–2004*	*2004–2005*	*2005–2006*	*2006–2007*	*2007–2008 (Adv)*
1	Agriculture	70738	74217	76857	81545	83238	87997	92809	97290	101987
2	Forestry	4180	4432	4974	5119	5750	6188	5840	6079	6328
3	Fishing	2010	2684	2109	2599	2112	2572	2467	2566	2668
4	Manufacturing	5022	5214	5123	8348	9387	10752	10659	11921	13156
4.1	Registered	2077	2130	2241	5386	6362	7964	7926	8846	9874
4.2	Un-Registered	2945	3084	2882	2962	3025	2788	2733	3075	3282
5	Mining	23706	27109	35516	26991	33034	Not available			

Source: NEDFI, Guwahati

Table 7(c)

Net State Domestic Product of Meghalaya at Current Prices (in ₹ Lakh)

Sl. No.	Industry	1999–2000	2000–2001	2001–2002	2002–2003	2003–2004	2004–2005	2005–2006	2006–2007	2007–2008 (Adv)
1	Agriculture	70738	78367	87397	92660	95538	96233	104044	108679	113521
2	Forestry and Logging	4180	4711	5453	5874	7053	7404	7278	7823	8408
3	Fishing	2010	2794	2426	2872	2795	3252	3112	3312	3525
4	Manufacturing	5022	5234	5281	8764	10556	14108	14770	16264	17502
4.1	Registered	2077	2239	2479	5902	7463	11233	11901	12609	13359
4.2	Unregistered	2945	2995	2802	2862	3093	2875	2869	3655	4143
5	Mining and Quarrying	23706	29191	40927	33704	44550	49199	50793	53611	56585
6	Construction	32376	40181	41720	44905	49546	57026	70188	81921	87628
7	Electricity, Gas and Water Supply	6628	6725	6708	7832	7893	9228	8273	8645	9034
8	Transport, Storage and Communication	20259	21644	23914	26165	28336	31957	35139	41797	48409
8.1	Transport by other means	17163	18610	20542	21992	24394	27404	29509	35599	41011
8.2	Storage	70	82	92	98	112	128	134	144	158
8.3	Communication	3026	2952	3280	4075	3830	4425	5496	6054	7240

Cont'd...

Cont'd…

9.	Trade, Hotel and Restaurant	33645	36843	43878	48406	57874	61420	66639	72698	81570
10	Banking and Insurance	9565	11345	12528	15016	17071	17407	19614	21940	24542
11	Real Estate, Ownership of dwelling and Business Services	35276	40019	46051	50614	54434	56754	60896	64844	71210
12	Public Administration	44300	47886	50035	53967	59156	68074	73319	78823	85300
13	Other Services Net State	33503	34770	38782	38977	40531	43233	47521	53494	57197
14	Domestic Product	321208	359710	405100	429783	475333	515295	561586	613851	664431
15	Population (000)	2237	2295	2353	2367	2397	2427	2458	2488	2518
16	Per Capita Income (in ₹)	14359	15674	17216	18157	19830	21232	22847	24672	26387

Sources: Central Statistical Organization (CSO).

Table 8
Sectoral Composition of NSDP in Meghalaya

Sector	*1981*	*1991*	*2002*	*2008*
Agriculture	78.74	68.62	61.69	54.50
Forestry	6.17	2.16	3.99	3.38
Fishing	0.75	1.52	1.69	1.43
Manufacturing	8.86	11.80	4.11	7.03
(a) Registered	2.44	4.08	1.80	5.28
(b) Unregistered	6.41	7.72	2.31	1.75
Mining and Quarrying	5.03	15.90	28.51	33.66

Table 9

Growth of Infrastructures in Meghalaya

Number of Vehicles

Year	*Trucks*	*Buses*	*Small 4–Wheelers*	*3–Wheelers*	*2–Wheelers*	*Others*
1980	1100	215	3131	–	1450	266
1991	7183	1502	13065	21	7404	3114
1998	10997	2012	19350	637	14734	2902

Road Length (kms)

Total Road Length				*Surfaced Road Length*				*Road per 100 sq. km.*				*Road per 1,000 Population*			
1979	1989	1992	1997	1979	1989	1992	1997	1979	1989	1992	1997	1979	1989	1992	1997
3690	5624	7832	8480	1475	3110	2931	3923	16.40	25.07	34.90	37.8	3.17	4.21	4.45	3.86

Per Capita Power Consumption (KWH)

1978	1979	1981	1985	1986	1987	1988	1989	1990	1992	1994	1995	1996	1999
25	35	31	61	76	83	84	98	108	129	110	140	143	150

Figure 1
Trends in the Birth Rate of Population in Meghalaya

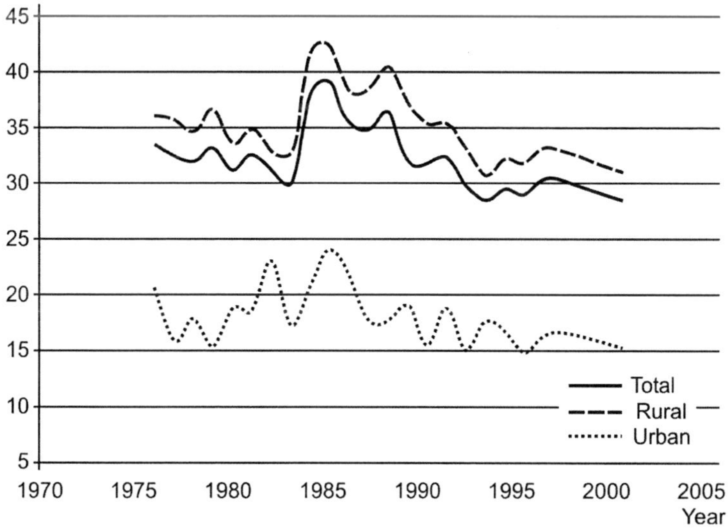

Figure 2
Trends in the Death Rate of Population in Meghalaya

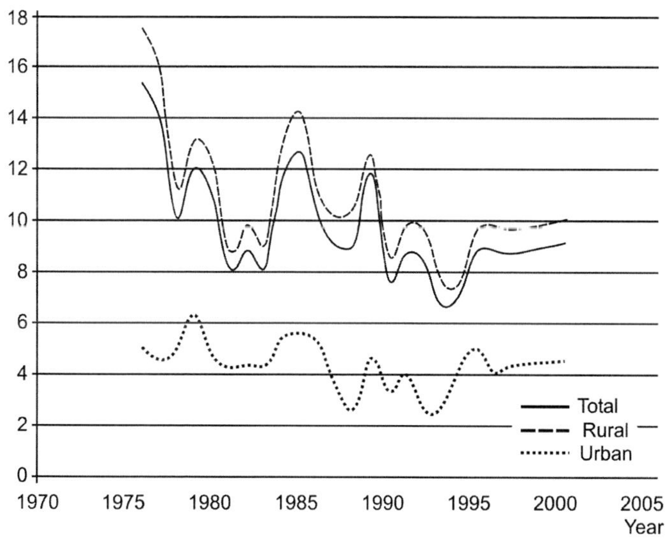

Figure 3

Trends in the Natural Growth Rate of Population in Meghalaya

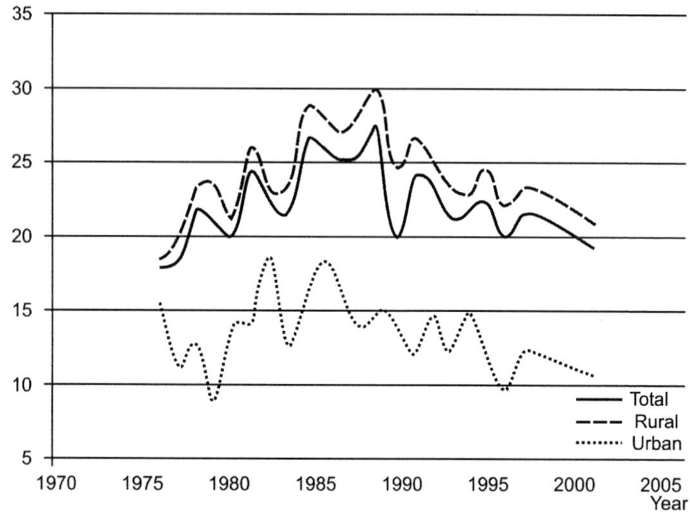

Figure 4

Changes in the Dependency Ratio in Meghalaya during 1991–2001

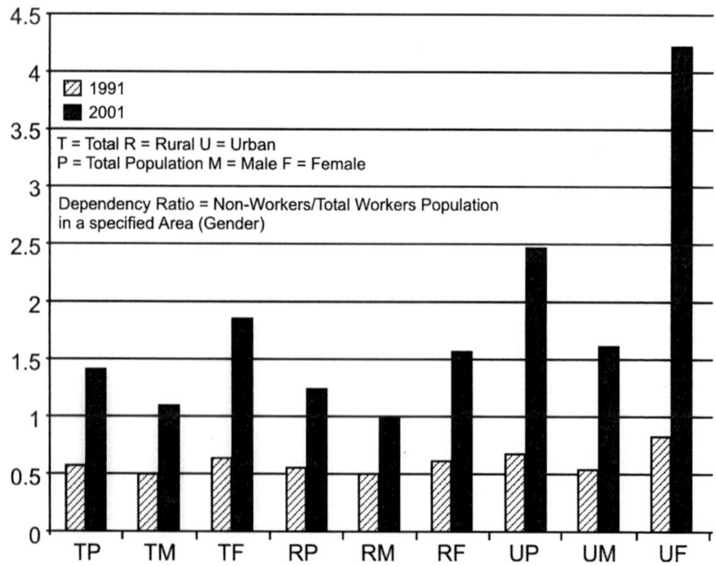

Figure 5

Changes in the Economic Participation Rate in Meghalaya during 1991–2001

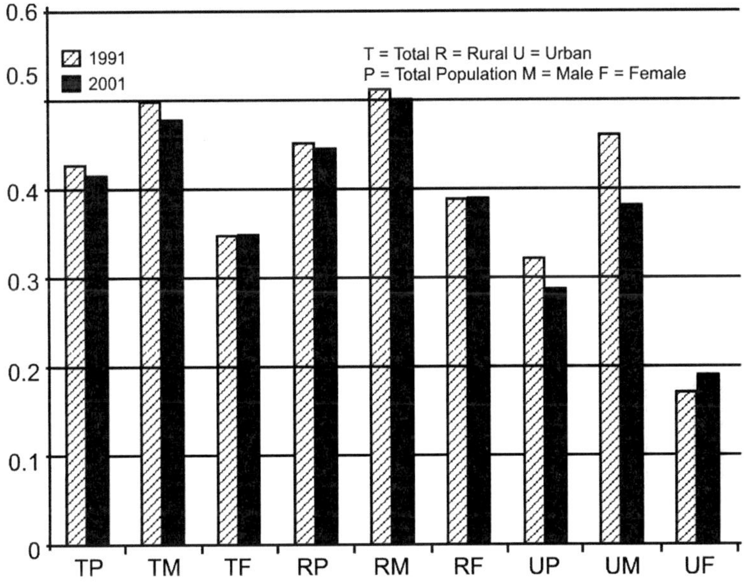

Figure 6

Changes in the Literacy Rate in Meghalaya during 1991–2001

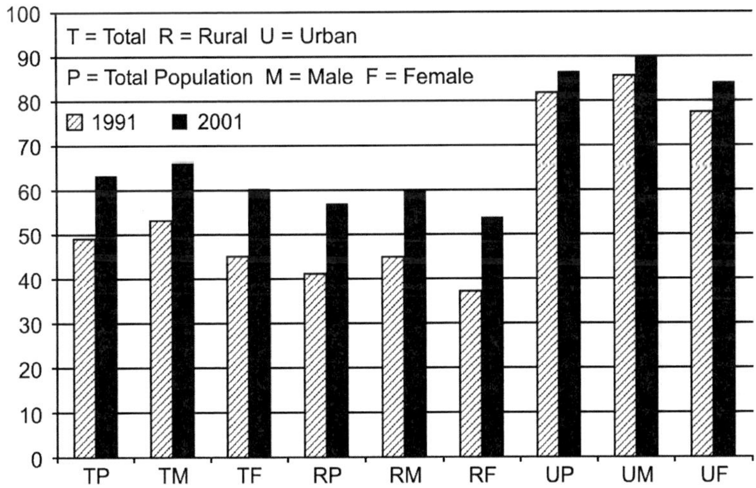

Figure 7

Changes in Net State Domestic Product in Meghalaya during 1981–2002

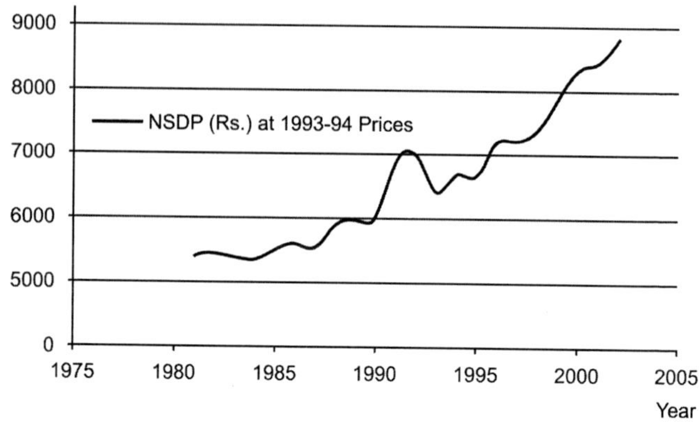

13

Industrialization and Socio-Cultural Transformation of Rural Community in Assam

B.N. BORTHAKUR

In sociology, development means many things which are invariably related and are all seen through the frame of change by action. Here, social development takes centre stage though with the clear understanding that it inevitably is hinged upon economic development. Thus, Smelser (1965) opines that economic development at the same instance has also to do with non-economic aspects which overlap and influence each other. In the modern era, economic development is never an automatic nor a spontaneous materialization. According to Borthakur (1994), economic development and its other intended implications are as a result of envisaged developmental policies emanating from the decision making and implementing bureaucratic structure.

Retrospectively, the sociology of economic development has had its roots in the writings of many scholars (Hagen, 1962; Hoselitz, 1960; Marx, 1970; McClleland, 1961; Moore, 1967; Weber, 1963, to mention some). Under these umbrella theoretical considerations, we keep in mind the development models of capitalism (A. Smith, J.S. Mills, Spencer) socialism (Marx, K.) and planning (K. Mannheim) that generally characterizes socio-economic development undertakings all across the globe today.

Planning in India

It can be arguably claimed that the seeds of the importance of planning within academic circles was planted by M. Visvesvarayyan's book in 1934. It led to stimulating many other scholars like P.S. Loknathan, K.N. Sen et al., to produce new formulations on planning. The first national plan for the country was formulated in 1938 by the National Planning Committee with Jawaharlal Nehru as its chairman. In spite of the II World War proving an interruption toward action, industrialists in Bombay further produced an economic plan for the country known as the "Bombay Plan" in 1944. A profusion of plans came about like the *Peoples Plan* drafted by M.N. Roy, *Gandhian Plan* by S.N. Agarwal, while the Government of India instituted the Planning and Development Department headed by A. Dalal. Following Indian Independence, the Planning Commission was constituted in 1950 with Pandit Nehru as its chairman to assess the country's need of capital and human resource and to plan for raid economic development.

Thus, under the auspices of economic planning and development with industrialization as one of the major focus envisaged by the Planning Commission, the present paper is an empirical study of the consequence of industrial establishment and social transformation of rural community in upper Assam. Here, the transformation is explained based purely on field data.

Candidly speaking, the administration in India during the British rule did nothing for industrialization in the country. The British took away the raw materials to their country and after processing those in industries/factories there brought the manufactured goods to India for marketing. India after her independence desired to achieve industrialization through her planned sector and to this end in view she laid her industrial foundation by establishing defence and heavy industries and permitting the private enterprises to establish agriculture based and large-scale consumer goods producing industries. India in her plan allocation by giving some incentives in the form of reduction in excise and custom duties and also by providing some subsidies to the private entrepreneurs has given a fillip to the industrial development in the country. Mention may be made here that in the last six decades of India's independence India has achieved a lot in the sphere of setting up of different kinds of industries. The North-East region of India also has witnessed a growth of industrialization. A few important industries of the North-East which came up after independence are fertilizer, oil, sugar, hard board, spun-silk, cycle, distillery, chemical, plywood and wood, cement, paper etc.

Industrialization entails change in many aspects of man and society. First, by replacing manual labour by machine in carrying out production it revolutionizes the system of production. Secondly, by transforming the mechanical solidarity to organic solidarity, it creates a number of specialized jobs. Thirdly, it creates a climate, which is congenial for imbibing the qualities like punctuality and discipline etc. by the individuals associated with the factory system of production. Finally, it changes the tastes of individuals in matters of dress and diet and mental outlook towards family and marriage, health practices, religious beliefs and practices and also with regard to savings.

In this paper, an attempt has been made to study the observable effects of an industry on the socio-cultural aspects of the people of a village named No. 1 Mohmara which is 5 km away from Oil India Ltd., Duliajan, an industrial establishment in the district of Dibrugarh, Assam. According to the old people of the village this village was established in about 1925. The earlier settlers of the village were from Tengakhat, which is 14 km away from the village. It was learnt that one late Tolon Ch. Tamuli was the first person to come to the present site in search of land who was the father of five sons and five daughters. Later on more persons from Tengakhat, Dibrugarh and Sibsagar came to settle in the present site. The present site of the village according to the old people was full of dense forest and in the forest there were beehives. The Assamese word for bee is *mou.* The earlier settlers while cutting the trees for their settlement annihilated the beehives and from this the village is named Mohmari. Another version of naming the village goes like this-after the establishment of the village the earlier settlers started buffalo farm for milching. The buffalo is called *moh* in Assamese. The buffaloes at one point of time were attacked by unknown disease and as a result all the buffaloes died and from this the village is named as Mohmari. With the passage of time more and more people started to come to settle in and around the village and those households who settled in the areas adjacent to this village named their village as No. 2 Mohmari and therefore the first village becomes popular as No. 1 Mohmari. The village No. 1 Mohmari has three Lower Primary Schools. The first L.P. School which is named as No. 65 Mohmari Primary School was established in 1935. The second L.P. School which is named as No. 73 Mohmari Primary School was established in 1942 and the third one established in 1970 is named as Naba Milan Primary School. There is no High School in the village. The distance to the nearest High School is 1.5 km which is situated at a place named Kothalguri. The children of this village pursue higher education in the college located at Duliajan. A health sub-centre of the state government functions in Merbil-Majuli which is just 1 km away from the village. The village falls under the Kathalguri Gaon Panchayat. There is one gaon panchayat women elected representative in the village. There are two women's organizations in the village. These are Jagriti Mohila Samiti formed in 1958 and the other one is Dibyajyoti Mohila Samiti formed in 1982. A music college was established in the village in July 2008. The only youth organization named as Ankuron Yuva Gosthi was formed in 1991. The village library named as Dipty Puthibhoral was established also in 1991. There are three *namghars* (temple) in the village. The total number of households at the time of our survey was found 258 and the total population was found to be 1,517. The village is connected by metalled road to the town.

The Oil India Limited was established in the year 1959 by M/s Burma Oil Company and Government of India as partners with 66.66 and 33.33 per cent share holding respectively. In 1961 the Government of India share holding was increased to 50 per cent and it became an equal partner. Later on the Burma Oil Company's share holding was also taken by Government of India, and from October 1981 the company became fully a Government of India owned company. After the setting up of the company at Duliajan much change has been taken place in the socio-cultural aspects of the rural community living on the fringe of the establishment. With a view to analyse the kind of change brought about by the Oil India Ltd we sought to elicit some information from the villagers.

In order to collect primary data from the villagers a brief interview schedule was prepared. The secondary data for the study were collected from the village headman *(gaonburah)* and village elders. Since the village is a big one, therefore, we decided to include one third of the households of the village within our sample. Thus, the total sample of our study consists of 86 households. The respondents of the study were selected from all corners of the village. The sample procedure we adopted in this study was random sampling. The data for the study were collected during July 2008.

During the visit to the households we interviewed whomever we met in the family. The respondents of our study belonged to different age groups ranging from 25 to 85. In all we interviewed 72 (83.72%) male and 14 (16.28%) females. The percentages of respondents belonged to the age group of 25–35 was 16 (18.60%), 18 (20.93%) in the age group of 35–45, 29 (33.72%) in the age group of 45–55, 13 (15.11%) in the age group of 55–65, 7 (8.13%) in the age group of 65–75 and 3 (3.48%) in the age group of 75–85. All the respondents we interviewed were found to be followers of Hinduism. The castes of the respondents were found to be Brahmin 4 (4.65%), Kalita 60 (69.76%), Chutia 10 (11.62%), Konch 5 (5.81%) and ex-tea garden labour community 7 (8.13%).With regard to marital status of the respondents it was found that 81 (94.18%) are married, 3 (3.48%) unmarried and 2 (2.32%) were widows. The educational qualification of the respondents varied from lower primary level to post-graduate level. In the sample households we surveyed the educational qualification of 14 (16.28%) was found to be primary level, of 30 (34.88%) ME standard, of 23 (26.74%) High School Leaving Certificate Examination passed, of 11 (12.79%) Higher Secondary passed, of 7 (8.13%) graduate level and of 1 (1.16%) post graduate standard. It is observed that the parents are interested to provide modern education to their children. In the village it is observed that the children of the families of the industrial workers and service holders are educationally advanced than the children of the agricultural families. It was further gathered that in most of the agricultural families the children help their parents in agricultural activities, in rearing cattle and nursing the young ones. On the whole, in the sample households nobody was found illiterate. It suggests that industrialization has created a climate, which generates a sense of value of education in the matter of job opportunities.

The impact of the industry in the village was observed in many aspects of life. Next to education it was the occupation of the people. In this village the economic base is composed of mixed occupations, the dominant being the industrial base. In our sample we found while 31 (36.04%) were engaged in agriculture, then 39 (45.34%) were found to engage in industrial occupation, 12 (13.95%) were found to engage in business, 1 (1.16%) in teaching, 2 (2.32%) in state government service and 1 (1.16%) enjoying state government pension. It is gathered that more and more men have engaged themselves in the industry leaving the farmland on lease to landless agricultural families and in some cases to contractual labour for cultivation under the care of women.

The food habits of the villagers though is not much different than prior to the establishment of the oil industry yet some new consumer items are found to enter into the village. Rice with vegetable and *dal* is taken by the villagers in lunch and dinner. In the breakfast and afternoon tiffin earlier they used to take *chira, muri, pithaguri, komolchaul* etc., prepared at home from paddy. But now-a-days these items are replaced by *roti* or *puri* made of atta or bakery made bread with butter or jelly. Further, consumer items like maggy, chao-chao, tomato sauce and lemon squash etc. are found to enter into the village. In this study the researcher desired to know from the respondents in what kind of hearth food is cooked in their households. To this query we came to know that in 28 (32.55%) respondents' house food is cooked in earthen hearth where firewood is used as fuel while in 58 (67.44%) respondents' houses gas burner is used as hearth and LPG is used as fuel. It was further learnt that these respondents' households where cooking is done in earthen hearth by using firewood, these households do not use pressure cooker instead they use steel or aluminium pot for cooking meal. On the other hand as many as 58 (67.44%) respondents were found to use gas burner, LPG and pressure cooker for cooking meals. In the sample households 45 (52.22%) respondents' were found to possess refrigerators.

With regard to dress pattern of the villagers it was observed that the old male folk of the village still wear *dhuti-punjabi* and the women folk *chador-mekhala.* The youths are quite modern with their dress. The young ones, the adults and the middle aged men while going out from homes for any kind of work, they dress themselves with long pants, shirts, shoes, socks and goggles. The dress of old women has not departed from traditional form while the traditional dress of the young women, i.e., *chadar-mekhela* is replaced by *salowar-kamij*. Moreover, the village women were found to be users of powder, snow-cream, lipstick and eye-brow pencils etc. This change in the style of dress among the younger people is due to their exposure to urban industrial situation and the mass-media including television and cinema.

In the sample households surveyed by the researcher as against 29.07 per cent joint family 70.93 per cent nuclear families were found. In the course of field enquiry it was gathered that as many as 10 persons of the sample households migrated to industrial town of

Duliajan, and out of these ten as many as six persons have been maintaining contact with the native families by participating in the festivals, two by regularly sending money and another two by visiting the families occasionally. It is observed that the change in the structure of families has been mainly due to industrialization. Regarding the matter of taking important decision in the family it was gathered that in 27 (31.39%) surveyed households decision is taken by the heads of the families, while in equal number of percentage of households the decision is taken by the head of the family in consultation with the adult members of the families, in 2 (2.32%) by the wives of the head of the households and in 30 (34.88%) by the head of the households in consultation with their wives. Another important finding of the study was that in every households women were accorded equal status. In the sphere of marriage it is gathered that marriage takes place within the caste. But, now-a-days, a tendency towards inter-caste marriage has developed among the young generation. In the surveyed households three inter-caste marriage and one inter-community marriages have taken place. The inter-community marriage was between an Assamese girl and a Bengali boy. Though the system of dowry is not prevalent in the Assamese society, the tradition of presenting some gifts to the bride by her parents still continues. Being exposed to industrial culture the villagers are now more conscious about their status. Hence, the parents start to present more gifts to the bride in the pretext of following the tradition. This is a marked shift from pre-industrial culture.

The village people now-a-days are seen to be more conscious about health and hygiene. From the surveyed households it is gathered that as many as 80.23 per cent had sanitary latrines and *pucca* bathrooms. The respondents were found to use tube-wells, and they formed the habit of drinking filtered water. It is further gathered that in the event of any family member falling ill 82 (95.34%) respondents consulted modern medical practitioners while only 4 (4.65%) instead of consulting doctors used to offer prayer to gods/goddesses for curing of disease. In regard to childbirth it was learnt that 79 (91.86%) respondents admitted the women in hospitals while 7 (8.13%) had it at home under the care and supervision of a midwife. Our further investigation revealed that the respondents in whose homes childbirth takes place belong to the ex-tea garden labour community. The respondents of the study were also found conscious about the health of their children. Of the surveyed households 82 (95.34%) respondents were found to provide anti-polio drugs and anti-measles vaccine to their children while only 4 (4.65%) did not provide these to their children.

Regarding the attitude of the villagers towards religion it is gathered that religion is emancipated from dogmatic beliefs and practices. In regard to this it can be said that industrialization leads to a decline of belief in supernaturalism. In the observance of any kind of religious function including purification ceremony of the new born, performance of marriage and death of a family member etc. as many as 84.88 per cent respondents have not followed the age old Brahmanical rituals. Instead, they resort *Nam-Kirton* (singing devotional songs of Lord Krishna composed by saint Sankardeva) for observance of any kind of function.

The respondents of the study were found to develop the habit of listening to radio, viewing TV and reading newspapers. It was gathered that 20 (23.25%) respondents regularly listened to radio, 60 (69.76%) regularly viewed TV and 70 (81.39%) regularly read newspapers. The respondents of the surveyed village further developed the habit of saving a portion of their earning in financial institutions. It was gathered that 86.84 per cent respondents used to save money in banks/Post Office/Life Insurance Corporation.

The Oil India at Duliajan thus has created situations for transformation of socio-cultural aspects of the people of the rural community. It affects almost every aspect of rural life including economy, food-habits, system of cooking, dress-pattern, family structure and attitude towards marriage, health practices, religious beliefs and practices etc.

References

Borthakur, B.N. 2004. *Communication and Village Development*. Kolkata: Institute of Social Research and Applied Anthropology.

—. 2004. *Social Aspects of Economic Development*. Dibrugarh: Upsana Publishing Company.

Hagen, E.E. 1962. *On the Theory of Social Change*. Homewood, Ill.: Dorsey Press.

Hoselitz, B.F. 1960. *Sociological Aspects of Economic Growth*. Glencoe, Ill.: Free Press.

Mannheim, K. 1940. *Man and Society in the Age of Reconstruction.* London: Routledge and Kegan Paul.

Marx, K. 1970. *Capital.* Vol. II. London: Lawrence and Wishart (first published in 1864).

McClelland, D. 1961. *The Achieving Society.* New York: D Van Nostrand Co. Inc.

Mills, J.S. 1959. *Elucidation of the Science of History: Theories of History.* New York: Free Press.

Moore, W.E. 1965. *Social Change.* New Delhi: Prentice Hall.

Smelser, N.J. 1959. *Social Change in the Industrial Revolution.* Chicago: Chicago University Press.

Smith, A. 1912. *An Inquiry into Nature and Causes of the Wealth of Nations.* London: G. Bell and Sons.

Spencer, H. 1898. *Principles of Sociology.* New York: Appleton.

Visvesvaraya, M. 1934. *Planned Economy for India.* Bangalore: Bangalore Printing Press.

Weber, M. 1963. *The Sociology of Religion.* Boston: Beacon Press.

14

Demographic Change and Ageing in the North-East India

Issues and Challenges

DEBENDRA KUMAR NAYAK

Few areas of research in social sciences, particularly in demography, have received as much attention in recent years as ageing. The subject is attracting increasing attention from Indian social scientists, too. This is not surprising considering the phenomenal increase in the proportion of the aged population as noticed since the results of Census of India 1991 was made public.

The term 'ageing' is somewhat ambiguous. Chronological ageing, referring to how old a person is, is perhaps the most straightforward definition of ageing and is often distinguished from 'social ageing' (society's expectations of how people should act as they grow older) and 'biological ageing' (an organism's physical state as it ages). In any case old age is a cultural construction, in much the same way as are the other phases ('vocations') of life. Concepts like chronological age, biological age, psychic or mental age, social age, and many others are frequently encountered in literature pertaining to ageing. Since these are our constructions, each of them is used separately in specific disciplines. Old age is also culturally constituted; its connotation in a simple society may be qualitatively different from that in a complex modern society.

Perhaps a more definitive connotation of the term 'ageing' has begun to appear in demographic literature which stands apart from chronological ageing or a mere increase in the number or proportion of old population as a consequence of increased life expectancy. Population ageing refers to shifts in the age distribution of the population in which the relative share of persons at older ages increases, and the share at younger ages decreases. This is distinct from absolute increases in the number of older persons that can occur even if their share does not increase (Leete and Jacobs, 2002). Demographers thus view ageing as a process inextricably linked to 'demographic transition' or 'fertility transition' leading to slow but a definite change from more youthful societies in many countries to more demographically mature populations. In strict demographic terms, the nations-states witnessing these transitions will be relieved of child dependency to a great extent while they will have to face a greater burden of old-age dependency. This shift of dependency as reflected in the changing age-structure of such nations may be similar in quantity – decrease in child dependency compensated by increase in old age dependency – but not in quality. It may be noted that the increase in life expectancy is not only due to greater life expectancy among the younger age-group but also rising life expectancy of the older segment.

While ageing research is fairly well developed and well documented in Europe and other developed countries including Japan not much interest in the past was shown by scholars and policy makers in most Asian countries including India. The reasons are not far to seek. This lack of research on ageing in Asia relates to the firm belief that the robustness and continuance of the family system 'is and will continue to be a full proof insurance against all problems faced during old age' (Dhar Chakraborty, 2004: 26). But we are now slowly waking up to the reality that joint family, long held as our answer to the problems of ageing, is neither as widespread as popularly believed, nor does it seem capable of accommodating pressures created by demands of a modern urban and industrialized lifestyle.

Initially observed in the more developed countries, the process of ageing is now rapidly approaching the developing world. Although not a global phenomenon yet, various predictions indicate that population ageing is going to become a major global issue in years to come. Virtually all countries will face population ageing, albeit with varying intensity and at different points of time. The inter-generational balance seen today may not be observed in future.

The changing balance between age groups would make the aged more of a burden on society and as resources are diverted from the young to the old, the world may experience unpleasant inter-generational conflicts and tensions. With improvements in life expectancy (and these improvements will take place at a faster rate for females than for males) there is, and will be, a progressive ageing of the older population, and interestingly, a majority of them will be females.

The issues that are likely to be confronted by all developing nation-states include the implications of an ageing population for socio-economic development programmes, health care, savings, investments, consumption patterns, work force participation, migration and social security. It may also include the role of the family in supporting the aged. According to Chakraborty, '... when the Western world is reshaping the world for the elderly, in order to contain costs as well as to mitigate the inter-generational conflict, many Asian countries have barely begun to think about their elderly, and given the pace of population ageing in Asia and the corresponding lack of adjustment mechanism, a 'time bomb' and 'agequake' may not be very far' (2004: 27).

Ageing in the Modern World

It may be noted however that all countries and regions are not experiencing these changes uniformly. Different countries and regions are at varying stages of this demographic transition. In most advanced countries, the ageing process is already well under way, and it is expected that a number of developing countries in the East and Southeast Asia and central and Eastern Europe will also experience significant ageing from about 2020. In other developing countries, however, the demographic transition is less advanced.

Prior to 1900, the world population growth was relatively slow. The age structure of the population too was broadly constant. Fewer people lived beyond age 65. Dramatic changes in life expectancy that was witnessed during the first half of the twentieth century resulted in unprecedented population growth. This unprecedented population increment however did not significantly alter the age structure of the population at least in the initial period. But phenomenal drop in the fertility rates in the second half of the 20th century significantly slowed down population growth resulting in a decline in the share of the young in the population with a corresponding rise in the share of the elderly. The last century thus has proved to be a watershed in terms of significant demographic transformation of the global population. The most significant of all developments is the phenomenal increment to the total size of the global population accompanied by unprecedented hike in population growth rate – a demographic event unlikely to be replicated in the coming years.

Table 14.1

Percentage Distribution of Population by Broad Age Groups

Year	*1950*	*1975*	*2000*	*2025*	*2050*
Age Group			*World*		
0–14	34.3	36.7	30.0	24.3	21.0
15–59	57.6	54.7	60.0	60.7	58.0
60+	8.2	8.6	10.0	15.0	21.1
			More Developed Regions		
0–14	27.3	24.2	18.3	15.0	15.5
15–59	60.9	60.4	62.3	56.8	51.0
60+	11.7	15.4	19.4	28.2	33.5
			Less Developed Regions		
0–14	37.6	41.1	32.8	26.0	21.8
15–59	56.0	52.7	59.5	61.4	59.0
60+	6.4	6.2	7.7	12.6	19.3
			Least Developed Regions		
0–14	41.1	44.7	43.1	37.9	29.1
15–59	53.5	50.3	52.0	56.2	61.4
60+	5.4	5.0	4.9	5.9	9.5

Source: United Nations (2001).

The spatial pattern of population growth was however not uniform across the developed and the less developed countries. Most developed countries had by the middle of the 20th century, witnessed major reduction in both in death rates and then in birth rates leading to not only slower population growth but also a phenomenal decline in child population (Table 14.1). Population began to age in such countries. In sharp contrast, the less developed countries continued to experience high fertility rates in spite of large decline in mortality and significant rise in life expectancy particularly in the post World War years. This contrasting population transitions resulted in significant population redistribution across countries and continents.

By the early 21st century a larger number of countries have joined the ranks of low fertility regime leading to a worldwide fall in growth rates to about 1.2 per cent per annum and is expected to fall further in years to come as more and more countries shall experience lower fertility. A net outcome of this vital demographic transformation is the slow but a definite change from more youthful societies in many countries to more demographically mature populations – a phenomenon variously described as the process of ageing or greying. In strict demographic terms, the nations witnessing these transitions will be relieved of child dependency to a great extent while they will be faced with a greater burden of old-age dependency. This shift of dependency as reflected in the changing age-structure of such nations may be similar in quantity – decrease in child dependency compensated by increase in old age dependency – but not in quality. It may be noted that the increase in life expectancy is not only due to greater life expectancy among the younger age-group but also rising life expectancy of the older segment.

A significant fact about ageing is that it increases the total number of aged persons compared to other age groups and that the pace of this change is more rapid now in developing rather than the developed countries (Table 14.2). Though all countries in the developing world have not uniformly received the full impact of this rise in the proportion of the aged and a corresponding decline in the young age population, it is expected that nearly all countries will experience, by the beginning of the next century, a gradual demographic shift towards an older segment exceeding the proportion of the young for the first time in history (UNFPA, 1998) – a situation that has already taken roots in more developed countries.

Table 14.2
Ageing Indicators

Regions	*World*	*More Developed Regions*	*Less Developed Regions*	*Least Developed Countries*	*Asia*	*China*	*India*
			Percentage in Old Age				
Total	10.0	19.4	7.7	4.9	8.8	10.1	7.6
Female	11.1	22.2	8.3	5.3	9.5	10.9	8.2
Male	8.9	16.5	7.1	4.5	8.1	9.4	7.1
Ageing Index	33.4	106.2	23.4	11.3	29.0	40.7	22.7
			Broad Age Groups (Percentage)				
0–14	30.0	18.3	32.8	43.1	30.2	24.8	33.5
15–59	60.0	62.3	59.5	52.0	61.0	65.0	58.9
60+	10.0	19.4	7.7	4.9	8.8	10.1	7.6
Median Age	26.5	37.4	24.3	18.2	26.2	30.0	23.7
			Dependency Ratio				
Total	58.4	48.3	61.1	86.0	56.5	46.4	62.5
Youth	47.5	27.1	52.9	80.2	47.3	36.4	54.4
Old Age	10.9	21.2	8.2	5.8	9.2	10.0	8.1
Potential Support Ratio	9.1	4.7	12.2	17.2	10.9	10.0	12.4
Growth Rate 60+	1.2	0.2	1.5	2.5	1.3	0.7	1.5
TFR	2.7	1.5	2.9	5.2	2.5	1.8	3.0
			Life Expectancy (Years)				
Total	66.0	75.6	64.1	51.4	67.4	71.2	64.2
Female	68.1	79.3	65.7	52.2	69.2	73.5	64.9
Male	63.9	71.9	62.5	50.6	65.8	69.1	63.6

Source: World Population Aging 1950–2050, United Nations, New York, 2002.

Notes: Ageing Index: Number of persons 60 years old or over per hundred persons under age 15.

Total Dependency Ratio: Number of persons under the age 15 plus persons aged 60 or older per one hundred persons 15 to 60.

Young Dependency Ratio: Number of persons 0–14 years per one hundred persons 15 to 60 years.

Old Age Dependency Ratio: Number of persons 60 years and over per one hundred persons 15–60 years.

Median Age: that age that divides a population into two groups of the same size, such that one half of the total population is younger than this age, the other half is older.

Potential Support Ratio: Number of persons aged 15–60 per every person aged 60 or older.

World Assembly on Ageing (United Nations, 2001) summarized the global trend in ageing as given below:

- One out of every ten persons is now 60 years or above; by 2050, one out of five will be 60 years or older; and by 2150, one out of three persons will be 60 years or older.
- The older population itself is ageing. The oldest old (80 years or older) is the fastest growing segment of the older population. They currently make up 13 per cent of the 60+ age group and will grow to 20 per cent by 2050. The number of centenarians (aged 100 years or older) is projected to increase 14–fold from approximately 2,65,000 in 2005 to 3.7 million by 2050.
- The majority of older persons (55%) are women. Among the oldest old, 64 per cent are women.
- Striking differences exist between regions. One out of five Europeans, but one out of twenty Africans, is 60 years or older.
- In some developed countries today, the proportion of older persons is already one in four. During the first half of the 21st century that proportion will be close to one in two in some countries.
- As the tempo of ageing in developing countries is more rapid than in developed countries, developing countries will have less time than the developed countries to adapt to the consequences of population ageing.
- Over the last half of the 20th century, 20 years were added to the average lifespan, bringing global life expectancy to its current level of 66 years. Large differences exist between countries, however. In the least developed countries, men reaching age 60 can expect only 15 more years of life and women, 17 more, while in the more developed regions, life expectancy at age 60 is 19 years for men and 23 years for women.
- The impact of population ageing is increasingly evident in the old-age dependency ratio, the number of working age persons (age 15–64 years) per older person (65 years or older) that is used as an indicator of the 'dependency burden' on potential workers. Between 2005 and 2050, the old-age dependency ratio will almost double in more developed regions and almost triple in less developed regions. The potential socio-economic impact on society that may result from an increasing old-age dependency ratio is an area of growing research and public debate.

The ageing process in India is no exception but reveals remarkable regional diversity in the manifestation of the process. The elderly population in India is the second largest in the world, next only to China and the older population has been steadily increasing in number and proportion. This segment numbered only 12.1 million in the year 1901 and it increased to 24.7 million by the year 1961. The 2001 census recorded 77 million elderly people in India (7.5% of the total population) which is projected to reach around 137 million by the year 2021. In a country where bulk of the population lives in rural areas, three out of every four elderly persons actually lives in rural areas. The fact that the elderly population is growing at a phenomenal rate in India is borne out from their annual growth rate (3%) which far exceeds the growth rate of the total population (1.9%). The proportion of the elderly population is likely to exceed the proportion in the child age group by the year 2050 as projected by the UN. The population of India is ageing in two ways: (i) ageing at the base due to lower fertility, and (ii) ageing at the apex due to reduced mortality and dramatic increase in life expectancy. The analysis of historical patterns of mortality and fertility decline in India indicates that the process of population ageing intensified only in the 1990s (Bose and Shankardass, 2004). All through the last four decades, the growth rate of the aged population has been consistently higher than that of the total population. During 1951–61, the decadal growth rate of the 60+ population in India was 26 per cent compared to the growth rate of 21.6 per cent for the total population. During the decade 1981–91, the comparable figures were 31.3 per cent and 23.9 per cent. The same story is repeated when we consider the male and female population separately (Bose, 2000). The process of ageing however is not spatially uniform in the country. Different regions are placed differently in the unfolding of this phenomenal demographic transition overtaking the population. The North-Eastern region experiences a very complicated pattern that merits a special attention.

The North-East

Demographic transition unfolding in the region is in sharp contrast to other regions of the country. The region has a very large concentration of scheduled tribes who have been exposed to urbanization in recent times only. Topographically, much of the region consists of hills and plateaus although some parts are located in plains notably, the Brahmaputra and Barak plains, the Manipur basin and the

Tripura plains. Economically, the region continues to be characterized by subsistence agriculture and the hills have the practice of shifting cultivation. Socially and culturally, the region presents extreme diversity characterized by tribal cultures in the hills and peasant culture in much of the plains. The tribal culture extends to the plains too though in many cases the tribal people living in the plains have been assimilated to the peasant cultures in some very important ways.

The region presents the complexities of the sub-Himalayan ranges, the Indo-Burmese hills of Nagaland, Manipur and Mizoram and the eroded surfaces of the Meghalaya plateau, all encircling the Brahmaputra valley. The hills are sharply marked from the plains, physically as well as culturally, though so linked that to some extent they must be treated together (Spate and Learmonth, 1972). The boundary between the hills and the plains often present themselves as demographic boundaries too. The region presents itself as a replica of the subcontinent both physically as well as culturally, only on a much smaller scale. The northern mountains are in fact an extension of the Himalayan ranges with modification introduced in the erosional features due to much heavier rainfall. The Indo-Burmese hills are much less imposing as a relief feature. Parts of Tripura and Imphal valley represent an area of low relief. The Assam valley is an alluvial expanse laid down by the mighty Brahmaputra and its numerous tributaries. The Meghalaya and Karbi Plateau, a fragment of the peninsular block, is a highly dissected tract.

The overall geographical setting of the region has provided an ideal habitat for a legion of tribal communities. "… the tribes of the North-East India have a world of their own. Having lived in the marchland between India and China and in the triangle where the Indian and the Chinese worlds meet, they have picked up the impression that they belong to none" (Ahmad, 1983). The peculiarity of the geographical and historical conditions of this region has offered relative isolation to the culture groups who found their way into the region through passes from the north and the east. The northern and the eastern mountain ranges and the southern plateau understandably provide more suitable tribal habitats compared to the Brahmaputra valley. However, the valley has not been totally averse to tribal people in providing them with a habitat. They have found suitable sites for settlement in the isolated hill features, forested portions of the valley and in marshy tracts. The northern bank of the river as well as the river islands still retains their predominantly tribal character. The area of the transition between the hills and the plains of Brahmaputra is also largely tribal in its ethnic composition. The plain tribals "generally represent the spillover communities from the hilly regions except for the Bodos who are a big tribal group largely confined to the plains (Sharma, 1984).

The process of population ageing, though less in magnitude than other states, has already begun in the North-East region. The population of persons aged 60 or over has almost doubled to 1.7 million persons by the year 1991. In some states like Manipur, Meghalaya and Mizoram, the growth rate of 60–plus persons has been faster than that of the overall population. In spite of the fact that the region is characterized by an overwhelming tribal population, majority of the elderly persons in a great number of states are males. In terms of birth rate, total fertility rate (TFR), death rate, infant mortality (IMR) and life expectancy at birth, there have been welcome improvements over the years. It may thus be interesting to analyse the patterns of ageing in the region with respect to a few important indicators of ageing. The indicators include (see *Notes* in Table 14.2) the proportion of people in the age group of 60 and over, the ageing index, the potential support ratio, old age dependency rate and the total dependency rate. The study is based on age distribution data available in successive census counts held between 1971–2001. No Census was held in the year 1981 for Assam and hence information for 1981 Census is excluded from the analysis for the purpose of comparability.

It is evident from the Table 14.3 that there are more districts in the region with lower proportion of aged females. Contrary to expectation the proportion of the aged has indeed declined in a few districts over time. In larger number of districts aged females are less compared to the males. The gender gap in the aged population is lower up to the year 1971, but increased substantially by 1991 and declined thereafter. This trend reveals lower survival of women, compared to their male counterpart in the region, beyond 60 years of age. Inter-district variation in the proportion of the aged increased over the years and much more for the female segment. Aged population, particularly among the women is very high in Tripura along with some districts of Manipur, Arunachal Pradesh, Nagaland, Assam and parts of Meghalaya. The distribution of the aged population is highly scattered over districts which preclude significant impact of regional factors.

Table 14.3

North-East: Distribution of Districts According to Proportion of the Aged

% aged	*1971*		*1991*		*2001*	
	Males	*Females*	*Males*	*Females*	*Males*	*Females*
2–2.9	–	–	–	2	1	1
3–3.9	5	15	5	10	4	7
4–4.9	27	19	21	30	15	18
5–5.9	18	25	24	17	31	24
6–6.9	17	13	16	9	17	14
7–7.9	2	–	5	4	4	6
8–8.9	–	–	1	–	–	2
9–9.9	3	–	–	–	–	–
Total	72	72	72	72	72	72

Source: Census of India, 1971, 1991 and 2001.

Table 14.4

North-East: Distribution of Districts in different Ageing Index Classes

Ageing Index (%)	*1971*		*1991*		*2001*	
	Males	*Females*	*Males*	*Females*	*Males*	*Females*
4–7.9	15	13	12	22	2	3
8–11.9	42	48	54	44	16	21
12–15.9	12	11	6	6	27	21
16–19.9	3	–	–	–	20	21
20–23.9	–	–	–	–	7	4
24–27.9	–	–	–	–	1	2
Total	72	72	72	72	72	72

Source: Census of India, 1971, 1991 and 2001.

When the ageing index is analysed, it is evident from Table 14.3 that there has been drastic fall in a number of districts with lower ageing index classes. This means that in a number of districts the ratio between the aged and the young is increasing over the years. This is a clear case of ageing manifesting in large parts of the region since the year 1991. However, the fall is far more in the case of males compared to the females. Number of districts with lower ageing index indeed increased till 1991 for the females, but began to fall by the year 2001.

Table 14.5

Distribution of Districts in Total Dependency Ratio Classes

Total Dependency Ratio	*1971*	*1991*	*2001*
50–50.9	0	1	3
60–60.9	3	5	11
70–70.9	11	24	23
80–80.9	15	29	24
90–90.9	19	9	9
100–109.9	15	4	2
110–119.9	9	0	0
Total	72	72	72

Source: Census of India, 1971, 1991 and 2001.

The total dependency ratio generally indicates economic burden on the adult population which has to support two dependent segments, i.e, the child and the old. Table 14.5 shows a generally declining number of districts over the years with higher dependency ratio. This means that in a large number of districts the overall dependence on the adult population is on the decline. In case the population is ageing, overall dependence normally declines. This seems to be happening in a number of districts particularly after 1991. In 2001 total dependency ratio is below 80 per cent in 37 (over 50%) districts. The number of such districts was 30 (41%) in 1991 and only 14 (19.5%) in 1971. On the other hand, the total dependency ratio continued to be exceedingly high (over 80) in as many as 35 (48%) districts in 2001, though it declined from 42 (58%) districts in 1991.

Table 14.6 reveals a generally decreasing proportion of districts with higher old age dependence. This is contrary to what happens in a situation when the population is ageing. Given that the total dependency is on the decline alongside declining old age dependency in a large number of districts poses an ironical situation with regard to the complex nature of ageing in this region. This is indicative of the fact that in many districts the adult population is growing at a much faster rate than the growth taking place in old age population. In 1971 there were a few districts with higher (over 18 per 100) old age dependency ratio. However, in 2001, no district shows such a high level of dependence.

Table 14.6

Distribution of Districts in different Old Age Dependency Ratio Classes

Old Age Dependence Ratio	*1971*	*1991*	*2001*
2–5.9	0	0	2
6–9.9	17	11	50
10–13.9	34	35	18
14–17.9	18	17	2
18–21.9	3	8	0
22–25.9	0	1	0
Total	72	72	72

Source: Census of India, 1971, 1991 and 2001.

Table 14.7

North-East: Distribution of Districts in Potential Support Ratio Classes, 1971–2001

Potential Support Ratio	*1971*	*1991*	*2001*
6–8.9	23	13	17
9–11.9	25	40	40
12–14.9	21	14	12
15–17.9	3	5	2
18–20.9	0	0	1
Total	72	72	72

Source: Census of India, 1971, 1991 and 2001.

The Potential Support Ratio is the number of persons aged 15–60 per every person aged 60 or older. This is exact opposite of old age dependency ratio. Table 14.7 reveals an increasing proportion of districts with lower potential support. In a great majority of districts (nearly 80%) the potential support ratio in 2001 is below 12 per aged. The proportion of such districts was lower at 74 per cent in 1991 and

67 per cent in 1971. Interestingly at least one district has experienced a large increase in potential support in the year 2001.

Regional/Social Contrasts

Patterns in ageing however differ drastically between the areas of tribal and non-tribal concentration. It is interesting to note that the aged component of the population in the tribal districts was higher in the year 1971 compared to the population living in districts dominantly inhabited by the non-tribal population. But the pattern reversed by the year 1991 and continued thereafter, when the non-tribal population contained a larger proportion of the aged. This reversal is the result of continued high fertility in the tribal population. Ageing process appears to be manifesting in areas of non-tribal concentration going by the proportion of the aged. The process appears to be highly muted in areas of tribal concentration.

Table 14.8

Ageing in the North-East: Comparison between the Tribal and Non-Tribal Districts

	Non-Tribal		*Tribal*	
	% aged	*Ageing Index*	*% aged*	*Ageing Index*
		1971		
Overall	5.1	10.1	5.3	9.9
Male	5.3	10.4	5.5	10
Female	4.8	9.9	5.2	9.9
		1991		
Overall	5.5	10	4.8	8.6
Male	5.7	10.3	5.2	9
Female	5.2	9.7	4.5	8.2
		2001		
Overall	6.0	16.5	5	13.3
Male	5.9	16.4	5.1	13.8
Female	6	16.5	4.9	12.8

Source: Census of India, 1971, 1991 and 2001.

Ageing index too reveals a similar trend though there was hardly any social or regional difference in the ageing index between areas of tribal and non-tribal concentration at least in the initial period, i.e., in the year 1971. The gap began to widen by the year 1991 and indeed increased thereafter as evident from the data available in 2001. The pace of increase in ageing index for the non-tribal population has been much faster in the 1991–2001 decade. Ageing index has increased much faster for the non-tribal female component than its male counterpart. On the other hand, the trend in increase in ageing index is far less in areas of tribal concentration.

Demographic parameters in the North-East region of India have improved remarkably reflecting interesting patterns over space (Nayak, 2009: 158). Population ageing has slowly but surely manifested itself against a background of continued high fertility in the region. However, the patterns are highly varied within different sub-regions and among different ethnic categories making it a highly complex phenomenon not lending itself to an easy explanation.

In terms of the proportion of the elderly population the entire region lags behind the country average of 7.6 per cent. The areas of tribal concentration show a very low proportion of elderly population in the total. The most significant aspect of ageing in the hilly and tribal areas refers to the fact of a declining trend in the proportion of elderly population over the three decades, which is surely linked to continued high fertility among the tribal segment. There is only a marginal increase in the proportion of the tribal elderly population since 1991.

Unlike the all-India average, the proportion of the aged among the female segment is lower than that of their male counterpart in the North-East. The elderly among the tribal males constitutes a higher proportion than their female counterparts in all the years. The gap however is reducing over the years.

If one goes by the most sensitive index of ageing, i.e., the ageing index, it is significant to note that the ageing process seems to have picked up momentum since the year 1991 in the country as a whole, but it is weak in the case of the areas of tribal concentration as evident in such areas of the North-East region of the country. There has been indeed a fall in the ageing index till the year 1991.

In terms of PSR, the areas of tribal concentration show a reverse situation of increasing PSR over the years. This is indicative of an increasingly larger proportion of adult population compared to the aged in the areas of tribal concentration. This is largely due to extremely high fertility level in the past. In terms of dependency, there has been a general decline in both the indicators over the years.

Going by international standards and comparing with the developed countries which have a longer history of ageing, it is expected that countries/regions beginning to age should experience an increase in the proportion of the aged, in ageing index and in old age dependency ratio, while there should be a fall in potential support ratio and total dependency ratio. The patterns observed in the North-East, particularly in the areas of tribal concentration do not conform to these parameters with equal vigour. The hilly and tribal areas experience an increase in ageing index only. The proportion of the aged in the total population is showing signs of an increase in recent years only and the PSR too is showing some signs of falling in recent years. All these indicators only suggest the beginning of the ageing process in hilly and tribal areas. This is supported by a drastic fall in total dependency ratio, but contradicted by equally drastic fall in old age dependency ratio. These features are perhaps common to a population that has just begun to experience ageing.

Issues and Challenges

It is clear from the analysis that the region as a whole is beginning to experience ageing in recent times though there are important regional variations in the pace. In the areas of non-tribal concentration, the pace appears to have picked up momentum whereas in the areas of tribal concentration there is some evidence of ageing to pick up momentum in the near future. This means that the problems that arise due to ageing may not have been felt in the region to the extent it has in the developed regions of the world or in the country. But the pace of the demographic changes is such that it can hardly be wished away. One needs to be prepared for the challenges before it is too late. The specificities of the geographical and social reality of the region need to be considered while discussing the issues. As has been noted earlier, the region supports a very high proportion of the scheduled tribes in the hilly areas and a legion of tribes who have their tiny worlds of their own. The plain and river valleys contain an overwhelming proportion of the non-tribal people. The complex ethnic composition in the region is also reflected in equally complex demographic transition experienced by the people. In the absence of in-depth anthropological studies on the joint family system, both regionally and for different socio-cultural groups, it will be difficult to assess the true impact of ageing and the aged. Some of the many issues and challenges thrown by ageing societies are outlined below in very broad terms:

Health and Health Care

Ageing is accompanied by biological changes increasing illness, disability and probability of dying. Greater proportion suffers from impairment and disability. Degenerative diseases afflict the older people. There are always limited Public health resources for degenerative diseases and are more confined to urban areas. Health issues of elderly require different approaches and cannot be combined with general health measures. Attitudinal changes are required as far as elderly health is concerned.

It is common to accept poor health conditions of the elderly as a 'natural', 'normal' or 'biological' manifestation with old age. However, aged persons can lead a normal healthy life through medical intervention, awareness, and public health measures sensitive to health problems of old.

Old age is also associated with psychological problems owing to poverty, neglect, loneliness, violence and abuse. Public health policy needs to address itself to these issues effectively for a better quality of life especially to the needs of older poor.

Gender and Ageing

Ageing is associated with a greater feminization of the aged (Stone, 1998). Although this phenomenon is not yet fully manifested in the North-East, the trends indicate that it is going to happen sooner or later. Older women are at a greater disadvantage particularly in less developed regions, due largely to patriarchal norms. Stereotypes of gender roles make the older women far more vulnerable. Though the region as a whole and particularly in tribal areas accords a better social status to women, the vulnerability of older women to a number of problems can be comparable to women living under strict patriarchal norms. Changes in marital status affect economic inequalities among the elderly. Most cultures encourage men to remarry, widows experience social stigma if they remarry. Widows are a larger group than widowers and a greater proportion of women are widowed at older ages than men. Older women's socio-economic status is largely rooted in the gender division of labour assuming their primary involvement in reproductive labour, unpaid household work, care-giving and unequal power relations at home. Such activities restrict women's employment opportunities, mobility, educational attainment and skills development. Thus most women are concentrated in low-wage, insignificant and demanding jobs, or to part-time employment with few benefits and little security. Women spend more time on combined unpaid and paid work than men do. Women also earn less and experience inequality at work, in the family and society. Thus, gender, ageing and poverty are interrelated.

The NFHS-3 reported 20 per cent marriages in Assam and Arunachal Pradesh wherein the age difference of the couple is 10 years or more (Kishor and Gupta, 2009: 40). Age disparity in marriages inevitably means that a great majority of women at older ages live the life of widows without the support from her husband. Large numbers of single, divorced or widowed older women are especially vulnerable. Problems of abandonment, loneliness and isolation tend to be more acute for women. Women's labour in the region is largely confined to the informal, agricultural and service sectors without access to social protection such as health insurance that can affect their health in old age. Throughout the world, older women are more likely to live in poverty than men and this group is increasing rapidly.

References

Ahmad, A. 1983. 'Education of the Scheduled Tribes: Some Aspects of Inequality', *Workshop on Indicators of Equity in Education*, October 24–28, New Delhi: NIEPA (mimeo).

Bhat, Anitha Kumari and Raj Dhruvarajan. 2001. 'Ageing in India: Drifting Intergenerational Relations, Challenges and Options', *Ageing and Society*, 21: 621–640.

Bose, Ashish and Mala Kapur Shankardass. 2004. *Growing Old in India: Voices Reveal, Statistics Speak*. New Delhi: B.R. Publishing Corporation.

Bose, Ashish. 2000. Demographic Transition. Paper presented at *Ageing: A Symposium on the Graying of Our Society*. Downloaded from website http://www.india-seminar.com/2000/488.htm

Dhar Chakraborty, Rajagopal. 2004. *The Greying of India*. New Delhi: Sage.

International Monetary Fund (IMF) (2004) *IMF World Economic Outlook*. Downloaded from website *www.imf.org/external/pubs/ft/weo/2004/02/*

Kishor, Sunita and Kamla Gupta. 2009. 'Gender Equality and Women's Empowerment in India', *National Family Health Survey (NFHS-3)*, India 2005–06, Ministry of Health and Family Welfare, Government of India.

Lee, Ronald. 2007. *The Economic Implications of Changing Age-Structure.* Downloaded from website *www.un.org/esa/population/cpd2007/presentations/lee.hz.shr.ppt*

Leete, R. and T. Jacobs. 2002. 'The Older Poor and the Excluded in the Developing World', in *Situation and Voice: The Older Poor and Excluded in South Africa and India.* New York: United Nations Population Fund, Population and Development Strategies Series No. 2, 1–18.

National Institutes of Health, Washington, DC. 2007. *Why Population Ageing Matters: A Global Perspective.* Downloaded from website *http://www.state.gov/g/oes/rls/or/81537.htm#over*

Nayak, D.K. 2007. *A Geographical Perspective on the Trends and Patterns in Ageing in India with a Special Reference to the Northeastern Region.* Research Monograph No. GE/UGC/DKN/7. Shillong: Department of Geography, North-Eastern Hill University.

—. 2009. 'A Geographical Perspective on the Patterns of Ageing in Northeast India with Special Reference to the Tribal Areas', in Ramesh Sharma and C. Joshua Thomas (eds), *Ageism: Problems and Prospects.* New Delhi: Akansha Publishers, 135–162.

Sharma, B.D. 1984. *Planning for Tribal Development.* New Delhi: Prachi.

Spate, O.H.K. and A.T.A. Learmonth. 1972. *India and Pakistan.* New Delhi: B.I. Publications.

Stone, Robyn. 1998. 'The Feminization of Poverty among the Elderly', *The New York Times,* 13 October, pp. A1–A8 (quoted in U.N. Economic and Social Council. 1999. *Gender and Ageing: Problems, Perceptions and Policies.* Commission on the Status of Women (Report of the Secretary-General). Downloaded from website *http://www.un.org/womenwatch/daw/csw/ageing.htm*

U.N. Economic and Social Council. 1999. *Gender and Ageing: Problems, Perceptions and Policies.* Commission on the Status of Women (Report of the Secretary-General). Downloaded from website http://www.un.org/womenwatch/daw/csw/ageing.htm

UNFPA. 1998. *The State of World Population.* New York.

—. 2002. *Population Ageing and Development: Operational Challenges in Developing Countries.* New York: Population and Development Strategies Series, No. 5.

United Nations. 2001. *World Population Prospects: The 2000 Revision.* New York: Department of Economic and Social Affairs, Population Division, Population Database. Downloaded from website *www.unpopulation.org*

15

Demography and Social Change in the Tribal Society of Tripura

K. DEBBARMA

This paper attempts to analyse the process of immigration that has affected the change in demographic structure and also the tribal society of Tripura, particularly in the post-partition and independent India. In fact, no society is static, it is in a state of constant flux. Social change in both developed and developing countries has been noticed either in revolutionary or evolutionary process. In pursuit of development and modernization, social change is inevitable. In a way, there is nothing called constant except the change itself. Human history is marked by constant efforts to bring about a change in the desired and progressive directions which affect societies at large. Social change, as a field of enquiry, has attracted attention among the researchers in social sciences. Social change may be understood as a universal phenomenon as there is no society whether primitive or modern that remains unaffected by the process of change. Social change in general terms refers to change in social structure like the social institutions, the social behaviour, or the social relations of a society and community of people. When behaviour patterns of a society change considerably and this change is visible and sustained, and when there is deviance from culturally-inherited values, rebellion against the established system, change in the social order may become quite inevitable.

It may also refer to any event or action which affects a group of individuals who have shared values or characteristics. At times even acts of advocacy for the cause of changing a society in a normative way may also be considered as a process of social change. Social change is a process whereby the values, attitudes, or institutions of society, such as education, family, religion and industry become modified. It includes both the natural process and action programmes initiated by members of the community. Charles L Harper defined social change as the 'significant alteration of social structure and cultural patterns through time' (Harper, 1993). He goes on to explain that this social structure is made up of 'a persistent network of social relationships' in which interaction between people or groups has become repetitive. The resultant changes can effect everything from population to the economy, which, as it so happens, alongside such others as industrialization and shifting cultural norms and values, are also established agents of social change.

Generally, there are two sources or dimensions of change (Shackman, Liu and Wang, 2002). One source is non-systematic change, such as climate change, some kind of technological innovation from the outside, or changes enforced by foreign countries. The other source is a systems change. Eisenstadt (1973) argued that modernization required a basic level of free resources and the development of standardized and predictable institutions, such as a stable but flexible market system and political process. An additional requirement was that governing institutions be flexible enough to adapt to the changes that come up. Most of the time, changes to society come about through some combination of both systematic and non-systematic processes (Shackman, Liu and Wang, 2002).

Social change may be understood as 'the significant alteration of social change that affect change in social values, institutions, property relations, economic pursuits, personnel and role distributions and hence, it refers to the modifications which occur in the life patterns of a people' (Koenig 1968). The concept of social change implies measurement of some characteristics of the group of individuals in any particular society. While the term 'social change' is usually applied to changes that are developmental and beneficial to society, it may at time result in negative consequences that undermine or eliminate existing ways of life that are considered positive.

Social change seeks to bring about all-round development in the right perspective. Every society wants to develop and, therefore, change is desirable. The level and degree of social change may differ from one society to another based on its socio-economic patterns. For instance, social change in developed countries is different from that of developing and tribal societies. Social change in a tribal society may take place due to combination of several factors such as large-scale migration resulting in a change in demographic structure and marginalizing the local population, introduction of new system but unfamiliar to the local population like religious practices, new market economy, process of globalization, etc. Tripura, a tiny state in North-East India is an example wherein the large-scale migration affected the demographic structure and the tribal society.

The post-independent India witnessed a tremendous social change in the tribal society (*Borok* Society) of Tripura which can be attributed to the large-scale immigration of non-tribal people from across the international border. The partition of Indian sub-continent based on two-nation theory created a fear psychosis in the minds of the Hindus and the Muslims falling in the territories of Pakistan and India. As a result, inter-migration of both the Hindus (from Pakistan) and the Muslims (from India) were allowed. But obviously such migration or interchange of population was not proportionate as the number of the Hindus and the Muslims living in both Pakistan and India varied. In North-East India, this process of migration mostly affected the international bordering states like Tripura and Assam.

Tripura shares the international border with the erstwhile East Pakistan and now Bangladesh in three sides and one side with Assam and Mizoram. The proximity of porous border greatly helped and facilitated migration and settlement of Hindu Bengalis from the erstwhile East Pakistan and now Bangladesh into this small state of Tripura. As per the record maintained by the state government, close to seven lakhs (6,09,998) non-tribal refugee populations were given settlement in the state from 1947 to 1971 (Bhattacharrya, 1988). Thereafter unrecorded immigration continued unabated from across the international border into the state that led to the growth of imbalance in demographic structure, thereby making the indigenous peoples into minority in their own homeland by 1960s. This situation obviously created a sense of insecurity for the local peoples that made the state witnessed youth movements, social unrest, political upheaval and ethnic conflicts and economic poverty since the early 1960s. Today, the ratio of tribal and non-tribal population is about 30 per cent and 70 per cent respectively. Such a dramatic change in demographic structure caused by the process of immigration brought about multi-dimensional effects on the tribal society in particular.

First, it affected the urban tribal community including the royal families who gradually lost their culture and tradition, and even forgot their mother tongue (*Kokborok*) mainly under the influence of alien Bengali culture, religion and tradition brought by the immigrants. The Bengali language, culture, Hindu religion and tradition was then considered more organized and standard and made the tribal people follow them as a sign of development. Second, having affected the royal families and urban dwellers, the wave of social change began to spread out fast in the rural tribal areas of the state cutting across tribal religion, culture and tradition even to the extent of creating an identity issue of the tribal people in the later stage.

The spread of education and entry of the Brahmin religious culture in the tribal society brought about change in the tribal society of Tripura. The change in the tribal society was noticed first in the individual names of the tribal people. With the entry of the Brahmin religious culture the royal families and urban people, tribal people began to give importance to Bengali language and culture. They stopped speaking in their mother tongue, the *Kokboro*k, even at home among the same family members and this was the starting point in the process of change in the tribal society. The performance of naming ceremony by the Hindu Brahmins in the tribal society obviously affected the names of the tribal people. In this process, the Bengali speaking Brahmins being not familiar with the tribal language, *Kokborok*, began to give sanskritized and Bengali names to the tribal people. This is evident from the fact that many tribal people even today bear *sankritized* names (first name) which became a confusing issue in their identity. This identity issue with regard to their names normally is realized when tribal people go outside the state either for study or other purposes like business, jobs, etc.

The process of *sankritized* name was accentuated in the entire tribal society not only by the entry of the Brahmins but also by the spread of education among the tribal people. For instance, when the tribal children started going to school for registration, their names would be changed from indigenous names to alien language as the non-tribal teachers were unable to either pronounce the local names or meaning of the names sounded not good to them. Tribal children then would return home happily with new names given by the teachers not knowing the long-term effect. The process of naming ceremonies conducted by the Hindu Brahmins and the tribal people having Bengali names gradually became the accepted norms in the tribal society until 1980s (Debbarma, 1996: 174–78).

Subsequently, due to constant interaction in daily sphere of life and business transactions between the tribal and non-tribal communities, the tradition and culture of marriage system, religious rites and mode of dressing of the tribal people were also influenced by the majority Bengali Hindu culture. Gradually marriage ceremonies and religious rites in the tribal society were performed by Hindu priests (Brahmins). These practices began to spread fast in not only among the urban tribal families but also in the rural tribal society. By the late 1960s, as the immigrants became a majority, their social norms and culture greatly influenced the tribal society. As a result, one could see married tribal women putting a red sticker (*sindur*) on the forehead, piercing the nose for wearing rings, wearing *sarees* and most tribal people speaking *Bangali* language which made them almost identical with the non-tribal people until the realization of identity issue in the early 1980s.

Immigration and their settlement also created a change in the traditional landholding pattern in the tribal society of Tripura. Traditionally, land used to be owned by the community of village as they practiced jhumming or shifting cultivation. Under the practice of shifting cultivation, the rights of tribal ownership of land enjoyed by an individual local person over a particular area of shifting cultivable land was neither permanent nor alienable nor transferable to any person nor inheritable from any person (Misra, 1976). However, with the increasing high growth rate of population mainly caused by the large scale immigration and their settlement that created scarcity of land, the tribal communities were compelled to practise settled cultivation. The scarcity of tribal land was further accentuated by the restriction of shifting cultivation and declaration of reserved forest land made by the government in 1952. The resultant scarcity of land in the state affected the tribal landholding system and the mode of cultivation. So the gradual shift from community landholding system to family landholding system and to members within the family began to appear in the tribal society. Today, such development in landholding pattern led the tribal society from community based landholding to family based and family to individual landholding system, which is one of the effects of immigration and the change in the demographic structure in the state.

In fact, to induce the *Boroks,* the local tribal people, to settled cultivation, all fertile and cultivable wetlands made reserved for the king's subject (Boroks), and many families were settled in reserved areas and taken to settled cultivation by late 1940s (Chakravarty, 1994). So each *Borok* family had huge areas of cultivable wetland under their possession. Subsequently, the introduction of land registration system by the government created hardship and legal problem that rendered many tribal families landless as they could not produce any evidence against their claims of land. As a result, tribal community/family lands that could not be registered, and were declared *khas* land or government land. Added to this, with the settlement of large-scale immigrants the introduction of money as medium of exchange and the growth of market began to take place, and this development gradually led to the process of alienation of tribal land. Although, a handful of *Boroks* had tried to adopt plough (settled) cultivation, the majority of them lost their wet lands to the non-tribal immigrants. As a result, many *Borok* families were compelled to retreat into interior hills and forests of the state.

On the other hand, many of the immigrants had taken to trading and money lending and steadily many *Boroks* (tribal people) became trapped under the exploitation of this system (Das Gupta, 1991). The failure of *jhum* products to meet the growing needs led the rural tribal people to borrow money from the moneylender and businessmen. Loans with compound interests to be repaid within a fixed period of time were given to the *Boroks* in the rural areas only against the mortgage of their plains cultivable lands. Meanwhile, during this fixed periods, the moneylenders could use the mortgaged lands for cultivation. Such practice of mortgaging of cultivable lands led to dwindling of production for the *Boroks,* and they failed to repay loan amount with interests within the stipulated time frame. The immigrant moneylenders and traders caught the *Boroks* in a debt trap of loan capital with compounded interests. Failure to pay the compounded amount within stipulated time enabled the moneylenders to have permanent possession of mortgaged lands. Hence, instead of wetlands yielding prosperity to the *Boroks* farmers, they found themselves victim of money lending system and alienation from their lands (Das Gupta, 1991). This development led to alienation of tribal lands and created a condition of general pauperization (S.R. Bhattacharrya, *Tribal Insurgency in Tripura*, 1989). Although, several land reforms acts were passed by the state government mainly to restore alienated lands and to prevent and protect from further alienation of tribal lands since the late 1960s, the process of alienation of land could not be prevented due to failure of implementation of these acts and also faulty provisions contained within the acts (Debbarma, *Eastern Quarterly*, 2007).

Hence, alienation of land became one of the major issues of tribal discontentment and social change in the tribal society of the state. As many tribal families were rendered landless, the tribal social structure also started to get fragmented. As the importance of money as medium of exchange began to increase many poor tribal people started selling whatever land they had under their possession. Very few tribal families, who had little money, could purchase lands from the poorer tribal communities which subsequently divided the tribal society into rich and poor. With the passage of time, tribal social structure became more fragmented whereby majority of tribal people by early 1980s were turned into daily wage labourers. Today, majority tribal families' sustenance became entirely dependent on the ability of their daily physical work.

This situation in the absence of assistance from the state government to provide the poor people with work creates severe hardship for the rural poor. In fact, there were reports of poverty, starvation and death of hundreds of rural tribal people in Longtrai Valley and other areas of Dhalai and North districts of Tripura during 1989–1992 (Debbarma, 1996: 221–28). In Tripura, while some urban areas have an access to development and welfare activities, the rural tribal areas are deprived of even basic amenities of life such as food, grains, drinking water, medical care facilities, etc. The uneven socio-economic development has aggravated the poverty-ridden tribal society into pauperization Further, the widespread rural poverty in Tripura may largely be attributed to the failure of government machineries to eradicate poverty and raise the living condition of the common masses. Since more than 95 per cent of the tribal population live in the rural areas and had not benefited much from whatever development schemes were undertaken by the government, the situation of widespread poverty had much adversely affected the tribal people and they became pauperized (Das Gupta, 1984: 450–51). Such a situation in tribal society of Tripura is also attributed to the failure of the state government to contain and overcome the problems associated with high growth rate of population caused by both immigration and natural growth.

The social change in tribal society largely caused by the process of immigration that brought about change in demographic structure and tribal society of Tripura however, became counter-productive with the growth of tribal movements in the early 1970s. Since this period a new dimension of development in tribal society began to take place. To better understand the new dimension of development in tribal society, one needs perhaps to go back to the genesis of tribal identity consciousness. The consciousness of tribal identity and a need to protect their interest led to the growth of political and social movements and the genesis of this development can be traced to the formation of organizations like the Tribal Students' Federation (TSF) and *Tripura Upajati Juba Samity* (TUJS, a regional political party) in 1967. The main objectives of forming these organizations were: (a) restoration of alienated lands to the tribal people, (b) introduction of *Kokborok* as official language, (c) deportation of refugees, and (d) introduction of tribal dress as school and college uniform. By and large, the movement led by these organizations was said to be successful in preserving the identity, culture and tradition of the tribal people, promotion and protection of *Kokborok* language and introduction of tribal dress as uniform among tribal girls in schools and colleges in the state.

However, some leaders were not satisfied with the performance of the regional political party, the TUJS, and they wanted to follow more stringent measures to achieve the goals. Thus, over the differences of views on the *modus operandi of* the organization, the TUJS was divided into moderate and extremist groups in 1977. The extremist breakaway group formed a separate organization known as Tripura National Volunteers (TNV) which was led by Mr B.K. Hrangkhawl. Soon this organization turned extremist and militant in its mode of operation. By now, the state and tribal society saw the emergence three tribal organizations namely the TSF, TUJS and TNV with more or less similar defined objectives. The tribal movement led by the TSF, TUJS and TNV strongly demanded the state government to initiate the creation of an Autonomous District

Council for the protection of overall tribal interest in the state. As the movement grew stronger, the state government led by the Left Front was pressurized to initiate measure towards establishing an autonomous district council for the tribal people in the state. On the other hand, this development generated fears in the minds of the non-tribal communities that led to a conflict between tribal and non-tribal communities in Tripura. The conflict was so culminated that it led to a riot and carnage in June 1980, which resulted in great loss of lives and properties of both the communities.

Following the June riot of 1980, the tribal society witnessed the decline of Hindu Brahmin's influence. More importantly, the post-riot of June 1980 has been marked by a strong renaissance of Borok culture and tradition. One of the effects of the riot is that most of the Boroks or tribal people living in the state capital and other urban areas who once lost their own culture and tradition including their own mother tongue, had started learning *Kokborok* language. Many educated affluent *Borok* people in Agartala were seen taking keen interest in learning and speaking in *Kokborok* and reviving their own culture. It may be mentioned here that due to the demand by various tribal movements, *Kokborok* was recognized as one of the official languages of the state.

Further, the beginning of 1990s was marked by emergence of various tribal socio-economic organizations. For example, the Kokborok Community Welfare Society (KCWS) was established in 1989 with the main objective of developing socio-cultural and economic aspects of the Borok community. Again, on June 27, 1989 the Tribal Socio-Cultural Development Organization was formed with the objectives of reviving the history of Tripura and development of socio-cultural identity among the indigenous people of state. This organization published the Tripura calendar called the *Tring* in *Kokborok* language in 1993–94 which depicts the Tripura era. In 1993, the *Kokborok Tei Hukumo Mission* (KOHM) was established with the purpose of initiating research and preserving *Borok* people's customs, traditions and cultural life styles.

The post-1980 saw the revival of tribal customs, practices and culture in marriage, naming children and performance of religious rituals in tribal society. Thereafter, naming children in *Kokborok* (indigenous name) has been found quite common. The identity consciousness among the tribal people led quite a few tribal elders legally changing their names from sanskritized to *Kokborok* through an affidavit in the Judicial Court (Debbarma, 1996: 179–80). This phase is marked: by a great consciousness of tribal identity so much so that at one point of time there was a tendency of identifying the capital city based tribal people who do not speak *Kokborok* as different from the rest of the tribal people in the state. This development to a certain extent compelled early city dweller tribal people to reinforce learning and speaking *Kokborok* language.

Following the June riot of 1980 child education in English medium of instruction by the middle class tribal people was also seen to be greatly emphasized. Since 1980s, education in English medium of instruction has been found encouraged by the spread of Christianity particularly in the rural areas of tribal society in the state. Although, the Christianity started spreading in the tribal villages since the early 1980s, its growth rate is not much significant as the ratio of tribal Christians in the state is found to be still very low. But Christianity seems to have brought about a revival of tribal culture and identity, and today many tribal Christian families are naming their children in their own language – *Kokborok*. Some tribal Christian parents are also found naming their children identical to Biblical names. Thus, one could see the social changes taking place from one phase to another.

The 1990s witnessed a paradigm shift of the tribal educated employees in buying either residential houses or plain land for construction of houses in the capital city of Agartala. Today one could see many rural educated tribal employees migrating to capital cities particularly in Krishnanagar, Banamalipur, Abhoynagar areas of Agartala. This pattern of rural to urban migration of the tribal people is also due to "push" and "pull" factors of absence and presence of needed educational facilities and other economic viabilities. The migration of rural tribal people to the capital city of the state brought about a renaissance of *Borok* culture in Agartala. The presence of tribal population in the city has also encouraged the rural tribal people to come and sell indigenous items in Agartala.

Under the initiative of the Tripura Tribal Areas Autonomous District Council, shooting of a *Kokborok* film called *Langami Haduk* depicting the socio-cultural and economic life of the indigenous people state was successfully completed. This film was shown in many cinema halls in the state thereby making *Boroks* realize the importance of reinforcing their identity through the practice of their culture and tradition. Thereafter, the successful production of *Kokborok* films like *Mathia, Yarung, Raima,* etc., depicting the culture and tradition of the tribal people is a reflection of the new dimension of social change in the tribal society of Tripura. Today, many audio-video CDs of tribal songs and dances in *Kokborok* language are found available in Agartala on sale.

The competition for education and job opportunities and the emerging tribal movements needed for survival and maintaining a separate identity vis-à-vis the non-tribal community have been reflected as the recent phenomenal of change in the tribal culture and society. Such a change challenging the tribal culture, society and identity became the offshoot of various socio-political movements through the formation of several organizations including resurgence of militancy in Tripura since the 1980s. Following the riot of June 1980, militant activities that include killings, attacks on security personnel, etc., became the order of the day till the TNV accord signed on September 12, 1988. Such a situation has greatly hampered the initiation and implementation of needed developmental schemes particularly in poverty ridden tribal society in Tripura.

Through the spread of education, entry of market economy, requirement of jobs for survival, etc., the tribal society today is found by and large fragmented than in the past. Emergence of a middle class in the tribal society is an example of fragmentation and social stratification. With the demographic change, the traditional tribal society of having a village chief and council is losing its ground and slowly getting replaced by institution of democratic decentralization in which village representatives are elected on the basis of adult franchise for a specific period. However, many of these elections are held only as a matter of formality as voters do not exercise their franchise on the basis of free and fair elections.

The youth and the tribal movements including militancy in Tripura are found to be the by-product of change in demographic, political and economic structures in the state. These changes brought about by the unabated process of immigration in the state had greatly made the tribal society fragmented and individualistic. Thus, the present tribal society has travelled a long way and has been constantly influenced by various socio-political and cultural movements. The resolution of tribal movement and militancy has been a major concern of the state. But, the measures and policies adopted by the successive state governments to contain the tribal movements have not been found effective for the protection and promotion of tribal interests. Added to this, the division of the indigenous tribal people on different political lines also hampered and weakened the tribal movements. It has also been noticed that the innocent youth have been subjected to various forms of suspicions, arrests, torture and killings. The tribal women and young girls too have become quite vulnerable to different forms of torture including rape and sexual harassment particularly in the hands of the Indian security forces deployed to combat militancy in the rural tribal areas. This calls for alternative approach to resolve the tribal issues. Therefore, both the state and central governments perhaps need to address the tribal issue in Tripura carefully which will facilitate peaceful situation in the State.

References

Bhattacharyya, Gayatri. 1988. *Refugee Rehabilitation and Its Impact on Tripura's Economy*. New Delhi: Omsons Publications.

Bhattacharyya, S.R. 1989. *Tribal Insurgency in Tripura: A Study in Exploration of Causes*. New Delhi: Inter-India Publications.

Chakravarty, Mahadev. 1994. 'Land in Tripura: The Tenurial System and Transfer', in J.B. Bhattacharjee (ed.), *Studies in the Economic History of North East India*. New Delhi: Har-Anand Publications, 43–52.

Choudhuri, J. Gan. 1985. *A Political History of Tripura*. New Delhi: Inter-India Publications.

Das Gupta, Malabika. 1984. 'Tripura: Tribal Unrest', *The Economic and Political Weekly*, 29(11): 34–37.

—. 1991. 'Land Alienation among Tripura Tribals', *The Economic and Political Weekly*, 26(36): 432–436.

Debbarma, Khakchang. 1996. *Trans-border Migration: A Study of Its Impact on Tripura Politics*. Ph.D. Thesis. Shillong: Department of Political Science, NEHU.

—. 2007. 'Politics of Land Alienation and Problem of Its Restoration in Tripura', *Eastern Quarterly*, 4(4): 101–111.

Eisenstadt, S.N. 1973. *Tradition, Change, and Modernity*. Malabar, Flo.: Krieger Publishing Company.

Ghosh, Kamalini. 1984. *Tribal Insurrection in Tripura: A Study in Relative Deprivation.* Hyderabad: Booklinks Corporation.

Giddens, A. 2006. *Sociology.* Cambridge: Polity Press.

Haralambos, M. and M. Holborn. 2004. *Sociology: Themes and Perspectives.* London: Harper Collins Publishers Ltd.

Harper, Charles L. 1993. *Exploring Social Change.* Englewood Cliffs, NJ: Prentice Hall.

Irwin, S. 2005. *Reshaping Social Life.* Oxford: Routledge.

Koenig, S. 1963. *Sociology: An Introduction to Society.* New York: Barnes and Noble.

Misra, Bani Prasanna. 1976. *Socio-Economic Adjustments of Tribals.* New Delhi: People's Publishing House.

Popenoe, D. 1995. *Sociology.* Englewood Cliffs, NJ: Prentice Hall.

Shackman, Gene, Ya-Lin Liu and George (Xun) Wang. 2002. Why does a society develop the way it does? The Global Social Change Research Project. Seen at *http://gsociology.icaap.org/report/summary2.htm*

—. 2005. Measuring quality of life using free and public domain data. Social Research Update, Issue 47, Autumn. Seen at *http://sru.soc.surrey.ac.uk/*

16

Non-Governmental Organizations and Social Change in the North-East

BISWAMBHAR PANDA

In a democratic state the role of civil society assumes significance as it acts as a pressure group to exert pressure on the state and its machinery. The constituents of civil society, i.e., voluntary organizations, media, and autonomous bodies contribute towards well-being of the people. Though the significance of civil society is uncontested there exists divergence of opinions amongst scholars about the very concept of civil society and its inherent constituents. The voluntary organizations or non-governmental organizations (NGOs) (as used synonymously) could be seen as one of the key constituents of civil society that work towards the strengthening of civil society through its people-oriented and people-centred approaches and initiatives that in turn bring about change and development in the society. The participatory modes of intervention, social activism, the awareness building measures of NGOs, coordination and networking with like-minded NGOs are some of the initiatives that NGOs undertake to achieve their objectives and in the process ensure people's active participation in the developmental programmes. Besides, their ability to mobilize the masses for the cause they fight for is an added advantage for them.

There has been a rapid rise of NGOs both in developed as well as in developing countries. NGOs of different size, nature and scope have emerged and grown. Apart from its heterogeneous nature the conceptual ambiguity continues to persist as synonymous terms such as voluntary organization, action group, voluntary development organization, etc. have been used in the literature to refer to the term NGO. India too has experienced a rapid rise of NGOs in recent times. The rich legacy of voluntarism, democratic polity, multi-party set-up, pluralism and a vibrant civil society have provided the conducive environment for NGOs to flourish in India. NGOs in India are actively participating in developmental activities and carrying out developmental programmes relating to poverty, education and health. In the field of activism and collective action too, they have demonstrated their ability in fomenting social movements. As an agent of social movement NGOs mobilize the people, generate awareness among them and provide platforms to raise their voice. Through their effective vertical and horizontal net-working they muster support from the like-minded NGOs and more importantly, make concerted efforts to obtain people's support in the areas of their operation. As catalysts NGOs motivate the target population to actively participate in the development programmes carried out by them. As an intermediary between the state and the people they are poised to bridge the gap between the people and the state. As pressure groups and the intermediary force between state and the people, they also influence the decision-making authorities to influence their policies, programmes, orientations and attitudes. Hence NGOs may be seen as an agent of social change that strives to bring about social change in the society.

The NGOs' rise into prominence and their active involvement in issues of contemporary relevance have made scholars and policy makers to analyse their significance in the society. Studies have been carried out; explorations have been made on organizational aspects of NGOs as well as on their functions in the society. In this paper an attempt has been made to discuss how NGOs as a potential social force can contribute towards development and change in the society. The paper outlines diverse roles that NGOs play in bringing about change in the society. Making use of both secondary and primary sources the paper delineates the programmes and activities of NGOs in India and also discusses the role and performance of some NGOs in the North-East India which are actively engaged in the process of development.

Voluntary Organizations: Emergence and Rise

The emergence and rise of voluntary organizations (VOs) can be perceived from various perspectives and attributed to various factors. The rise of VOs can be seen as a consequence of inevitable social change in the society due to industrialization and urbanization processes resulting the growing individualism and thus replacing the primary group relations. In this context voluntary organization can be perceived as a counter force to espouse and uphold voluntarism and collectivism, thus, promoting group relations (Oommen, 1975: 162). The NGOs' rise can also be attributed to the role of state and the growing importance of civil society particularly in a democratic polity and a pluralistic society. They could be seen as intermediary organizations in the civil society which seeks to mediate between the state and the public at large. Increasing importance attributed to decentralized form of governance is another reason for their rise as it provides the scope for the NGOs to operate at the grassroots level. Besides, the urge for charity, reform and philanthropy also contribute in the formation of voluntary organizations to carry out the social work. Another socially significant factor – the role of intellectuals, ideologues who are always in constant search for a space in the society to engage them in a development debate find this sector viable and suitable for them to create a niche for themselves and use this platform to espouse their activities. As Dhanagare (1988: 48) argues, the young middle class intellectuals who increasingly associate themselves with several action groups and micro level movements that have developed in India since 1970s are poised to fill the political space outside the mainstream party politics and state power. Such intellectuals can use ideology to initiate collective action in a structured world.

The NGOs' emergence as a formidable force may also be due to the effective net-works that they forge. Formation of net-works both vertically and horizontally with like minded voluntary organizations help the NGOs to form pressure groups. When NGOs having different structure and size, cutting across geographical boundaries come together can be called as vertical networking of NGOs whereas the NGOs of similar structure and strategy forge links can be called as horizontal networking. Networks are formed at regional, national and international levels. Networks are also formed on the basis of issues such as women empowerment, human rights, environment, etc. wherein like-minded NGOs create a common platform to fight for their cause. The NGO net-works such as FEMNET (African Women's Development and Communications Network), PAN (Pesticides Action Network), APPEN (Asia Pacific People's Environment Network) can be seen some of the instances of formidable NGO net-works (Potter, 1996: 28–30). These networks help the NGOs to reach across sectors, i.e., intellectual, press, community organizations and the decision-making authorities. Hence, networks are the building blocks of social movements and change (Korten, 1990). The NGO sector comprising a large network of voluntary agencies, associations, social action groups have a vital role to play in bringing about socio-economic development in the society.

The rise and growth of the NGOs in India can be seen in three stages of development namely the stage of social welfare, the stage of radical nationalism and the stage of social orientation. During the first stage the NGOs were involved in community welfare and work with social workers at micro level. In the second phase they were engaged in establishing alternative structures through mass mobilization, and during third stage they worked for building alternative social order through localized struggle of marginalized sections (Dhanagare, 1988: 43). In India, though there is no complete census on the NGOs yet, many organizations have come out with their own estimation and documentation. Different government offices, government sponsored autonomous organizations such as CAPART, Central Social Welfare Board, etc. and the NGOs themselves maintain their own database to suit their purpose. Pointing out the steady rise of the NGOs, Lalitha and Kohli, (1982, cited in Garain, 1998) observe that the number of the NGOs have grown from 1,739 in 1953 to 8,052 in 1980 with uneven geographical distribution. Central Social Welfare Board has succeeded in promoting more than 10,000 NGOs engaged in different aspects of social development (Nanavatty, 1987; Paulchowdhry, 1987).

NGOs and Civil Society

Civil society could be seen as an independent domain which maintains its independence from two other prime domains such as public and private and gets strengthened by intermediary institutions such as the NGOs. In an expanded concept of civil society (Hasenfeld and Gidron, 2005) three diverse forms are formulated, such as Civil Society I, Civil Society II, and Civil Society III. Civil Society I consists of organizations that have a neutral relationship with the state. Their indifferent nature ensures that they neither openly support nor oppose state political institutions and policies. Social clubs and SHGs that carry out welfare programmes can be seen as examples under this form. Civil Society II consists of organizations that arise in direct opposition to the state's political institutions and policies and make efforts to change these by using non-conventional political means. Various social movement organizations can be considered under this category. Civil Society III consists of organizations that legitimate and reinforce state regimes and policies through their programmes and activities. They often depend on the state both for legitimacy and financial resources. These organizations include mostly non-profit service organizations that receive benefits of tax exemption, seek and obtain resources from the state. Some argue that 'non-governmental organizations are perhaps the most authentic voice of a civil society' (Plender, 2000; Dhanagare, 2001). According to Beteille (2001: 298) the voluntary action, voluntary movements and voluntary associations have brought about a new lease of hope and also concerns for creation of viable civil society and these organizations can be seen as new institutional faces in an organized and responsive civil society. He however argues that only modern secular and open organizations can find place in the civil society. Strengthening of civil society means enhancing basic grassroots organizing skills, making the way to participate in the political process and creation of institutions. Their apparent diversity, flexibility, efficiency and participatory nature provide a contrast to formal bureaucratic organizations and profit oriented corporate sector. In this context, NGOs may be perceived as a catalytic force which addresses issues such as poverty alleviation, environmental preservation and issues relating to human development. Hence, the NGOs can contribute towards strengthening of civil society by (i) promoting capacity building at the community level, (ii) providing inputs to policy debates, (iii) bridging the gap between masses and the state, and (iv) making efforts to ensure people's participation in development process. Advocating a similar line of argument Bava (1997) argues that there is a need to appreciate and accommodate the NGOs as legitimate and dynamic institutions of civil society. As Korten (1990) articulates there are several key democratic functions, i.e., empowering, educative and advocacy that the civil society organizations and associations can perform. By playing advocacy role and striving for institutional innovation, as a whole, the NGOs play an integrative role in society (Brett, 1993).

NGOs-Government Relationship

The NGOs, seen as a formidable force emanating from civil society, its relationships with other sectors particularly with the state/government assumes significance as the primary objective of these two is to work for the welfare of the people. Though perceived as contradictory forces, both the sectors can complement each other on various developmental programmes and issues. The NGOs seek various help and support from the government to effectively carry out their programmes. Pertinent is Najam's (2000: 375–396) 'four C' model which has outlined the nature of the NGO-GO relations. The four C model is comprised of four possible forms of government-NGOs relations, i.e., Co-operation, Confrontation, Complementarity and Co-optation. Under the Co-operation form of relationship the government and the NGO tend to share similar goals, policies, and strategies to achieve the set objectives thus leading to the convergence of ends and means. Under confrontation form of relation there exists a divergence of strategies of the government and the NGOs. Each follows a different set of means and strategies to achieve the goals. In complementarity form of relation the government and the NGOs share similar goals but follow different strategies where as in Co-optation form the government and the NGOs aim to achieve different goals by following similar strategies. Depending on their interests, principles and strategies the NGOs forge their relation with the government. Keeping aside their confrontational nature of relations there are reasons for both the NGOs and the government to have reciprocal relationship with each other. While the confrontational NGOs may seek collaboration with the government (i) to have an access to technical, managerial and financial resources; (ii) to gain legitimacy or recognition; (iii) to jointly address the people's problem and encourage people's participation, government agencies may find it beneficial to work with the

NGOs (i) to enhance people's participation in their programmes, (ii) to cover more areas particularly in remote areas, and (iii) to apply innovative approaches devised by the NGOs to achieve the objectives in more cost effective manner. Therefore, the collaboration between these two sectors may bring about better results and accelerate the process of development.

Developmental Orientations of the NGOs

The NGOs follow different strategies and approaches to achieve their objectives. With their basic aim to bring about integrated development in the society, their strength lies in the public support. They deploy various people-centred approaches to muster support from the people. Encouraging people to participate in development projects undertaken by them, creating awareness among the people, involving them in the execution of their project strategies, mobilizing them to form pressure blocks are some of the measures taken by the NGOs towards achieving people's support. While people's overwhelming support is the key, the resource generation particularly financial resources become necessary for an organization to survive and sustain. Apart from voluntary contributions from the members and the public the NGOs seek financial support from various donor agencies. They also seek financial support from the government along with training and professional assistance to achieve their objectives. Therefore, the strategies that the NGOs follow can broadly be divided into top-down and bottom-up approach. While bottom-up strategy emphasizes people's participation, and the mechanisms adopted to win the trust and confidence of the people, the top-down strategy basically emphasizes lobbying and bargaining with decision-making authorities and to obtain support from the government (Panda, 2007). Grassroots voluntary organizations particularly carry out bottom-up strategies to empower the disadvantageous sections of the society and motivate them to participate in the community action. This community participation brings about significant impact on the local situations (Edwards and Hulme, 1992).

The NGOs employ participatory modes of intervention such as Participatory Rural Appraisal (PRA), Rapid Rural Appraisal (RRA) and through the application of these methods they provide opportunities for villagers to discuss, interpret, apply, and also invent methods themselves (Chambers, 1995: 15). This approach becomes useful when applied to issues such as community management of common property resources, child labour, security, poverty, health issues, farmers' attitude and cropping pattern, forest issues such as Joint Forestry Management (JFM), Social Forestry (SF). Some of the NGOs who have pioneered PRA in India are MYRADA based in Bangalore, Action Aid, Bangalore, SPEECH Madurai, Youth for Action Hyderabad, etc. while among international NGOs Intercooperation (Berne), and Action Aid, London are prominent (Chambers, 1995: 8).

NGOs' Initiatives to Promote Social Change

The NGOs perform diverse functions for various stakeholders. The functions that the VOs perform can broadly be classified as manifest and latent functions. Benefits that individuals accrue from the organization in form of sociability, recreation, service can be seen as manifest functions of the VOs for individuals whereas social integration, interpersonal relations can be seen as latent functions. Individuals draw the benefits of interaction such as easing loneliness, learning new norms, acquiring relevant information (Shils, 1968), which in turn integrate individuals with the society. In other words, the VOs can be seen as a force that performs social integrative functions. Similarly, at the societal level, the organizational skills that individuals develop from the organization not only provide satisfaction for them but also incorporate fresh cadres of leaders with new perspectives on problems, innovative ideas to the society which in turn stimulate social change. Another sociologically significant aspect which needs to be discussed at the backdrop of the contributions of the VOs is the avenue that these organizations provide for upward social mobility. These organizations through their programmes and activities create conducive situations that promote the upward mobility of the people in the society. The upward mobility brings about a significant change in the nature and structure of the society. The VOs offering the space to fill in the void created by other two prime sectors in carrying out public functions, welfare activities can be seen as some of the manifest functions of the VOs oriented towards the society.

Further, the strategies of the NGOs deployed to bring about change and development in the society can be categorized into internal and external. While the NGOs who work in tandem with the government and business establishments to foster changes in the society tend to follow internal strategies. At times they also challenge the programmes and policies of the government by resorting to confrontational approach which may be referred to as external strategies. However, the convergence of strategies is important for the NGOs to become effective.

Korten (1990) asserts four critical roles that the VOs perform within broader framework of people's development movement, i.e., catalysing the transformation of institutions, policies and values; monitoring and protesting abuses of power; facilitating reconciliation; and providing essential community services. The roles of the NGOs that aim to promote social change and transformation in the society can be classified as philanthropic, developmental, advocacy, reformative, collaborative and radical activism.

Philanthropic: Rooted with the values of voluntarism and altruism, the NGOs with philanthropic undertone carry out various social welfare activities. Running programmes for disadvantageous sections of the society such as disabled, aged, women, orphans, etc. they try to instill confidence among these. Establishing and running schools and hospitals, old age homes, rehabilitation centres, etc. and such initiatives taken by them can be seen under this role of the NGOs.

Developmental: The NGOs who contribute towards accelerating the developmental process and are concerned with development-related issues such as poverty alleviation programme, human development, empowerment programmes, i.e., formation of self-help groups, micro finance schemes, undertaking community development programmes construed to play developmental role. Emphasizing participatory mode of development and sustainable development while they encourage people to participate in their developmental initiatives they also take initiatives to maintain the pristine ecosystem.

Advocacy: The NGOs make efforts to influence the decision-making bodies through bargaining, building up of pressure on decision making authorities through its intense campaigning, effective net-working, offering suggestions, providing feedback to policy debates in order to bring modifications are some of the efforts taken by the NGOs which could fall under this role.

Collaborative: Though the NGOs maintain a separate and distinct entity, they also collaborate with other two prime sectors such as government and corporate sectors.

Radical activism: The NGOs through their widespread net-working and mobilization programmes can resort to organize protest campaigns that may culminate in the formation of social movements thereby bringing about social transformation in the society.

Through awareness campaign the NGOs make people aware of their rights and responsibilities. They take measures to educate the ignorant mass and in the process fight against the structured inequalities. By exerting pressure on decision-making bodies, mobilizing opinion and net-working the NGOs tend to bring about changes in the policies and programmes which otherwise go against the interests of the common people. The NGOs through innovative strategies and methods address the needs of local communities. Through participatory approaches they ensure people's participation in their programmes despite operating in difficult terrains. While they bring about changes at the micro level through awareness campaigns, creation of grassroots institutions; at macro level they induce changes through their mobilization programmes. The NGOs who canvass for social change and transformation on different issues through intense campaigns and people's mobilization can also be seen as facilitators of New Social Movements (Mencher, 1999: 2085). The collective action forms the basis of the social movement and the NGOs may be seen as an agent that mobilizes and organizes people to contribute to such collective action. Thus, the NGOs can be considered as agents of social movement and social change. It is assumed that as one of the actors that promote development, the NGOs' relations with the state/government assumes significance. The mobilization of the people results in the expression and formation of popular protests such as silent protest marches, peaceful protest marches, demonstrations, etc. and eventually results in social movements. Therefore, the NGOs could be seen as networking agents which encourage and translate popular participation in their programmes into popular mobilization in a direction resulting in a movement. Korten (1990: 117) asserts that the NGOs employ fourth generation strategies such as awareness building, networking and mobilization programmes to empower people. The inherent philosophy of the NGOs which is rooted in voluntarism, altruism and non-profit the ultimate goal of the NGOs remain to bring about social change and transformation.

It will be worth mentioning the efforts that some of the NGOs have undertaken to bring about change and development in the society. The NGOs' involvement in promoting various environmental movements such as Chipko, Narmada Bachao are well known. The Self-Employed Women's Association (SEWA) having an all India membership of 2.2 lakh continue to organize women and help them to participate in the mainstream of the economy. The SEWA bank has demonstrated how it is profitable to run a bank of and for poor women (Bhatt, 1998). The study (Gore, 2004) observes that the projects carried out by four NGOs such as Shramajivi Sanghatana, Gramayan, Satpuda Adivasi Shikshan Mandal and Vanrai in different parts of Maharashtra which have brought about qualitative changes in the form of rehabilitating bonded labourers through the formation of cooperatives, promoting and strengthening voluntary action in rural development, spread of education among tribal population, promoting afforestation and watershed development in the areas of their operation respectively. Mane (2004) presents the work done by Maharashtra Arogya Mandal in Pune on community development by addressing issues such as drinking water, agricultural development, education, vocational training thereby targeting the integrated development of the people of the region. Vidyavathi (2004) presents the efforts of Women Voluntary Organizations particularly the work done by Andhra Mahila Sabha in Hyderabad. Pundir (2004) provides case studies of voluntary organizations initiated and established by scheduled castes to bring about development in their community.

In the Context of the North-East India

The NGOs in North-East India can contribute significantly towards socio-economic development of the region through their developmental initiatives and participatory development approach. A concerted effort of the government, the NGOs and the community is indeed warranted for the integrated development in the region. A discussion forum comprising representatives of the government, the NGOs and community leaders can help approaching the common problems. The issues relating to micro finance, health, human development assume significance in the context of the North-East India.

Even though there is no proper documentation on the NGOs' contribution and activities in the North-East region of India, there is a great deal of scope and space for them to assert and contribute towards the development of this region. The voluntarism and activism displayed by some of them through their developmental initiatives are praiseworthy. The data gathered from some of these NGOs such as Bethany Society, Bosco Reach Out and NEICORD reveal that initiatives taken by these organizations on areas such as empowerment, disability, health issues have been implemented effectively to ascertain qualitative changes in the areas of their operation. These organizations have made efforts to create awareness among the people, generate enthusiasm among them and elicit the hidden innovative ideas and methods in them. Let us discuss some of the major initiatives taken by these organizations in this region particularly in Meghalaya.

Bethany Society with a vision to improve the quality of life of the most vulnerable sections of society is engaged in various developmental activities to meet its objectives. The objectives it has set to achieve are (i) to organize programmes on disability which are inclusive, barrier free and rights based; (ii) to organize, establish support, develop and consolidate educational, vocational, social, cultural, charitable and economic activities for the holistic development of people and communities in vulnerable situations; and (iii) to create sustainable livelihoods particularly among rural communities and to care for the environment. In one of its significant ventures, it has worked towards empowerment of persons with disability in all districts of Meghalaya, covering 400 villages and reaching out to 5,000 persons with disability. Rural livelihood programmes have been carried out in five districts of Meghalaya, i.e., East Khasi Hills, West Khasi Hills, West Garo Hills, East Garo Hills and South Garo Hills in over 500 villages. Significantly, more than 400 SHGs have been established (Annual Report, Bethany Society).

The North-East India Committee on Relief and Development (NEICORD) has been involved in relief and development works in the North-Eastern states of India. With a focus on issues such as micro enterprise development, health, HIV-AIDS, peace building in partnership with the churches in the North-East, like-minded NGOs and the government, the organization strives for integrated development. Through its people oriented programmes it continues to contribute towards development and change in the society. Let us discuss some of the projects that the organization has implemented. The Raphaelhas Project emphasizes information sharing and distribution of information, education and communication (IEC) materials in an effort to disseminate the information and in the process educate the mass and make them aware. Under the project Urban Community Development Project (UCDP) in slum of Pynthorumkhrah area of Shillong, Meghalaya 12 SHGs have been formed out of which 10 are women's group and two are men's group. Various capacity building training programmes have been conducted which include SHG, leadership, team building, book keeping, agriculture, floriculture, skill training on handicraft in order to help them in sustainable livelihood opportunities. Another project Patharkhamah Community Development Project (PCDC) implemented in the Ri-Bhoi district, Meghalaya has covered 12 villages that serves the Khasi, Rabha and Garo people through its programmes, i.e., group formation and community leadership development, functional literacy, primary health care and income generating programme. At present there are 40 SHGs consisting of 20 each from women and men group. In another project, Livelihood Improvement Project for the Himalayas (LIPH), Umsning Block was started in 2007 at Umsning, Ri Bhoi District, Meghalaya in partnership with Meghalaya Rural Development Society. Under this project 46 villages are being covered where the main focus of the project is SHG mobilization and formation. In one year the project team has successfully formed 76 SHGs out of which 22 are women's groups 26 are men's group and 18 are mixed group (Annual Report, NEICORD).

Bosco Reach Out (BRO) has been carrying out capacity building programmes in order to empower the people in the areas of its operation. To meet the needs of the different target groups BRO has adopted different approaches which can be categorized into four phases such as Phase I: Institutionalized Charity Approach to Development through Individuals (1983–1994) (development of vocational schools, relief operations); Phase II: Participatory Project Approach to Development (1995–1998) (integrated programme approach, focus on SHGs); Phase III: Strengthening People's Institutions (1999–2005) (strengthening SHGs, grassroots governance); and Phase IV: Creating awareness, facilitating people's movement) Rights Based Approach to Development (2006 onward). BRO through the implementation of various development oriented projects is engaged in bringing about change and transformations in the society.

Brisoh Project is an intensive resource utilization programme for the tribal mass, which is being implemented in 20 villages of

Marmain Region at Ri-bhoi district in Meghalaya. The project supported by NABARD and government of Meghalaya is in the second year of implementation. The improved quality of life through appropriate and effective management of resources by the poor tribal people is the focus of this project.

As one of its major initiatives, 4,000 SHGs have been formed with more than 41,677 members. BRO has been working with District Rural Development Agency (DRDA) in seven blocks in Meghalaya, spreading over to 1,014 villages. Apart from community health programme, BRO with its implementing partner Ferrando Integrated Women Development Centre, Durtlang, Mizoram is working on the issue of drug addiction and working towards rehabilitating the drug addicts. It is implemented through its centres in the four districts such as Aizawl, Champhai, Lawngtlai and Saiha and also at Guwahati in Assam. BRO has adopted women empowerment as part of its growth and development initiative. Integrated Women Empowerment (IWEP) is a collaborative programme of BRO in Umling Community and Rural Development Block, Meghalaya. This project so far has benefited 55 villages (Bosco Reach Out, 2008).

Three awareness programmes on Malaria and its preventive measures were held at Nongshluid and Phlangsynnei villages, Mawkyrwat and Mawlai, Shillong on 28, May, 16 June and 21 June 2008 respectively. The SHG members, village durbars and villagers attended the programme. Entrepreneurship Development Programme, a three day training on Entrepreneurship Development was conducted at Agricultural Training Centre, Corpora, East Garo Hills, Meghalaya from 27 to 30 June 2007. Two one-day capacity building programmes for SHG members were conducted by CLF members on 20 and 23 May 2008 at Umran and Nongpoh regions respectively. Two one-day awareness programmes on National Rural Health Mission Programme were held on the 21 and 31 May 2008 in Sylein village, Mawsynram and Tynnai villages of Meghalaya respectively. In one of its innovative strategies the organization has tried to create business units in the specific area. Keeping in mind the market value of the commodity that people produce in a given area the business units help marketing the local products. Awareness programme on various government schemes and programmes have made rural people conscious about their rights and claims, and they do not hesitate to seek information under the RTI. It has created awareness on general health issues, particularly issues relating to mother and child care, malaria awareness programmes, right based awareness programmes, livestock management programme, micro-enterprise development programme, etc.

BRO makes its members aware through in-house training, providing exposure to other groups and villages which are doing well. CLF (Cluster Level Federation) identify issues, runs RTI programmes through the clusters, work towards strengthening of traditional governance system and establish rapport with the village headman. Nongstoin Cluster Level Federation of West Khasi Hills districts, Meghalaya in a workshop prioritized corruption issue that affecting the society in the district. To combat this menace, it has taken initiatives such as creating awareness about the RTI Act 2005 in collaboration with BSO. CLF members along with local leaders seek information relating to delay of implementation of government schemes as well as on implemented schemes in the area (BSO, 2008). BRO's involvement in the Child Line Project, a project of Women and Child Development of the Government of India in partnership with State Governments, international donors, the corporate sector, shows the collaborative work that the NGOs do along with other sectors. The composition of SHG groups shows that 78 per cent SHG members are women which indeed is socially significant. This shows that women have shown keen interest to participate in developmental activities and the organization has been able to motivate them a lot. With the commitment to social cause, strong bond and rapport with people, formation of SHGs and addressing socially relevant issues these organizations are indeed making efforts to bring about social transformations in the society.

Owing to the increasing rise and growing importance of NGO sector, the intervention of NGOs in the process of development one can argue that NGOs have indeed emerged as a potential social force in India and in the North-East region of India. However, despite the increasing importance of the NGOs, the accountability and sustainability issues remain crucial for the NGO sector. As an organization will an NGO maintain its distinctiveness? Will the NGOs sustain as a potential force? How they become accountable to multiple stakeholders, i.e., donors, beneficiaries? These are some of the concerns that the NGO sector is confronting with. For the NGOs to remain as distinct organizations, a lot would depend on its leadership, the staff and its commitment to its core goal. The deviation from its core values, i.e., voluntarism and altruism, social service will lead to the confusion. The NGOs today are becoming more donor-centric and professional. There have been charges of corruption, miss utilization of funds, etc. levelled against the NGOs. Charges have also leveled that the NGOs are going in corporate ways. The mushrooming NGOs have also led to doubts about their credibility as many NGOs which are not genuine try to take advantage. But what is needed is more accountability and assertiveness on the part of the NGOs. As Dhanagare (1988: 59) articulates, 'only a careful blend of ideological commitment and pragmatism, macro perspective and micro-level involvements, discourse with outsiders but awareness of self autonomy, and discretion in accepting both allies and financial help can unfold the inherent strength of action-groups if they are to become a viable as well as a stable alternative in the social transformation process in India'.

Conclusion

The NGOs certainly have emerged as a social force in the domain of development and have made their presence felt in developmental programmes and activities. The people centred approaches and strategies deployed by these organizations have proved to be a boon for them. They have demonstrated their ability in mobilizing masses for the cause they fight for and projecting themselves as intermediary to establish the link between the amorphous mass of people and the state. As social service providers and active actors in civil society the NGOs have the capacity to empower socio-economically deprived communities and build social capital in the society. No doubt, many NGOs struggle to live up to the expectations, many of them in the process to fade away, many of them work contrary to their basic principles, yet the NGO sector as a whole has created a niche for itself and has emerged as a formidable social force to reckon with in India. The NGOs in the North-East region of India have been engaged in socio-economic development of the region. Some of them have indeed made significant contributions in their chosen developmental issues. However, at the organizational level, better networking and proper documentation are warranted in order for them to project as a viable channel to address the developmental and welfare issues.

References

Bava, N. 1997. 'Towards an Integrated Theory of People's Participation through NGOs: Nation Building and Decentralized Development', in N. Bava (ed.), *Non-Governmental Organizations in Development: Theory and Practice*. New Delhi: Kanishka Publishers, 255–274.

Beteille, A. 2001. 'Civil Society and the Good Society', *Sociological Bulletin*, 50(2): 286–307.

Bethany Society. Annual Report 2007–2008.

Bhatt, E.R. 1998. 'Empowering the Poor through Micro-finance: The SEWA Bank', in M.L. Dantwala, Harsh Sethi and Pravin Visaria (eds), *Social Change through Voluntary Action*. New Delhi: Sage, 146–161.

—. 1993. 'Voluntary Agencies as Development Organizations: Theorizing the Problem of Efficiency and Accountability', *Development and Change*, 24: 269–303. New Delhi: Sage.

Chambers, R. 1995. 'Rural Appraisal: Rapid, Relaxed and Participatory', in Amitava Mukherjee (ed.), *Participatory Rural Appraisal: Methods and Applications in Rural Planning*. New Delhi: Vikas Publishing House, 1–63.

Dhanagare, D.N. 1988. 'Action Groups and Social Transformation in India', *Lokayan Bulletin*, VI (5): 37–59.

—. 2001. 'Civil Society, State and Democracy: Contextualising a Discourse', *Sociological Bulletin*, 50(2): 167–191.

Edwards, M. and D. Hulme. 1992. 'Scaling-up the Developmental Impact of NGOs Concepts and Experiences', in Michael Edwards and David Hulme (eds), *Making a Difference: NGOs and Development in a Changing World*. London: Earthscan, 13–27.

Focus: Newsletter of Bosco Reach Out. Vol. XII. May-September, 2008.

Garain, S. 1998. *Organizational Effectiveness of Non-governmental Organizations*. Jaipur: University Book House.

Gore, S.D. 2004. 'Role of NGOs in Social Transformation', in S.N. Pawar, J.B. Ambekar and D. Shrikant (eds), *NGOs and Development: The Indian Scenario*. New Delhi: Rawat Publications, 186–199.

Hasenfeld, Y. and B. Gidron. 2005. 'Understanding Multi-purpose Hybrid Voluntary Organization: The Contributions of Theories on Civil Society, Social Movement and Non-profit Organizations', *Journal of Civil Society*, 1(2): 97–112.

Korten, D. 1990. *Getting to the 21st Century: Voluntary Action and the Global Agenda*. West Hartford: Kumarian Press.

Mane, M. 2004. 'Voluntary Organization and Community Development: A Case Study of Maharashtra Arogya Mandal', in S.N. Pawar, J.B. Ambekar and D. Shrikant (eds), op. cit., 169–176. Voluntary Organisations.

Mencher, J. 1999. 'NGOs: Are They a Force for Change?', *Economic and Political Weekly*, 34(30): 2081–2086.

Najam, A. 2000. 'The Four C's of Third Sector-Government Relations: Cooperation, Confrontation, Complementarity and Co-optation', *Non-Profit Management and Leadership*, 10(4): 375–396. New Delhi: Kanishka Publishers.

NEICORD. Annual Report 2007–2008.

Oommen, T.K. 1975. 'The Theory of Voluntary Associations in a Cross Cultural Perspective', *Sociological Bulletin*, XXIV (2): 163–180.

Panda, B. 2007. 'Top Down or Bottom Up? A Study of Grassroots NGOs' Approach', *Journal of Health Management*, 9(2): 257–273.

Potter, D. 1996. 'Non-Governmental Organizations and Environmental Policies', in A. Blowers and P. Glasbergen (eds), *Environmental Policy in an International Context: Prospects for Environmental Change*. London: Arnold, John Wiley Sons Inc., 26–49.

Pundir, J.K. 2004. 'Voluntary Efforts of Scheduled Castes and Their Development: Select Evidence from North-India', in S.N. Pawar, J.B. Ambekar and D. Shrikant (eds), op. cit., 223–239.

Sills, D.L. 1968. 'Voluntary Associations: Sociological Aspects', in David L. Sills (ed.), *International Encyclopedia of the Social Sciences*. Vol. 16. New York: The Macmillan Company and Free Press, 362–379.

Vidyavathi, A. 2004. 'Women Voluntary Organisations and Social Change: A Case Study of Andhra Mahila Sabha, Hyderabad', in S.N. Pawar, J.B. Ambekar and D. Shrikant (eds), op. cit., 200–213.

17

Forests and the Tribal Life

Roots of Environmental Change Among the Khasis

REKHA M. SHANGPLIANG

Since time immemorial, forests have played a vital role in the determination of the ways of life and culture of societies across the world. Human ingenuity and nature's generosity have conspired into numerous ways of usages born out of forests. During the Indian mythological period, certain distinct forest territories – '*Aranyas*' were identified as abodes of sages (Sinha, 1993: 34). In the forestlands of western Africa of the Sahelian states, Africans lived in small communities known as 'Forest Kingdoms' under the rule of their tribal chiefs. For the local forest dwellers of Amazonia, the "Caboclos", the 'Punan' hunter-gatherers of Borneo and the 'Pygmies' of Central Africa, tropical forests provide them nearly with all their needs, from medicinal plants and protein-rich game to fire-wood and building materials; flour resins and dyes to fruits and mushrooms. The forests are both a shelter and a food larder (CIFOR, 2003: 2). These are but, a few examples to show the myriad ways in which forests have intricately coalesced with human life and culture which makes it the most important biological entity of all eco-systems.

Knowledge of Forests among the Tribal People

Although tribal societies across the world have been known for their special kinship with forest and forest products, the mainstream view, about tribal cultures, since colonial times upto the present, is extremely negative and seems to bear almost no shred of reality. It starts from ideas that tribal cultures are 'primitive' and 'backward'. This negative perception about tribal people that was built during British rule remains unquestioned in India till today, and denies the existence of tribal forest lore, their culture and values. But what exactly constitutes tribal knowledge of forest? While schools and universities have taught us to value one kind of knowledge ('factual', 'rational' or 'scientific') as against another kind – 'intuitive' and 'instinctive knowledge' (Padel, 1992: 1), there is a second kind of knowledge that is based solidly in 'experience' and not 'experiments' that harbours tribal knowledge. Tribals depend on this knowledge to fulfill most of their day-to-day needs (their 'economy') through agriculture, hunting, fishing, and gathering a huge range of forest foods and materials; with these they make most of their articles of daily use, from houses to ploughs, baskets to leaf-plates; they possess an ancient lore of herbal medicine, as well as knowledge about many aspects of nature and human life that is more highly developed than ours (Padel, 1992: 1). The knowledge of forests of the tribal people is a 'real' knowledge, that is deeply linked to their day-to-day experience and survival needs, and so there is a lot we may learn from them. Today, the tribals have come a long way since the British rule was imposed on tribal areas and a new set of administrative process have been established which aimed at economic and industrial development. With the rapidly increasing population, the economic pressure fell on the forests and this pressure had to be borne by a land-based economic system, which did not achieve a better growth rate of agriculture because of the lack of marketing facilities. As a result, forests, as common property resource was privatized because of the continued reliance on land-based activities. Added to this problem for the tribes is their high dependence on forest to meet their needs for survival. According to an estimate, roughly 95 per cent of India's tribal population are located in the rural areas where agriculture and forestry traditionally constitute the main source of livelihood (Nongbri, 2003: 2). Indeed, the tribal development policies of the government would do better than consider them as 'museum pieces' (Shukla et al., 1990: 12). In Jenny Diski's novel *Rainforest*, an anthropologist/ecologist goes mad when she begins to feel the forest she has been studying scientifically. Official knowledge of the forest compartmentalizes it, an analysing that kills the heart – kills our relationship with it (Padel, 1992: 9).

An understanding of this so-called 'real' knowledge about the forest among the Khasi of Meghalaya and making an appraisal of the changes in the parameters of resource use that have emerged in recent times as a result of the gradual spread of government policies and legislations would make an interesting study.

"U Khasi u im bad ka mariang,
bad ka mariang ka im bad u ..."

This resounding declaration of the famous Khasi writer H.O. Mawrie, which literally means, 'A Khasi lives with nature and nature lives with him', sums up the strong emotional bond that has ever sustained between the Khasi and nature. The Khasi Hills is a plateau of rolling grasslands, meandering rivers, green rolling hills gently sloping towards the plains and valleys with deep gorges and precipitous ravines (Giri, 1990: 3). Situated in the North-Eastern State of Meghalaya known as the 'abode of clouds',[1] the East and the West Khasi Hills have both earned a name for its temperate climate, which is neither too hot nor too cold with a plentiful rainfall in summer which helps the growth of gorgeous and luxuriant vegetation.

From a historical retrospective the forest wealth of the Khasi was diverse, ranging from tropical to temperate type of forests. Besides the indigenous pine tree (*Pinus khasiana*), which still dominates the natural vegetation, 'Sal' is also a valuable timber in the region. Bamboo or '*siej*' as it is locally called has served as a good source of traditional craftsmanship ever since long centuries past. From cane and bamboo, the Khasi created several articles of daily use such as cones, baskets, mats, cages, sun and rain shades etc. (Bareh, 2001: 26). Bamboo was so much in use and modelled into so many articles of value that 'there was once among the Khasi a widespread bamboo culture' (Bareh, 2001: 27). Much of Khasi timber in the past was also used for making bridge-piles, railway sleepers, boat building and furniture. For a Khasi, the forest has been a natural store-house from where he derives everything needed for his daily life, shelter, fodder, food and medicine. The forest is a well-loved home, a game sanctuary and also a shrine of worship around which his social, cultural and religious activities revolve.

The natural wisdom of the ancient Khasis is a God-given gift to them, an inborn quality which could be interpreted as the result of their close contact with mother-earth.[2] Much of this ancient wisdom is today the result of oral tradition (Mawrie, 2001: 78). A basic element present in such legends is the personification of elements of nature as mother, son, husband and wife, friend and foe, according to their natural behaviours, their love, hate, jealousy, pride and vanity which are projected out before the listeners with the sole purpose of teaching moral and spiritual values. Forest myths and legends have played an important role in enriching the ecological history of societies around the world.[3] One such legend which is very popular among the Khasis is the legend of "U Diengiei". According to this legend there was a very tall and gigantic tree at "Lum Diengiei" which had its branches spread far and wide and covered the sun overshadowing the earth. The whole world became dark, damp and gloomy and the people were deprived of the warmth of the sun and light resulting in ill-health, disease and death. So they held their village council and decided to cut down the tree. Accordingly they felled the tree and it was only after they had felled the tree that they could enjoy good health, peace and happiness (Gurdon, 1975: 23). This folktale throws ample light on the perception and attitude of the ancient Khasi towards trees and forests. They considered the forest as the home of gods and evil spirits, as something dreadful and look upon it with a sense of awe and reverence.

Thus, for the Khasi, nature itself is like a great book with infinite leaves. Each page contains valuable lessons which every Khasi adheres to (Mawrie, 2001: 40). It is known that in the reckoning of time, months of the year, days of the week, the Hindus looked at the planets like sun, moon, Jupiter, Saturn etc. while the Greeks followed the mythological names of gods and goddesses. The Khasi ancestors, however, had no knowledge of astronomy, but they had their mother nature close to them. They looked at the changes that took place in nature from season to season and named the months of a year according to their natural characteristics.

Objects of nature have occupied a central place in the *sanctum sanctorum* of Khasi tradition. They are indispensable in the performance of religious rites and rituals amongst the followers of traditional Khasi religion.[4] Whatever may be the occasion, either naming ceremony (*Ka jer ka thoh*), marriage (*Ka poikha poiman*) or death (*niam ïap*) there is an explicit usage of natural objects with a sense of necessity and sacredness. To cite an example, during the naming ceremony of a child, a banana leaf (*'la-kait*) is placed on the floor with five pieces of dry fish (*Khapiah*) on it. Beside this, is placed a bow and three arrows if the child is a boy and if the child is a girl, a bamboo basket (*khoh*) with a carrying belt (*star*) is placed. As the priest summons God to witness the function and give his blessing, the relatives present in the ceremony mention a few names for the child. The priest repeats each name while pouring out the liquor from the gourd container (*u klong*) on the floor. The name at the repetition of which the last drop of liquor from the gourd adheres to the spout of it, is the selected name for the child (Gurdon, 1975: 124–125). The role played by nature in its various forms in Khasi ethos and tradition is thus an embodiment of their socio-cultural heritage.

Khasi literature is replete with thoughts and ideas that express and communicate what nature means to them. One finds that most of the idioms and phrases commonly used by them in ordinary course of conversation are derived from the beauty of a flower, the lofty mountains, the cascading waterfalls and various forms of nature which attract their imaginations. To cite a few examples here – a person with good reputation and respect is often compared to a flower called '*Tiew-pathai-khubor*' (flower that sends messages) a kind of flower which emits a sweet smell around it. A boy who grows very tall is compared to a tender bamboo plant shooting straight to the sky.

The indigenous system of folk medicine prevalent in the Khasi society accounts for the rich ecological heritage of the Khasis. Over the centuries, the Khasis have developed an indigenous ethno-medical knowledge which has served well the Khasi community and has been handed down from generation to generation. A study conducted by the North-Eastern Biodiversity Research Cell of NEHU, Shillong, revealed that the total volume of medicinal plants or their products used or consumed per year was 80 to 120 tonnes, involving an amount of ₹ 2.5 crore per annum within the three districts of Khasi and Jaintia Hills (Syiem and others, 1999: 2).

Traditional System of Forest Management Among the Khasis

For the Khasis, the traditional system of forest management emerged as a natural response to their deep sense of eco-consciousness. This is evident in their unique system of ownership, control and management of forests that has formed the basis of forest culture of the Khasis since time immemorial. In spite of British possession of the 25 Khasi states, there was no instance of the British substantially interfering with the tribal rights to land and forest. British administration showed considerable respect for customary land laws of the Khasis and never stood in the way of its normal operation. The Meghalaya Land and Revenue Manual while expressing its viewpoint on this matter noted, 'the customs of the Khasis in regard to land was respected by the British from the day they came to these hills in 1,829 till the day they departed in 1947. We may be surprised by the magnanimity of the British, strange though it may sound that they never thought it necessary to interfere in the customs of the Khasis. For their needs and requirements of land the British went through proper negotiations. After due agreements, paid for the land in cash' (Phira, 1989).

The three categories of land identified by the Land Reforms Commission of Meghalaya which was appointed in 1973 are Ri Raid Land, Ri Kynti Land and Government Land. This categorization presents a logical order of the Khasi land tenure system and its related concepts of ownership; control and occupancy rights of land.

The Ri Kynti Land is a private land acquired by a particular clan which has proprietary, heritable or transferable right over such land. Such land can also be inherited by a woman from her mother.[5]

The Ri Raid Land which is a community land is managed and controlled by the concerned community. Every member of the community has the right to use and occupy the Ri Raid land without payment of land revenue. However, such rights revert back to the community when the person ceases to occupy or use the land for a consecutive period of three years or more. The forest-lands that fall under the category of Ri Raid land are:

1. *Ri 'Law Kyntang, Ri 'Law Niam or Ri 'Law Lyngdoh*

   There are forest lands that are set apart for religious purposes, managed and controlled by the Raid or the village or in the case of Ri 'Law Lyngdoh by the Lyngdoh (Priest) of the community.

2. *Ri 'Law Adong, Ri 'Law Sang, Ri 'Law Shnong*

   These are village forests reserved by the villagers so that any member could obtain timber or firewood for personal needs or for use as water catchment areas.

3. *Ri 'Law Sumar*

   There are forests which belong to the individual or clan or village who had first occupied and afforested them and maintains them thereafter.

The attitude reflected in the above observation exhibits the apparent trend of land and forest ownership pattern prevalent among the Khasis and the traditional methods of conservation strategies evoked by them as a response to their eco-consciousness.

The Emerging Trend

The concept of 'change' and emerging trends in relation to the environment have acquired a new dimension today. It goes beyond the description of the nature and extent of environmental degradation; it has little to say about the rates of tropical deforestation in the extinction of species or the build-up of carbon in the atmosphere. These facts are properly the reserve of the scientist (Guha, 2002: 2). Rather to make an assessment of the emergent trends in forest-man relationship would mean to examine the changes in the parameters of resource use that have emerged in recent times as a result of the gradual spread and rigidity of government policies and legislations.

The parameters of resource use among the Khasis have been defined largely by their traditional belief systems, concepts and perceptions about nature, its resources, their usage and conservation. These parameters basically revolve around the social, religious, economic as well as recreational life of the Khasis whereby the forest is considered as their total life-situation from where they derive almost everything for their basic needs. Land and forests are the integral parts of their habitat to which they belong, hence from time immemorial tribes have exercised complete control over these, and whatever else is contained above and beneath them (Nongbri, 2003: 122). Among the Khasis the right to use, control and management of lands or forestlands within the society is defined at the village level or '*shnong*' where there are categories of forestlands owned by the village community or privately. The village council acts as the highest authority which accordingly respects and abides by the customary beliefs and practices. These councils have done a good job of protecting the forest reserves and taking action against those violating the rules.

The apparent trend, eco-consciousness and deep sense of eco-spirituality of the Khasis have no doubt generated a liberal use of resources and allowed the emergence of rational concepts of resources and their behaviour. Had it not been for the existence of village forests (*'law-shnong*) and sacred groves (*'law-kyntang* or *'law-lyngdoh*) the forest wealth of the hill areas would have long ago been irremediably lost (Simon, 1991: 79). The widely talked about issue of Common Property Resource Management (CPR) has acquired an important place in the traditional economy of the Khasis, particularly of the rural masses. Common Property Resources (CPRs), broadly speaking are the resources accessible to the whole community of a village and to which no individual has exclusive property right (Jodha, 1986: 1). Subject to seasonal variation, the local Khasi villagers, especially women, engage themselves in collection of Non-Timber Forest Products (NTFP) such as fruits, edible roots, vegetation, mushroom, bamboo, broomstick, dried pine leaves, pine cones, bamboo-shoots, etc. which cater to the needs for food and other daily requirements. Every Khasi village has two categories of rules of right over forestlands. One rule is for the permanent residents of the village, "*Trai-shnong*" and the other is for the non-permanent residents of the village, "*Bar-shnong*". The second category of persons cannot enjoy equal rights on the village CPRs. They are not allowed to cut grass or collect wood from any of the community forests. But they are allowed to use the springs, ponds and rivers to get water and to wash their clothes and collect wild vegetables.

Systematic management of forests in the Khasi Hills began over a hundred years ago, specifically in the period immediately following the visit of Lord Northbrook, the Viceroy of India to the Khasi Hills in 1874. Steps were then taken to reserve certain tracts for the regeneration and preservation of timber trees and 37 'reserved' and 'protected' forests varying in size from 0.65 to 18 sq. kms were created in several of the then Khasi states (Allen, 1905: 82). In addition, a number of "Green Blocks" for protecting the water supply of Shillong and providing firewood were also set up in the neighbourhood of the town (Simon, 1991: 80).

This is just the tip of the iceberg in the light of the major achievements of the colonialists in bringing about systematic forest management in the country. This has largely been a result of colonial rule and the process of development that followed soon after India's Independence (Nongbri, 2003: 12).

Unlike other areas of the country, the Khasi Hills have a diarchical system of forest management managed by the state government on one hand and the Autonomous District Council on the other. In accordance with the provisions laid down under the Sixth Schedule of the Indian Constitution, the first District Council was inaugurated in 1952.Under Section 3 of the Sixth Schedule to the

Constitution of India, the Autonomous District Council is empowered to make laws on a range of subjects, which include:

1. the allotment, occupation or use, or the setting apart of land other than any land which is a reserved forest for the purposes of agriculture or grazing or for residential or other purpose likely to promote the interests of the inhabitants of any village or town.
2. the management of any forest not being a reserved forest.
3. the use of any canal or water course for the purpose of agriculture; and
4. the regulation of the practice of *jhum*, or other forms of shifting cultivation.

In addition to these, the District Council is also equipped with other legislative powers relating to the establishment of town or village committee, town and village administration, appointment and succession of chiefs and headman, inheritance of property, marriage and divorce and social customs (Nongbri, 2003: 145). However, a major setback of the Sixth Schedule has been its failure to bring a clean-cut distinction in the working of the State Government and the District Council. In matters relating to forest management, the existing diarchy between the two has posed problems on two counts. Firstly, the forest being the principal source of revenue the District Councils cannot afford to stop giving permits for forest operations under prevailing fund constraints. Most of the forests in the district being under the management of the District Council, the Government does not have much of a say in the affairs of controlling forest operations. Secondly, the District Councils are paranoidly wary that their powers under the Sixth Schedule may be over-stepped by the State Government on the ground of protection and preservation of environment. In fact, the claims of State Forest officials that all tree permits issued by the District Council authorities must have a corresponding marking of the forest department is termed by the District Council authorities as a curtailment of their powers (Shangpliang, 1995: 99). In addition to this, the enactment of the Assam Reorganization Act, 1969 and the North Eastern Reorganization Act, 1971 further undermined the powers of the District Council by rendering the laws passed by it as subservient to those of the State legislature. All this has led to a strain in the relationship between the two, and added constraints to their functioning, especially in areas pertaining to the protection of customary rights and practices of the people (Nongbri, 2003: 146).

In the field of judiciary powers entrusted to the State Government, the Supreme Court order empowering the government to bring all forests under working plans and evict encroachers from forestlands seemed to be an encroachment on their customary rights and systems of resource management and land use. The passing of the Supreme Court interim order on December 12, 1996 putting a blanket ban on "all on-going activity within any forest in any state throughout the country, without the prior approval of the central government", has put many states in the North-Eastern region in a quandary, as a major part of their economic activity, including revenue earnings, is based primarily on forest based activities (Apphira, 1997: 1). What comes to the fore is that a large chunk of forested areas in the region are under the control of the Autonomous District Councils (ADCs) whose main revenue earnings come from royalty from forest based produce. It is also pertinent to note here that the Apex Court had taken into consideration the Forest Conservation Act of 1980 which "must apply to all forests irrespective of the nature of ownership or classification thereof". All this leads one to ponder upon the question, 'what impact has the timber ban had on the indigenous communities?' The forest has always been an important source of livelihood to the Khasi community and so the most visible impact of the ban has been on the economy of the Khasi rural people, a major chunk of whom depended on forest as the primary source of subsistence. For forest owners and loggers the ban has become the proverbial Sword of Damocles, which they want to cut off and throw into the dark sea. But for the environmentalists the ban came as a much needed respite (Mukhim, 2000: 3). While one can appreciate the humble motive behind the Supreme Court order to protect environmental degradation, one can also point out its shortcomings in understanding tribal knowledge about forest. What needs to be recognized and understood is that the tribals have their own wisdom – a different way of understanding nature. In this juncture, the solution lies only on working together in close cooperation between the government and the District Councils giving way to a more pragmatic approach, and if necessary even by providing additional fund to District Councils to compensate their revenue losses.

In short, an appraisal of the roots of environmental change in these hills has revealed that it has largely been a result of modern forces of development, faced by a challenge to identify to implement a development process that will lead to greater equity, growth and sustainability. But development can take place at the cost of the environment only upto a certain point. Beyond that point it will be like the foolish man who was trying to cut the very branch on which he was sitting (Agarwal, 1984: 4).

Far from knowing that is best for them, our planners and policy makers had better learnt a lot from them. With such an awareness perhaps the Government will develop a policy for safeguarding the forest based on a recognition of tribal knowledge of it, instead of a constraint that alienates them from it (Padel, 1992: 9).

Notes

1. The British colonialists referred to Shillong, the capital of Meghalaya as the 'Scotland of the East'.
2. Mother earth is personified by the Khasis as '*Ka mei ramew*' and her husband was called '*U Basa*'. Having no off-spring, they pleaded the creator to give them children. Finally *Ka Mei Ramew* gave birth to five children – *U Bnai* (moon), *Ka Um* (water), *Ka Lyer* (air) and *Ka Ding* (fire).
3. The Khasis have a large collection of fables and folktales called '*Khanatang* and *Puriskam*' which carry moral lessons for the people and most of them are connected with nature.
4. The traditional Khasi religion is holistic and has to parts – one is based on *Ka Niam-im* (religion for the living) and *Ka Niam-ïap* (religion for the dead). The Khasis uphold the theandric commandment of their religion namely – '*Tip briew-tip blei*' and '*Tip-kur tip kha*' (know man and know god and know the kinsmen).
5. The Khasis are a matrilineal tribe.

References

Agarwal, Anil. 1982 *Status of India's Environment. The Second Citizen's Report,* CSS, New Delhi.

Allen, B.C. 1905 Gazetteer of Khasi and Jaintia Hills, Shillong.

CIFOR report. 1993–2003 *Forests and People.* Indonesia: Communications Unit Information Services Group, Indonesia Printers.

Jodha, N.S. 1986. 'Common Property Resources and Rural Poor in Dry Regions of India', *Economic and Political Weekly,* 21(27): 1–3

Mawrie, B.L. 2001 *The Khasis and their Natural Environment.* New Delhi: Academy Press

Mukhim, P. 2000 *Shillong Times,* June 4: 4

Nongbri, Tiplut. 2003 'Poverty and Indigenous Peoples with special reference to India', in *Indigenous People.* International Workshop for Indigenous People (IWGIP) January, 2003.

Nongkynrih, A.K. 2000 Human Development in Khatar Shnong. Shillong: Don Bosco Press.

Padel, Felix. 1992 Forest knowledge: Tribal People, their Environment and the Structure of Power (Presented at the First International Workshop on the Environmental History of South and South East Asia, New Delhi, 18–21 February 1992).

Shangpliang, R. 1995 Environmental Management in the Socio-economic dimension of Meghalaya A case study of Mawsynram Village. Unpublished M. Phil Dissertation, NEHU. Shillong

Shillong Times, February 11, 2000, Vol. LV No. 180.

Index